Contents

ENGAGING IDEAS

The Professor's Guide to Integrating Writing, Critical Thinking, and Active Learning in the Classroom

Second Edition

John C. Bean

Foreword by Maryellen Weimer

JOSSEY-BASS
A Wiley Imprint
www.josseybass.com

Published by Jossey-Bass
A Wiley Imprint
989 Market Street, San Francisco, CA 94103-1741—www.josseybass.com

Readers should be aware that Internet Web sites offered as citations and/or sources for further information may have changed or disappeared between the time this was written and when it is read.

Jossey-Bass books and products are available through most bookstores. To contact Jossey-Bass directly call our Customer Care Department within the U.S. at 800-956-7739, outside the U.S. at 317-572-3986, or fax 317-572-4002.

Jossey-Bass also publishes its books in a variety of electronic formats. Some content that appears in print may not be available in electronic books.

Library of Congress Cataloging-in-Publication Data

Bean, John C.
   Engaging ideas : the professor's guide to integrating writing, critical thinking, and active learning in the classroom / John C. Bean. – 2nd ed.
      p. cm. – (The Jossey-Bass higher and adult education series)
   Includes bibliographical references and index.
   ISBN 978-0-470-53290-4 (pbk.)
   ISBN 978-1-118-06231-9 (ebk.)
   ISBN 978-1-118-06232-6 (ebk.)
   ISBN 978-1-118-06233-3 (ebk.)
   1. Critical thinking–Study and teaching.   2. Academic writing–Study and teaching.   I. Title.
   PE1404.B35 2011
   808'.042–dc23

2011021319

Printed in the United States of America

SECOND EDITION

PB Printing   10 9 8 7 6 5 4 3

The Jossey-Bass Higher and
Adult Education Series

Foreword

I still remember the first incarnation of this book I saw. It was an in-house manual John had written to help faculty at his institution incorporate writing in their various courses. It was one of those proverbial diamonds in the rough. I remember constructing a list of reasons why Jossey-Bass should publish it as a book, which I presented with some passion to the then higher education editor, Gale Erlandson. I kept my fingers crossed, unsure whether the in-house manual would realize its potential as a full manuscript. When John submitted it, I couldn't believe how good it was. The years since its publication have confirmed that this book is better than good. It is one of the best books on teaching and learning published during the last twenty-five years. It has become the book that cemented the legacy of writing across the curriculum in countless classrooms. To write the Foreword for a new edition is indeed a privilege.

I was a bit surprised when I reread my Foreword in the first edition. The conditions described there are darker than I remember them. Could this be an even bleaker time? The lack of resources and devaluing of teaching described there are still realities today. Faculty continue to contend with large classes, students with pressing learning needs, and pressure to do lots of scholarship and service in addition to teaching. Higher education's days of wine and roses have yet to arrive.

Something positive can be said about the differences between those days and these. College teachers everywhere now understand that teaching students to write is a shared responsibility, not one to be relegated to those faculty assigned composition course instruction. Faculty have incorporated writing in courses from introductory to capstone in a long list of disciplines. The results haven't always been pretty. Many faculty have struggled more than they anticipated with designing writing assignments, reading what students write, providing constructive feedback, and assessing its merit. Teaching writing in any field is a labor-intensive, time-consuming endeavor. This book has helped many faculty members accomplish those tasks more productively. There is no need to start working on student writing skills without knowing what to do or how to do it when a book like this offers a plethora of ideas, information, and resources that can dramatically increase the success of those who are teaching and learning to write.

The features that contributed to this book's enormous success remain in this edition. John sees writing as more than a necessary communication skill, more than the skillful management of grammar, spelling, and punctuation. He believes that writing promotes critical thinking, and he makes that case most convincingly. When students write, their writing and their thinking improve. As a writer struggles with word choice, sentence structure, and paragraph composition, thinking occurs. Writing forces the clarification of ideas, attention to details, and the logical assembly of reasons. You can write without thinking—students often do. But as this book so ably shows, writing activities and assignments can be designed so that they are very difficult to complete without mind engagement, and when that occurs, critical thinking skills are being developed.

As in the first edition, this one showcases the many different ways writing can be used in assignments and activities, all illustrated with concrete examples from a wide range of disciplines. Beyond writing, there are other classroom activities with potential to develop writing and thinking skills—things like reading, working in groups, essay exams, and course projects. This edition concludes with a section of pragmatic advice on ways of dealing with student writing, including how to provide feedback and develop grading criteria. This is a book that addresses all the issues faculty face when they incorporate writing in their courses. This book not only persuades you that you should incorporate writing; after having read it, you are convinced that you can.

Most faculty do not read a lot of pedagogical material. We are not expected to grow our pedagogical knowledge the same way we are expected to keep current in our fields. No special rewards come to those few faculty who are pedagogically well-read. Even so, most faculty are readers, and, if you give them a book on a topic they care about (or think they should care about) that is written with voice and style by an author who knows and believes in the material, faculty will read that book and pass it on to others. I refer to this book when I need an example to support that claim.

If you have read the previous edition of this book, perhaps you even have a copy in your collection, there are lots of reasons to read the new edition. Every chapter has been updated with current references, and new chapters have been added. Those chapters address the need to get students thinking rhetorically, "sizing their audience and purpose," as John describes the topic. Another new chapter explores genre—the various kinds of writing that can expand critical thinking and promote deep learning. Students benefit when they do different kinds of writing—not just the typical academic, thesis-driven structure that usually ends up as some form of a term paper.

It's hard to imagine college teachers in any field reading this book and not finding some kind of writing assignment or activity that could be used in the courses they teach. But most how-to books don't make you think, and this book definitely does. Most how-to books don't usefully blend theoretical and practical knowledge, and this book does. Most how-to books don't develop a commitment to do what's being proposed, and this book does. Most how-to books don't end up being classics, that kind of timeless resource with dog-eared corners on the cover, turned-down pages, and a wide array of underlines, stars, and marginalia—all signs of hard use and high regard.

Those of us committed to writing across the curriculum have been after John to do a second edition for some time now. Yes, the content merits updating and enriching with new ideas and information that have emerged since the first edition, but more important than making the book current is the continuing need to work with students to develop their writing and thinking skills. Many now arrive at our colleges and universities deficient in both. And to graduate from college without good writing and thinking skills is to embark tenuously on a professional career. The need for faculty to teach writing and thinking in every course across the curriculum has never been more crucial. Fortunately, there is a book that can guide your efforts and contribute to your and your students' success.

Maryellen Weimer

Preface

I have been both gratified and humbled by the success of the first edition of *Engaging Ideas*, which has proven helpful to teachers across a wide range of disciplines. My aim in the second edition, as in the first, is to help teachers design engaging writing and critical thinking activities and incorporate them smoothly into their disciplinary courses. The goal of these activities is to transform students from passive to active learners, deepening their understanding of subject matter while helping them learn how disciplinary experts ask questions, conduct inquiry, gather and analyze data, and make arguments.

What's New in the Second Edition?

Much has changed since 1996, when the first edition was published. Readers of the second edition will notice (and I hope appreciate) how the second edition responds to recent developments in scholarship, teaching practice, and campus cultures. Particularly, the second edition has been influenced by changes in and interest in:

The Scholarship of Teaching and Learning (SoTL)

Although scholars working in learning theory and pedagogy have long struggled to find a respected place in the research university, the impact of SoTL is increasingly felt throughout academia—in faculty development workshops, in training of graduate teaching assistants, in national teaching conferences, in the growing presence of centers for teaching and learning on campuses, and in spectacular new research in teaching and learning published in recent books and scholarly journals. Nurtured by the Carnegie Foundation, the Professional and Organizational Development Network (POD), the International Society for the Scholarship of Teaching and Learning (ISSOTL), the Association of American Colleges and Universities (AAC&U), the National Science Foundation, major granting agencies, and many other organizations and forces, the scholarship of teaching and learning has provided theoretical foundations for pedagogical research along with empirical evidence for teaching practices that promote deep learning. A glance at my references list will reveal the number of recent SoTL publications that have helped shape the second edition.

Recent Scholarship in Rhetoric, Composition, and Writing in the Disciplines

The first edition of *Engaging Ideas* is rooted in the writing process paradigm that dominated composition theory in the 1980s and 1990s—the belief that most problems with student writing could be alleviated if teachers encouraged student writers to spend more time-on-task, going through the stages of the writing process, doing multiple drafts, and learning the principles of global revision. The second edition still emphasizes process but adapts a more broadly rhetorical view of writing based on novice/expert theory, which shows how experts in a field think rhetorically about genre, audience, and purpose. To write "expert insider prose" in their majors—a term I have adopted from Susan Peck MacDonald (1994)—students need to enter their field's discourse community, especially learning how disciplinary genres embody disciplinary ways of thinking and making knowledge. In the second edition, these influences are particularly felt in an entirely new chapter, "Helping Writers Think Rhetorically" (Chapter Three), an extensively revised and newly named chapter, "Using a Range of Genres to Extend Critical Thinking and Deepen Learning" (Chapter Four), and a new approach to teaching undergraduate research, "Designing and Sequencing Assignments to Teach Undergraduate Research (Chapter Thirteen).

The Assessment Movement

In 2000, my institution received what we might euphemistically call a "bad mark" for assessment during its accreditation visit from the Northwest Association of Schools and Colleges. Our provost hired an outside consultant—Barbara Walvoord, one of the first proponents of writing across the curriculum and the coauthor of *Effective Grading: A Tool for Learning and Assessment* (now in its second edition, 2009), whose work on our campus has influenced me profoundly. Walvoord showed us how embedded writing assignments anywhere in the curriculum can be used for systematic outcomes assessment—not just for assessing writing but for assessing disciplinary outcomes connected to inquiry, research, problem solving, critical thinking, or subject matter knowledge. We soon discovered that if assessments of senior papers revealed patterns of weaknesses, disciplinary faculty could use the principle of backward design to make pedagogical changes earlier in the curriculum to improve student performance—particularly short "scaffolding" assignments in lower level courses to teach targeted disciplinary thinking skills. Walvoord's visits led to a renaissance in writing across the curriculum at Seattle University—a story my colleagues and I have told in Bean, Carrithers, and Earenfight (2005) and in a number of subsequent articles and conference presentations. Ways to use embedded writing assignments for outcomes assessment are suggested in numerous places in the second edition, particularly in Chapter Thirteen, "Designing and Sequencing Assignments to Teach Undergraduate Research."

Quantitative and Scientific Literacy Across the Curriculum

Modeled partially on the writing-across-the-curriculum movement, new programs in quantitative and scientific literacy are having an impact on general education. Among the pioneers are the Quantitative Methods for Public Policy program at Macalester College, the Quantitative Inquiry, Reasoning, and Knowledge program (QUIRK) at Carleton College, and our own work with rhetorical mathematics at Seattle University. These programs generally do not focus on higher mathematics but on what the Mathematical Association of America defines as the "quantitative reasoning capabilities required of citizens in today's information age" (http://www.maa.org/features/QL.html). One of the best ways to promote quantitative literacy is to design disciplinary writing assignments that ask students to make arguments using numbers. This second edition has numerous examples of quantitative writing assignments, many of which ask writers to design their own graphs and tables that serve as visual arguments reinforcing the text's verbal argument.

Use of Classroom Technology

The first edition of *Engaging Ideas* appeared during the early age of e-mail, long before the advent of classroom management software, drop boxes, class discussion boards, social networking sites, text messaging, Twitter, PowerPoint, or YouTube. The second edition is updated to reflect this new technological universe—including online and blended learning—although I must confess that I have depended on my wired, linked, and gadget-loving younger colleagues to guide me into this new age.

Teaching Undergraduate Research

Although the "research paper" has long been a traditional college assignment, faculty across the curriculum increasingly realize that learning to write a research paper in first-year composition does not teach students the kinds of disciplinary thinking, genre knowledge, and specialized research skills needed for actual undergraduate research in the major. Programs that require a senior thesis, a capstone project, or some other kind of "expert insider prose" in their discipline need to develop a curriculum in which research skills are taught intentionally within the undergraduate major. In this second edition, I propose a new approach to teaching undergraduate research. (See Chapter Thirteen, "Designing and Sequencing Assignments to Teach Undergraduate Research," which is a complete revision of the first edition's chapter on research papers.)

What Hasn't Changed?

Throughout I have tried to retain the strengths of the first edition, which aims to integrate two important movements in higher education—the writing-across-the-curriculum movement and the critical thinking movement. A basic premise of both editions, growing out of the educational philosophy of John Dewey, is that critical thinking—and indeed all significant learning—originates in the learner's engagement with problems. Consequently, the design of interesting problems to think about is one of the teacher's chief behind-the-scenes tasks. Equally important are strategies for giving critical thinking problems to students and for creating a course atmosphere that encourages inquiry, exploration, discussion, and debate while valuing the dignity and worth of each student. Teachers of critical thinking also need to be mentors and coaches, developing a range of strategies for modeling critical thinking, critiquing student performances, and otherwise guiding students toward the habits of inquiry and argument valued in their disciplines.

Unique Features of This Book

In keeping with these premises, therefore, this book has the following unique features:

- It takes a pragmatic nuts-and-bolts approach to teaching critical thinking, giving teachers hundreds of suggestions for integrating writing and other critical thinking activities into a disciplinary course.

- It integrates theory and research from the writing-in-the-disciplines literature with the broader scholarship-of-teaching-and-learning literature on critical thinking, intellectual development, active learning, and modes of teaching.

- It gives detailed practical assistance in the design of formal and informal writing assignments and suggests time-saving ways to coach the writing process and handle the paper load.

- It treats writing assignments as only one of many ways to present critical thinking problems to students; it shows how writing assignments can easily be integrated with other critical thinking activities such as use of small groups, inquiry discussions, classroom debates, and interactive lectures.

- It has a separate chapter devoted to academic reading, exploring the causes of students' reading difficulties and offering suggestions for promoting more engaged and deeper reading.

- It has separate chapters devoted to small groups, to increasing critical thinking in discussion or lecture courses, and to evoking more learning from essay exams.

- It devotes a separate chapter to teaching undergraduate research and proposes alternatives to the traditional term paper.

- It assumes that there is no one right way to integrate writing and critical thinking into a course; it therefore provides numerous options to fit each teacher's particular personality and goals and to allow flexibility for meeting the needs of different kinds of learners.

- It emphasizes writing and critical thinking tasks that focus on the instructor's subject matter goals for the course, thus reducing, and in some cases perhaps even eliminating, the conflict between coverage and process.

- It offers a wide array of ways to use writing in courses, ranging from short write-to-learn "microthemes" to major research projects and from formal academic writing to personal narratives; it also offers numerous ways to work exploratory writing into a course, including in-class freewrites, blogs, practice exams, and thinking pieces posted on class discussion boards.

- It devotes a separate chapter to the creation of rubrics for grading student writing, discussing both the upside and downside of rubrics. It also devotes a chapter to the art of commenting on student papers to minimize teacher time while maximizing helpfulness and care.

- Throughout it suggests ways that embedded writing assignments can be used for assessment.

Link Between Writing and Critical Thinking

Although this book examines a wide range of strategies for promoting critical thinking in the classroom, it assumes that the most intensive and demanding tool for eliciting sustained critical thought is a well-designed writing assignment on a subject matter problem. The underlying premise is that writing is closely linked with thinking and that in presenting students with significant problems to write about—and in creating an environment that demands their best writing—we can promote their general cognitive and intellectual growth. When we make students struggle with their writing, we are making them struggle with thought itself. Emphasizing writing and critical thinking, therefore, generally increases the academic rigor of a course. Often the struggle of writing, linked as it is to the struggle of thinking and to the growth of a person's intellectual powers, awakens students to the real nature of learning.

Intended Audience

Engaging Ideas is intended for busy college professors from any academic discipline. Many readers may already emphasize writing, critical thinking, and active learning in their classrooms and will find in this book ways to fine-tune their work, such as additional approaches or strategies, more effective or efficient methods for coaching students as writers and thinkers, and tips on managing the paper load. Other readers may be attracted to the ideas in this book yet be held back by nagging doubts or fears that they will be buried in paper grading, that the use of writing assignments does not fit their disciplines, or that they will have to reduce their coverage of content. This book tries to allay these fears and help all professors find an approach to using writing and critical thinking activities that help each student meet course goals while fitting their own teaching philosophies and individual personalities.

It may be helpful to realize that this book is aimed primarily at improving students' engagement with disciplinary subject matter and *not* at improving student writing. Whenever I conduct writing-across-the-curriculum workshops, I always stress that a teacher's purpose in adding writing components to a course is *not* to help English departments teach writing. In fact, improvement of student writing is a happy side effect. Rather teachers should see writing assignments and other critical thinking activities as useful tools to help students achieve the instructor's content and process goals for a course. The reward of this book is watching students come to class better prepared, more vested in and motivated by the problems or questions the course investigates, more apt to study rigorously, and more likely to submit high-quality work. A serendipitous benefit for teachers may be that their own writing gets easier when they develop strategies for helping students. Many of the ideas in this book—about posing problems, generating and exploring ideas, focusing and organizing, giving and receiving peer reviews of drafts, and revising for readers—can be applied to one's own scholarly and professional writing as well as to the writing of students.

Structure of the Book

Chapter One, designed for the busy professor, gives the reader a nutshell compendium of the whole book and provides handy cross-references enabling readers to turn to specific parts of the book that concern their immediate needs. It also addresses four misconceptions that tend to discourage professors from integrating writing and critical thinking assignments into their courses.

Part One (Chapters Two through Five) presents the general theoretical background and pedagogical principles on which the book is based. Chapter Two examines the principles that relate writing to critical thinking and argues that good writing is both a process and a product of critical thought. Chapter Three suggests ways that teachers can help students think rhetorically about writing, particularly about purpose, audience, and genre. Doing so helps students develop transferable skills related to titles, introductions, tone, and reader expectations based on genre. Chapter Four introduces readers to the debate in the writing-across-the-curriculum literature between professional writing and personal or experimental writing and argues that students benefit from practicing both kinds. In Chapter Five, I focus on the problem of error in student writing, examine the debate among linguists and others over the role of grammar in writing instruction, and offer concrete suggestions about ways to reduce the incidence of error in students' writing.

Part Two (Chapters Six and Seven) focuses on the design of problem-based writing assignments. Chapter Six focuses on the design of formal writing assignments and Chapter Seven on ways to use informal, exploratory writing both inside and outside of class to enhance learning and promote critical thinking.

Part Three (Chapters Eight through Thirteen) examines a wide variety of strategies for stimulating active learning and for coaching students as writers and critical thinkers. Chapter Eight provides a heuristic for designing critical thinking problems and illustrates them with examples from across the disciplines. These problems can then be used in a wide variety of ways—as formal or informal writing assignments, as problems for small groups, as topics for class debates, and so forth. Chapter Nine, which focuses on teaching academic reading, explores the causes of students' difficulty with academic texts and suggests coaching strategies to help students improve their skills in comprehending and responding to difficult readings. Chapters Ten and Eleven together discuss ways to use class time for active inquiry and critical thinking. Chapter Ten focuses on the use of small groups in the classroom, and Chapter Eleven suggests ways to make lectures more interactive and whole-class discussions more productive. Chapter Twelve examines the strengths and weaknesses of essay exams as writing assignments and suggests ways to promote more student learning from essay exam settings. Chapter Thirteen, on teaching undergraduate research, opens with a discussion of students' alienation from research writing—an alienation that often results in uninspired cut-and-paste writing or even plagiarism—and offers suggestions for engaging students in undergraduate research that is truly productive and inquiry-based. Particularly, it explains the principle of backward design so that skills needed for advanced research writing at the end of the major are taught through strategically designed scaffolding assignments earlier in the curriculum.

The final section of the book, Part Four (Chapters Fourteen through Sixteen), concerns strategies for coaching the writing process and for marking and grading student papers. Chapter Fourteen offers advice on creating and using rubrics, which can clarify an instructor's grading criteria and, in many cases, decrease an instructor's time spent grading and commenting on papers. Chapter Fifteen offers ten time-saving strategies for coaching the writing process while avoiding burnout. Finally, Chapter Sixteen focuses on ways to write revision-oriented comments that guide students toward significant revision of their work.

Thanks and Acknowledgments

I have been fortunate over my teaching career at three different institutions to have been supported by major writing-across-the-curriculum grants from foundations or public agencies: Lilly Endowment for its support of a pioneering WAC project at the College of Great Falls (Montana) in the late 1970s; the Fund for the Improvement of Postsecondary Education (FIPSE) for supporting the Montana State University Critical Thinking and Writing Project (Bozeman) in the early 1980s; the Consortium for the Advancement of Private Higher Education (CAPHE) with matching support from the Ackerley Foundation at Seattle University in the early 1990s; and the Teagle Foundation for a recent project entitled Using Embedded Assignments to Assess Writing in the Majors and the Core Curriculum at Seattle University and Gonzaga University (2008–2011). The interdisciplinary conversations and ensuing research and scholarship from these grant-supported projects have created a wide network of colleagues to whom I am deeply indebted.

I wish particularly to thank W. Daniel Goodman in the Department of Chemistry at the College of Great Falls and Dean Drenk, John Ramage, and Jack Folsom for our FIPSE-grant days at Montana State University. At Seattle University, I thank my SoTL colleagues (many of whom have been coauthors with me on WAC or SoTL publications): economists Dean Peterson, Gareth Green, and Teresa Ling; finance professors David Carrithers and Fiona Robertson; chemists P. J. Alaimo, Joe Langenhan, and Jenny Loertscher; historian Theresa Earenfight; English professors Charles Tung, Nalini Iyer, June Johnson Bube, and David Leigh, S.J; and SoTL scholars Therese Huston and David Green of Seattle University's Center for Excellence in Teaching and Learning. Thanks also to Larry Nichols, Director of the Writing Center at Seattle University, my longtime friend, workshop cofacilitator, and fellow advocate for good writing assignments and engaged learning.

A larger network of WAC friends has also nurtured and inspired my work: Joanne Kurfiss Gainen, former director of the Center for Teaching and Learning at Santa Clara University; Linda Shohet, the Centre for Literacy in Montreal, Canada; John Webster, SoTL scholar and Director of Writing for the College of Arts and Sciences at the University of Washington; Michael Herzog, Teagle Grant co-investigator and longtime SoTL colleague at Gonzaga University; Carol Rutz, Director of the Writing Program at Carleton College; Carol Haviland, former Director of the Writing Center at California State University at San Bernardino; and nursing professor Rob van der Peet of the Netherlands, who translated the first edition of *Engaging Ideas* into Dutch.

I owe a special debt of gratitude and warm thanks to pioneering SoTL scholar Maryellen Weimer, Emeritus Professor of Teaching and Learning at Pennsylvania State University, whose faith in my work, whose encouragement, and whose extraordinary generosity of time gave me the confidence to produce the first edition of *Engaging Ideas* and the persuasive push to write the second. Her contribution to the book is explained in the opening narrative to her Foreword, for which I am most honored and grateful. Finally, I'd like to thank my editors at Jossey-Bass: Gale Erlandson for the first edition of *Engaging Ideas* and now David Brightman for the second. David has been extraordinarily supportive and flexible in providing the space, timing, and guidance that made the second edition possible. His generous, unflappable spirit has been a comfort throughout the process.

My deepest thanks and love go to my wife, Kit, who is also a professional writing teacher at South Seattle Community College, and to our children Matthew, Andrew, Stephen, and Sarah for their patience and good humor in enduring parents who can turn any occasion into a writing assignment.

John C. Bean
Vashon Island, Washington
June 2011

About the Author

John C. Bean is a professor of English at Seattle University, where he holds the title of Consulting Professor of Writing and Assessment. He has an undergraduate degree in English from Stanford University (1965) and a Ph.D. in Renaissance literature from the University of Washington (1972). He has been active in the writing-across-the-curriculum movement since 1976—first at the College of Great Falls (Montana), then at Montana State University (Bozeman), and, since 1986, at Seattle University. Besides *Engaging Ideas*, the first edition of which has been translated into both Dutch and Chinese, he is the coauthor of four composition textbooks with varying focuses on writing, argumentation, critical thinking, and rhetorical reading. He has also published numerous articles on writing and writing across the curriculum as well as on literary subjects including Shakespeare and Spenser. He has done extensive consulting across the United States and Canada on writing across the curriculum, critical thinking, and university outcomes assessment. In 2001, he presented a keynote workshop at the first annual conference of the European Association of Teachers of Academic Writing (EATAW) at the University of Groningen in The Netherlands. More recently, he and his wife Kit (who is also a college teacher of writing) spent three weeks in Dhaka, Bangladesh, facilitating workshops on critical thinking for Bangladeshi educators at BRAC University. His current research interests focus on problems of transfer of learning as students move through and across a curriculum and on the development of institutional assessment strategies that promote productive faculty conversations about teaching and learning. In 2010 his article "Messy Problems and Lay Audiences: Teaching Critical Thinking within the Finance Curriculum" (coauthored with colleagues from finance and economics) won the 2008 McGraw-Hill–Magna Publications Award for the year's best scholarly work on teaching and learning.

ENGAGING IDEAS

1

Using Writing to Promote Thinking

A Busy Professor's Guide to the Whole Book

In his now classic study of pedagogical strategies that make a difference, Richard Light (2001) examined the connection between writing and student engagement. "The results are stunning," he claims:

> *The relationship between the amount of writing for a course and students' level of engagement—whether engagement is measured by time spent on the course, or the intellectual challenge it presents, or students' level of interest in it—is stronger than the relationship between students' engagement and any other course characteristic. . . . [p. 55]*

More recent research, conducted jointly by the National Survey of Student Engagement (NSSE) and the Council of Writing Program Administrators (WPA), has shown that for promoting engagement and deep learning the number of writing assignments in a course may not be as important as the design of the writing assignments themselves (Anderson, Anson, Gonyea, and Paine, 2009). Good assignments, this research has shown, give students opportunities to receive early feedback on their work, encourage meaning-making, and clearly explain the instructor's expectations and purpose. (I discuss this research in depth in Chapter Six.)

The aim of this book is to give professors a wide range of options for bringing the benefits of engaged learning to students. My premise, supported by an increasing body of research, is that good writing assignments (as well as other active learning tasks) evoke a high level of critical thinking, help students wrestle productively with a course's big questions, and teach disciplinary ways of seeing, knowing, and doing. They can also be designed to promote self-reflection, leading to more integrated, personally meaningful learning. Moreover, the benefits do not accrue only to students. Professors who successfully integrate writing and other critical thinking activities into their courses often report a satisfying increase in their teaching pleasure: students are better prepared for class, discussions are richer, and student performance improves.

But the use of writing and critical thinking activities to promote learning does not happen through serendipity. Teachers must plan for it and foster it throughout the course. This chapter suggests a sequence of steps that teachers can take to integrate writing and critical thinking into their courses. It then addresses four negative beliefs that often discourage teachers from taking these steps—the beliefs that integrating writing into a course will take time away from content, that writing assignments are not appropriate for some disciplines or courses, that assigning writing will bury a teacher in paper grading, and that assigning writing requires specialized expertise. Because these beliefs raise important concerns, I seek to supply reassuring responses at the outset.

This chapter provides, in effect, a brief overview of the whole book; subsequent chapters treat in depth each of the suggestions or issues introduced briefly here.

Steps for Integrating Writing and Critical Thinking Activities into a Course

This section surveys eight steps teachers can take to integrate writing and critical thinking activities into a course.

Step 1: Become Familiar with Some of the General Principles Linking Writing to Learning and Critical Thinking

To appreciate how writing is linked to learning and critical thinking, we can begin with a brief discussion of how we might define critical thinking.

Critical Thinking Rooted in Problems

Although definitions in the pedagogical literature vary in detail, in their broad outlines they are largely elaborations, extensions, and refinements of the progressive views of John Dewey (1916), who rooted critical thinking in the students' engagement with a problem. Problems, for Dewey, evoke students' natural curiosity and stimulate both learning and critical thought. "Only by wrestling with the conditions of the problem at first hand, seeking and finding his own way out, does [the student] think" (p. 188).

Part of the difficulty of teaching critical thinking, therefore, is awakening students to the existence of problems all around them. Meyers (1986), who agrees with Dewey that problems are naturally motivating, argues that teachers ought to begin every class with "something that is a problem or a cause for wonder" (p. 44). Meyers quotes philosopher and chemist Michael Polanyi, who claims that "as far down the scale of life as worms and even perhaps amoebas, we meet a general alertness of animals, not directed towards any specific satisfaction, but merely exploring what is there: an urge to achieve intellectual control over the situations confronting [them]" (p. 41).

Presenting students with problems, then, taps into something natural and self-fulfilling in our beings. In his fifteen-year study of what the best college professors do, Ken Bain (2004) shows that highly effective teachers confront students with "intriguing, beautiful, or important problems, authentic tasks that will challenge them to grapple with ideas, rethink their assumptions, and examine their mental models of reality" (p. 18). Set at the appropriate level of difficulty, such "beautiful problems" create a "natural critical learning environment" that engages students as active and deep learners. Similarly, Brookfield (1987) claims that critical thinking is "a productive and positive" activity. "Critical thinkers are actively engaged with life" (p. 5). This belief in the natural, healthy, and motivating pleasure of problems—and in the power of well-designed problems to awaken and stimulate the passive and unmotivated student—is one of the underlying premises of this book.

Disciplinary Versus Generic Domains for Critical Thinking

Not all problems, however, are *academic* problems of the kind that we typically present to students in our classrooms or that we pose for ourselves in doing scholarly research. Academic problems are typically rooted within a disciplinary conversation: to a large extent, these problems are discipline-specific, as each discipline poses its own kinds of questions and conducts inquiries, uses data, and makes arguments in its own characteristic fashion. As Anne Beaufort (2007) has shown, to think and write like a disciplinary professional, students must draw not only on subject matter knowledge, but also on knowledge about the discipline's genre conventions, its methods of argument, its typical kinds of evidence, its ways of referencing other researchers, and its typical rhetorical contexts and audiences. Chapter

Thirteen on teaching undergraduate research addresses Beaufort's novice-to-expert schema in more detail.

But certain underlying features of critical thinking are generic across all domains. According to Brookfield (1987), two "central activities" define critical thinking: "identifying and challenging assumptions and exploring alternative ways of thinking and acting" (p. 71). Joanne Kurfiss (1988) likewise believes that critical thinkers pose problems by questioning assumptions and aggressively seeking alternative views. For her, the prototypical academic problem is "ill-structured"; that is, it is an open-ended question that does not have a clear right answer and therefore must be responded to with a proposition justified by reasons and evidence. "In critical thinking," says Kurfiss, "all assumptions are open to question, divergent views are aggressively sought, and the inquiry is not biased in favor of a particular outcome" (p. 2).

The Link Between Writing and Critical Thinking

Given this view of critical thinking, what is its connection with writing? Quite simply, writing is both a process of doing critical thinking and a product that communicates the results of critical thinking. As I show in Chapter Two, writing instruction goes sour whenever writing is conceived primarily as a "communication skill" rather than as a process and product of critical thought. If writing is merely a communication skill, then we primarily ask of it, "Is the writing clear?" But if writing is critical thinking, we ask, "Is the writing interesting? Does it show a mind actively engaged with a problem? Does it bring something new to readers? Does it make an argument?" As Chapters Two and Three explain, experienced writers begin by posing two kinds of problems—what we might call subject matter problems and rhetorical problems. Subject matter problems drive the writer's inquiry. The writer's thesis statement is a tentative response to a subject matter problem; it poses a contestable "answer" or "solution" that must be supported with the kinds of reasons and evidence that are valued in the discipline. But writers also think critically about rhetorical problems: Who is my audience? What genre should I employ and what are its features and conventions? How much do my readers already know about and care about my subject matter problem? How do I want to change my audience's views? What alternative views must I consider? Writers produce multiple drafts because the act of writing is itself an act of problem solving. Behind the scenes of a finished product is a messy process of exploratory writing, conversation, and discarded drafts. Chapters Two and Three deal with these issues in depth.

Step 2: Design Your Course with Critical Thinking Objectives in Mind

Once teachers are convinced of the value of critical thinking, the next step is to design a course that nurtures it. What is such a course like? In her comprehensive review of the literature on critical thinking, Kurfiss (1988) examined a wide range of successful disciplinary courses devoted to the teaching of both subject matter and critical thinking. In each case, she explains, "the professor establishes an agenda that includes learning to think about subject matter. Students are active, involved, consulting and arguing with each other, and responsible for their own learning" (p. 88). From this review, she derives eight principles for designing a disciplinary course that supports critical thinking:

1. Critical thinking is a learnable skill; the instructor and peers are resources in developing critical thinking skills.

2. Problems, questions, or issues are the point of entry into the subject and a source of motivation for sustained inquiry.

3. Successful courses balance challenges to think critically with support tailored to students' developmental needs.

4. Courses are assignment centered rather than text and lecture centered. Goals, methods, and evaluation emphasize using content rather than simply acquiring it.

5. Students are required to formulate and justify their ideas in writing or other appropriate modes.

6. Students collaborate to learn and to stretch their thinking, for example, in pair problem solving and small group work.

7. Several courses, particularly those that teach problem-solving skills, nurture students' metacognitive abilities.

8. The developmental needs of students are acknowledged and used as information in the design of the course. Teachers in these courses make standards explicit and then help students learn how to achieve them [pp. 88–89].

This book aims to help teachers develop courses that follow these guidelines. Of key importance are Kurfiss's principles 2, 4, and 5: a good critical thinking course presents students with "problems, questions, [or] issues" that make a course "assignment centered rather than text [or] lecture centered" and holds students responsible for formulating and justifying their solutions orally or in writing. This book particularly emphasizes writing assignments because they are perhaps the most flexible and most intensive way to integrate critical thinking tasks into a course and because the writing process itself entails complex critical thinking. But much attention is also given to class discussions, small group activities, and other teaching strategies that encourage students to work collaboratively to expand, develop, and deepen their thinking. Attention is also given throughout to the design of problems at appropriate levels of difficulty, to the developmental needs of students, and to the importance of making expectations and criteria clear (principles 1, 3, and 8).

Step 3: Design Critical Thinking Tasks for Students to Address

A crucial step in teaching critical thinking is to develop good problems for students to think about. Tasks can range from enduring disciplinary problems to narrowly specific questions about the significance of a graph or the interpretation of a key passage in a course reading. The kinds of questions you develop for students will depend on their level of expertise, their current degree of engagement with the subject matter, and the nature of question asking in your own discipline.

When I conduct workshops in writing across the curriculum, I like to emphasize a disciplinary, content-driven view of critical thinking by asking faculty to write out one or two final examination essay questions for one of their courses—questions that they think require both subject matter knowledge and critical thinking. We then discuss the kinds of critical thinking needed and the relative difficulty of each question, sometimes offering suggestions on ways to improve questions to elicit the kinds and levels of critical thinking the teacher seeks. When we have appreciated the value of these questions for promoting critical thinking, I suggest that it is a shame to waste them on a timed exam, where students spend only an hour or so on task. Such questions and dozens more like them can be integrated into the fabric of a course, where they can stimulate curiosity, drive inquiry, and promote learning. Chapters Six, Seven, and Nine focus specifically on the design of critical thinking tasks to serve as formal or informal writing assignments or as starting points for other critical thinking activities.

Step 4: Develop a Repertoire of Ways to Give Critical Thinking Tasks to Students

Once you have developed a stockpile of critical thinking problems based on your course's subject matter, you can choose from dozens of ways to integrate them into your course. This book presents numerous options for giving critical thinking problems to students. These include the following:

1. *Problems as formal writing assignments.* Formal writing assignments, which require revision and multiple drafts, keep students on task for extended periods and are among our most powerful tools for teaching critical thinking. They can range in length from one-paragraph "microthemes" (see Chapter Six) to major research projects within a disciplinary genre (see Chapter Thirteen). As these chapters show, effective academic assignments usually require that the student formulate and support a thesis (or test a hypothesis) in response to a problem. Such problem-centered assignments, which are primarily argumentative or analytical, are more effective for developing critical thinking than topic-centered assignments, which students often interpret as asking for information ("Write a research paper on one of the following topics").

2. *Problems as thought-provokers for exploratory writing.* Although students normally write only a few formal papers for a course, they can do behind-the-scenes exploratory writing on a daily basis. Chapters Two and Seven provide a rationale for this kind of low-stakes writing, which is a seedbed for generating and growing ideas. Exploratory writing records the actual process of critical thinking while simultaneously driving it forward. Perhaps more than any other instructional tool, exploratory writing transforms the way students study for a course because it can make active critical thinking about course subject matter part of each day's homework. Chapters Seven and Eight give numerous suggestions for integrating exploratory writing into a course, ranging from various kinds of journals or "thinking pieces" to postings on an electronic discussion board.

3. *Problems as small group tasks.* Disciplinary problems make powerful collaborative learning tasks. Small groups can be given a set time to brainstorm possible solutions to a problem or to seek a best solution by arriving at a consensus or a reasoned "agreement to disagree." In a plenary session, groups report their solutions and present their justifying arguments using appropriate reasons and evidence. The instructor usually critiques the groups' solutions and often explains how experts in the discipline (for whom the teacher is spokesperson) might tackle the same problem. During plenary sessions, the instructor both models and coaches disciplinary ways of making arguments, also attending to the generic critical thinking skills of looking at the available evidence and considering alternative views. Chapter Ten focuses on the uses of small groups to promote critical thinking.

4. *Problems as starters for class discussions.* Discussion classes can begin with one or two critical thinking problems written on the chalkboard or posted in advance on an electronic discussion board as "questions of the day." The teacher guides the discussion, encouraging students to appreciate and manage complexity. (If students have addressed these questions the night before in an exploratory thinking piece, they will be both eager and prepared for class discussion.) Other ways to get students actively addressing critical thinking problems include classroom debates, panel discussions, and fishbowls. See Chapter Eleven for suggestions on bringing more critical thinking into lectures and class discussions.

5. *Problems as practice exam questions.* Chapter Twelve suggests ways to coax more student learning and critical thinking out of essay exams. One of the best approaches is to give practice exams that students write for homework on a self-timed basis. Feedback is provided through in-class discussion of representative essays.

The point of all these strategies is to model for students a view of knowledge in which inquirers must develop and support provisional answers to disciplinary problems. By actively using new concepts and information, students engage course material on a deeper level.

Step 5: Develop Strategies to Include Exploratory Writing, Talking, and Reflection in Your Courses

Good writing, I like to tell my students, grows out of good talking—either talking with classmates or talking dialogically with oneself through exploratory writing. A key observation among teachers of critical thinking is that students, when given a critical thinking problem, tend to reach closure too quickly. They do not suspend judgment, question assumptions, evaluate evidence, imagine alternative answers, play with data, enter into the spirit of opposing views, and just plain linger over questions. As a result, they often write truncated and underdeveloped papers. To deepen students' thinking, teachers need to build into their courses time, space, tools, and motivation for exploratory thinking. Closely connected to exploratory tasks are reflective tasks aimed at encouraging students to think metacognitively about their own thinking processes, to connect learning in one course to other courses or to their own lives, to transfer skills from one setting to another, and to integrate their learning. Chapters Seven through Twelve suggest numerous ways to make exploratory writing, talking, and reflection a habit of students in your courses.

Step 6: Develop Strategies for Teaching How Your Discipline Uses Evidence to Support Claims

To grow as critical thinkers, students need to learn how different disciplines use evidence to support arguments. According to Richard Light (2001), "A surprising number of undergraduates describe learning how to use evidence to resolve controversies in their field, whatever their field, as a breakthrough idea" (p. 122). Light describes the bafflement of first-year students as they shift from discipline to discipline, encountering different ways that disciplines gather and use evidence to address problems. Some disciplines derive their evidence from observations of natural or cultural phenomena, sometimes converted to numbers, subjected to statistical analysis, and displayed in graphs and tables. Other disciplines use qualitative data from ethnographic observations, focus group transcripts, or interviews. Still others analyze aural, visual, or verbal texts housed in libraries, historical archives, art galleries, museums, popular media archives, or websites.

What new students don't see is how these different kinds of data function as evidence in support of a claim. Teachers can accelerate students' understanding of a field by designing assignments that teach disciplinary use of evidence or that help students analyze the thinking moves within an evidence-based argument. Closely related to disciplinary use of evidence is use of disciplinary genres such as experimental reports, ethnographies, design proposals, or disciplinary papers suitable for presentation at an undergraduate research conference. Part Two of this book (particularly Chapter Thirteen on teaching undergraduate research) treats the use of disciplinary evidence and genres in more detail.

Step 7: Develop Effective Strategies for Coaching Students in Critical Thinking

Besides giving students good problems to think about, teachers need to critique students' performances and to model the kinds of critical thinking they want students to develop. According to Meyers (1986), teachers of critical thinking will often spend much of their class time as "referees, coaches, and mentors rather than as lecturers and purveyors of the truth . . . For most of us," he continues, "this is a worthwhile but difficult shift" (p. 39). This book suggests numerous ways that teachers can coach critical thinking, including guiding discussions, critiquing solutions developed by small groups, writing comments on student drafts, holding conferences, sharing autobiographical accounts of their own thinking and writing processes, discussing strengths and weaknesses of sample papers, breaking long assignments into stages, and stressing revision and multiple drafts. An equally important aspect of coaching is providing a supportive, open classroom that values the worth and dignity of students. Suggestions for coaching writing and critical thinking are integrated throughout the book but occur especially in Chapters Ten and Fifteen. Chapter Nine focuses specifically on coaching students as critical readers of academic texts, and Chapter Sixteen focuses entirely on ways to comment on student papers to promote critical thinking.

Step 8: When Assigning Formal Writing, Treat Writing as a Process

In most kinds of courses, the student "product" that most clearly exhibits the results of critical thinking is a piece of formal writing addressing an open-ended problem. Too often, however, what the student submits as a finished product is in an unrevised draft, the result of an undeveloped and often truncated thinking process that doesn't adequately confront all the available evidence, consider alternative views, examine assumptions, or imagine the needs of a new reader. Much of the thinking promoted by writing occurs during the messy process of revision when the writer's ideas gradually become focused and clarified. No matter how much we exhort students to write several drafts and to collaborate with peers, most of our students will continue to write their papers on the night before they are due unless we structure our courses to promote writing as a process.

Teachers can get better final products, therefore, if they design their courses from the outset to combat last-minute writing, to promote exploratory writing and talking, and to encourage substantive revision. Promoting such exploration is one of the functions of progressive writing centers, where experienced tutors or consultants can help students understand the demands of an assignment, brainstorm ideas, and revise their papers through multiple drafts. On many campuses the director of the writing center is one of an instructor's most important resources for developing ways to incorporate writing into a course. Chapters Fifteen and Sixteen offer many suggestions for encouraging students to deepen and extend their writing processes.

Four Discouraging Beliefs and Some Encouraging Responses

The steps just described can help teachers integrate writing and critical thinking activities into their courses. However, many teachers who are tempted to do so may be held back by negative beliefs or misconceptions about what happens when a teacher begins developing a pedagogy using writing and critical thinking. It will be helpful, therefore, to address these beliefs at the outset. Based on discussions with faculty from across the disciplines, I find the following four misconceptions the most pervasive and potentially discouraging.

Misconception 1: Emphasizing Writing and Critical Thinking in My Courses Will Take Time Away from Content

Many faculty, understandably concerned about coverage of material, do not want to shift class time away from content. In addressing this conundrum, one must first distinguish between how much a teacher "covers" in a given course and how much students actually learn in a meaningful and usable way. Much of the literature on best pedagogical practices suggests that less is more. For example, Robert Zemsky (2009), founding director of the University of Pennsylvania's Institute for Research on Higher Education, argues that "no one has sufficient time or gray matter to master a knowledge base that is growing exponentially every decade or so." Rather than focus exhaustively on content coverage, Zemsky urges educators to prioritize content, focusing on high-priority material while simultaneously teaching the critical thinking and problem-solving skills needed to acquire and apply new knowledge:

> *Discussions of the changing nature of knowledge often morph into what a successful learning outcome would be if detailed content were actually becoming less important than a well-executed learning process. The former is static; the latter is dynamic in the sense that learning processes change as the learner seeks new knowledge and tackles new problems.*

In my experience, integrating writing and critical thinking components into a course can increase the amount of subject matter that students actually learn. My assertion may seem counterintuitive until one realizes that these assignments can restructure the way students study outside of class. Critical thinking tasks—which require students to *use* their expanding knowledge of subject matter to address disciplinary problems—motivate better study habits by helping students see their learning as purposeful and interesting. If tasks are designed to improve academic reading (see Chapter Nine), students often learn to read textbooks more powerfully and to interact more critically with primary source readings. With more confidence that students can learn from assigned readings, teachers can, if they choose, redirect some class time away from lecturing over the readings toward critical discussions, small group problem solving, or other critical thinking activities. The emphasis throughout this book is on helping students learn the subject matter of a course at a deeper and more intellectually mature level.

Misconception 2: Writing Assignments Are Unsuitable in My Course

Most teachers believe that writing applies naturally to English courses, to liberal arts courses, and to certain specialized courses in their fields. They may not, however, believe that writing is equally appropriate in their own courses. These doubts are frequently expressed by teachers of quantitative or technical courses or ones that focus on basic facts, concepts, or algorithmic procedures that, according to the teacher, must be "committed to memory" before the student can move on to problem solving and analysis. If we apply some conceptual blockbusting, however, we see that writing assignments can be used profitably in any course. (My point is exemplified by the wide range of disciplines represented in this book—accounting, physics, chemistry, all levels of mathematics, nursing, business, education, and engineering, as well as the humanities and social sciences.) By conceptual blockbusting, I mean primarily rethinking what constitutes a *writing assignment*. Many of the assignments in this book are nongraded or are very short formal tasks designed to help students understand an important course concept. Others have a metacognitive aim—helping students reflect on their own thinking processes or productively altering their methods of studying or reading. Still others have a procedural aim—helping students learn disciplinary methods of inquiry and analysis. Whatever a teacher's goals for a course, writing assignments can be designed to help students meet them.

Misconception 3: Adding More Writing to My Course Will Bury Me in Paper Grading

Many teachers would gladly require more writing in their courses if it were not for the need to mark and grade all those papers. If teachers do not currently assign any writing in their courses, adding a writing component will admittedly require extra work, although not necessarily more total time devoted to teaching if some of the teacher's current preparation or conference time is shifted toward responding to writing. If teachers already require writing in their courses (say, a couple of essay exams and a term paper), following the suggestions in this book might *reduce* the total time they spend on student writing while simultaneously making that time more rewarding for themselves and more productive for students.

The NSSE/WPA research cited at the beginning of this chapter (Anderson, Anson, Gonyea, and Paine, 2009) has shown that what matters in using writing to promote deep learning is not the amount of writing in a course but the quality of the writing assignments themselves.

There are many ways to work writing into a course while keeping the paper load manageable. Some methods require no teacher time (for example, in-class freewriting); some, minimal time (perusing a random selection of entries from a guided journal or class discussion board); and some, very modest time (assigning write-to-learn microthemes using models feedback). Even when you require several formal essays or a major research paper, you may employ any number of timesaving strategies to reduce the paper load (see Chapter Fifteen). The key is to decide how much time you are willing to spend on student writing and then to plan your courses to include only what you can handle—always remembering that you do not have to read everything a student writes.

Misconception 4: I Am Not Knowledgeable Enough About Writing and Grammar to Help Students with Their Own Writing

Many teachers across the curriculum will admit that English was not their favorite subject. Although they produce competent professional writing in their own fields, they believe that because they struggle with their own writing and because they do not know grammatical terminology or composition theory, they lack the skills to help students. This book aims to allay these fears. Because the best teacher commentary focuses primarily on ideas and development, no special terminology is needed. Teachers simply need to be honest readers, making comments like these:

"I got lost in this part."

"You need more evidence here."

"You seem to be overlooking Baker's research on this problem. Can you summarize and respond to Baker's views?"

"Excellent point!"

A main key to teaching writing, as Chapter Two argues, is teaching students how to revise. The more teachers struggle to revise their own writing, the more they can serve as role models for students. In short, your own experience as an academic writer and reader, combined with your expertise in how scholars in your field inquire and argue, should be all the background you need to help your students with their writing.

Conclusion: Engaging Your Students with the Ideas of Your Course

The steps suggested here for integrating writing and critical thinking assignments into a course can increase students' engagement with subject matter and improve the quality of their work. Moreover, these suggestions do not call for rapid, complete makeovers of a course. It is possible to make changes in a course gradually—trying a few new activities at a time, looking for strategies and approaches that fit your discipline and subject matter, that work for your students, and that accord with your own personality and teaching philosophy.

Some teachers make only minimal changes in their courses. I know of one teacher, a brilliant lecturer, who has changed nothing in his courses except for adding a series of nongraded "practice essay exams." He collects the exams (written out of class, self-timed by students), keeps a record of who submits them, reads randomly selected ones in search of representative problems as well as models of excellent exams, and then holds class discussions of what constitutes a good answer. He is very happy with this minimalist approach and offers persuasive anecdotal evidence that this practice has improved students' study habits as well as the quality of their actual essay exams.

But I know of other teachers who have radically transformed their classrooms, moving from a teaching-centered to a learning-centered pedagogy, from lecture-based courses to inquiry-based courses using exploratory writing, collaborative learning, lively discussions, and other strategies for engaging students in inquiry and debate.

In the pages that follow, I invite readers to find what works for them and for their students.

PART ONE

Understanding Connections Between Thinking and Writing

2

How Writing Is Related to Critical Thinking

The writing-across-the-curriculum movement—along with a surge of new interest in composition theory and practice—began in the 1970s as a reaction against traditional writing instruction that associated good writing primarily with grammatical correctness and style and thus isolated writing instruction within English departments, the home of the grammar and style experts. The problem with traditional writing instruction was that it led to a view of writing as a set of isolated skills unconnected to an authentic desire to converse with interested readers about real ideas.

A classic "Shoe" cartoon from the late '80s illustrates the traditional view. Skyler, a bright young bird of a student, sits at his school desk writing essays—an activity that he apparently relishes. "They give me an opportunity to perfect a verbal skill I can use all my life," he says with a self-satisfied smile. In the last frame of the cartoon, his smile turns to a triumphant grin as he discloses the skill he has in mind: "the ability to disguise total ignorance with good writing."

To the general public this is a funny cartoon; to me it symbolizes what was wrong with traditional writing instruction. Skyler believes that the act of writing can be separated from thinking, that writing is merely packaging and thus a separate thing from "content," which he assumes exists independently, apart from language. To put it another way, writing is like the box and wrapping paper into which we put our already formulated ideas. Once writing is imagined as "packaging," students find little use for it. Separated from the act of thinking and creating, writing becomes merely a skill that can be learned through grammar drills and through the production of pointless essays that students do not want to write and that teachers do not want to read. This is the view of writing held by many first-year students when they show up at our gates to begin their college careers. It is the challenge of faculty across the disciplines, along with their colleagues in writing programs and writing centers—to show them other ways of imagining writing.

To gain a different perspective on writing, let's see what writing looks like through the metaphors of a different language. In French, the word for a rough draft is *brouillon,* derived from a verb meaning "to place in disorder, to scramble." This metaphor suggests a writing process that begins as a journey into disorder, a making of chaos, out of which one eventually forges an essay. Perhaps driven by their awareness of disorder in the term *brouillon,* the French place an equally strong emphasis on a *plan* (roughly equivalent to the English *outline*), which is the principle of order that the mind must impose on the scrambled *brouillon.* Together the metaphors *plan* and *brouillon* reveal a creative tension between order and disorder. In English, we have no equivalent word for a *brouillon.* Our phrase "rough draft" suggests something that must be smoothed and polished, but not something deliberately scrambled, something placed in disorder, something that must be wrestled into form. Nor is our word *outline*— suggesting an inert structure—exactly equivalent to *plan,* which like the English word *plan* implies a sense of human purpose and intention.

Viewed in the light of the metaphorical *brouillon* and *plan,* traditional writing instruction seems impoverished indeed. Traditionally, we have seldom suggested to students that writing has a *brouillon* stage, a creative period of confusion and disorder; rather, we have taught that writing begins with an outline (which we dutifully correct for proper indentation and placement of periods and capital letters). Without the *brouillon,* we have eliminated from our writing classes the rich, creative source of ideas and substituted instead a sterile order that leaves us obsessed with correctness, neatness, and propriety. The message from our schools has often been that writing is a joyless activity, an opportunity mainly for displaying errors for teachers to red-pencil. The social cost is incalculable: when writing gets separated from what the writer really thinks, the experience of "really thinking" can be quickly lost from the curriculum.

The writing-across-the-curriculum movement is thus rooted in a radical reenvisioning of what it means to be a writer. It is the purpose of the four chapters in Part One to sketch for the reader a general overview of the theory, principles, and rationale that underlie a revised approach to writing, one that can accelerate students' growth as thinkers and learners. The present chapter discusses how writing can be best understood as a process of critical thinking. Chapter Three examines the role of critical thinking in addressing rhetorical problems of audience, purpose, and genre. Extending the ideas developed in Chapters Two and Three, Chapter Four shows how different genres—for example, an academic article versus a personal reflection—promote different kinds of critical thinking. Finally, Chapter Five examines current theory about the best way to respond to grammatical problems and errors in student writing. Together, these chapters provide the underlying theory for the rest of the book's pragmatic focus on classroom strategies for improving students' writing and critical thinking.

Overview of the Writing-Across-the-Curriculum and Critical Thinking Movements

Before we turn to the way that writing promotes critical thinking, let's take a brief look at the overlapping histories of the writing-across-the-curriculum and critical thinking movements. Since its origins in the 1970s, writing-across-the-curriculum has developed into a nationwide (and increasingly a worldwide) network of practitioners and researchers, often loosely organized into programs shaped by local exigencies and culture. (For a history of writing across the curriculum, see Bazerman and others, 2005, and Russell, 2002.) Sometimes a distinction is made between writing-across-the-curriculum (WAC) and writing-in-the disciplines (WID). The former is often associated with "writing to learn," the aim of which is to use a variety of writing activities to promote deep learning of a course's ideas, concepts, and skills. The latter is more often associated with "learning to write," particularly with learning to write within the discipline-specific genres and styles of the student's major. In places where speaking is paired with writing, programs are often designated as "communication-across-the-curriculum" (CAC). A related movement emerging in Europe, sponsored by the European Association of Teachers of Academic Writing (EATAW), focuses specifically on academic writing in specialized settings, often targeting graduate students writing theses. Lately, many institutions have added quantitative literacy to this mix so that students often write papers analyzing quantitative data and using numbers or other empirical data to support claims. What this kaleidoscope of movements has in common is a commitment to the empowerment of students through a constructivist view of knowledge that demands critical thinking rather than memorization and regurgitation.

A parallel movement has focused on teaching critical thinking. The literature reveals considerable consensus on how critical thinking can be defined. A widely cited definition comes from Paul and Elder (2009), who characterize critical thinking as follows:

> *A well cultivated critical thinker:*
>
> - *raises vital questions and problems, formulating them clearly and precisely*
>
> - *gathers and assesses relevant information, using abstract ideas to interpret it effectively*
>
> - *comes to well-reasoned conclusions and solutions, testing them against relevant criteria and standards*
>
> - *thinks open-mindedly within alternative systems of thought, recognizing and assessing, as need be, their assumptions, implications, and practical consequences; and*
>
> - *communicates effectively with others in figuring out solutions to complex problems. [p. 2]**

In Chapter One, I summarized the definitions of Brookfield (1987) and Kurfiss (1988). Similarly, Perkins, Jay, and Tishman (1994) argue that critical thinkers question assumptions and seek out alternative perspectives that they analyze open-mindedly. All theorists agree that skilled critical thinkers demand justification of claims, seek to disconfirm hypotheses, avoid hasty conclusions, and provide reasons and evidence for their own claims.

Although experts largely agree on what critical thinking means, they often disagree on how to teach it or to assess it. One approach, which we might characterize as "psychometric," disaggregates critical thinking into a variety of subskills such as making inferences, recognizing assumptions, and detecting fallacies. Practitioners then design exercises aimed at developing each subskill. Different scholars identify different sets of subskills. For example, Ennis (2006, 1996) has developed a taxonomy categorizing dozens of subskills under the headings of "dispositions" (three kinds) and "abilities" (fifteen kinds), while one researcher, as reported by Fawkes (2001), identifies 250 subskills. (For a comprehensive bibliography of the research literature and critical thinking textbooks arising from this approach, see Ennis, 2006.) Psychometric researchers have developed a variety of machine-gradable multiple-choice instruments to assess critical

---

*   From *Miniature Guide to Critical Thinking Concepts and Tools* by Richard Paul and Linda Elder, 2009, Dillon Beach, CA: Foundation for Critical Thinking Press, p. 2. www.criticalthinking.org. Used by permission.

thinking skills. The most widely used of these are the Watson Glaser Critical Thinking Appraisal, the California Critical Thinking Skills Test, the Cornell Critical Thinking Test (Levels X or Z), and the California Critical Thinking Disposition Inventory (see Fawkes, 2001, for information about these tests).

However, this approach to critical thinking doesn't illuminate the relationship of critical thinking to writing—that is, to the generation of ideas and to the production of one's own arguments. Another strand of the critical thinking movement—focused on making arguments—is more helpful. Within this approach, critical thinking is both taught and assessed by asking students to construct arguments in response to what cognitive psychologists call "ill-structured problems"—that is, problems that cannot be solved algorithmically to yield a single right answer. Kurfiss (1988) defines critical thinking as "an investigation whose purpose is to explore a situation, phenomenon, question, or problem to arrive at a hypothesis or conclusion about it that integrates all available information and that can therefore be convincingly justified" (p. 2). According to Kurfiss, an effective assessment of critical thinking would typically ask students to develop a "best solution" to an ill-structured problem and to justify the proposed solution with appropriate reasons and evidence. This approach has influenced the developers of the Collegiate Learning Assessment (CLA) to design a critical thinking assessment based on writing rather than a multiple choice test (see Hersh, n.d.).

The rest of this chapter explores in more detail the relationship between writing and critical thinking. It focuses first on the dialogic view of knowledge that characterizes academic writing. It then describes students' difficulties in producing thesis-based organizational structures, explores various theoretical explanations for these difficulties, and suggests pedagogical strategies for overcoming them through improved critical thinking. It concludes with an examination of the writing processes through which experienced writers, in a series of drafts, discover, complicate, and clarify their ideas.

Writing, Thinking, and a Dialogic View of Knowledge

Our friend Skyler believes that he can disguise total ignorance with "good writing" because he sees knowledge as discrete bits of information to be studied and stored in memory. Before he can connect thinking with writing, he needs to understand "knowing" in a different way. Asking a first-year student to write a college-level essay is really asking for a baffling new view of knowledge itself.

The View of Knowledge Underlying Academic Writing

For the most part, formal academic writing requires analytical or argumentative thinking. Such writing is initiated by a problem or question and is typically characterized by a controlling thesis statement supported by a hierarchical structure of reasons and evidence. The thesis statement is the writer's one-sentence summary of his or her argument—the writer's "answer" or "solution" to the question or problem that drives the essay. Thesis-governed writing entails a complex view of knowledge in which differing views about the nature of truth compete for allegiance.

However, as William Perry (1970) has shown in his influential study of students' cognitive growth through college, most of our students do not come to college seeing the world this way. Perry shows that most beginning college students view education dualistically, imagining knowledge as the acquisition of correct information and right answers. They see themselves as empty buckets being filled with data by their professors. To dualists, the only academic use of writing is to demonstrate one's knowledge of the correct facts—a concept of writing as information rather than as argument or analysis. Students in Perry's middle stages of multiplicity are beginning to accept the notion of opposing views, but they see these simply as "opinions"; because "everyone has a right to his or her own opinion," they see little purpose in defending any particular view and thus are not compelled through the process of rigorous thinking that intellectually mature writing demands. It is not until they reach Perry's highest stages of development that a real need for reasoned argument begins to emerge.

What our beginning college writers do not understand, therefore, is the view of academic life implied by writing across the curriculum, where writing means joining a conversation of persons who are, in important ways, *fundamentally disagreeing with each other*, or, to make the matter less agonistic, *jointly seeking answers to shared questions that puzzle them.* In other words, they do not see that a thesis implies a counterthesis and that the presence of opposing or alternative voices implies a view of knowledge as dialogic, contingent, ambiguous, and tentative.

It follows that teaching thesis-governed writing means teaching students an unfamiliar way of looking at their courses and at knowledge itself. For a brief glimpse of a student being initiated into this uncomfortable world, consider for a moment the following transcript of a writing center conference in which the student had been asked to support one of two opposing theses: "The U.S. involvement in Central America is or is not imperialism."

Tutor: If I said, "Tell me whether or not this is imperialism," what's your first gut reaction?

Writer: There are very strong arguments for both. It's all in how you define it.

Tutor: Okay, who's doing the defining?

Writer: Anybody. That's just it—there's no real clear definition. Over time, it's been distorted. I mean, before, imperialism used to be like the British who go in and take Hong Kong, set up their own little thing that's their own British government. That's true imperialism. But the definition's been expanded to include indirect control by other means, and what exactly that is I guess you have to decide. So I don't know. I don't think we really have control in Central America, so that part of me says no, that's not imperialism. But other parts of me say we really do control a lot of what is going on in Central America by the amount of dollars and where we put them. So in that sense, we do have imperialism . . . So the other big question on that, and why I brought in the balance of power, is, where are we allowed to cross the line and where are we not?

Tutor: Okay then, if you're going to ask that question—where are we allowed to cross the line?—it implies that a line is drawn. So what I guess I'm trying to get you to say is [pause]

Writer: Whether I'm for or against.

Tutor: Yes!

Writer: The reason why I'm undecided is because I couldn't create a strong enough argument for either side. There are too many holes in each side. If I were to pick one side, somebody could blow me out of the water.

The student writer, obviously engaged with the assignment, is keenly aware of the tentativeness of both positions, either of which can be "blown out of the water" by the other side. Both the facts of the case and, more troublingly, the definition of imperialism are open-ended problems. The student longs for a "right answer," resisting the frightening prospect of having to make meanings and defend them. Good writing assignments produce exactly this kind of discomfort: the need to join, in a reasoned way, a conversation of differing voices.

We thus need to help our students see that academic writing involves intellectual and often emotional *struggle.* The struggle is rooted in the writer's awareness that a problem exists—often dimly felt, unclarified, and blurry—and that the writer's thesis must be a tentative, risky proposition in response to that problem, a proposition that competes for readers' allegiance with other differing propositions.

Teaching Multiple Drafts as a Thinking Process

Fortunately, the writing process itself provides one of the best ways to help students learn the active, dialogic thinking skills valued in academic life. Students need to understand that even for the most skilled writers, composing an essay is a tortuous process because, as writing theorist Peter Elbow (1973) has argued, "meaning is not what you start out with but what you end up with. . . . Think of writing then not as a way to transmit a message but as a way to grow and cook a message" (p. 15). Thus, the elegance and structure of thesis-governed writing—as a finished product—evolves from a lengthy and messy process of drafting and redrafting. An across-the-curriculum emphasis on multiple drafts encourages the messy process whereby writers become engaged with a problem and, once engaged, formulate, develop, complicate, and clarify their own ideas. The habit of problem posing and thesis making does not come naturally to beginning college students, who write more clearly when given assignments that do *not* challenge them as thinkers. The next sections explore this phenomenon in more detail.

Avoiding a Thesis: Three Cognitively Immature Essay Structures

To see more clearly the relationship between a dialogic view of knowledge and the approach to writing instruction advocated here, let's examine several cognitively immature organizational structures that students often resort to when unable to produce thesis-governed prose.

"And Then" Writing, or Chronological Structure

By "and then" writing I mean a chronological narrative in which the writer tells what happens between time point A and time point B without focus, selection, pacing, or tension. Students produce "and then" writing when they resort inappropriately to chronological organization. Typical examples are students' writing a plot summary of a film or short story instead of an analysis. Another example, commonly encountered in the sciences, is students' writing a literature review that simply summarizes articles in the order in which the student read them without creating an argument about what's known or unknown.

"And then" writing can be illustrated by the following student's difficulty in producing an interpretive argument about Shakespeare's *The Tempest*. This excerpt is from the introduction of the student's first draft:

> *Prospero cares deeply for his daughter. In the middle of the play Prospero acts like a gruff father and makes Ferdinand carry logs in order to test his love for Miranda and Miranda's love for him. He is also very cruel to the servant Caliban. In the end, though, Prospero is a loving father who rejoices in his daughter's marriage to a good man.*

Here the student seems to be summarizing the plot of *The Tempest* without forecasting an argument or proposing a thesis. The body of this draft contained similar passages of lengthy plot summary. However, in an office conference the instructor discovered that the student actually intended an argument. She thought that Prospero was a loving father, in contrast to several of her classmates who thought that Prospero was a tyrannical ruler and parent. The instructor helped her recast the introduction to set up a thesis.

> *Many persons believe that Prospero is an evil person in the play. They claim that Prospero exhibits a harsh, destructive control over Miranda and also, like Faust, seeks superhuman knowledge through his magic. However, I contend that Prospero is a kind and loving father.*

The student is now prepared to make an argument. The paper poses a problem (What kind of father is Prospero?), indicates an opposing view (Prospero is harsh and hateful), and asserts a contestable thesis (Prospero is loving). She now needs to develop her reasons for arguing that Prospero is loving and organize her paper hierarchically to support these reasons with appropriate textual details.

It must be noted, however, that it is not just inexperienced writers who produce chronological structures. In their classic study, Linda Flower and John R. Hayes (1977) show that long passages of chronological writing characterize the early drafts of expert writers (see also Flower, 1979). In fact, they argue that chronological thinking provides a natural way of retrieving ideas and details from long-term memory. But experienced writers convert "and then" material into hierarchically focused material as they revise, whereas novice writers seem satisfied with the draft at the "and then" stage.

"All About" Writing, or Encyclopedic Order

Whereas the "and then" paper strings details on a chronological frame, the "all about" paper tries to say a little bit of everything about a topic. When well written, such papers may seem organized hierarchically because the writer usually groups data by category or topics. But the categories do not function as reasons in support of a thesis. Rather, like the headings in an encyclopedia article, they are simply ways of arranging information that do not add up to an argument.

Unfortunately, educators in America have a long tradition of rewarding "all about" writing. We encourage such writing when we assign a "report on North Dakota" in fifth-grade social studies, a "library paper on General Rommel" in eleventh-grade history, or "a term paper on schizophrenia" in college psychology. Assignments like these have endured because they have one major virtue: they increase students' general store of knowledge about North Dakota, General Rommel, or schizophrenia. But they often do little to increase students' maturity as writers and thinkers.

Consider the difference between a student who is asked to write a traditional "term paper" on, say, Charles Darwin versus a student who is asked to write a research paper on Darwin that must begin with the presentation of a problem or question that the writer will investigate and try to resolve.

Without guidance, the first student will tend toward "all about" writing, perhaps producing an initial outline with headings like these:

I.   Early childhood

II. How Darwin became interested in evolution

III. The voyage of the *Beagle*

IV. An explanation of Darwin's theory

V.   Darwin's influence

This paper promises to be encyclopedic and devoid of surprise. But when the student is guided toward a focus on a significant question that grows out of the writer's interests and that demands critical thinking, undergraduate research writing can spring to life. Flower (1993, p. 299) describes a successful undergraduate term paper on Darwin written at Carnegie Mellon University for a course in cognitive psychology. Flower's student Kate, a sophomore, posed the following problem about Darwin at the end of her introduction:

In this paper I will look at the creativity of Charles Darwin by asking two questions. Does Darwin's work support or contradict current psychological definitions of creativity? And secondly, what is the best way to account for Darwin's own kind of creativity? Which of the major theories best fits the facts of Darwin's life and work?

Within her paper, Kate presented different theories of creativity and examined Darwin's work in the light of each theory. She proposed that Darwin was indeed creative and that his creativity could best be accounted for by the "problem-solving theory" of creativity, as opposed to the "romantic imagination theory," the "Freudian sexual energy theory," or "Wallis's four-stage theory."

Kate's essay reveals how successful undergraduate writing can be when students are actively engaged in posing and exploring questions. Emphasizing inquiry and question asking is thus a promising antidote to "all about" writing.

Data Dump Writing, or Random Organization

Both "and then" writing and "all about" writing have discernible organizational plans—chronological in the former case and encyclopedic in the latter. Data dump writing, by contrast, has no discernible structure. It reveals a student overwhelmed with information and uncertain what to do with it. Commonly encountered in research papers, data dump writing patches together quotes, statistics, and other raw information without a thesis or a coherent organizational plan. It takes all the data the writer gathered about topic X and dumps it, as it were, on the reader's desk. Data dump writing is particularly facilitated by the Internet because it is so easy to cut and paste material from websites; students often lift material word for word without assimilating it into their own language. Data dump papers can create nightmares for teachers with their exasperating mix of incomprehensible structure and possible plagiarism. Because data dump writing is familiar to all teachers, it needs no specific illustration here.

What Causes These Organizational Problems?

The "and then" paper, the "all about" paper, and the data dump paper all reveal a retreat, in some manner, from the kind of reasoned analysis and argumentation that we value in academic writing. Why do these problems occur? A number of explanations have been posed. For example, writing theorists influenced by the Swiss psychologist Jean Piaget have hypothesized that the immature organizational patterns just described are symptomatic of concrete operational reasoners, who tend to focus on data, objects, or things as opposed to propositions or forms (Lunsford, 1979; Bradford, 1983). In writing, concrete operational reasoners can string details together chronologically ("and then" writing) or arrange them in simple informational categories ("all about" writing). But creating the kinds of nested hierarchical structures required in propositional writing requires the abstract thinking that characterizes formal operations.

Other explanations focus on theories of intellectual development such as Perry's developmental theory (1970) based on research with male students at Harvard or by Belenky, Clinchy, Goldberger, and Tarule (1986), who focus on women. In both schemas, students come to college imagining knowledge as the acquisition of correct information rather than the ability, say, to argue a position. Eventually, students develop a complex view of knowledge, where individuals have to take stands in the light of their own values and the best available reasons and evidence. Composition scholars using these theories have hypothesized that students will produce cognitively immature prose as long as their attitude toward knowledge remains in the early stages of intellectual growth (Hays, 1983; Lunsford, 1985). The best teaching strategies for accelerating students' growth are tasks that ask students to consider multiple points of view, to confront clashing values, and to imagine, analyze, and evaluate alternative solutions to problems. Many of the assignments used as illustrations throughout this book have these aims.

Still other explanations focus on the different cognitive processes of novices versus experts (Beaufort, 2007; Graff, 2004; Alexander, 2003; Bransford, Brown, and Cocking, 2000; Voss, 1989; Kurfiss, 1988; Sommers, 1980; Flower and Hayes, 1977). Novice/expert theory provides perhaps the most hopeful of all explanations because it implies fairly quick improvements in student writing derived from improved teaching practices. In this view, students simply have not been taught the kind of writing admired in the academy. "And then" structures, "all about" structures, and data dumping are the result of poorly designed writing assignments and uncoordinated teaching.

For example, many teachers report improvement in their students' writing when they use Booth, Colomb, and Williams (2008) to explain how expert academic writers construct an introduction: early in the introduction the writer must identify a problem, show why the problem is problematic, and motivate readers to see the problem's importance. Other teachers report the benefits of teaching students what Graff and Birkenstein (2009) call "the moves that matter in academic prose." Building on Graff's

(2004) earlier analysis of students as outsiders to academic prose, Graff and Birkenstein set out to demystify academic prose by showing students how to insert their own voices into academic conversations. (Later in this chapter I summarize some of the "moves" taught by Graff and Birkenstein—see pages 31–32.)

Pedagogical Strategies for Promoting Critical Thinking

This overview of writing and critical thinking points toward a consistent set of teaching practices aimed at promoting critical thinking about subject matter problems. If we are to create a pedagogy truly aimed at the development of thinking skills, we should consider adopting the following strategies.

Create Cognitive Dissonance for Students

According to Meyers (1986), "Students cannot learn to think critically until they can, at least momentarily, set aside their own visions of the truth and reflect on alternatives" (p. 27). A good way to promote this process is to create what psychologists call *cognitive dissonance*, which undermines students' confidence in their own settled beliefs or assumptions. Research in neuroscience, as summarized by Zull (2002), offers a material explanation for how cognitive dissonance helps restructure neuronal networks in the brain. Zull explains how knowledge exists as elaborate networks of neurons and synapses. Because learners build new knowledge on existing neuronal networks, these existing networks must be partially dismantled if the learner is to create new networks that embrace fuller, more detailed knowledge. To encourage new networks, Zull recommends assignments that help students dismantle an older mistaken or inadequate view. Thus a physics teacher might facilitate this process by giving an assignment like this:

> *Many people believe, mistakenly, that summer is hotter than winter because the summer sun is closer to the earth. Imagine someone who holds this mistaken belief (your kid brother, for example). Send this person an e-mail attachment that explains why this belief seems logical but is in fact wrong. Then offer a better explanation.*

In similar fashion, a teacher might challenge views that oversimplify a concept or make the concept too comfortable. Here is a professor's assignment for a first-year seminar on the nature/nurture controversy in gender identity:

In class yesterday, almost 90 percent of you thought that Lawrence Summers was wrong in offering a biological hypothesis for why there are so few tenured female professors in math and physics at major research universities. Tomorrow's homework asks you to read the article by Harvard psychologist Steven Pinker, who supports Summers' biological hypothesis. Write a one-page thinking piece in which you summarize Pinker's argument and then explore ways that the research he cites causes you to view this issue more complexly.

Another strategy is to create "decentering" tasks that encourage students to see a phenomenon from an unfamiliar perspective or to teach them to play what Peter Elbow calls the "believing and doubting game" (1973, p. 147), a strategy that I explain in detail in Chapter Nine. The point of these strategies is to present students with conflicting interpretations of material and to encourage them to confront the inadequacies and contradictions lying dormant in the views they bring to college.

Present Knowledge as Dialogic Rather Than Informational

In addition to creating cognitive dissonance for our students, we need to show them that our course readings (and our lectures) are not "information" but arguments. In many academic disciplines—particularly the humanities and social sciences—introductory courses often initiate students into disciplinary examples of opposing views (Plato versus the pre-Socratics in philosophy, competing interpretations of *Hamlet* in literature, behaviorism versus humanism in psychology). In other disciplines—particularly the physical sciences and engineering—introductory courses must build up a disciplinary knowledge base presented largely as information. But much of what is now "known" in the sciences—and passed on to students as current knowledge—was once unknown and subject to theory, hypothesis, and empirical study. If science teachers can promote awareness of the historical development of knowledge—the original questions that gave rise to the currently accepted facts—they will be foregrounding what I mean by a dialogic or questioning epistemology.

To dramatize the difference between information and argument, teachers can situate readings and lectures within a dialogic structure. A master of this approach at my own institution was a much loved and now deceased historian who, in advance of a unit of lectures, gave his students a series of controversial theses that brought the course's subject matter into problematic focus. The students knew in advance that they would need to use what they learned from lectures and readings to attack or defend each thesis in a short writing assignment. Typical theses used by my colleague included the following:

- The *essential* theme of the French Revolution was human freedom; Napoleon Bonaparte killed the French Revolution by reversing its thrust toward freedom.

- The Industrial Revolution created unprecedented wealth at the expense of brutalizing European labor and colonial producers.

- The ultimate victors in the English Revolution of 1688, the American Revolution, and the French Revolution were the economically conservative property-owning classes.

In all cases, the writing assignment is the same: "Present an argument that supports, rejects, or modifies the given thesis, and support your response with factual evidence." My colleague's goal was to help students see the difference between history as one damn thing after another and history as a constructed argument based on data and interpretation.

Teach the Academic "Moves" and Genres That Are Important in Your Discipline

Chapter Three on rhetorical problems and Chapter Thirteen on teaching undergraduate research will develop this strategy in more detail, but the general principles are relevant here. Certain "moves" of academic writing may be generic across all disciplines. For example, Graff and Birkenstein (2009) have identified the moves that help students position their own claims within a conversation of alternative views. Here are some examples of particularly important moves:

- "They say/I say"—which teaches students to summarize the views to which they are responding. In some cases, the "they say" is an opposing view (for example, a "mistaken critic"). In this case the "they" sets up a problem and becomes the exigency that prompts the writer's argument. In other cases, the "they say" sums up the current state of knowledge on a question (the literature review) prompting the "I say," which is the writer's contribution aimed at advancing knowledge.

- "Yes, no, OK but"—which teaches students three main ways to respond to another writer's view: to accept it and extend it (yes), to disagree with it (no), or to complicate it (OK but).

- "Plant a naysayer in your text"—which teaches students to role-play alternative moves by imagining and responding to the perspective of skeptics.

- "So what?"—which teaches students to articulate why the writer's argument matters by showing what is at stake.

Closely related to Graff and Birkenstein's academic moves are prototype templates for the deep structure of an academic argument (see Bartholomae, 1985):

- Many scholars have argued X, but I am going to argue Y.

- Scholars have frequently asked questions X, Y, and Z. But curiously they have neglected to ask A. This essay poses question A and proposes a solution.

- Researchers are currently confident in their understanding of X and Y. But we don't yet understand Z because a component of Z is unknown. This paper tests a hypothesis relevant to that component.

Simply helping students understand these prototype structures goes a long way toward helping them envision a purpose for their writing.

In many cases, instructors also need to teach the genres of a given discipline, such as the experimental report, the ethnography, the research proposal, the business plan, or the interpretive argument in literature. Strategies for introducing students to the genres of their major fields are examined in Chapter Thirteen.

Create Opportunities for Active Problem Solving That Involve Dialogue and Writing

Homework and other activities for a course should engage students in complex thinking about significant problems. To accomplish this end, teachers need to structure activities to help students become personally engaged with questions addressed by the course. As we have seen, teachers can do so by designing good problems for students to think about—problems that cause students to reflect on course readings and to use course concepts and data actively in writing assignments and in class discussions and debate. (Recall that by "writing assignments," I mean anything from formal term papers to one-minute freewrites.) The rest of the chapters in this book discuss numerous strategies for integrating teacher-designed problems into a course.

Teaching Thinking Through Teaching Revision

Composition research confirms that most students do not revise their essays, as the term *revise* is understood by expert writers. Of course, students *think* they are revising, but usually they are merely editing—checking spelling, making word substitutions, tinkering with sentences, deciding on punctuation. (Classic early studies of the revising behavior of novices versus experts include Faigley and Witte, 1981; Sommers, 1980; Flower, 1979; and Beach, 1976. Recent works on teaching revision include Booth, Colomb, and Williams, 2008; Harris, 2006; and Gopen, 2004.)

What our students need to understand is that for expert writers the actual act of writing causes further discovery, development, and modification of ideas. If one examines the evolving drafts of an expert writer, one sees the messy, recursive process of thinking itself as new ideas emerge during the drafting process. Expert writers do extensive rewriting, the final products often being substantially different from the first drafts. (To encourage this kind of global revision, I often tell students that a "C" paper is an "A" paper turned in too soon.)

The foregoing description differs from an older positivist model of the writing process that many of us of a certain age were taught in school. The old model looked like this:

A Positivist Model of the Writing Process

1. Choose a topic.

2. Narrow it.

3. Write a thesis.

4. Make an outline.

5. Write a draft.

6. Revise.

7. Edit.

This description presupposes what Elbow (1973) calls the "think, then write" model of composing in which writers discover, clarify, and organize their ideas before they start to write. But it seriously misrepresents the way most academic writers actually compose. For example, few scholars report starting an article by choosing a topic and then narrowing it. Rather, academic writers report being gradually drawn into a conversation about a question that does not yet seem resolved. The writer-to-be finds this conversation somehow unsatisfactory; something is missing, wrongheaded, unexplained, or otherwise puzzling. Similarly, having focused on a problem, only rarely does a skilled academic writer write a thesis statement and outline before embarking on extensive exploration, conversation, correspondence with colleagues, and even, on some occasions, writing one or more drafts. A thesis statement often marks a moment of discovery and clarification—an "aha!" experience ("So *this* is my point! Here is my argument in a nutshell!") rather than a formulaic planning device at the very start of the process.

Presenting students with this problem-driven model of the writing process has a distinct advantage for teachers. It allows them to link the teaching of writing to their own interests in teaching the modes of inquiry and discovery in their disciplines. Their goal is to get students personally engaged with the kinds of questions that propel writers through the writing process. Thus the writing process itself becomes a powerful means of active learning in the discipline.

Why Don't Students Revise?

If one of our major goals is to teach thinking through revision, we need to understand more clearly why students do not revise. Our first tendency may be to blame students' lack of motivation or their ineffective time management. They do not revise because they are not interested in their work or do not care about it or simply put off getting started until the night before a paper is due. But other explanations should also be considered.

For example, one hypothesis, influenced by Piagetian theory, argues that revision requires the ability to "decenter" (Kroll, 1978; Bradford, 1983)—that is, to think like a reader instead of a writer. One of Piaget's observations is that persons identified as concrete operational reasoners have difficulty switching perspectives. If sitting in the back of a classroom, for example, a person may have trouble sketching the room from the perspective of a lecturer standing in front. By analogy, novice writers may have difficulty imagining their drafts *from a reader's perspective*. If a passage seems clear to the writer, he or she believes that it ought to be immediately clear to the reader also. Novice writers may simply not recognize their reader's confusion and consequently not recognize the need to fill in gaps, to link new information to old information, or to arrange material in the order needed by readers.

Related theories emphasize students' lack of familiarity with academic genres or with the complexity of addressing rhetorical problems (purpose, audience, genre) as well as subject matter problems. What drives revision for mature writers is their awareness of the complex conversation that a piece of writing must join—how its argument must accommodate opposing views, for example, while also contributing something new to the conversation. Thus, mature writers need multiple drafts because, in the face of many different goals and rhetorical constraints, they can concentrate on only one or two problems at a time.

Another contributing factor may be the increasingly common strategy of composing and revising on a computer screen without paper drafts. When word processing first came into vogue, several researchers (Daiute, 1986; Hawisher, 1987) showed that although word processing facilitates sentence-level revision as well as some larger-scale revisions such as additions, deletions, and block moves of text, it may actually discourage major reconceptualizing of a text—the kind of global revision that leads to substantial dismantling and rewriting. By revising from the screen rather than from a hard copy, writers see only narrow windows of their text rather than the whole. Global revision often requires the writer to revisit earlier passages, to compare, for example, a topic sentence on page 5 with what was forecast on page 2. Such a bird's-eye overview of a text is easier with hard copy than on screen, where scrolling backward is time-consuming.

Whatever the cause of students' failure to revise, teachers need to create an academic environment that encourages revision. The importance of revision has been highlighted by the NSSE/WPA research on writing assignments that contribute to deep learning (Anderson, Anson, Gonyea, and Paine, 2009). This research identifies the presence of "interactive elements" in an assignment as the first of three criteria for best practices. These interactive elements include building into the assignment opportunities for in-class brainstorming, peer review, teacher feedback on drafts, or visits to a writing center. (See Chapter Six for further discussion of the NSSE/WPA research.)

Fifteen Suggestions for Encouraging Revision

In the spirit of this research, I offer fifteen suggestions for promoting revision by building interactive elements into an assignment or a course.

1. *Profess a problem-driven model of the writing process.* Instead of asking students to choose "topics" and narrow them, encourage students to pose questions or problems and explore them. Show how inquiry and writing are related.

2. *Give problem-focused writing assignments.* Students are most apt to revise when their essays must be responses to genuine problems. See Chapter Six for advice on creating writing assignments that guide students toward a problem-thesis structure.

3. *Create active learning tasks that help students become posers and explorers of questions.* Students need to be seized by questions and to appreciate how the urge to write grows out of the writer's desire to say something new about a question or problem. Through classroom activities that let students explore their own responses to questions, students rehearse the thinking strategies that underlie revision. Chapters Eight through Thirteen focus on strategies for active learning.

4. *Incorporate low-stakes exploratory writing into your course.* Chapter Seven suggests numerous ways to incorporate exploratory writing into a course. Exploratory writing gives students the space, incentive, and tools for more elaborated and complex thinking.

5. *Build talk time and writing center conferences into the writing process.* Student writers need to talk about their ideas with others by conversing with classmates, friends, or writing center consultants/tutors. Writers need to bounce ideas off interested listeners, to test arguments, to see how audiences react, and to get feedback on drafts. In this regard, consider having students talk through their ideas in small groups before they write their first drafts. On many campuses, the writing center director can arrange for writing center consultants/tutors to conduct tutor-led brainstorming or draft workshops in class. Also encourage one-on-one writing center consultations. One of the most important services offered by writing centers is the opportunity for students to talk through their ideas in the early stages of drafting.

6. *Intervene in the writing process by having students submit something to you.* Take advantage of the summarizable nature of thesis-based writing by having students submit to you their problem proposals, thesis statements, nutshelling statements, or self-written abstracts. Use these brief pieces of writing to identify persons who need extra help. Much of this work can be done online through electronic bulletin boards or other courseware. See Chapter Fifteen for further details.

7. *Build process requirements into the assignment, including due dates for drafts.* If students are going to stay up all night before a paper is due, make that an all-night session for a mandatory rough draft rather than for a finished product.

8. *Develop strategies for peer review of drafts, either in class or out of class.* After students have completed a rough draft, well in advance of the final due date, have students exchange drafts and serve as "readers" for each other. See Chapter Fifteen for advice on conducting peer reviews.

9. *Hold writing conferences, especially for students who are having difficulty with the assignment.* Traditionally, teachers in American universities

spend more time writing comments on finished products than on holding conferences earlier in the writing process. As a general rule, time spent "correcting" finished products is not as valuable as time spent in conference with students at the rough draft stages. See Chapter Fifteen for suggestions.

10. *Require students to submit all drafts, notes, and doodles along with final copies.* Have students staple their final copies on top of draft material arranged chronologically like geological strata. Not only will you have evidence of your students' writing process, but you will also set up a powerful defense against plagiarism.

11. *Allow rewrites, or make revision-oriented comments on typed next-to-final drafts.* Many students are motivated toward revision by the hope of an improved grade. If students have an opportunity to revise an essay after you have made your comments, you will strike a major blow for writing as a process. See Chapters Five, Fifteen, and Sixteen for advice on writing marginal and end comments that encourage revision rather than cosmetic editing.

12. *Bring in examples of your own work in progress so that students can see how you go through the writing process yourself.* Students like to know that their teachers also struggle with writing. The more you can show students your own difficulties as a writer, the more you can improve their own self-images.

13. *Give advice on the mechanics of revising.* If students compose entirely online, explain the advantages of revising on a double-spaced hard copy rather than on the screen. This strategy leaves plenty of room on the page for crossing out and revising while making it easier to look back at earlier pages for inserting large-scale mapping statements, signposts, and other structural cues.

14. *Don't overemphasize essay exams.* Symbolically, essay exams convey the message that writing is a transcription of already clear ideas rather than a means of discovering and making meaning. They suggest that revision is not important and that good writers produce acceptable finished copy in one draft. Although essay exams obviously have an important place in liberal education, they should not substitute for writing that goes through multiple drafts. See Chapter Twelve for further discussion of essay exams.

15. *Hold to high standards for finished products.* Teachers are so used to seeing early drafts as final copy that they often forget how good a globally revised essay can be when teachers demand excellence. Students do not see much point in revision if they can earn A's or B's for their quickly edited first drafts.

Conclusion: The Implications of Writing as a Means of Thinking in the Undergraduate Curriculum

As this chapter has tried to show, teaching thesis-based analytical and argumentative writing means teaching the thinking processes that underlie academic inquiry. To use writing as a means of thinking, teachers need to make the design of writing assignments a significant part of course preparation and to adopt teaching strategies that give students repeated, active practice at exploring disciplinary questions and problems. Additionally, it is important to emphasize inquiry, question asking, and cognitive dissonance in courses and, whenever possible, to show that scholars in a discipline often disagree about answers to key questions. By teaching a problem-driven model of the writing process, teachers send a message to the Skylers of the world that good writing is not a pretty package for disguising ignorance. Rather it is a way of discovering, making, and communicating meanings that are significant, interesting, and challenging.

3

Helping Writers Think Rhetorically

Some years ago I had the opportunity to participate in a statewide assessment of student writing in upper-division courses across the curriculum. Researchers collected several hundred papers written by juniors and seniors from a wide range of disciplines at six public universities. Our goal for this first-stage project was descriptive: we were to determine what kinds of papers students were being asked to write and to classify them into whatever categories seemed to emerge. What we discovered as we puzzled over many of the papers was that we should have asked for an assignment sheet to be attached to each paper.

Our confusion indicated that students were not thinking rhetorically about audience. Without the assignments, we struggled to understand what many of the papers were doing. Students tended to write directly to the teacher, whose background knowledge we didn't share. We were plopped down in the middle of a conversation to which we hadn't been introduced. As outside readers, we needed papers with effective titles that identified the subject and promised something new or challenging. We also needed introductions that explained the problem to be addressed, filled in needed background, and offered some kind of thesis statement or purpose statement to indicate the writer's intentions and to forecast the argument.

Clearly students across the disciplines were not being coached to transfer into their upper division writing the rhetorical knowledge introduced in first-year composition. A goal of most first-year composition programs is to show students how a writer's decisions are often functions of the writer's rhetorical situation—the writer's purpose, audience, and genre. Particularly, expert writers pose the following kinds of questions about their rhetorical context:

- Who are my intended readers?

- How much do my readers already know and care about my topic? What is their stance toward my topic?

- What is my purpose for writing? What kind of change do I want to bring about in my readers' understanding of my topic? When my readers finish my paper, what do I want them to know, believe, or do?

- What genre is most appropriate for my context? What are the features and constraints of this genre? What style, level of language, and document design does this genre require?

My goal in this chapter is to suggest ways that disciplinary instructors can help students practice these rhetorical skills when they write papers in any field. Recent scholarship has shown that helping students situate their writing within a rhetorical context helps them transfer knowledge from one writing situation to another (Beaufort, 2007; Carter, 2007; Carroll, 2002). Because thinking rhetorically is such an important skill, writing theorists recommend that teachers build a rhetorical context into every writing assignment. (I offer suggestions for doing so both in this chapter and in Chapter Six.) When students learn to wrestle with questions about purpose, audience, and genre, they develop a conceptual view of writing that has lifelong usefulness in any communicative context.

Helping Students Think About Audience and Purpose

An important difference between novice and expert writers is that experts think about audience early in the writing process whereas novices don't (see Sommers's classic study, 1980). Closely related to audience is the concept of purpose. One way to think about purpose is through the writer's aim—such as to inform, to explain, to analyze, to persuade, to reflect, to entertain, and so forth. But another useful way to understand purpose is to articulate the kind of change the writer hopes to bring about in the readers' view of his or her topic. Instructors can help students understand purpose in this way by having them do the following nutshell exercise while planning their papers:

Before reading my paper, my readers will think this way about my topic: _____.

But after reading my paper, my readers will think this different way about my topic: _____.

Here are some examples:

- Before reading my paper, my readers will think that Hamlet lives in a traditional Christian universe inherited from the Middle Ages. But after reading my paper, my readers will see that Hamlet lives in an absurdist world similar to Sartre's existentialism.

- Before reading my paper, my little brother will think that summer is hotter than winter because the earth is closer to the sun. But after reading my paper, he will see that summer is hotter than winter because the tilt of the earth's axis causes the "summer hemisphere" to receive more concentrated overhead sun rays and the "winter hemisphere" to receive more slanted, diffused sun rays.

- Before reading my paper, my readers will think that wind power is a viable alternative energy source for the United States. But after reading my paper, my readers will see that wind power can never provide more than 4 percent of the nation's electricity needs.

- Before reading my experimental report, my readers will be uncertain whether 1940s Mickey Mouse cartoons have less or more gender stereotyping than recent *SpongeBob SquarePants* cartoons. After reading my report, readers will see that *SpongeBob SquarePants* cartoons have less gender stereotyping with a statistically significant level of confidence.

Articulating purpose in this way is particularly valuable in settings calling for thesis-governed prose. When the thesis pushes against an alternative view, it creates the kind of tension encouraged by Graff and Birkenstein's (2009) template "They say/I say." Because the writer must defend a contestable thesis against a background of what others say, readers can appreciate that something is at stake in the argument. Moreover, articulating purpose in terms of changing the audience's view is an effective antidote against "and then" papers, "all about" papers, and data dumps as described in Chapter Two (pages 24–27).

When helping students imagine an audience, therefore, I want them to imagine simultaneously the audience's initial stance toward the writer's topic. It is this stance that creates for the writer an implied purpose or role. Here are some typical kinds of audiences and initial stances that instructors can use:

Naïve audience: Here the instructor specifies a naïve audience who needs new information or a clear explanation of something. The student plays the role of expert relative to the assigned audience.

- Explain the difference between velocity and acceleration to a student who missed last week's lectures.

- Your batty uncle thinks it is unfair and stupid that passengers sitting in the same section of an airplane probably paid different prices for their tickets. As an economics student, help your uncle see why all these different prices make perfect economic sense and are not unfair.

- Your boss needs an informative report on competitors' marketing and pricing strategies for selected items that are not selling well in your stores. Do the research and write your report for the boss.

- A nine-year-old diabetic child needs to understand the glycemic index of foods. As a pediatric nurse, prepare a short talk that will explain glycemic index in language the child will understand.

Puzzled audiences with skeptical tendencies: Here writer and reader of equal status confront a shared question or problem. The writer's role is to present, through critical thinking and analysis, a "best solution" to the problem while attending to counterviews. The audience will be interested in your solution but will raise skeptical questions.

- What kind of bearings should we use in our design for a circumferentially mounted radiator fan? Write a proposal to fellow engineers uncertain about the best approach but likely to raise objections to your solution.

- Does Hamlet change in the last act? Write to classmates who are apt to be skeptical of your answer.

- You are a research assistant to a state legislator who needs to decide whether to support a new sales tax on soda and candy. Using the economic analysis tools we have learned in class, write a recommendation memo to your boss.

Resistant or hostile audiences: Here students must imagine an audience whose views of the subject are well formed and opposed to the writer's view. The writer's purpose is more clearly argumentative and persuasive.

- The design team for the circumferentially mounted radiator fan has recommended air bearings, but you believe that this decision is a mistake. Write a memo to your project manager laying out your best case against air bearings.

- Next week there will be a public hearing on whether to use taxpayer dollars to build a new sports arena for a professional basketball team in your city. Because you have been researching public financing of sports stadiums, you have been asked to present your position in a formal speech at the beginning of the hearing. Prepare your PowerPoint presentation for a five-minute speech. Try to sway those most opposed to your position.

Helping students think rhetorically about audience and purpose can lead to substantial improvements in their writing. I'll cite two recent examples from my own research with colleagues across the disciplines. In a sophomore organic chemistry course, chemists Peter J. Alaimo and Joseph Langenhan decided to eliminate traditional lab reports in order to teach students how to write authentic professional papers in chemistry (Alaimo, Bean, Langenhan, and Nichols, 2009). To do so, they replaced cookbook lab experiments with newly designed experimental problems that simulated discovery research. For all their writing assignments—aimed at teaching each of the sections of a scientific report—they specified a professional audience of practicing chemists who were interested in the assigned experimental problem but not familiar with it. Here they describe their rationale:

> The problem with conventional lab reports is that they encourage students to think and behave like students rather than like professionals. . . . Also [students'] assumption that the audience for their reports is the instructor contributes to a novice style. In many cases this assumption is highly visible: Students [often referred] to the instructor directly in their writing (e.g., "Professor Alaimo said we should use 1 M NaOH rather than the 1.2 M NaOH that the lab manual recommended") [p. 20].

To address this problem, Alaimo and Langenhan emphasized writing to an outside professional audience rather than the instructor. "When students write to their instructor as audience, they see lab reports as homework, not as professional documents. In contrast, imagining professional scientists as the audience orients students to adopt the persona of expert insiders who are communicating with other expert insiders" (p. 22). Writing to a professional audience, they explain, requires students to "provide scientific context, construct well-formulated ideas, and build persuasive arguments for readers who have a professional interest in but no prior knowledge of the specific experiment" (p. 22). The authors show how imagining a professional audience led to substantial improvements in the quality of the papers.

Whereas our chemistry project focused on writing to professionals, a second project, led by finance professor David Carrithers, asked students to write to a lay audience—in this case a small business owner with no background in finance or quantitative analysis. Carrithers asked students to analyze the owner's finance problem (requiring professional expertise) and then to write a memo to the owner recommending a course of action (Carrithers and Bean, 2008; Carrithers, Bean, and Ling, 2008). Carrithers specified a lay audience not only because finance professionals often work with nonexpert clients but also because addressing a lay audience forces students to avoid finance jargon—a constraint that requires an extra dimension of critical thinking. Here is his reasoning (Carrithers and Bean, 2008):

> At first glance, finance faculty might consider overuse of jargon to be primarily a rhetorical problem resulting from insufficient focus on audience. But we believe it may also indicate an underlying critical thinking problem. When students use financial jargon, including abbreviations, [illustrated in a previous example], it may indicate that they are not comfortable in their knowledge of the concept—especially when they provide no explanation of the tool or how it is employed in the analysis. Students, we surmise, tend to find comfort in jargon. They can memorize the terms and thus feel that they sound like finance professionals without fully understanding the concepts they represent. However, it takes considerable control of the concepts to be able to explain them to a nonexpert audience. Besides revealing weak communication skills, use of jargon may thus be evidence of a fundamental inability to use financial concepts in unfamiliar settings [p. 19].

What we discovered in the initial phases of our finance project is that students were surprisingly resistant to writing to a lay audience. With few exceptions, despite the assignment's admonition to address an owner who had no insider knowledge of finance, students wrote directly to the teacher. Students loaded their memos with finance jargon and even attached pages of Excel spreadsheets that would make sense only to a finance expert. We interviewed a representative sampling of students to discover why they didn't adapt their message to the assigned audience. Their reasons were instructive:

- They didn't think the instructor was serious about writing to a lay audience. They didn't see the assignment as an authentic, open-ended problem requiring an argument; rather they thought the assignment was simply a "story problem" to be solved algorithmically to find a right answer.

- They didn't think they would sound professional unless they used jargon; they felt they would be dumbing down their knowledge if they took the lay audience requirement seriously.

- They didn't realize the importance of walking in the shoes of business owners who needed bottom-line advice for making a decision but didn't need to know the analytical steps that yielded the information. Until prompted by our interview questions, they didn't realize that the owner—unlike the instructor—would be confused by the finance jargon and Excel spreadsheets. They also didn't realize that they often buried (or didn't supply at all) the actual information that the owner needed.

- They didn't see the relevance of a previous course in business writing, which stressed analysis of audience and purpose as the first step in producing a memo. Students didn't transfer knowledge from the business writing course to the finance course, apparently because they regarded the curriculum as a sequence of isolated courses with little connection to each other.

These findings support the frequently encountered observation that students write to the teacher even when they have been assigned a "real world" audience. As Anne Beaufort (2007) puts it in her own study of students' gradual acquisition of rhetorical knowledge, "School takes precedence; it is more immediate, so the more distant target audience cannot be fully imagined" (p. 132). However, Beaufort shows how students make progress, sometimes quickly, when teachers stress the importance of imagining the needs of the reader. Our own research supports Beaufort's conclusion.

EXHIBIT 3.1

Sample Questions to Spur Rhetorical Thinking

Question to Ask	Purpose or Value of This Question
What is my level of expertise relative to my assigned audience? (Note: A student may be a novice relative to the instructor but an expert relative to someone else.)	Helps writer determine an appropriate level of vocabulary and syntax as well as amount of background and development needed.
How do I want to change my readers' view of my topic?	Helps writer establish a contestable thesis in conversation with alternative views.
How much does my audience already know about the problem/issue I am addressing? How much do they care about it?	Helps writer compose an effective introduction. The less an audience already knows about the writer's subject, the more the writer must provide background and context. To motivate the audience to care, the writer needs to make the problem vivid and to show why addressing the problem matters.
What's the "news" in my paper? What constitutes old information and new information for my audience?	Helps writer connect new information to old information. Readers need to know the "news" quickly—usually in the title or subject line and certainly early in the introduction. But the news makes sense only when linked to the reader's previous knowledge and interests (old information).
How resistant is my audience to my thesis?	Helps the writer accommodate resistant readers. Resistant audiences need assurance that the writer has thought about and respects alternative views; they'll expect the writer to anticipate possible objections and respond to them.
How busy is my audience?	Helps writer think about reader's environment. Busy audiences often prefer concise documents with easy-to-scan structures and meanings up front.

Helping students think rhetorically teaches concepts with great explanatory power. Exhibit 3.1 gives examples of the kinds of questions that instructors can encourage students to pose about any disciplinary writing assignment.

Helping Students Think About Genre

Besides purpose and audience, another important rhetorical concept is genre. The term *genre* refers to recurring types of writing identifiable by distinctive features of structure, style, document design, approach to subject matter, or other markers. Genres usually arise from recurring cultural occasions or situations with their own recognizable patterns. Certain cultural contexts or situations might invite a writer to, say, compose a syllabus, a text message, a letter to the editor, or a scholarly article (all examples of genres) or to purchase a birthday card or a bumper sticker (genres that let you say your piece without having to put your own pen to paper). Any given genre has prototypical members that exemplify the most common features of the genre as well as outlier or borderline members that push the limits of the genre, playing creatively with its features. Some genres, such as the APA research report, are governed by strictly prescribed rules set forth in an organization's publication manual. Other genres are more diffuse or open to a wide range of structures and style (popular magazine articles, blogs, the personal essay). Exhibit 3.2 shows some typical examples of genres.

The concept of genre is often confusing to students. One way I try to explain genre is to create an analogy between genres and dress codes. Just as some social occasions create writing genres, I explain, other social occasions create clothing genres. I place on the board some typical social occasions such as "wedding," "job interview," "high school prom," "'70s party," or "exam week" and invite discussion of appropriate kinds of dress. I want students to see that social occasions create clothing

---

EXHIBIT 3.2

Examples of Genres

Personal Writing	Academic Writing	Popular Culture	Public Affairs/Civic Writing	Professional/ Workplace Writing
Letter	Scholarly article	Magazine article	Letter to the editor	Cover letter
Diary/journal	Book/chapter	Advertisement	Op-ed piece	Résumé
Reflection	Abstract	Hip hop lyrics	Advocacy website	Business memo
Autobiographical essay (literary nonfiction)	Review article	Bumper sticker	White paper	Legal brief
	Experimental report	Graffito	Political blog	Brochure
Blog		Fan website	Advocacy poster	Technical manual
Text message	Poster	Comic book	Magazine article on civic issue	Proposal
E-mail	Ethnography	Newspaper article		Marketing plan
Tweet		Greeting card	Policy brief	Management report
Personal essay		Trade book	Documentary film	Press release
Facebook page				

expectations that operate as genres—invitations to dress in a certain way along with corresponding limits or constraints. One can express individuality at a job interview by choosing a particular style and quality of necktie or handbag but not by choosing a favorite sweatshirt or pair of flip-flops. Similarly, one can express individuality in an APA research report by asking a particularly shrewd research question or developing an elegant methodology, but not by creating a fun cover page or organizing the report as a personal narrative.

To operate successfully in a written genre, students need to learn the genre's expectations, possibilities, limits, and constraints. Many of the questions that concern novice writers (such as *Can I use "I" in my paper?* or *Do I need a thesis statement in the introduction?*) are functions of the assigned genre rather than of the teacher's whims. But genres are more than a set of guidelines for formatting and style. According to recent theorists, they are forms of "social action" (Miller, 1984)—that is, they help produce the ways that certain communities think and act (Wardle, 2009; Nowacek, 2009; Beaufort, 2007; Carter, 2007; Russell and Yanez, 2003; Bawarshi, 2003; Russell, 1997; MacDonald, 1994; Swales, 1990; Bazerman, 1987, 1981; Myers, 1986a). The concept of genre creates strong reader expectations, which in turn place demands on a writer to fulfill those expectations. When one writes in a certain genre, one's structure, style, and approach to subject matter are influenced by the hundreds of previous writers who have employed that same genre. The existence of the genre invites us to generate the ideas that meet the genre's expectations. Every genre is thus an invitation. For example, the existence of the genre "grant proposal" invites us to find problems that might be solved through grant funding. The existence of the genre "letter to the editor" invites us to insert our own voices into the public arena.

It often takes years to become an expert user of a genre. Teachers in the physical and social sciences, for example, appreciate how difficult it is for a novice science student to understand the difference between the "Results" and "Discussion" sections of an experimental report, particularly to see how the Discussion section constructs an argument (usually drawing data from the Results section as evidence) that tries to answer the research question presented in the introduction, a question that in turn grows out of the literature review and the scientist's theoretical orientation. As rhetorician Charles Bazerman has shown (1988), the genre of the experimental report helped constitute the practices of modern science (see also Greg Myers, 1986b, 1985). This empirical way of thinking about the world, embodied in the genre of the research report, is what expert insider scientists, as teachers, must pass on to their new students. Other disciplines have analogous genres that embody their discipline's ways of thinking and that students must learn in order to become disciplinary insiders. In Chapter Thirteen on teaching undergraduate research, I suggest strategies for teaching students how to write within the main genres of a discipline. But knowledge of genres is important even in introductory courses where students need to appreciate the difference between, say, an academic argument and a personal reflection, or a news story and an op-ed column.

I conclude this section with one final point about genres: while some genres call for closed-form prose, others call for alternative or open forms. Let me explain.

By *closed-form prose,* I mean the kind of conventional thesis-governed, points-first prose that we typically think of as good writing. Closed-form prose typically has the following features:

- An explicit thesis statement, usually in the introduction
- Clear forecasting of the structure to follow
- Unified and coherent paragraphs introduced by topic sentences
- Clear transitions and signposts throughout (in some cases facilitated by various levels of headings)
- Coherently linked sentences aimed at maximum clarity and readability

Such structures are called "closed" because after the introduction the reader expects the argument to follow the plan announced in the introduction, with no digressions, gaps, or other organizational surprises. Because its structure and style aim for maximum clarity, the value of closed-form prose rests on the quality of the ideas it presents. The closed-form structure aims to make those ideas as clear and transparent as possible. The high school five-paragraph essay is a by-the-numbers way of teaching closed-form writing to beginning writers.

Readers expect closed-form prose in most kinds of academic writing, particularly in conference papers, journal articles, book chapters, research proposals, and so forth. It is also the expected norm in most workplace and professional writing—memos, reports, white papers, grant proposals, policy briefs, civic arguments, and other occasions that call for transparency, clarity, and readability. Clearly success in academic and professional life depends on students' learning to produce closed-form prose.

But there are other ways also to produce "good writing." Many genres typically break the rules of closed-form prose. These genres, which I call *open form*, often celebrate playfulness, digressions, personal voice, the narrative strategies of literary nonfiction, or other characteristics that resist the smoothly mapped structure, predictability, and argumentative confidence of closed-form prose. These open-form genres often have a reflective, personal, exploratory, or inquiring stance; they often try to heighten or deepen a problem or show its human significance, rather than offer a thesis-governed solution.

One kind of open-form writing is belletristic prose. Sometimes called literary or creative nonfiction, it applies literary techniques to nonfiction subjects. Such essays, which often resist easy summary, surprise the reader (pleasurably) with digressions, gaps, and purposeful structural fissures such as flashbacks or changes of scene, causing the reader to momentarily lose bearings and then reconstruct the "plot." Some iconic examples are George Orwell's "Shooting an Elephant," Joan Didion's "The Santa Ana," and Annie Dillard's "Living Like a Weasel."

Another kind of open-form prose is the highly theorized academic writing associated with postmodernism or critical theory. The complex, difficult, and sometimes playful prose of writers like Jacques Derrida or Jacques Lacan seems to rebel philosophically from the logocentric structure of closed-form prose. New students encountering these styles are often confused about how they themselves are expected to write in response to them. As a Ph.D. candidate at the University of Copenhagen lamented: "If Lacan tried to hand this book in as a Ph.D. project at my university, would he even pass? Am I supposed to write *like* Lacan, or *about* him, but in a very different style?" (Rienecker and Stray Jorgensen, 2003, p. 106). Before writing his seminar paper on Lacan, this graduate student needs to determine the genre in which he or she is expected to write.

Still other kinds of open-form prose include the hypertext genres of digital culture. The reader/viewer's often maze-like, branching journey through hypertext sites or through multimodal digital artifacts is very different from the reader's linear journey down the clearly marked paths of closed-form prose.

It is important, therefore, that students appreciate where their assigned genre is situated on the continuum from closed-form to open-form prose. Likewise, teachers must choose what mix of genres they want to assign in their courses. These concerns—the strengths and limitations of different genres—are the subject of the next chapter.

Conclusion: Thinking Rhetorically as a Transferable Skill

As students move from course to course through a curriculum or from writing project to writing project in their professional lives, they must develop usefully portable skills that transfer from setting to setting. The most powerful of these skills is the ability to think rhetorically—to size up a writing situation in terms of audience, purpose, and genre—and then to make appropriate composing decisions based on this analysis. Teachers can help students develop these skills by including a rhetorical context in their writing assignments.

4

Using a Range of Genres to Extend Critical Thinking and Deepen Learning

One of my favorite books is *Grasshopper Dreaming: Reflections on Killing and Loving* (2002) by entomologist Jeffrey A. Lockwood. This book is an extended autobiographical reflection that I would classify as literary nonfiction (see the discussion of open-form genres in Chapter Three). In *Grasshopper Dreaming*, Lockwood explores his deep connection to grasshoppers—indeed, his love for them—in ironic tension with his scientific identity as a grasshopper "assassin":

> *My job is to extinguish life. I am expected to do it well—efficiently and professionally. This year I will direct the killing of no fewer than 200 million grasshoppers and more than a billion other creatures, mostly insects. Their accumulated bodies will weigh more than 250 tons and fill twenty dump trucks. That's a lot of killing, and each year it gets harder [pp. 27–28].*

As a scientist, Lockwood has devoted his life to finding more efficient and environmentally friendly ways to destroy grasshoppers. His scientific articles range from research reports to more theoretical work on the edge between science and ethics, with academic titles such as "Ecological Theory and Zadeh's 'Law of Incompatibility': Incorporating Contingency-Based Models into Metatheories." His scholarly articles address a narrow academic audience. But *Grasshopper Dreaming* reaches readers from all walks of life—readers interested in questions about life's meaning and our personal place on a fragile planet that humans share with grasshoppers. The differences between Lockwood's closed-form scholarly articles and his reflective musings in *Grasshopper Dreaming* illustrate the tensions I would like to explore in this chapter—what we might call the tension between academic versus alternative forms.

Many academic writers have felt this tension. For example, here's a note from a friend of mine: "I'm blanching a little at holding up academic writing as any kind of exemplar—what with its jargon, excessive reliance on the passive voice, excessive qualification of conclusions, nonstylized redundancy. The last thing I want to teach my students is how to write a 'scholarly' article." Other academics have even deeper reservations about academic prose. When Stanford political science professor Richard Fagen (1990) was asked why he switched late in his career from writing academic articles to writing a novel, he explained that a key motive was "frustration born of more than thirty years of trying to express myself within the constraints of the language of the academic social sciences." He goes on to explain:

> *Lest I be misunderstood, when I speak of this language I am not talking about turgid prose, vapid topics, twisted logic, or banalities paraded as breakthroughs. These are the sins of third-rate scholarship, and although they abound in the academy, they are not intrinsic to the enterprise. No. My frustration stems from canons of propriety and evidence, from rules of the game that outlaw satire, indignation, passion, love, hate—in short, most of the feelings that are at the heart of our humanity [p. 41].*

Fagen also observes that the centrality of academic prose (both reading it and writing it) "suggests a very widespread problem of undergraduate education in the social sciences: How to get the human beings, warts and all, back into a curriculum that emphasizes abstraction, generalities, methods, and theory at the expense of people." He turned to fiction, he says, because "I wanted a different voice, an uninhibited voice, a voice that spoke from the heart without being filtered through the screens and cautionary devices that are part and parcel of scholarly writing" (p. 41).

Fagen's concern for lost "voice"—the sound of an individual human being, warts and all, with a life and passions—is at the heart of the concerns that I address in this chapter. My thesis is that across the curriculum it is possible for instructors to assign a range of genres that allow students to learn not only academic and professional forms of writing but also alternative genres that draw on different talents, passions, and ways of seeing. In their landmark study of writing in the disciplines at George Mason University, Chris Thaiss and Terry Myers Zawacki (2006) asked their informants (college professors from across the curriculum) about the kinds of writing they most valued from their students. They discovered a refreshingly wide range of answers to this question:

> [M]ost of our informants, while they may themselves write within the conventions of their disciplines, do not necessarily want undergraduates to learn to write within these conventions. Rather, for many, it is important for students to connect what they are learning in school with either their outside experience and/or ideas in the popular media and to write about these connections in a variety of forms [p. 46].

The researchers placed their informants loosely into three categories, which I paraphrase as follows:

- One group expected their students to produce straightforward academic writing, characterized typically by a closed-form structure following the conventions of a disciplinary genre. These teachers expected well-reasoned analyses or arguments, an appropriate academic voice and disciplinary style, and a scholarly *ethos* characterized by a disciplined, open-minded, thorough examination of the question-at-issue.

- A second group also valued well-reasoned arguments, but allowed students to write in a more generic style, with looser expectations about academic voice and disciplinary formats.

- Finally, a third group, while respecting and often assigning academic genres, tended to value alternative forms—often highlighting the personal voice and passion of the writer. These teachers' assignments ranged from reflective, exploratory essays to stories, dialogues, popular media articles, visual/verbal texts, or multimedia/hypertext digital projects.

What I hope to show in this chapter is the strengths of both academic and alternative forms. Writing in different genres and rhetorical contexts to different kinds of audiences can help students think and see in more diverse and complex ways. Particularly, work in more personal, exploratory, or experimental genres can lay the groundwork for deeper thinking in professional academic genres. In this chapter I highlight the particular strengths of different genres. I then use insights from the scholarship of teaching and learning to show why students benefit from writing in a variety of genres as they move through a four-year curriculum.

The Value of Teaching Closed-Form Academic Prose

The most obvious value of teaching closed-form academic prose is that it helps students learn to conduct academic inquiry, make academic arguments, and enter the discourse communities of their majors. Skill at producing closed-form prose also transfers to professional and civic life, where many workplace or civic advocacy genres follow the same closed-form structures.

Let's consider first how such prose advances students' thinking skills. The problem-thesis structure of most academic prose provides a simple and powerful heuristic for students. Thus we can explain to students that the academic writer typically begins an article by engaging the reader's interest in a question, problem, or issue. The writer usually explains why the question is significant and why it has not yet been solved, often by reviewing the relevant literature. Following the presentation of the problem, the writer presents his or her thesis, which is the writer's tentative solution to the problem. Typically, the thesis is in tension with other perspectives or alternative theses. (See Chapter Thirteen for further elaboration on the generic pattern of academic introductions.)

The advantage of teaching this pattern to undergraduates is that it reflects the deep structure of academic thinking, which is rooted in questioning and problem posing. As we saw in Chapter Two, the presence of a true problem is at the heart of academic writing; it is what drives critical thinking and sends the writer through multiple drafts in search of conceptual clarity. The thesis statement that the writer places confidently in the introduction of a finished product may have been discovered late at night in the conclusion of an earlier draft.

Additionally, traditional academic writing teaches students valuable skills of organization and clarity. Its closed-form structure teaches students to write for busy readers, who can most quickly comprehend prose that announces its thesis early, proceeds through unified and coherent paragraphs with topic sentences, and reminds readers of the unfolding progress of the argument through transitions and other coherence cues. In aiming at maximum clarity for readers, closed-form writing requires maximum clarity from writers, who must be able to put their meaning, their purpose, and their structure in a nutshell in order to write an introduction. The effect of closed-form writing is to stress meanings up front. By summarizing the whole before presenting the parts, closed-form writing produces a cognitive framework that helps readers process information and store it in long-term memory. (For an elaboration on the connections between cognition and closed-form structure see Colomb and Williams, 1985.)

Finally, teaching academic prose within disciplinary genres teaches students how to think within a discipline. It teaches students how a discipline asks questions, gathers and uses evidence, and makes arguments. These benefits I will develop in more detail in Chapter Thirteen on teaching undergraduate research.

To be sure, many teachers and scholars raise objections to academic prose. Some find the closed-form pattern of academic prose formulaic. Others raise political and philosophical objections to academic prose, often seeing it as a Western or patriarchal form that silences other ways of knowing. (For an overview of political objections to academic prose, including feminist objections, see Thaiss and Zawacki, 2006; Villanueva, 2001; Flynn, 1988; Meisenhelder, 1985). These objections will find fuller voice in the next section on alternative genres and styles.

The Value of Teaching Alternative Genres and Styles

The literature on writing across the curriculum often values alternative forms. Particularly important is the expressivist movement popularized in the United States by James Britton's influential study of children's writing development in British schools (Britton and others, 1975). The term *expressivism* comes from Britton's classification scheme, which identifies three categories of prose: the "expressive," the "transactional," and the "poetic." The latter two categories are generally familiar. Transactional writing, which includes most academic or scholarly discourse, refers to writing that "transacts" the world's business by conveying messages from writer to reader, usually in closed-form style. Poetic writing, in contrast, is what Americans call "creative writing." Britton's first category—expressive writing—is much less familiar. Britton calls it writing that is close to the self. One of its main functions is to help the individual assimilate new ideas by creating personal contexts that link new, unfamiliar material to what one knows or has experienced. It is writing to discover and explore, to mull over, to ruminate on, to raise questions about, to personalize. It is often fragmentary and disorganized, like talking to oneself on paper. Although intended for the self, it seems to be the seedbed for ideas that later emerge in products written for others. Britton noticed how frequently professional writers explore ideas in notebooks, journals, daybooks, memoranda to themselves, and letters to colleagues about ideas in progress. He further noticed how extensively expert writers revise their ideas through multiple drafts in which the earliest drafts have the characteristic inchoateness of expressive writing.

Britton's work has strongly influenced contemporary composition practice by emphasizing expressive writing across the curriculum in the form of journals, in-class freewriting, thought letters to classmates, blogs, personal reflection, and so forth. (For a review of the emotional and physical benefits of expressive writing, see Baikie and Wilhelm, 2005.) The effect of this emphasis can be startling in the classroom in terms of the changed nature of learning, in the increased validation of the personal experience of the individual writer, and in the increased creativity and elaboration of ideas that can emerge in students' writing (Herrington and Moran, 1992; Belanoff, Elbow, and Fontaine, 1991; Connolly and Vilardi, 1989; Fulwiler, 1987a; Fulwiler and Young, 1982). More recently, expressive writing has been connected specifically to reflective writing, which can bring what Donna Qualley (1997) calls an "essayist stance" (open and inquiring rather than agonistic or persuasive) to bear on intellectual problems. Expressive writing gives students an opportunity to think on paper and to connect their learning to their own experiences and concerns. (Chapter Seven discusses expressive writing in detail and offers numerous suggestions for incorporating it into courses across the curriculum.)

Although expressivism is often associated with "behind-the-scenes" journals and other kinds of exploratory writing, many scholars also want to integrate a more expressive voice into their scholarly prose. They often find their ideas and their passions constrained by what Bridwell-Bowles (1992) calls "the standard academic essay" (p. 350). Acknowledging that she had to write "in conventional language, in traditional rhetorical patterns, using accepted research methodologies" (p. 366) in order to get published and achieve tenure, Bridwell-Bowles explains her desire to write also in "alternative" or "experimental" forms, which give her "a more personal voice, an expanded use of metaphor, a less rigid methodological framework, a writing process that allows me to combine hypothesizing with reporting data, to use patterns of writing that allow for multiple truths, what Dale Spender has called a 'multidimensional reality,' rather than a single thesis, and so on" (p. 350).

Bridwell-Bowles's objections to the standard academic essay are echoed by various informants in Thaiss and Zawacki's (2006) research on writing in the disciplines at George Mason University (see my summary of their work in the introduction of this chapter, page 54). They studied several teachers who took academic risks by publishing (or trying to publish) scholarly articles in alternative formats and styles. Their commentary on anthropologist Roger Lancaster (author of *Life Is Hard*, a 1994 book about life in Nicaragua during the Sandinista regime) illustrates what is at stake:

> *[Lancaster saw his work] as both politically and compositionally alternative. In the preface, he asserts that the book is deliberately written "against the grain," that "it misbehaves," and that it is "better to see the ethnographer in the ethnography." Better because, he argues, "Partisan analysis is the only resistance to power that a writer, as writer, can effectively offer" (xvii-xviii). To make his text "mirror the discombobulation of a failed revolution," Lancaster created a kind of postmodern collage, composed of journalistic and impressionistic passages, raw fieldnotes, chapter-length interviews and life histories, newspaper articles, and letters. Though he thought at the time that he was "gambling with [his] career," the book is now mainstream reading in many anthropology classes [p. 44].*

The enthusiasm for alternative forms documented by Thaiss and Zawacki is shared by many teachers on my own campus. For example, psychologist Therese Huston, in her course on investigating popular "myths" about human behavior, asks students to create a multimedia blog instead of a traditional research paper. Here are her instructions to students in the "overview" section of her assignment handout:

> *You've all selected a popular myth about human behavior and over the next five weeks, you'll be creating a blog to investigate that myth. As I explained in the syllabus, I've chosen a blog instead of a final paper so that your research and insights can be public. This is your chance to shine! Your goal will be to correct a common misunderstanding and connect readers to better information. The online format means you can include links to other web sites, images, video clips, or audio recordings.*

In a nutshell, her assignment asks students to investigate myths about human behavior (such as "adolescent brains are prone to impulsive behavior" or "positive attitudes can cure cancer") and to report their research in a public interest blog. I've perused several of her students' blogs and attest to her claims about student engagement. The blogs have creative "about me" entries and are highly personalized. They are written in an informal style suitable for a nonspecialized audience and have numerous links to YouTube videos, advertisements, and other websites. For the most part, they successfully translate the dense academic style of the peer-reviewed literature into a tone and style that works for the blog.

Genre Awareness and Student Learning

The previous sections have suggested the value of teaching students to write in different genres. In this section I hope to show how genre awareness can promote transfer of learning from one context to another. Additionally, assigning different genres can draw out the strengths of different kinds of learners and may provide cognitive benefits revealed by recent research in brain imaging.

Genre Awareness Promotes Transfer

Let's look first at the particularly puzzling problem of why students have difficulty transferring writing skills from one course to the next. A student who produces strong papers in first-year composition course may struggle mightily with a political science or art history paper. Students often produce remarkably uneven writing performances from course to course, making it hard to determine whether any given student is a "good writer" or even whether the student is making progress in writing. In fact, one writing theorist, Lee Ann Carroll, drawing on the psychological development theory of Urie Bronfenbrenner, argues that writing improvement should be measured not by students' ability to produce increasingly better papers on the same kind of assignment but instead by the ability to produce flawed but passable papers on increasingly diverse and complex assignments within a variety of rhetorical contexts:

> *The college students in my study . . . did not necessarily get better at some predetermined type of academic writing. Instead, they acquired a "more extended differentiated, and valid conception of the ecological environment" (Bronfenbrenner, 1979, p. 27). These successful students learned to accommodate the often unarticulated expectations of their professor readers, to imitate disciplinary discourse, and, as juniors and seniors, to write in forms more diverse and complex than those they could produce when they entered college [Carroll, 2002, p. 22].*

Carroll's research suggests the importance of introducing students to increasingly "diverse and complex" forms. Research in genre theory suggests that this developmental process can be facilitated by greater genre awareness. Both students and instructors need to understand that the criteria for good writing are contextualized within genres—an insight that runs counter to the common belief that "good writing is good writing." As Thaiss and Zawacki have shown, teachers may not realize how much their views about good writing are shaped by their own disciplinary or subdisciplinary genres. Although teachers across the curriculum tend to describe good writing in the same way—exhorting their students to write "clear prose" with a "strong thesis" and "well organized paragraphs"—they often aren't envisioning the same thing. When Thaiss and Zawacki interviewed teachers about their assignments, they discovered underlying differences in the definition of good writing. They argue that bringing these differences to the surface and explaining them to students helps students transfer their writing knowledge from one context to another.

This insight suggests that students benefit when instructors explain specific features of a required genre and differentiate these features from those of other genres. Instead of saying, "Be sure to use evidence to support your thesis," a teacher can be more helpful by explaining what counts for evidence in a particular disciplinary genre. Thus a sociology professor who has just assigned a research project on gendered differences in behavior (say, snacking habits at a party) might tell students: "Whereas in your history course you probably used quotations from primary sources to support your point, for this sociology assignment your evidence will come from close observation of males versus females at the snack table. You'll need to learn to observe gender differences in behavior (if any) and describe them in sociological language." This explanation, in helping students understand what makes a sociology paper different from a history paper, promotes transfer of a generic skill (using evidence to support a point) from one discipline to another.

A particularly cogent example of disciplinary difference comes from Nowacek (2009), who shows how a literature professor and a history professor view the term *thesis statement* differently. The literature professor wants students to write an explicitly argumentative thesis that "sticks its neck out." In contrast, the history professor, downplaying agonistic argument, wants a student's thesis to emerge from research in primary sources. As the history professor puts it, "You don't set out to prove something; you set out to see where the evidence leads you" (p. 500). Consequently, the history professor doesn't insist on an argumentative thesis in the introduction. In fact, the thesis might not be stated explicitly until the end, or it might simply be implied. Nowacek shows how these differences emerge from deeper disciplinary differences, particularly the history professor's belief that "historians like to think that they're finding reality" (p. 505) in contrast to the literature professor's emphasis on the student's interpretive stance. Nowacek argues that students can transfer knowledge more effectively when teachers make these disciplinary differences explicit rather than implying that teachers mean the same thing by *thesis statement.*

In the following list, I attempt to summarize the advice of various genre theorists about the use of different genres as students progress through the curriculum (see especially Beaufort, 2007; Bawarshi, 2003; and Carroll, 2002):

- *Advice to teachers of first-year composition:* Ask students to analyze different genres and to write in several different genres in order to develop rhetorical flexibility and to practice adjusting their writing to different rhetorical contexts. Learning to analyze different genres helps students size up a new rhetorical context and adapt to its demands.

- *Advice to teachers of general education courses or early courses in the major:* Show students how writing in the present discipline may differ from the writing they have done previously. Often teachers can develop short assignments to teach students how disciplinary experts incorporate evidence into an argument, whether in the form of textual quotation, field or laboratory observation, data analysis using tables or graph, or other strategies. Also stress what may be similar to what students did in first-year composition; show them what transfers.

- *Advice to teachers of advanced courses in the major:* Help students learn to write in one or more of the primary genres of the discipline, perhaps leading to a capstone paper in the senior year. Chapter Thirteen on undergraduate research focuses on how to help students move from the status of the novice to the status of disciplinary expert.

Different Genres Tap Different Kinds of Strengths, Allowing More Students to Succeed

Another benefit of assigning different genres—especially mixing academic with more personal or creative forms—is that it draws out different kinds of strengths from students. Often students do their best work when instructional methods and assignments match the way they like to learn. Although learning style research has lost some of its popularity from its heyday in the 1980s and 1990s, the research reveals important differences in the ways students approach writing tasks.

For example, Jensen and DiTiberio (1989) used the Myers-Briggs inventory to reveal different assignment preferences among writers. Along the Myers-Briggs thinking/feeling continuum, they found that "thinkers" excel at writing logical, well-organized essays requiring analysis and argumentation. In contrast, "feelers" prefer assignments that allow for personal voice, conviction, and emotion. They are unlikely to be motivated by an assignment unless they can relate to it personally, and they are attuned to a reader's desire for lively, interesting prose. They like to put their own personal experiences into a paper and often prefer autobiographical or narrative approaches rather than an abstractly reasoned approach.

Differences across other continua reveal other insights that are helpful to teachers when designing assignments. "Sensing" types, for example, want writing assignments with very detailed instructions and guidelines and find comfort in teacher-prescribed organizational patterns such as the "five-paragraph theme." In contrast, "intuitive" types rebel against prescribed patterns and like looser assignments that give them room for their own unique or creative personal touches. Along the perceiving/judging scale, "judgers" tend to arrive quickly at a thesis and are often bored with personal exploratory writing such as journals, which they dismiss as "busywork." In contrast, "perceivers" like to play with ideas endlessly, have trouble deciding on a thesis, and will explore ideas forever in their journals unless a deadline forces them to quit. Finally, along the extrovert/introvert continuum, "extroverts" prefer to explore ideas through class discussions or small groups, whereas "introverts" like solitude, preferring a journal for exploration rather than group conversation.

Jensen and DiTiberio's research suggests that some students are apt to do their best work within closed-form, academic genres, whereas others will do best on open-form, more personal or creative writing tasks. Students who rush to closure might benefit from low-stakes exploratory writing that encourages them to explore all sides of an issue. Students who feel stifled by "rules" might profit from explanations that rules are often constraints imposed by genres rather than by the idiosyncrasy of the teacher. By asking students to write in several different genres or styles, teachers give students more opportunity to find one or two that are particularly effective for them; likewise, students get to discover that they can learn significantly from doing an assignment that is not, by nature, their preferable way of operating.

The Value of Writing in Different Genres Seems to Be Supported by Brain Research

Although I have not myself studied the primary literature on brain research, several secondary works make a persuasive case (to me) that different kinds of writing tasks stimulate different parts of the brain. Kellogg (2008) explains that the frontal lobes of the brain, which seldom reach full maturity until age twenty-three to thirty, are needed for complex writing tasks that require writers first to wrestle with advanced, domain-specific knowledge and then to read their emerging texts from the audience's perspective. The strain on working memory can be reduced, Kellogg argues, by earlier scaffolding exercises that encourage students to take notes, generate ideas during prewriting, make an outline, or learn the structural features of different genres. These different kinds of tasks apparently activate different parts of the brain.

Another study, by biologist James Zull (2002), shows that all new learning must be linked to preexisting neural networks already in the learner's brain. Teachers can't simply transfer a concept from their own brains into students' brains, because a teacher's neural networks are the products of his or her own life history and don't exist within the learner's brain. Consequently, the learner must build the new concepts on neural networks already present. Informal writing assignments aimed at helping students probe memory, connect new concepts to old networks, dismantle blocking assumptions, and understand the significance of the new concept are particularly valuable.

Zull links his analysis of brain research studies to David Kolb's (1985) research on cognitive styles. Kolb plots an individual's cognitive style along four axes: concrete experience (feeling), reflective observation (watching), abstract conceptualization (thinking), and active experimentation (doing). Kolb recommends that for each learning unit in a course the instructor cycle through activities that focus on each of these learning styles, thus helping learners find at least one approach that most appeals to them while giving all students practice at thinking in less natural ways. Zull draws on brain imaging studies to argue that each of Kolb's quadrants corresponds with different regions of the brain, so that the kind of thinking or writing task associated with each quadrant particularly fires neurons in that region. Each phase of the cycle suggests a different kind of writing assignment, as shown in Exhibit 4.1.

In sum, Zull's study suggests that different genres engage different parts of the brain and that teachers can deepen student learning by mixing personal writing (expressive, exploratory, reflective pieces) with academic

EXHIBIT 4.1

Assignments Throughout the Learning Cycle

Kolb's Learning Style Phase	Corresponding Brain Cortex (Zull, 2002, p. 18)	Suggested Writing Assignments
Concrete experience phase: Learners are introduced to new concepts and issues through watching a film or demonstration, playing a game, doing field observations, and so forth.	Sensory cortex	Nongraded personal writing that records the learner's personal observations, thoughts, and feelings during the initial experience and that raises questions and expresses puzzlement
Reflective observation phase: Learners consider the concepts and issues again after doing readings, listening to lectures, participating in class discussions, and hearing different points of view.	Temporal integrative cortex	Personal exploratory writing, such as journal entries that allow the students to connect new material to their personal experiences and previous knowledge Personal pieces based on autobiographical experiences with a topic or concept Personal reflection papers that encourage a questioning, open-ended, thinking-aloud-on-paper approach rather than thesis-with-support writing
Abstract conceptualization phase: Learners try to achieve abstract understanding of the concepts and issues by mastering and internalizing their components and seeing the relationship between new material and other concepts and issues.	Frontal integrative cortex	Formal academic papers calling for thesis-based analyses and arguments
Active experimentation phase: Learners actively use the new concepts to solve problems by applying them to new situations.	Motor brain	Position papers based on cases that use the new concepts Write-ups of a student's laboratory or field research using the concepts Proposals applying new concepts and knowledge to solve real-world problems Creative pieces demonstrating understanding of new material

and professional writing (mainstream academic papers, proposals, and persuasive pieces).

Conclusion

In this chapter I have addressed the question of what kinds of genres we should assign our students. Based on the studies reviewed in this chapter, I have tried to propose a consensus answer: students' growth as writers will be enhanced if, throughout their college careers, they have the opportunity to write in a variety of genres—a goal that can be achieved by a mix of assignments drawn from the following categories:

1. *Informal exploratory writing in an expressive mode*: journals, in-class free-writes, thought letters, reflections, electronic postings to a class discussion board, reading responses, and so forth. This personal exploratory writing is a seedbed for ideas out of which committed academic or professional writing can emerge. Such writing can often be nongraded or low-stakes.

2. *Closed-form thesis-governed academic or professional writing*: analyses, arguments, proposals, research reports, and other forms of mainstream academic or workplace discourse. Specific genres will vary according to subject matter, discipline, or professional field.

3. *Alternative genres and styles:* Essays written in other styles and forms that create different ways of "seeing": open-form personal essays or reflections, blogs, posters, experimental pieces, dialogues, interviews, magazine articles for popular audiences, pamphlets, op-ed pieces and white papers, satires, short stories or poems, web pages, multimodal projects, and the like.

Although no one course is likely to require the full range of these assignment types, as students pass through a curriculum they should have an opportunity to experience as many of them as possible. Individual teachers need to find a balance that works for their students and for them.

5

Dealing with Issues of Grammar and Correctness

When teachers across the disciplines complain that students "haven't learned to write," they often think first of sentence-level errors. The horror stories we hear of college graduates who make sentence errors on job application letters make us all cringe. One of the goals of any writing program ought to be the reduction of the number of college graduates who embarrass themselves and their alma maters through careless editing errors or through unfamiliarity with the usage conventions of standard edited English. As an example of many teachers' passionate concern for error, I quote here a memorandum from a colleague on my own campus. It addresses the provost, who had asked teachers for their "top three academic priorities" for long-range budget planning and mentions me in my role of director of writing. I retain the writer's emphatic use of capital letters.

> *Priority 1: ADDRESS THE MISERABLE STATE OF THE UNDERGRADUATE CONTROL AND USAGE OF ENGLISH, BOTH ORAL AND WRITTEN.*
>
> *Priorities 2 and 3: There is no Second Choice and, to me, all other possibilities rank a distant Third.*
>
> *ANYONE IN THE UNIVERSITY WHO FEELS THAT THIS SUGGESTION IS MERELY IDLE SHOULD SPEND A FEW DAYS CORRECTING PAPERS OR EXAMINATIONS.*

WE NEED AN EXTENDED COURSE IN ENGLISH STRUCTURE AND GRAMMAR, A CONSISTENT EFFORT TO IMPROVE SPELLING, AND A STAFF OF ASSISTANTS WHO WILL PATIENTLY GO OVER THE WORK OF OUR STUDENTS AND EXPLAIN TO THEM HOW ENGLISH—A MAGNIFICENT TOOL—WORKS. THEY SIMPLY DO NOT KNOW (unless they come from the bloc of lucky ones whose parents and teachers constantly and carefully corrected and guided their efforts to learn to use English).

DR. JOHN BEAN HAS RIGHTFULLY CAUTIONED US AGAINST BEING SO OVERLY CRITICAL THAT WE DISCOURAGE THE STUDENTS AND I AM SYMPATHETIC TO THAT POINT OF VIEW: HOWEVER, the students' work can be discouraging to the instructors and the only way they seem to pay attention is to have every error pointed out and to be told to correct every error and TOLD WHY THERE IS AN ERROR AND HOW TO GO ABOUT CORRECTING IT. FAR TOO MANY OF OUR STUDENTS SIMPLY DO NOT HAVE A GOOD 8TH GRADE KNOWLEDGE OF ENGLISH.

My colleague's frustration with student writing (and with my own caution against overemphasizing errors) extends to our whole first-year composition program, which does not provide an "extended course in English structure and grammar." Consequently, writing teachers at my own institution—and I am sure these politics are played out on other cam puses across the country—are often seen as "soft on error" and perhaps even professionally remiss in not teaching the basics of grammar. There is a genuine conflict here between what composition teachers do and what many disciplinary instructors wish they would do. The purpose of this chapter is to examine the problem of error in enough depth so that non-English faculty can appreciate the reservations that many composition teachers have about teaching grammar in a writing course. At the same time, I hope to assure faculty across the curriculum that composition teachers are not "soft on error" and to suggest strategies that faculty in all disciplines can use to reduce the incidence of error in their own students' writing.

The Difficulty of Teaching Sentence Correctness

For reasons no one fully understands, improvement of students' grammatical competence in writing is a difficult goal to achieve. Weak writers seem to make more progress in their mastery of generating ideas, improving fluency, and organizing and developing arguments than they do in sentence correctness. It may well be, in fact, that competence in editing and correctness is a late-developing skill that blossoms only after students begin taking pride in their writing and seeing themselves as having ideas important enough to communicate.

Whatever the cause of the errors in students' prose, eliminating them is a slow and difficult process. Partly as a response to this difficulty, contemporary composition theory has changed the way writing teachers approach sentence correctness. The old model was to teach formal grammar, which students then applied to writing through workbook exercises in punctuation, usage, sentence construction, and so forth. Teachers supplemented this workbook approach by dutifully red-penciling all errors on student essays.

Although this model may have helped relatively skilled writers improve their control of the fine points of punctuation and usage, it has been largely discredited as a method of teaching composition to most writers. In a landmark research review that helped change the direction of composition studies in the mid-sixties, Braddock, Lloyd-Jones, and Schoer (1963) concluded that teaching grammar does not improve writing: "In view of the widespread agreement of research studies based upon many types of students and teachers, the conclusion can be stated in strong and unqualified terms: the teaching of formal grammar has a negligible or, because it usually displaces some instruction and practice in composition, even a harmful effect on the improvement of writing" (pp. 37–38). To teachers outside of composition, this statement may seem perplexing and counterintuitive, but it corroborated what many veteran composition teachers secretly felt, and it had a profound influence on the emergence of the process movement described in Chapter Two. (It should be noted here that not all composition scholars are swayed by the research summarized by Braddock and colleagues and that debates about grammar still occur in the literature. For a pro-grammar critique of the anti-grammar research, see Kolln, 1981. For a critique of Kolln and a passionate anti-grammar argument from a variety of linguistic perspectives, see Hartwell, 1985. For an attempt to synthesize the views of the pro- and anti-grammarians, see Mulroy, 2003; Devet, 2002; and Noguchi, 1991. For a comprehensive review of twenty years' worth of articles on grammar appearing in *Teaching Writing in Two-Year Colleges,* see Blaauw-Hara, 2007; for an approach to teaching editing skills similar to that proposed in this chapter, see Blaauw-Hara, 2006.)

What Does It Mean to "Know Grammar"?

When my colleague complained that today's students "simply do not have a good 8th grade knowledge of English," he opened up a complex question: What does it mean to "know" a language's grammar?

Linguists distinguish between a tacit, preconscious "knowing how"—the unfathomably complex ability to produce language by internalizing the rules for word formation, inflection, and ordering that all native speakers of a language learn as toddlers—and a conscious "knowing about" that provides a nomenclature for describing and analyzing the structural features of an utterance. It is the difference between being able to throw a curve ball and being able to explain the physics of the ball's motion.

To appreciate the complexity of the internal grammar (the "knowing how" knowledge) that native speakers learn as toddlers, consider the following two exercises. The first is a little quiz I give my first-year composition students. I have them read the following sentence:

Flobbing sallably, glotty yofs sambolated in the wickersnacks.

Here is my quiz, with the answers in brackets:

What were the yofs doing? [They were sambolating.]

Were the yofs norgy or glotty? [These yofs were glotty.]

Do we have one yof or more than one? [There were at least two yofs.]

What else were they doing besides sambolating? [They were flobbing sallably.]

I have yet to encounter any group of students, including students in remedial writing classes, who could not easily pass this test. They evidently know how the English language works, even if most of them could not label *glotty* as an adjective or *flobbing sallably* as a participial phrase.

For a second exercise, you might try your hand at a problem we give writing center consultants at my institution as part of their training:

Explain to a native speaker of Japanese when English speakers use the articles a, an, *and the* the *in front of nouns and when they don't. Consider utterances such as these: Here is a cookie. Here is the cookie. Where are the cookies? I think I smell cookies. I like sugar. He brought the sugar (but not He brought a sugar).*

Native speakers know instinctively how to use these articles, but unless they are trained as linguists or ESL specialists, they are baffled when they try to formulate rules that can accurately describe their performance, just as speakers of most Asian languages are baffled in trying to learn the rules.

When we talk about knowing grammar, therefore, it is important to understand as precisely as possible what we mean by both "knowing" and "grammar." To help clarify these matters, Hartwell (1985) identifies five different meanings for the word *grammar,* which I summarize as follows:

○ *Grammar 1.* The internalized, preconscious knowledge of word arrangement and inflectional endings shared by all native speakers of a language. Hartwell calls grammar 1 the "grammar in our heads" (p. 111). It is this grammar that allows us to talk, hear with comprehension, read, and write.

○ *Grammar 2.* Scientific attempts to understand and describe the preconscious rules of grammar 1. The cumulative work of linguists—whether structuralists, generative transformationalists, or whatever—gradually increases our conscious knowledge of grammar 1 through increasingly improved models (grammar 2). Hartwell argues persuasively that expertise in grammar 2 does not increase one's ability to use grammar 1.

○ *Grammar 3.* The grammar of linguistic etiquette. Grammarians in this third sense are on the lookout for *ain't, brung, he don't,* and other dialectical features that signal class or social distinctions. To linguists, these are issues of usage rather than grammar. Grammar 2 calls "he brung the luggage" a grammatical utterance (a nongrammatical utterance would be "brung the he luggage"); grammar 3 calls it "bad grammar." (I will deal with this issue at greater length shortly.)

○ *Grammar 4.* Traditional school grammar associated with the "8th grade" and perpetuated in textbooks and college handbooks. It analyzes language into eight parts of speech, identifies various kinds of clauses and phrases, and describes function slots in sentences as subjects, verbs, objects, complements, modifiers, and so forth. Based on ill-fitting Latin categories, traditional school grammar has very little explanatory power as a scientific grammar (grammar 2) and is used largely in the service of grammar 3.

○ *Grammar 5.* Stylistic grammar. This grammar studies language beyond the sentence level and is concerned with such matters as coherence, gracefulness, and rhetorical effectiveness. Strunk and White's *Elements of Style* or the style chapters of college handbooks are examples of grammar 5. When used in the service of grammar 3, grammar 5 introduces such "errors" as wordiness, weak verbs, and lack of emphasis.

My purpose in summarizing Hartwell's five kinds of grammar is to emphasize two points. First, the ability to use language flexibly and fluently is a function of grammar 1, which grows out of our participation in a rich language environment and is independent of our ability to describe language either with scientific grammars or traditional school grammar. Second, the common meaning of the concept "bad grammar" (as in *he brung it*) has nothing to do with grammar itself; rather, it is concerned with conformity to social conventions and is properly called a usage matter rather than a grammar matter. To this issue we turn next.

The Politics of Grammar and Usage

The sentence *He brung it*, though grammatical, is produced in a nonstandard dialect of English. Those who speak this dialect probably do so because it is the dialect of their parents and peers. Unfortunately for their success in college and professional life, their parents and peers do not speak the prestige dialect of our culture—a sociological and political issue, not an issue of intelligence or verbal skill.

Some persons, such as those seeking higher social status, want to expurgate all vestiges of their home dialects in order to speak (and write) standard English. Others resist standard English as a badge of pride, defiance, and social identity. Consider Black Panther Stokely Carmichael's "Declaration of War" ([1968] 1970), published in the *San Francisco Express Times:* "Take the English language. There are cats who come here from Italy, from Germany, from Poland, from France, in two generations they speak English perfectly. We have never spoken English perfectly, never, never, never. And that is because our people consciously resisted a language that did not belong to us . . . Anybody can speak that simple honkey's language correctly. Anybody can do it. We have not done it because we have resisted, resisted" (p. 180). As Carmichael makes vividly clear, to change usage is to change one's social identity. The linguist Noguchi (1991) explains:

> *Like other primates of the animal kingdom, humans seek, in one way or another, to signal, enhance, and, ultimately, protect status . . . Language partakes in these activities insofar as linguistic form conveys not just cognitive meaning but often social status as well—high, low, in between, insider, outsider. People usually gauge the status of speakers (and writers) by socially and culturally determined surface criteria. Japanese speakers, for example, gauge it principally by the presence of polite forms; British English speakers, principally by pronunciation; American English*

speakers, principally by "grammar." Whether we care to admit it or not, American English speakers employ various grammatical shibboleths (e.g., use of ain't, brung, double negatives) not only to affirm their current status within a social group but sometimes also to distance themselves from other social groups [p. 114].

As a general rule, middle-class Americans (especially those with upwardly mobile desires) strive to avoid any grammatical shibboleths that would identify them as poorly educated. They explain their behavior as a desire for "good grammar," unaware of the distinction Hartwell makes between grammars 1 and 3. To appreciate the underlying issues of etiquette and class, consider the most common grammar 3 error made by middle-class college professors: using a nominative pronoun in compound constructions requiring the accusative (for example, saying "Let's you and I go to the conference together" rather than "you and me"). Linguists call this error "hypercorrection," stemming from the middle-class fear of usage mistakes (grammar 3). Having been reprimanded for saying "Sally and me are playing marbles" in grade school, we now overcorrect by always saying "Sally and I": "The dean wants Sally and I to serve on this committee" or "The dean wants to see Sally and I first thing in the morning." Upon reflection, we all know that these are grammar 3 errors, but that knowledge does not stop our brains from generating the wrong forms. To change, we do not need grammar lessons so much as behavior modification, perhaps by enlisting a grammar 3 friend to stop us each time we make the error. But what drives us to change is not the innate demands of grammar 1; we want to change to avoid social embarrassment (grammar 3).

Where one stands on social embarrassment is, of course, a political issue. My own personal stance is conservative: I want to avoid grammar 3 errors in my own speech and writing. My stance as a composition teacher is to empower students to make their own decisions about social embarrassment by describing very clearly those language practices that cause embarrassment in different rhetorical contexts and by giving them the power to avoid unintentional errors in whatever dialect their audience expects. This stance obviously leads to a conservative position on error in academic, business, or professional writing where audiences expect standard edited English that obeys the rules of grammar 3. Because writing involves many more opportunities for error than does speech, students need to study grammar 4 (handbook grammar) and grammar 5 (stylistic grammar beyond the sentence level) in order to follow standard punctuation practices, avoid dangling modifiers or nonparallel constructions, and appreciate the stylistic value of conciseness or varied sentence structure. Most composition courses spend time on these issues, but they are only a small part of learning to be a good writer. To see an excellent strategy for explaining grammar 3 errors to students in terms of embarrassment, professional ethos, and power, see Blaauw-Hara (2006), especially p. 171, where he compares editing for Standard English to putting on a business suit for a job interview.

What Teachers Across the Curriculum Need to Know About Recent Studies of Error

Teaching students to avoid errors in standard edited English is, of course, more easily said than done. Although most contemporary theorists doubt the value of teaching school grammar (at least in the traditional diagramming-sentences way) as a strategy for avoiding error, the study of error remains an important branch of research in composition studies. (For reviews of the research on error, see Blaauw-Hara, 2007; Robinson, 1998; Hull, 1985.) Drawing on work from a number of related disciplines including speech communications, cognitive psychology, linguistics, brain research, sociology, early childhood development, and first- and second-language acquisition, this branch of the discipline addresses a number of puzzling questions about grammatical error. Some of the findings of this research, which I review in this section, may prove useful to faculty across the curriculum in developing effective strategies for dealing with errors in their own students' writing.

College Teachers Have Always Railed Against Errors in Student Writing

It might be comforting to know that teachers have a long tradition of complaining about errors in their students' writing and that the frequency of errors has not risen appreciably. Connors and Lunsford (1988) compared the types and frequency of errors of 1980s students with earlier studies from 1917 and 1930. They found surprising consistency in the frequency of errors across time. The error frequency rate in 1917 was 2.11 errors per hundred words; in 1930, it was 2.24 errors per hundred words; and in 1986, it was 2.26 errors per hundred words. Their conclusion: "College students are not making more formal errors in writing than they used to" (p. 406).

There are interesting differences in the kinds of errors observed, however. For one thing, what is perceived as an error shifts as the language evolves. Connors and Lunsford report that two Harvard professors, writing in 1901, identified confusion about the rules for *shall* and *will* as the most common grammatical error in their first-year students' papers. The most significant difference discovered by Connors and Lunsford is that today's students make substantially more errors in spelling and in confusing of homonyms (*to, two, too; it's, its*), a phenomenon they attribute to "declining familiarity with the visual look of the written page" (p. 406). Thus the poor spelling of today's students, according to this hypothesis, reflects a decline in the amount of time spent reading. Since Connors and Lunsford's study, the advent of spell-checkers has eliminated most spelling errors in students' word-processed work (but not in their in-class writing, or, alas, in their e-mail messages to their professors), but homonym errors continue.

Students' Prose Contains Fewer Mistakes Than Teachers Sometimes Perceive

Even in an error-laden essay, an actual count of the errors reveals that there are many more correct sentences than flawed ones and many more correctly spelled words than misspelled ones. When we throw up our hands at a "miserable" student essay, therefore, we need to acknowledge that at least some of our own perception of error is shaped by our psychology of reading. Williams (1981), writing about the phenomenology of error, notes that many teachers read student essays with the primary purpose of finding errors, whereas they read their own colleagues' drafts-in-progress for ideas. When Williams stealthily embedded errors in a professional essay, readers noticed far fewer of them than they noticed when the same errors occurred in a student essay. Moreover, Williams points out as an illustration that the renowned essayist E. B. White unwittingly violates in his own essays various "rules" from his own *Elements of Style* (written with William Strunk). "Now I want to be clear," says Williams; "I am not at all interested in the trivial fact that E. B. White violated one or two of his own trivial rules. That would be a trivial observation . . . What I am interested in is the fact that no one, E. B. White least of all, seemed to notice that E. B. White had made an error" (p. 156). Williams's point here is that we are less apt to notice errors if we are not looking for them.

Moreover, readers vary widely in the kinds of errors that bother them. Some teachers mark every instance of an apostrophe error but do not notice comma splices; others rail at fragments but apparently do not notice dangling modifiers. Some teachers get livid over "Everyone in the room raised their hands," while others prefer this form over the sexist "his hand" or the unwieldy "his or her hand." Thus, if we are looking for certain errors, they leap out at us, even though another reader might not notice any of the errors that bothered us.

Finally, we should note that much of what constitutes "error" really involves stylistic choices—issues of rhetorical effectiveness and grace rather than right-or-wrong adherence to rules. For purposes of definition, we might label as an error any unintentional violation of a stable convention of standard edited English, such as a wrong pronoun case, a comma splice, or an awkwardly dangling participle. However, it is less helpful to think of wordiness or choppy sentences or excessive use of the passive voice as errors in the same sense. Yet many teachers lump all violations of their own stylistic pet peeves into the "error" category.

Our Students Have More Linguistic Competence Than the Surface Features of Their Prose Sometimes Indicate

Our tendency, when we see an error-ridden student paper, is to consider the student hopelessly lacking in skills. Composition researchers, however, in studying the etiology of error, have discovered that often students have far more linguistic competence than the surface features of their texts might indicate. In this section, I offer three signs of an encouraging competence beneath the surface tangle.

1. *At least half of student errors result from inattentive editing and proofreading.* Haswell (1983) discovered that students found and corrected approximately 60 percent of their own sentence errors (misspellings, comma splices, dangling modifiers, and so forth) when he quit circling mistakes and simply marked an X in the margin next to lines that contained errors. Haswell's system of "minimal marking," which I describe more fully later in this chapter and again in Chapter Sixteen, withholds a grade on an essay until students have found and corrected as many of their own errors as possible. Haswell thus creates a classroom environment that motivates better habits of editing and proofreading. This system can easily be implemented across the curriculum and will go a long way toward teaching students to take personal responsibility for the surface features of their prose.

2. *When asked to read their drafts aloud, students unconsciously correct many of their mistakes.* Bartholomae (1980) discovered that when developmental writers read their drafts aloud, their oral rendering of the text unconsciously corrected most of their written errors, even though the students were often unaware that their spoken version differed from their written version. Here is an example based on Bartholomae's research (pp. 261–262):

What the Student Wrote

The school suspense me for being late ten time. I had accummate ten dementic and had to bring my mother to school to talk to a conselor and Princicable of the school what when on at the meet took me out mentally period.

What the Student Said When Reading Aloud

The school suspended me for being late ten times. I had accumulated ten demerits and had to bring my mother to school to talk to a counselor and the Principal of the school (full stop) what went on at the meeting took me out mentally (full stop) period (with brio).

Bartholomae's work helps us keep faith in the tacit power of Hartwell's grammar 1. When reading aloud, this student pronounced correctly all his misspelled words (the student did not stumble over the unfamiliar nonword *dementic* but simply said "demerit"); he also corrected past tense formations (by adding *-ed*), punctuation (through intonation—coming to a full stop between sentences), and wrong-word errors (*when* for *went* and so forth). What Bartholomae puzzles over is why the student does not notice or "see" the differences between the oral sounds and the written symbols on the page.

Whatever the cause—and surely this student's lifetime of nonreading is an essential factor—the pedagogy that emerges is hopeful. Teachers can help struggling writers rely more trustingly on the preconscious grammar that generates their speech—to talk their writing, as it were. Bartholomae's strategy with developmental writers is to teach students to "hear" their own voices and to master gradually the skills of transcribing oral language into the written code. The strategy of reading drafts aloud also helps more skilled writers and has widespread application across the curriculum. Students should be asked to read their drafts aloud—both to themselves and to peer audiences—and to note places where their oral reading differs from what they have written. Often the simple act of reading a draft aloud can clear up a large number of errors. (See the discussion of peer review workshops in Chapter Fifteen.)

3. *Student errors are systematic and classifiable.* The late Mina Shaughnessy, who founded modern research into the problems of developmental writers, discovered that students seldom make random errors. Shaughnessy (1977) demonstrated that many of the errors in a typical student's essay are reiterations of a few consistent mistakes, often stemming from a misunderstood, misapplied, or idiosyncratic rule or from second-dialect or

second-language interference. By helping students classify their errors and understand their causes, teachers can make order out of tangled texts and teach the specific skills needed to overcome each student's particular pattern of errors. Thus Bartholomae (1980), using Shaughnessy's strategy, analyzes a student's error-laden text as follows: "The passage contains 41 verbs; only 17 of them are used incorrectly. With the exception of four spelling errors, the errors are all errors of inflection and, furthermore, these errors come only with regular verbs. There are no errors with irregular verbs. This would suggest, then, that when John draws on memory for a verb form, he gets it right; but when John applies a rule to determine the ending, he gets it wrong" (p. 260). Chapter Sixteen describes ways that teachers across the curriculum can use a nonspecialist version of this strategy to make their comments on student papers more helpful and productive.

Errors in Student Writing Increase with Greater Cognitive Difficulty of the Assignment

A particularly illuminating discovery of composition research is the extent to which students' apparent skill level varies according to the cognitive complexity of the writing task. Schwalm (1985) has noted the relationship between error production and the difficulty level of a communication task in the examinations used by government language schools to categorize students' skill levels. An examinee might seem totally fluent in a foreign language when making small talk; however, grammatical competence begins to drop off as the tasks become more complex and decreases dramatically when the examinee is asked to advance arguments, hypothesize, or handle abstractions. The more cognitively difficult the task, the more an examinee's sentence structure breaks down. Using insights from second-language examination procedures, Schwalm designed an experiment in which sixty developmental writers who could produce error-free prose when writing descriptions or personal narratives were given a simple academic task requiring the analysis of new information. Almost all the students, reports Schwalm, "experienced partial or total linguistic collapse . . . Grammatical, lexical, and syntactic skills that they *seemed* to have mastered disintegrated. The papers were nearly incomprehensible . . . *Their skills developed in personal writing, especially sentence level skills, were not adequate to simple academic writing tasks*" (p. 633, emphasis in the original). In a workshop presentation, Joseph Williams of the University of Chicago noted a similar phenomenon in his study of the writing of first-year law students, where grammatical problems, supposedly eliminated in undergraduate work, begin cropping up again in their first attempts to write legal briefs. Williams's finding accords with my own experience with students who wrote well for me in first-year English going on to produce poorly written papers the next term in philosophy or political science. Longitudinal studies of student writing (see especially Carroll, 2002) note the same phenomenon.

This research points to a relationship between grammatical competence and a writer's control over the ideas being expressed and the features of new genres. As each new course immerses students in new, unfamiliar ideas and rhetorical contexts, the quality of students' writing predictably degenerates. Teachers can help counter this phenomenon by building requirements for multiple drafts into their assignments so that students can use early drafts to clarify their thinking. This last suggestion leads to the next point.

Errors Often Disappear in Students' Prose as They Progress Through Multiple Drafts

Here is a common scenario. A student writes a paper containing many sentence errors. The teacher, treating the paper as a draft rather than a finished product, notes that the paper also has problems with organization and focus. Instead of working on errors, teacher and student focus on clarifying the ideas in the paper. The writer leaves the conference with a newly formulated thesis and an improved organizational plan. On the next draft, many of the grammatical errors disappear. This phenomenon suggests that the early error-laden draft is a necessary step toward the writer's eventual mastery of the ideas and that once the ideas have become clearer, the sentence structure begins to clear up also. In our desire for students to produce correct sentences, then, we must trust the writing process and not ask for premature editing.

Teachers Can Expect to See Sentence Problems in First Drafts and on Essay Exams

Based on my own experience, I can classify students loosely into four skill categories with regard to error production. Writers in category 4—my top category—come to college blessed with the ability to write error-free prose at both the rough-draft and finished-product stages. Whatever accounts for their skill at correctness—heredity, home environment, early reading habits, a tough old bird of an eighth-grade grammar teacher—they show few sentence problems, and the errors they do make are often the result of lack of knowledge about a specific rule, not a deficient level of skill. A brief explanation from a handbook clears up the errors.

Students in my categories 3 and 2 write rough drafts marred by numerous sentence-level errors, often serious ones. Looking at their rough drafts (or their essay exams), one might be dismayed at their lack of sentence-level competence. Category 3 students, however, can usually edit these problems out of their drafts without assistance (if they have the time and the motivation to do so). Category 2 students, by contrast, need guidance—often the patient editing help of a tutor or teacher. The most severe writing problems occur with category 1 students, who need the intense extra help provided by developmental courses in basic writing.

It follows, then, that unless a student is consistently a category 4 writer, we can expect to see sentence-level problems in early drafts. We will see even more problems on essay exams—the more cognitively taxing the question, the more convoluted the errors.

The converse of this phenomenon is this: if teachers are consistently besieged with error-ridden writing, they are probably not seeing their students' best work, because all but category 1 students ought to be able to submit finished products with relatively few errors. The appropriate intervention for teachers across the curriculum, as the rest of this book tries to show, is to design better assignments, to build a process approach into the requirements, and to coach that process so that students submit thoroughly revised and edited work. It is more difficult to improve the quality of writing on essay exams (which in timed situations is necessarily first-draft writing), but Chapter Twelve suggests ways to build process components into an exam setting.

Traditional Procedures for Grading and Marking Student Papers May Exacerbate the Problem

Category 4 writers benefit from having teachers correct errors on their papers. These students usually produce few errors, and they can quickly learn the rules needed to correct them once they are pointed out. When there are more than a few errors in a paper, however, it can be demoralizing to have every one circled in red ink. More importantly, for category 3, 2, and 1 writers, marking errors on papers can be counterproductive because it deprives them of needed practice in finding and correcting their own errors.

In the final section of this chapter, we turn to considering more effective strategies for dealing with error than the traditional red-ink approach.

Responding to Error: Policies and Strategies for Teachers Across the Disciplines

With this brief review of research on error as background, we now face the pragmatic question of what instructors across the curriculum should do about errors in their students' papers. The remaining pages of this chapter present my own answer to this question, based on what I believe the research recommends.

Help Students Appreciate That Unintentional Sentence-Level Errors Will Harm the Rhetorical Effectiveness of Their Writing

Faculty members across the disciplines might consider conveying to students a message something like this: "It is socially unacceptable to submit written work with an annoying level of error. You may damage yourself irrevocably in business and professional life if you do so. You might as well learn the habits of careful editing and proofreading now while you are in college."

Many students think that only English teachers care about sentence errors. Therefore I like to make my students aware of the research of Beason (2001) and Hairston (1981), both of whom studied the reactions of business professionals to sentence errors in business prose. Both studies reveal that business people are bothered by errors, sometimes quite heatedly. Beason's study, based on interviews with fourteen business professionals, showed how errors hurt the ethos of writers. According to one of Beason's respondents:

> *If this [piece of business writing] was something important that [the writer] wanted me to read . . . and had a lot of these little sloppy errors, then that would probably affect the way I thought about that person and how important that proposal was to them as well [p. 51].*

Another respondent had a similar reaction to error:

> *What [these errors] say is that if a person doesn't care more about themselves than to not present themselves in the best possible light, how in the world can you expect them to care about you and your business? [p. 51]*

Beason's analysis reveals three ways that business professionals categorize "sloppy" writers: they are hasty or careless, they are not trustworthy or dependable as business colleagues (not detail persons, poor thinkers), or they are persons who might harm a company's image.

Likewise, Hairston's research showed that business professionals indeed recognize sentence errors and react strongly against many of them. She divided the errors into status-marking errors (errors that tend to indicate the writer's social, educational, or ethnic status, such as "them apples" or "he brung it") and non-status-marking errors of various levels of seriousness. Status-marking errors received the strongest negative reactions from her respondents, followed by non-status-marking errors in the categories she labeled "very serious" and "serious." I list these here.

Status-Marking Errors

Nonstandard verb forms in past or past participle: *brung* instead of *brought*, *had went* instead of *had gone*

Lack of subject-verb agreement: *we was* instead of *we were, he don't* instead of *he doesn't*

Double negatives

Objective pronoun as subject: *him and Richard were the last ones hired*

Very Serious Errors

Sentence fragments

Run-on sentences

Noncapitalization of proper nouns

Non-status-marking subject-verb agreement errors

Would of instead of *would have*

Insertion of comma between the verb and its complement

Nonparallelism

Faulty adverb forms

Use of transitive *set* for *sit*

Serious Errors

Verb form errors

Dangling modifiers

I as object pronoun

Lack of commas to set off interrupters such as *however*

Lack of commas in series

Tense switching

Use of a plural modifier with a singular noun: *these kind of errors*

EXHIBIT 5.1

Exercise: Commenting on Student Papers

Background. Students in a lower-division philosophy course are assigned to evaluate opposing arguments by Peter Singer and Garrett Hardin on the issue of an affluent person's obligation to help the poor.

Task. Suppose that the following passage occurs in the middle of a student essay submitted about halfway through the term. How would you mark this passage? [The first part of the paper summarizes Hardin and Singer. This passage is the beginning of the evaluation section.]

> *Garit Harden and Peter Singer have both writen essays that are thought provoking. Hardin has the strongest argument, on the other hand, Singer has some good things to say too but his arguements arent as strong as Hardins because he is to idealistic. Meaning he believes people will give up things like color TV and stereos to thrid world poor people even though they (the rich people) will have earned these things (TV and stereos) through their own hard work. This is what I don't like about Singer. Hardin believes in private property and I do too.*
>
> *Another weakness of Singer is . . .*

Shift from "Editing-Oriented" Comments on Papers to "Revision-Oriented" Comments

In addition to explaining to students why professional writing requires careful proofreading and editing, teachers need to develop marking and commenting strategies that encourage those skills. To help instructors appreciate differences in teachers' commenting styles, I often give the exercise in Exhibit 5.1 to participants in writing-across-the-curriculum workshops. You might try spending five minutes or so doing the exercise yourself.

In general, two different philosophies of commenting emerge from these workshops. The most common philosophy—which reflects an editing orientation—produces a marked paper like that shown in Exhibit 5.2. The teacher identifies and circles errors, often with few comments (or none) about ideas or structure. The more numerous the errors, the less apt the teacher is to comment on anything else. A quite different philosophy—which is oriented toward revision—largely ignores sentence errors and concentrates on ideas and structure with the aim of evoking a revised draft exhibiting greater complexity and sophistication of thought (see Exhibit 5.3).

The editing-oriented philosophy sends the message that the student mainly needs to correct errors (even though the draft, if perfectly edited, would be weak in ideas and structure). The revision-oriented philosophy sends the message that the current draft needs to be dismantled and the ideas thought through again. Note, too, that the revision-oriented

---

EXHIBIT 5.2

Editing-Oriented Commenting Strategy

Spell author's name correctly!

Ga(r)it) Har(d)en) and Peter Singer have both
wri(te)n essays that are thought provoking.
                                    comma splice
Hardin has the strongest argument, on the

other hand, Singer has some good things to say

too but his arguements ar(en't) as strong as

Hard(i)ns) because he is (to) idealistic. Meaning   Lookup to,
                                                     too, two
he believes people will give up things like

frag.   color TV and stereos to thrid world poor

people even though they (the rich people) will

have earned these things (TV and stereos)   Don't put
                                             antecedents
through their own hard work. This is what I   of pronouns in
                                             parentheses
don't like about Singer. Hardin believes in   after the
                                             pronoun.
private property and I do too.

Another weakness of Singer is . . . .

---

philosophy takes the writer's ideas seriously and finds something to
praise. To the extent that the errors in this paper reflect haste, carelessness,
and alienation, the revision-oriented comments may result in a new draft
in which the writer's emerging pride in his work may lead to a marked
decrease in the number of sentence errors. Chapter Sixteen deals at length
with ways that faculty across the curriculum can adopt revision-oriented
commentary in their own courses.

Hold Students Responsible for Finding and Fixing Their Own Errors

The best way to make students responsible for finding and fixing their own
errors is to adopt some version of Haswell's (1983) strategy of "minimal
marking," explained in Chapter Sixteen. Using this system, teachers do
not mark and correct errors; instead, they withhold or lower a grade until
the student revises, reedits, and resubmits the paper for a new reading.

In not marking errors, the instructor hopes to create an environment
that forces students to develop their own mental procedures for finding
and correcting errors. Circling errors points out mistakes but does not
teach students how to acquire new mental habits. Also, by not marking

---

EXHIBIT 5.3

Revision-Oriented Commenting Strategy

Garit Harden and Peter Singer have both
writen essays that are thought provoking.
Hardin has the strongest argument, on the
other hand, Singer has some good things to
say too but his arguements arent as strong as
Hardins because he is to idealistic. Meaning
he believes people will give up things like
color TV and stereos to thrid world poor
people even though they (the rich people)
will have earned these things (TV and
stereos) through their own hard work. This is
what I don't like about Singer. Hardin
believes in private property and I do too.
↱ Another weakness of Singer is . . .

Is this your first point about Singer —"A first weakness of Singer is that he is too idealistic" (?) Expand and explain

Excellent insight here—different attitudes about private property are at the heart of their differences— but you raise the point and then drop it without development

Good transition but implies that previous paragraph was about a "first weakness"— e.g., Singer's idealism?

In your next revision break the weaknesses of Singer into separate chunks and develop each. Also edit for sentence errors!

---

errors, instructors avoid sending the misleading message that a poorly written essay simply needs editing rather than revision. Time and again, the best advice to give students about a passage is not to edit it for errors but to rewrite it for clarity and coherence.

A Note About Nonnative Speakers of English

Second-language speakers present extra challenges to teachers across the curriculum. Awareness of a student's cultural background is particularly helpful in dealing with this population because second-language speakers may be unfamiliar not only with the disciplinary discourse of specific fields but also with academic discourse in general. In her study of international students struggling with writing in American academies, Fox (1994, p. xxi) concludes that "the dominant communication style and world view of the U.S. university, variously known as 'academic argument,' 'analytical writing,' 'critical thinking,' or just plain 'good writing,' is based on assumptions and habits of mind that are derived from western—or more specifically U.S.—culture . . . This way of thinking and communicating is considered the most sophisticated, intelligent, and efficient by only a tiny fraction of the world's peoples." Fox then shows how cultural differences explain much of the characteristic difficulties that second-language speakers have with academic prose—reluctance to come to a point, digression and irrelevancies, a tendency to transmit the wisdom of others rather than do original critical analysis, and bafflement about the sin of plagiarism. Fortunately, the best way to help second language speakers is by providing a rich language environment created by the kinds of writing and critical thinking activities recommended throughout this book. We need to remember that we are teaching not simply a way of writing but a style of thinking. When we develop assignments to teach the thinking processes we value, we help all our student populations simultaneously.

Working with the ideas of second-language speakers also helps lessen our focus on their sentence-level errors, which are apt to differ from those of native speakers. Many second-language speakers, particularly international students as opposed to recent immigrants or refugees, have adequate classroom knowledge of English grammar and can avoid comma splices, fragments, nonparallel constructions, and so forth. But research suggests that we should expect—and not worry about—what ESL teachers call written "accent"; problems with articles, count versus non-count nouns, verb tenses, and word formations such as using a noun form in a verb slot ("I hope to success in this course"). My best advice for responding to the writing of nonnative speakers is to focus on ideas and organization, as one would do with native speakers, but to use a somewhat different approach for handling error. Generally, I expect second-language speakers to avoid punctuation and sentence structure errors that depend on grammar 4 handbook rules (such as dangling participles, comma splices, or nonparallel constructions), but I am very forgiving of "accent" errors arising from the absence of a native speaker's grammar 1 knowledge. Expecting nonnative speakers to produce fluent, unaccented English is an unrealistic goal.

A Note About Spell-Checkers and Grammar-Checkers

Teachers across the disciplines often ask about my view of spell-checkers and grammar-checkers. Spell-checkers, of course, are extremely valuable, even if they can't pick up homonym errors. They have saved me from embarrassment on many occasions. But I must confess that I think my own native spelling has gotten worse since I have come to rely on spell-checkers. I used to keep a dictionary with me and would regularly look up my nemesis words such as *weird*, *accommodate*, and *idiosyncratic*. Now I just let the spell-checker correct the error as I type. I am particularly surprised at the number of spelling errors I make in rapidly composed e-mails and breathe a sigh of relief when the e-mail spell-checker finds them.

Grammar-checkers are an entirely different matter. If a writer is already a grammar whiz, grammar-checkers may usefully catch a careless error. I generally keep my grammar-checker turned on and look carefully at marked sentences. But a writer absolutely cannot depend on grammar-checkers either to find errors or to correct them. In one study, Kies (2008) built twenty common errors into a passage and ran it through five grammar-checking programs. Only one program (Grammarian Pro-X) found at least half of the errors, with other programs faring much worse. Moreover, in some cases the program's suggested "corrections" were howlers. Unless you are confident in your ability to override the advice of a grammar-checker—which after all isn't really "reading" but only applying complex algorithms to data—you are better off ignoring them. The occasional grammatical mistakes made by real writers are preferable to the egregious errors suggested as "corrections" by the grammar-checker. In short, I tell my students to turn off their grammar-checkers.

Conclusion: Keeping an Eye on Our Goals

The elimination of error from student writing is an enormously complex project. Teachers across the curriculum can best help with error by learning to live with it on essay exams but by not accepting it on final products that have gone through multiple drafts. By emphasizing ideas and organization and by making students find and fix their own errors, instructors will be doing the best we can hope for in light of our current knowledge about language competence.

This approach may not be exactly what my colleague hoped for in calling for an "extended course in structure and grammar." But it will best lead, I think, to the goals that my colleague and I emphatically share: the goal of helping students produce intelligent, graceful, well-argued, and largely error-free essays.

Designing Problem-Based Assignments

6

Formal Writing Assignments

Part Two of this book focuses on the design of problem-based assignments to promote critical thinking and active engagement with course subject matter. The present chapter concerns the design of formal writing assignments, which call for finished prose. Formal writing usually requires multiple drafts and is thus distinguished from equally important informal, exploratory writing aimed at generating, developing, and extending thinking on a subject. (How to use informal exploratory writing in your courses is the subject of Chapter Seven.)

Formal writing can range in length from microthemes (one or two paragraphs) to substantial research projects. The chapter's initial focus is on thesis-governed academic writing, but the concluding section surveys other kinds of assignments that let students write in alternative genres, often with a more personal voice and style.

Let's begin by comparing the traditional method of assignment writing with alternative methods.

The Traditional Method

In American universities, a traditional way to assign writing goes something like this: "There will be a term paper due at the end of the semester. The term paper can be on any aspect of the course that interests you, but I have to approve your topic in advance." About halfway through the term, students may be asked to submit proposals for topics—usually stated as a topic area rather than as a research question or tentative thesis. The instructor either approves the topic or advises that it be narrowed or otherwise refined. In many cases, there is no further contact between teacher and student. (Sometimes the professor may ask for an outline and make comments on it.) At the end of the term, the teacher collects and grades the papers. Some teachers mark the papers copiously; others make only cryptic end comments. Much to teachers' disappointment, many students never pick up their papers from the teacher's office.

Alternative Approaches to Assigning Writing

Early in my career in writing across the curriculum, I witnessed the power of alternative approaches to assigning formal writing. A memorable example came from my colleague at Montana State University, finance professor Dean Drenk, who asked his students to write a series of short essays, each of which must support either the positive or the negative side of a thesis on a controversial question in finance (Drenk, 1986; Bean, Drenk, and Lee, 1986). Drenk constructed the theses, which he sequenced from easy to more difficult, to cover various key issues in the field, such as the following:

The market is/is not efficient in strong-form, random-walk terms.

Bonds are/are not more risky investments than stocks.

Random diversification is/is not more reliable than selective diversification.

Each thesis support assignment requires students to understand and use key course concepts while simultaneously practicing the methods of inquiry, research, and argumentation in finance. Students must use research skills to find relevant data on their assigned issues, analyze the data, develop reasoned positions, and produce empirically supported arguments. Students are required to meet minimal standards on each thesis support essay before progressing to the next, and they are encouraged to rewrite their essays for higher grades, a bonus that stimulates revision. To provide feedback, Drenk developed an evaluative rubric focusing on the quality of critical thinking, the clarity of writing, and the adequacy of empirical support.

Traditional and Alternative Methods Compared

The first of these methods—the traditional research paper—can be excellent for skilled upper-division students who have already learned the conventions of inquiry and argumentation in a discipline. At some point in their undergraduate careers, we want to turn students loose and say, "Okay, now talk and write like a new member of this discipline. Go find your own topic and do something interesting with it." But even for advanced students in the major, this "term paper" assignment could be improved by clearer specification of genre, audience, purpose. (See Chapter Thirteen on teaching undergraduate research.)

But for many college writers, the freedom of an open-topic research paper is debilitating. Not yet at home with academic writing or with the discourse conventions of a new discipline, these students are apt to produce either wandering "all about" papers (see pages 26–27) rather than arguments, or quasi-plagiarized data dumps with long quotations and thinly disguised paraphrases. Even worse, students may resort to outright plagiarism. Because the traditional term paper assignment does not guide students toward formulating a problem, developing a thesis, or arguing within the conventions of a disciplinary genre, it often does not stimulate the complex thinking (and hence the need for multiple drafts) that teachers desire. In addition, traditional term papers often do little to enhance learning of course content. They supplement a course but do not focus students' mental energies on the most important or most difficult course concepts or issues.

In contrast, Drenk's thesis support assignments focus directly on course concepts and teach thesis-governed argumentation in the discipline. In investigating a series of issues in finance, students see that knowledge in this discipline is not an assemblage of inert concepts and data but rather an arena for inquiry and argument. Moreover, because Drenk's thesis support essays are short (one to two pages), students can rework them through multiple revisions and transfer what they have learned from one essay to the next. Furthermore, Drenk's emphasis on standards, combined with his allowing of rewrites, often leads to a surprisingly high level of student work. "Although doubts always accompany teaching," Drenk says, "I know that I am successful as a teacher when students confess that they learned more through my writing assignments than through any other academic activity" (Drenk, 1986, p. 55).

EXHIBIT 6.1

Considering the Effects of Small Variations in Assignment Design

Suppose that you are a nursing professor with two goals for a research assignment: (1) you want to deepen students' thinking about controversies in alternative medicine and (2) you want to create a writing assignment that will help your students learn to read the professional literature with sophistication and to do the kind of critical thinking, inquiry, analysis, and problem-solving required of nurses. You decide to have your students investigate the controversy over therapeutic touch (TT), a form of alternative medicine in which the healer is said to effect therapeutic changes in the patient's energy field by moving his or her hands slightly above the patient's body. Consider the following five assignment options and the discussion questions that follow:

Assignment Option 1

Write an eight- to ten-page research paper on therapeutic touch. Follow APA conventions for documentation.

Assignment Option 2

You are a staff nurse at a large urban hospital. Recently the hospital became embroiled in a major controversy when several nurses were discovered to be practicing TT on patients without the permission or knowledge of their supervisors or of attending physicians. The hospital governing board reprimanded the nurses and issued a general statement forbidding the practice of TT, which they called "non-scientific quackery." Research the professional literature on TT, looking especially for evidence-based studies. Then write a four- to five-page argument, addressed to the hospital governing board, supporting or attacking the board's decision to forbid the practice of TT. Support your position with reasons and evidence based on the professional literature.

Assignment Option 3

Assume that you and several colleagues seek grant funding to do a controlled research study on the efficacy of TT for reducing anxiety and pain in surgery patients. Research the current professional literature on TT and then write the "review of the literature" section of your grant proposal.

Assignment Option 4

Do a literature search to find several empirical studies of TT. Choose one of these studies for this two- to three-page paper. Write a critical review of your selected article in which you (1) summarize the purpose, method, and results of the study (in your own words—don't copy the abstract) and (2) write a critical review of the article in which you analyze the extent to which it provides or doesn't provide a scientific basis for regarding TT as evidence-based medicine.

Assignment Option 5

Should schools of nursing and major nursing organizations give their imprimatur to TT? In some quarters, nurses are being ridiculed for their attraction to "new age mysticism." In other quarters, nurses are praised for their openness to modalities of healing other than Western science. For this assignment write an eight- to ten-page exploratory research paper that describes chronologically your own search for a personal answer to this question. The paper should start with a reflection on where you stood on this issue before you began your research, and why. (Being confused or uncertain is OK.) Then write a first-person, reflective narrative of your thinking process as you investigated your question by researching the professional literature, talking with classmates, and drawing on your own personal experiences, memories, and observations. Your narrative should include a summary of at least three professional articles, followed by your own intellectual wrestling with that article's ideas. By the end of your essay, sum up how your ideas evolved during your process of research and reflection. You will be rewarded for the quality of your exploration and thinking processes. In other words, your goal is not to take a stand on this issue, but to report on your process of wrestling with it.

Discussion Questions

1. What differences in thinking processes are apt to be encouraged by each option?

2. What are the advantages and disadvantages of each option?

3. Which assignment or sequence of assignments would you choose were you the nursing professor?

Thinking Rhetorically: Five Variations on the Same Assignment

When designing formal writing assignments, instructors should consider how variations in the rhetorical context—purpose, audience, genre—can create significant differences in students' writing and thinking processes as well as in their final products. As an illustration, consider the small group task I sometimes present at writing-across-the-curriculum workshops (Exhibit 6.1).

When I give this task, I often find surprising consensus among participants about the strengths and limitations of each assignment. Almost universally, faculty reject the first option—the "research paper"—which they see as a pseudo-academic or "school" genre that invites "all about" reports rather than higher-order critical thinking. Because it provides no guidance about purpose, audience, or genre, students are led simply to gather and report information. In contrast, option 2 (the civic argument) and option 3 (the literature review) are important real-world genres, the first aimed at public policy making and the second at producing academic scholarship. Both require a high level of critical thinking. Participants also recognize that option 5 (the exploratory paper), while not a typical academic genre, links academic subject matter to the genre of the "personal essay," drawing on the values of open-form expressive writing that is "close to the self." (See Chapters Three and Four.)

The assignments also differ in the kinds of critical thinking they are apt to evoke. Whereas option 2 demands an argumentative thesis, option 5 rewards uncertainty and inquiry. Option 3 seems to invite both inquiry and argument. It invites inquiry in that its goal is to find gaps or remaining unknowns in the literature and to establish a new research question worthy of funding; it requires argument in that it must show why the new research question is both problematic (no one else has solved it) and significant (it is worth solving). This assignment, faculty tend to agree, is the most difficult of all the options.

Option 4 also stimulates interesting discussion. Everyone agrees that it is the most basic of the assignments, teaching the skills of summary and critical analysis needed for any of the more difficult options. Participants often suggest that this assignment could become a preliminary skill-building or "scaffolding" assignment given early in the term. After students have produced an option 4 paper and received feedback from the instructor, they would be better able to complete the research and do the critical thinking needed to produce options 2, 3, or 5.

So which option would participants choose for their own classrooms? Participants are usually divided in about the same proportions as those revealed in Thaiss and Zawacki's (2006) research on faculty preference for academic versus alternative forms (see Chapter Four, page 54). Many participants are attracted to option 2, which requires closed-form, thesis-governed writing in a civic rather than academic context. They argue that nurses should be encouraged to join public debates about health care and develop strong leadership voices in the civic arena. Others are attracted to the personal reflective writing evoked by option 5, which gives students space to connect their professional training to their personal lives and to wrestle with the philosophic issues that underlie controversies about Western medicine. Still others value the literature review because it is so central to mainstream academic writing. Some, however, believe that option 3 as written is too difficult for undergraduates—that doing grant proposal literature reviews would be more appropriate for graduate school. (These faculty want to develop an assignment more extended than option 4 but less difficult than a professional literature review.) Others argue that undergraduates can do quite sophisticated research that engages the professional literature, and they welcome the challenge of teaching students to do a literature review.

My point in doing this exercise is to show instructors that they have a range of options in designing formal assignments and that the rhetorical context they build into their assignments influences the thinking and writing processes of their students. When planning assignments, therefore, teachers need to consider not only their conceptual learning goals but also the thinking and writing processes that they want their assignments to encourage.

The remaining sections of this chapter focus on issues of planning, designing, and giving formal writing assignments.

Articulation of Learning Goals as Preparation for Designing Assignments

Teachers can build more learning power into their writing assignments and other critical thinking tasks if they focus first on their learning goals for students. Prior to designing assignments, teachers can develop their learning goals by considering answers to the following questions:

1. What are the main units or modules in my course? (For example, two weeks on X, four days on Y, and another two weeks on Z.)

2. What are my main learning objectives for each of these modules and for the whole course? What are the chief concepts and principles that I want students to learn in each unit or module?

3. What thinking skills am I trying to develop within each unit or module and throughout the whole course? (Such skills include ways of observing, habits of mind, questioning strategies, use of evidence—whatever thinking processes are important in your course or discipline. To put it another way, what ways of thinking characterize a historian, an accountant, a chemist, a nurse, and so forth?) Teachers often consolidate their highest level conceptual and disciplinary thinking goals into five or six key learning outcome goals for the course.

4. Based on previous students' experience, what are the most difficult aspects of my course for students? When have students most struggled? When have I been most unhappy with student performance? What concepts or ways of thinking are most challenging?

5. If I could change my students' study habits, what would I most like to change?

6. What difference do I want my course to make in my students' lives—in their sense of self, their values, their ways of thinking? What is my unique stamp on this course? Ten years later, what do I want them to remember most about my course?

Of course, it is impossible to design assignments that have an impact on every facet of a course. But teachers can put together a combination of formal and informal writing assignments and other kinds of critical thinking tasks that will help students achieve many of the course's learning goals. (For a more detailed approach to articulating course goals, see "The Teaching Goals Inventory" in Angelo and Cross, 1993, pp. 13–23.) In designing formal assignments, teachers have numerous options. Before looking specifically at these options, first we'll discuss the principle of "backward design" or "reverse engineering" of a course or curriculum.

Planning Your Course Backward by Designing the Last Assignment First

The final writing assignment in a course can build on the skills of thinking, seeing, analyzing, and arguing that students have been developing through the whole course. It encourages students to synthesize earlier work and to focus on problems more complex than those encountered earlier in the course. If teachers design this last assignment first, they can analyze its level of difficulty, determine the kinds of problems students are apt to encounter, and then design earlier assignments that help students build the skills needed for the final assignment. (These earlier assignments are often called "scaffolding" assignments based on the metaphor of platforms that workers can climb to reach higher levels of a wall.) Suppose the nursing professor discussed earlier wanted to use option 2 in Exhibit 6.1 for the final assignment for the course (the civic argument for or against allowing nurses to offer TT to patients). By designing the course backward, the teacher might assign option 4 (a critical review of one article) and perhaps option 5 (the exploratory paper) early in the term as scaffolding assignments aimed at promoting deeper thinking and delaying closure.

Of course, a professor might prefer not to sequence assignments in this way. Rather than having a series of scaffolding tasks that lead to a final major paper, a teacher might prefer two or three shorter assignments of equal weight focusing on different course goals. But even in such cases it is possible to apply backward design to each short assignment. What in-class or out-of-class exploratory tasks could help students generate ideas for this assignment? What small group exercises or in-class debates would give students the kind of analyzing or arguing practice demanded in the assignment? What kinds of assignments in lower-level courses would prepare students to write more complex disciplinary papers when they are seniors? (I'll return to the principle of backward design in Chapter Thirteen, which considers the backward design of a department's whole curriculum for majors. For more on the concept of backward design, see Wiggins and McTighe, 2005, and Fink, 2003.)

Best Practices in Assignment Design

Scholarship in teaching and learning has led to considerable consensus on the design of effective writing assignments.

The NSSE/WPA Research on Writing and Deep Learning

Particularly important is research from the Consortium for the Study of Writing in College—a joint project of the Council of Writing Program Administrators (WPA) and the National Survey of Student Engagement (NSSE) headquartered at the University of Indiana. Using extensive data compiled from NSSE surveys at a variety of institutions, the researchers conclude that the use of writing to promote deep learning depends less on the amount of writing assigned in a course than on the design of the writing assignments themselves (Anderson, Anson, Gonyea, and Paine, 2009). Effective assignments, this study concludes, have the following three features:

○ *Interactive components:* An assignment's "interactive components" give students opportunities to brainstorm ideas prior to drafting, to get feedback on drafts from the instructor or peers, to visit a campus writing center, or otherwise to see writing as an interactive exchange between writers and readers. Interactive activities situate writing as a process of inquiry and discovery, promote productive talk about the writer's emerging ideas, and encourage multiple drafts and global revision. For assignments early in the term, allowing students to rewrite an assignment for a new grade can particularly motivate deep learning about both subject matter and writing as a process.

○ *A meaning-constructing task:* A "meaning-constructing" task asks students to bring their own critical thinking to bear on problems that matter to both the writer and the intended audience. A meaning-constructing task typically presents students with a disciplinary problem, asks students to formulate their own problems, or otherwise engages them in active critical thinking. Meaning-constructing tasks discourage the kind of alienation we examined in Chapter Two, in which students resort to "all about" reports, data dumps, or cut-and-paste collages from the Web.

○ *Clear explanations of writing expectations:* Often an assignment that seems clear to the instructor can be confusing to students. Effective assignments clearly present the instructor's expectations for a successful performance. Ideally the assignment prompt also explains the purpose of the assignment in terms of the course's learning goals and presents the instructor's grading criteria, often in the form of a rubric.

The NSSE/WPA research accords well with theoretical thinking about assignment design in the WAC literature; I refer to it regularly throughout this chapter and elsewhere in the book.

EXHIBIT 6.2

The Two Dimensions of a "Meaning-Constructing" Task

GIVE YOUR STUDENTS A "RAFT" . . . AND A "TIP"

Role (or purpose)	**T**ask as
Audience	**I**ntriguing
Format (or genre)	**P**roblem*
Task	

The instructor can set the problem or ask students to formulate their own problem.

RAFT and TIP: Further Explanation of "Meaning-Constructing" Tasks

An effective meaning-constructing task has two dimensions: (1) it presents students with an authentic problem requiring their own critical thinking or invites them to pose their own problem, and (2) it presents the problem within a rhetorical context that gives students a role or purpose, a targeted audience, and a genre. To make these dual dimensions "sticky," I like to refer to the mnemonic shown in Exhibit 6.2.

This mnemonic stresses both the subject matter dimension of a good assignment (the TIP) and the rhetorical dimension (the RAFT). Some teachers might object to the apparent constraints of RAFT and TIP in that they may seem to limit students' freedom and creativity. Teachers often resist formulating the problem for students or specifying a genre and audience, on the premise that students need to be free to choose their own topics or find their own way into a subject. These are important objections. Giving students more open-ended assignments can work beautifully so long as the teacher guides students toward formulating a problem (rather than writing about a topic) and encourages them to write to a targeted audience for some purpose within some genre. I'll return to the problem of assigned problems versus student freedom later in this chapter.

Designing an Effective Assignment Handout

Following the NSSE/WPA criteria and the RAFT/TIP dimensions of a meaning-making assignment, a formal writing assignment handout typically has the following features:

Task

The task itself sets forth the subject matter dimension of the assignment. For thesis-driven essays requiring disciplinary ways of thinking and arguing, tasks are best presented as disciplinary problems that the student must address, unless the teacher wants students to formulate their own problems. An alternative is to imply the disciplinary problem by providing a contestable thesis for the student to support or attack, a data set that might lead to competing interpretations, or a genre that requires a disciplinary way of thinking. (Suggestions for alternative kinds of tasks—including reflections, exploratory papers, or expressive or creative writing tasks—are listed later in this chapter.)

Role or Purpose

As part of the rhetorical context, the "role" or "purpose" helps students understand the kind of change they hope to bring about in their audience's view of the subject matter. Are they supposed to bring new information to the reader (informative purpose)? Clarify something that puzzles the reader (analytical purpose)? Change the reader's stance on an issue (persuasive purpose)? Deepen a reader's sense of an issue's complexity (reflective or exploratory purpose)? The writer's role or purpose is closely connected to the audience's opening stance on the writer's subject, as shown in the next section.

Audience

Specifying an audience further sets the rhetorical context. When specifying an audience, the instructor needs to help students visualize the audience's initial stance toward the writer's subject. The instructor's goal is to move students toward a thesis with tension—what Graff and Birkenstein (2009) summarize as the "They say/I say" move: "Many people think X, but I am going to argue Y" or "Before reading my paper, my reader will think X. After reading my paper, my reader will think Y." The writer's goal is to change in some way the reader's initial stance or view. The implied stances of audiences can be presented in ways such as these:

- Several classmates who missed last week's lectures are confused about X. Write them a letter that . . .

- You are a research assistant to Senator Smith, who needs to decide X. Write a policy brief that . . .

- Scholars are divided about X. Write a formal academic paper presenting your position on this disciplinary problem. Imagine presenting the paper at an undergraduate research conference where listeners are apt to be skeptical of your thesis.

Audiences such as these allow students to write either from a position of power (to audiences who know less about the topic than the writer) or of equality (to audiences whose views on the topic differ from the writer's).

Format or Genre

By specifying a genre (academic paper, op-ed piece, memo, proposal, experimental report), the assignment helps students transfer earlier genre knowledge to the current task and make decisions about document design, organization, and style. Here the instructor can also specify expectations about length, manuscript form, documentation style, and so forth.

Interactive Components

By building into the assignment a time schedule for completion of drafts, peer review workshops, revisions, and so forth, the instructor encourages writing as a process of discovery and clarification. Instructors might also consider asking students to save all doodles, notes, outlines, and drafts and to submit these along with the final essay. (This requirement rewards students for following the recommended process and effectively discourages plagiarism.) Providing opportunities for students to brainstorm ideas before drafting or for getting feedback on drafts from the instructor particularly promotes deep learning. (See Chapter Fifteen for strategies on coaching the writing process.)

Evaluation Criteria

This section explains how the instructor will grade students' work. Attaching a rubric is particularly helpful (see Chapter Fourteen on developing grading criteria and designing rubrics).

Examples of an Effective Assignment Handout

In this section, I provide an example of an assignment handout that follows the NSSE/WPA criteria and the RAFT and TIP guidelines. I also analyze some of the issues the professor faced in designing his course and creating the assignment. The example handout (shown in Exhibit 6.3) comes from my colleague at Seattle University, historian Marc McLeod, who designed the assignment for a first-year seminar in Latin American history. His discussion of "interactive components"—particularly the invitation to get

EXHIBIT 6.3

McLeod's Assignment Handout for First-Year Seminar

One of the most prominent topics in the historiography of colonial Latin America has been the nature of the encounter between Amerindians and Europeans beginning in 1492. According to a recent review essay by historian Steve J. Stern, one of the three main paradigms or frameworks for interpreting the conquest has been that of the conquest as an "overwhelming avalanche of destruction," characterized by the military defeat and demographic collapse of indigenous populations, the brutal treatment and ruthless economic exploitation of surviving natives by rapacious conquistadors, and the forced disappearance of pre-Columbian cultural, political, and social ways. Based on your reading of Inga Clendinnen, *Ambivalent Conquests: Maya and Spaniard in Yucatán, 1517–1570,* would you agree with this view of the conquest as one of extreme destruction and trauma? If so, why? If not, what is the best way to describe the nature of the encounter between Spaniards and Amerindians in colonial Latin America?

Using Clendinnen, *Ambivalent Conquests,* as well as the other readings, lectures, and discussions we have had in this course, write a **4–6 page (typed, double-spaced, stapled) essay** answering the above question. The assignment is due **October 10**. Assume that you are writing an academic paper for an undergraduate conference on Latin America. Also assume that your audience has NOT read this assignment and will attend your conference session because your title hooked their interest. Your introduction should explain the problem-at-issue before presenting your thesis. Because this is an academic paper in history, follow the manuscript form of the *Chicago Manual of Style* and Kate L. Turabian, *A Manual for Writers of Term Papers, Theses, and Dissertations.* I will grade your paper using the following rubric:

Introduction and Thesis Statement

10 9 8	7 6 5 4	3 2 1 0
Explains problem to be addressed; provides necessary background; ends with contestable thesis statement; thesis answers question	Problem statement missing; problem poorly focused; thesis unclear, not contestable, and/or does not fully answer question	Paper begins without context or background; paper lacks thesis statement; reader confused about what writer is attempting to do

Quality of ideas and argument

20 18 16	14 12 10 8	6 4 2 0
Strong insights; remains focused on question; effectively links course materials to question; good historical reasoning	Some good insights; loses focus on question or gaps in argument; connections between question and course materials vague; unsupported generalizations	Fails to adequately answer question; contains no clear argument; descriptive rather than analytical; tends to summarize course materials

Use of evidence

10 9 8	7 6 5 4	3 2 1 0
Excellent use of different course materials to support argument; effectively provides relevant examples, evidence, and appropriate quotes	Uneven use of evidence and examples; evidence not always directly relevant; over-reliance on a single source; significance of quotes not readily apparent	Lack of evidence and examples; evidence, if provided, not related to overall argument; limited reference to course materials

(Continued)

Organization and Clarity

10 9 8	7 6 5 4	3 2 1 0
Clear, well-organized paper; paragraphs begin with topic sentences related to thesis; topic sentences fully developed in each paragraph; paper flows logically, reader doesn't get lost	Generally sound organization; some topic sentences strong, others weak; some paragraphs not fully developed; reader occasionally confused by awkward organization, unclear sentences, fuzzy ideas	Poor organization, lacks clarity; paper not organized around coherent paragraphs; paragraphs lack topic sentences; prose is hard to follow and understand

Editing and Manuscript Form

10 9 8	7 6 5 4	3 2 1 0
Flawless paper, or an occasional minor error. Looks like a professional history paper; notes follow assigned format; contains an academic title.	Distractions due to spelling, punctuation, grammar errors; writer seems a bit careless. Varies from assigned style and format in a few ways; contains non-academic title.	Paper seriously marred by mistakes in grammar, spelling, and punctuation; lack of editing. Paper does not follow assigned style and format; papers lacks a title.

feedback on drafts—was in the syllabus rather than in each writing assignment handout.

Although there are many ways to think about writing assignments and overall course design, I particularly value some of the choices McLeod made for this assignment. Let's go behind the scenes for a moment to analyze some of the decisions McLeod had to make.

Problem-Focused Versus Topic-Focused Task

McLeod could have presented the assignment as a topic rather than a problem: "Write a paper on a topic of your choice connected to Clendinnen's book." Topic-focused tasks, however, often lead to "all about" reports or unfocused data dumping unless the student is able to convert a topic into a disciplinary problem. McLeod's problem-focused assignment puts students on the right track from the start by helping them see how academic writing is rooted in controversies or unknowns within an academic community.

Task-Only Versus Task-with-Rhetorical-Context

Because teachers across the disciplines focus primarily on subject matter, they may not consider the importance of specifying a rhetorical context within an assignment. However, providing a rhetorical context helps students develop transferable rhetorical skills that are essential to any writing situation (see Chapter Three). McLeod creates a rhetorical context for this assignment by asking students to write an academic paper for an undergraduate conference on Latin America. When students realize that conference participants choose the papers they want to hear on the basis of their titles, they begin to see how titles serve an important rhetorical purpose. Likewise, they appreciate how readers need to be introduced to the problem-at-issue before they can understand the writer's thesis. This assignment also introduces first-year students to a genuine academic genre—the scholarly conference paper—and gives McLeod an opportunity to explain how scholarship is advanced in an academic culture.

Disciplinary Versus MLA Documentation Style (for a General Education Course)

Students tend to see academic documentation as a baffling maze of arcane, anally compulsive rules. Because students at my institution learn the Modern Language Association (MLA) style in first-year composition, it might seem more logical and efficient for McLeod to let students use MLA instead of Chicago in this first-year history course. But to do so would be to mask useful-to-learn differences between disciplines. In my view, the takeaway knowledge about documentation that students should learn in first-year composition is not how to follow MLA style but how to adapt efficiently to different styles. Students need to understand why each discipline has its own characteristic systems. (Historians prefer Chicago style because it welcomes footnotes and provides detailed guidelines on how to document archival sources.) In specifying Chicago style, McLeod helps students see documentation rhetorically. He's telling students, in effect, "to get used to it"—documentation varies from discipline to discipline. Instead of memorizing one system, students need to learn to follow the directions of different style manuals. I thus applaud McLeod's specification of Chicago style, not because he personally prefers it or because it is better than another style but because it marks the discourse community of historians.

Same Task for All Students Versus Freedom of Choice

In designing a syllabus, instructors often wrestle with the dilemma of how much freedom to provide in individual assignments—whether to have the whole class work on the same problem-based task or allow students to choose their own problems. For this course, McLeod assigned three four- to six-page papers on assigned problems rather than giving students a choice.

There are advantages either way. When students choose their own topics, they may become more invested in the assignment. Moreover, learning to pursue one's own passions and to find problems that connect with one's own interests is crucial for a liberal education. Yet there are also disadvantages in giving students this freedom. Freedom of choice places extra work on the instructor, who often needs to monitor students' choices and help them convert broad topic areas into a problem focus. Additionally, when students pursue their own problems the instructor has only limited ways to connect the paper assignment to in-class work. In contrast, when all students work on the same problem, class time can be devoted to debates, brainstorming sessions, and small group exercises on thinking like a historian (examples of the NSSE/WPA "interactive components" that promote deep learning). Although it may seem that students have less nominal freedom when given an assigned problem, they often feel a kind of existential freedom in having to stake out a claim and make an argument, especially when confronted with classmates' alternative claims. From this perspective, students' individual voices are expressed in the distinctiveness of their thesis statements and methods of argument rather than in their choice of topic.

McLeod opted to give students assigned problems because this approach promoted, in his view, the most effective way to maximize active learning while giving him an efficient means of coaching disciplinary ways to use evidence and make arguments. (Of course, it is possible to mix and match methods also—for example, to give students an assigned problem for the first paper and then to let them pose their own problems for a second or third paper.)

A Common Problem: Asking Too Many Questions

Some instructors, in an understandable effort to stimulate students' thinking, include in their assignments a whole series of "you might want to think about" questions instead of a single focusing question. My experience suggests that this practice confuses students more than it helps. Exhibit 6.4 is an example of too many such questions.

EXHIBIT 6.4

Confusing Task Statement

In the graveyard scene of *Hamlet*, Shakespeare calls to mind the medieval *memento mori* ("remember thy death") philosophic tradition by having Hamlet contemplate the meaning of a human skull. But Shakespeare alters his sources by adding the clownish gravediggers. How does the presence of the gravediggers influence the way you read this scene and perhaps the play itself? Why did Shakespeare add the gravediggers? Do you think "comic relief" is an adequate explanation? Do you think the gravediggers are funny? Absurd? Blasphemous? How does Hamlet's attitude toward the gravediggers affect the scene? Do you think it is appropriate to sing while digging a grave? You might also want to think about the jokes they tell. Do these jokes comment on themes in the play? Do you think that Yorick was more like the gravediggers or more like Hamlet? Does Hamlet seem like a Christian in this scene or something else? You may want to do some research to help you with this topic, but you don't need to. If you do use research be sure to cite your sources.

Although the instructor probably regards these questions as suggestions to stimulate thinking, students may believe they are supposed to answer all of them in some way. Because the questions seem parallel rather than hierarchical, students are apt to produce a series of short answers, addressing each question in turn, rather than a unified essay.

In Exhibit 6.5, the assignment is phrased as a single question and now forces the student to frame a single answer as a thesis statement for the essay. (Some of the "you might want to think about questions" could be used as informal exploratory assignments earlier in the course to stimulate thinking about the gravediggers.)

Asking a Colleague to "Peer-Review" Your Assignment Handout

A good way to fine-tune an assignment is to ask a colleague to read it and role-play a student, trying to predict how students would react. Then discuss with your colleague questions such those as in Exhibit 6.6.

Such discussions with colleagues may help you see ways to revise the assignment to make it both stronger and clearer.

Giving the Assignment in Class

When giving the assignment in class, allow plenty of time for students to ask questions. No matter how clearly you think you have explained the assignment, students will ferret out ambiguities. If possible, show students an A paper from a previous class on a slightly different but related topic.

EXHIBIT 6.5

Improved Task Statement

In the graveyard scene of *Hamlet*, Shakespeare calls to mind the medieval *memento mori* ("remember thy death") philosophic tradition by having Hamlet contemplate the meaning of a human skull. But Shakespeare alters his sources by adding the clownish gravediggers. What do you think is the function of the gravediggers in this scene? Imagine readers who believe in the "comic relief" theory: "The function of the gravediggers is to supply comic relief. When we laugh at the grave diggers, we are temporarily relieving some of the tragic tension that has been building up." Your goal is to show these readers that the gravediggers serve a deeper, more complex function than comic relief. But what is that function? We'll be debating this question in class, so you'll have plenty of chances to generate ideas.

EXHIBIT 6.6

Questions for Collegial Peer Review of an Assignment Handout

- Is the assignment clear? How might a student misread the assignment and do something not anticipated?

- Does the assignment focus on an "intriguing problem"—either directly or implied?

- Does the assignment specify a rhetorical context for the writer (that is, a purpose, audience, and genre)?

- Are my grading criteria clear? Does my rubric adequately explain criteria to students? Is my rubric too sketchy or too detailed?

- If you were a student, would you find the assignment interesting and challenging?

- If you were a student, how difficult would this assignment be? How long do you think it would take?

- If the assignment is quite difficult, could it be preceded by a simpler "skill-building assignment" that would serve as scaffolding?

- To what extent does this assignment stimulate critical thinking? Does it cause students to wrestle with key concepts or key thinking skills in the course?

- Is the purpose of the assignment clear? Does it seem to tie into my course goals? Would it seem like busy work to some students?

- Are the mechanics of the assignment clear (due dates, expected length, single versus double spacing, manuscript form, documentation style, and so forth)?

- Is the process students should go through as explicit as possible?

- Should I build more "interactive components" into the assignment to keep students productively on task? Some possibilities:

  - Class time for brainstorming

  - Submission of a thesis, title, and introduction

  - Mandatory conference

  - Annotated bibliography

  - Opportunities for rewriting

- How easy will it be for me to coach and grade this assignment? What problems can I anticipate?

Even better, if you can afford the class time, pass out a set of representative essays, strong and weak, and ask students to grade them for themselves in an in-class collaborative session. (See Chapter Ten, page 194, for a discussion of group norming sessions.) You can then explain how you would grade the papers in order to clarify your expectations. Be prepared for a lively discussion!

In the rest of this chapter, I offer a variety of options for designing formal assignments. I have placed them loosely into four categories:

- Assignments leading to closed-form thesis-governed writing
- Microtheme assignments for writing-to-learn (includes an analysis of student microthemes in physics)
- More open forms: alternatives to the thesis-governed paper
- A potpourri of other kinds of alternative assignments

Assignments Leading to Closed-Form Thesis-Governed Writing

Chapters Two and Four provide a rationale for closed-form, thesis-governed writing—the prototypical structure for most academic prose. Because thesis-governed writing does not come naturally to students, teachers need to encourage it. The following strategies suggest ways that you can teach students to write closed-form prose that addresses a problem with stakes.

Present a Proposition (Thesis) for Students to Defend or Refute

In this strategy, the teacher's task is to develop arguable propositions that engage students with disciplinary controversies.

In recent years, advertising has (has not) made enormous gains in portraying women as strong, independent, and intelligent. [Cultural studies]

. . .

The overriding religious view expressed in *Hamlet* is (is not) an existential atheism similar to Sartre's. [Literature]

. . .

Prescribing Ritalin and other psychotropic medications is (is not) an appropriate treatment for behavioral problems of children. [Nursing]

. . .

This proposed bridge design does/does not meet the criteria set forth by the city in its request for proposal. [Civil engineering]

. . .

Schizophrenia is a brain disease/schizophrenia is learned behavior. [Psychology]

Thesis-support writing, as exemplified in these assignments, works best when students are urged to consider opposing views and to sift and weigh evidence on all sides. Teachers can help students consider opposing views by showing them how to add an "although" clause to a thesis statement along with appropriate qualifiers: "Although there is some evidence to suggest that schizophrenia is a learned behavior, the preponderance of current research favors the theory that schizophrenia is a brain disease." In addition, teachers can allow students to revise the provided thesis to represent their own arguments more accurately. (For further examples of thesis support assignments, see Chapter Nine, pages 152–153; see also, in Chapter Eleven, the "believing/doubting" strategy, page 192; and the "evidence-finding" strategy, pages 192–193.)

Give Students a Problem or Question That Demands the Student's "Best Solution" Answer

Unlike the previous strategy, in which the instructor provides a controversial thesis to defend or attack, this strategy avoids a pro/con framework by inviting a variety of different thesis statements arguing different conceptual positions. In the following examples, the instructor's focusing question is italicized:

What should Project Manager Hisako Hirai propose to her supervisor in response to the problems that have cropped up in Week Three? Role-playing Ms. Hirai, write a memo to your supervisor presenting and justifying your recommendations. [Part of a business management case]

. . .

So far, your team has examined four alternative design solutions for the circumference-mounted radiator fan. *Which solution do you think your team should propose to the project manager as the most optimal?* Write a brief technical proposal to the project manager explaining your proposed solution and justifying it with reasons and evidence. [Mechanical engineering]

. . .

Gauss's law relates the field at the surface to the charge inside the surface. But surely the field at the surface is affected by the charges outside the surface. *How do you resolve this difficulty?* [Mullin, 1989, p. 207] [Physics]

. . .

At the end of Act I of *As You Like It*, Celia says, as they contemplate leaving for the Forest of Arden, "Now go in we content/ To liberty, and not to banishment." This assignment asks you to analyze the meaning of "liberty" in *As You Like It* by contrasting Touchstone's view of liberty with that of Rosalind. Write a three- to four-page critical argument addressing this question: *How does Rosalind's view of liberty differ from Touchstone's?* [Literature]

Assign a Thesis-Governed Paper Requiring Analysis of Raw Data

Another effective way to guide students toward thesis-governed arguments is to give them raw data (such as lists, graphs, tables) to analyze and have them write a thesis-governed paper based on the data. The meaning induced from the data becomes the writer's thesis. Selected pieces of the data serve as evidence.

To what extent do the attached economic data support the hypothesis "Social service spending is inversely related to economic growth"? First create a scattergram as a visual test of the hypothesis. Then create a verbal argument analyzing whether the data support the hypothesis. [Economics]

• • •

You and your friend are looking over the attached table and note that in 1998 the median income for all families was $33,400 but the mean income was $53,000. Your friend was confused about the difference between median and mean and didn't see any significance in this difference. Send your friend a well-structured email message, about one screen in length, that explains the difference between median and mean and then gives your answer to the following question: What can we say about the distribution of income in the United States if we know that mean income is considerably higher than median income? [General education mathematics]

Create "Strong Response" Assignments Based on One or More Scholarly Articles or Other Readings

For this strategy ask students to read one or more scholarly articles or other texts. Then ask them to summarize each article's argument and provide a "strong response" that speaks back to the texts through closed-form prose. This strategy teaches skills of academic reading while showing students how to position themselves within a conversation of alternative views.

Do animals have rights? Read the assigned article by Peter Singer. In a short essay that sets up the question about whether animals have rights, summarize Peter Singer's argument in response to that question and then set forth the strongest objection that a naysayer might make to Singer. Don't for this paper reveal your own view. [First year seminar]

• • •

Read the speech President Barack Obama delivered at Cairo University in Egypt on June 4, 2009. Summarize the main argument of his speech and then analyze the rhetorical strategies he used to appeal to Muslim listeners and readers. [Communication]

• • •

(Continued)

In the introduction to a conference paper, you want to show that critics disagree on how to read the ending of Hawthorne's *The Scarlet Letter*. Read the two scholarly articles that I have placed on our course website. Then write the section of your introduction that will show the critical controversy over the ending of the novel. Devote about two hundred words to your summary of each critic. Note that I'm not asking for your own argument about the ending—just set up an interpretive problem by showing that critics disagree. [Literature]

Let Students Develop Their Own Questions

This strategy gives students the greatest amount of free choice. Often, however, students need help learning how to pose appropriate questions.

Now that we have practiced asking interpretive questions about poems, consider Yeats's "Among School Children." Propose your own interpretive question about this poem, and then write an explication of the poem that tries to answer your question.

• • •

The Generic Term-Paper Assignment: Write a researched argument [specify length] on any topic related to the subject matter we have been studying. Early in your research process you must identify within your topic area a problem, question, or controversy that requires from you a contestable thesis statement supported by your own critical thinking. Use the introduction of your paper to engage your reader's interest in the problem or question you plan to address, showing why it is both problematic and significant. The body of your paper should be your own contestable response to this question made as persuasive as possible through appropriate analysis, argumentation, and use of evidence. Midway through the course, you will submit to the instructor a prospectus that describes the problem or question that you plan to address and shows why the question is (1) problematic and (2) significant.

This last assignment, which I have called "the generic term paper assignment," has a number of advantages. First, for teachers who like to give students as much freedom as possible, the generic assignment permits free choice of topics while guiding students toward thesis-governed prose that addresses a real problem. By requiring that the introduction set forth a problem, the assignment implies both an audience and a purpose, thus helping inexperienced writers overcome their tendency toward "all about" papers. Second, in its focus on question asking, the assignment encourages teachers to discuss the process of inquiry in their disciplines. Finally—and this is an advantage not to be taken lightly—the assignment is easy to coach. Well before the assignment due date, students can be asked to submit a prospectus explaining and focusing the question to be addressed (the prospectus later serves as a rough draft of the introduction). In responding to the prospectus, the instructor can guide the student toward an appropriately delineated question and thesis. (See Exhibit 13.9, page 246, for an example of how I have used the generic term-paper assignment as the final project for a course designed to teach research writing to literature majors.)

For shorter assignments, an even simpler method of screening is possible: teachers can ask students to submit two sentences—their introductory question and their thesis statement—which can be quickly checked for focus and direction. Conceptual problems noted at this stage can often be solved through individual or group conferences or through referral of the student to a teaching assistant or writing center consultant. (See Chapter Fourteen for further discussion of this screening technique.)

Microtheme Assignments for Writing-to-Learn

Although writing-to-learn is often associated with informal, exploratory writing such as journals, in-class freewriting, or "thinking pieces" (the subject of Chapter Seven), teachers can also design short formal assignments (I call them "microthemes") that help students learn important concepts in a course (Bean, Drenk, and Lee, 1986). I define a microtheme as a very short piece of formal, closed-form writing usually less than 250 words.

Examples of Microtheme Assignments

In the following cases, consider how a physics professor and a psychology professor developed assignments focusing on key course concepts—acceleration versus velocity in physics and operant conditioning in psychology.

Microtheme assignments like these can prompt intense, purposeful rereading of textbooks and class notes while stimulating out-of-class discussions among students. Furthermore, students report that the act of writing often alerts them to gaps in their understanding. In the operant conditioning problem, for example, students reported in interviews with me that it was easier to explain how the professor conditioned the cats than how the cats conditioned the professor, yet the latter case is essential for full understanding of the concept.

[Physics] You are Dr. Science, the question-and-answer person for a popular magazine called *Practical Science*. Readers of your magazine are invited to submit letters to Dr. Science, who answers them in "Dear Abby" style in a special section of the magazine. One day you receive the following letter:

Dear Dr. Science:

You've got to help me settle this argument I am having with my girlfriend. We were watching a baseball game several weeks ago when this guy hit a high pop-up straight over the catcher's head. When it finally came down, the catcher caught it standing on home plate. Well, my girlfriend told me that when the ball stopped in midair just before it started back down, its velocity was zero, but its acceleration was not zero. I said she was stupid. If something isn't moving at all, how could it have any acceleration? Ever since then, she has been making a big deal out of this and won't let me kiss her. I love her, but I don't think we can get back together until we settle this argument. We checked some physics books, but they weren't very clear. We agreed that I would write to you and let you settle the argument. But, Dr. Science, don't just tell us the answer. You've got to explain it so we both understand because my girlfriend is really dogmatic. She said she wouldn't even trust Einstein unless he could explain himself clearly.

Sincerely,

Baseball Blues

Can this relationship be saved? Your task is to write an answer to Baseball Blues. Because space in your magazine is limited, restrict your answer to 250 words or less. Don't confuse Baseball and his girlfriend by using any special physics terms unless you explain clearly what they mean. [Adapted from Bean, Drenk, and Lee, 1986, p. 35]

· · ·

[Psychology] Consider the following problem:

In the morning, when Professor Catlove opens a new can of cat food, his cats run into the kitchen purring and meowing and rubbing their backs against his legs. What examples, if any, of classical conditioning, operant conditioning, and social learning are at work in this brief scene? Note that both the cats and the professor might be exhibiting conditioned behavior here.

You and some fellow classmates have been discussing this problem over coffee, and you are convinced that the other members of your group are confused about the concepts. Write a one-page essay (250 words or less) to set them straight.

From a teacher's perspective, these assignments—because they are short—have the additional benefit of being easy to grade. They use what we might call the "principle of leverage": a small amount of writing preceded by a great amount of thinking. Such assignments can be very effective at maximizing learning while minimizing a teacher's grading time. (For a discussion of how to grade microthemes quickly using "models feedback" rather than writing comments on the essays, see Chapter Fifteen, pages 314–315).

Using Microthemes for Formative Assessment

Another benefit of microthemes is their use as formative classroom assessments of student learning. In designing write-to-learn assignments, we obviously hope that writing a microtheme will help students learn the desired concepts. Often—to our disappointment and chagrin—this is not the case. What many students reveal in their microthemes is the depressing variety of ways that they can misunderstand the very concepts we hoped they would learn.

Nevertheless, students' errors, mistakes, and misunderstandings can give us valuable insights into their thinking processes and provide clues about how to redesign and sequence instruction. Teachers who assess their students' understanding of concepts as a course progresses can adjust instruction to improve the quality of learning (Stewart, Myers, and Cully, 2010; Angelo and Cross, 1993). For assessing students' learning, short write-to-learn assignments are particularly effective because they provide direct windows into students' thinking processes.

Consider the following three student responses to the physics microtheme on acceleration versus velocity. The teacher graded the microthemes on a 1 (lowest) through 6 (highest) scale using the grading rubric shown in Chapter Fourteen (page 283). The following microtheme received a top score of 6:

High-Scoring Microtheme

Ask your girlfriend's forgiveness because she is absolutely right. An everyday definition of acceleration means speeding up. But the scientific meaning is more precise. It means the rate at which *speed* or *direction* changes over a certain period of time—two things really. Thus it is indeed possible for the ball to still be accelerating even when it has zero velocity. If the baseball had no acceleration when it stopped in midair, it would float in the air where it stopped forever. A baseball can accelerate in either of two ways. It can change its speed or it can change its direction of travel. If it does either or both of these things over a period of time, it has accelerated. As the baseball stopped in midair its speed—or velocity—became zero. Yet the acceleration was not zero because, like a stretched out spring, gravity was pulling at it. As you noticed, it soon turned around from going up and came plummeting straight down toward the catcher's mitt. During any given interval of time, it was changing direction or speed (velocity). Because of this, its acceleration (a measurement taken over a period of time) was never zero.

In giving this microtheme a 6, the instructor felt that the student both understood the concept accurately and explained it well in his own words to a new learner.

In contrast, the following microthemes were rated in the 1 to 2 range because their writers failed to apply the concepts accurately. But the significantly different patterns of thinking in these low-success microthemes helped the teacher understand each writer's difficulty.

Student A's Microtheme

Acceleration is defined as the ratio of the change in velocity to the time over which this change occurs. When the pop-up left the hitter's bat it had a certain acceleration in the upward direction. This acceleration soon became deceleration (a decrease in speed with time) as the downward pull of the earth became strong enough to decrease upward acceleration to 0. This force is called gravity and by definition accelerates a free falling body at 32 ft./sec.^{2} in the downward direction. When the ball paused at the peak of its flight, before beginning its descent, the upward acceleration and the downward acceleration were equal, even though the ball was stationary.

Student B's Microtheme

It makes me sad to hear that you have lost your girlfriend over such a trivial problem. I have some good news for you, though. You are right. An object cannot have 0 velocity and have acceleration too. I hope that with the arguments I lay forth in the next few paragraphs you two can reconciliate.

First, velocity is defined as how far an object moves during a certain time. If an object is moving then, in any direction, it has velocity. An airplane is a good example of this. It flies at a certain velocity such as 160 miles per hour, which means it covers 160 miles every hour it is in the air. Next we need a definition of acceleration. This is simply the change in velocity over a certain period of time. If you have an object that is moving at a constant velocity, and covers the same amount of distance during each time period, then it cannot have any change in velocity and thus any acceleration. Going back to the airplane we see acceleration when it speeds up or slows down.

Now we can use these two above concepts to give an answer to your question. If you have an object having no velocity it can have no change in that velocity, thus it cannot be accelerating. If this is still not clear think of the airplane sitting in its hangar. It has no velocity just sitting there, right? Therefore it cannot be accelerating or it would run through the side of the building! The baseball is the same way. I hope that the explanation above will help your girlfriend to see the light.

Student A's microtheme reveals a problem-solving strategy commonly encountered among novices in any discipline—what one of my colleagues calls "text-parroting." Unsure of the answer, the student uses the textbook as a crutch, attempting to imitate its authority by creating a dense, academic-sounding style complete with impressive technical data ("This force is called gravity and by definition accelerates a free falling body at 32 ft./sec.^{2} in the downward direction"). To nonspecialist readers, this strategy is often successful—what students in my part of the country call a "snow job." When shown student A's microtheme, beginning physics students (and many faculty members outside of science) often give it a top-ranking score of 5 or 6. When it is pointed out that student A never actually answers the question (is the girlfriend right or wrong?) and that there is no such thing as upward and downward acceleration, the weakness of this microtheme starts to emerge. To help text-parroters make progress on their next microtheme assignment, the instructor can urge them to replace their current strategy ("When in doubt, sound like the textbook") with a more productive one in which they explain the answer in their own words. (To see how a history professor helps students overcome text-parroting, see Walvoord and McCarthy, 1990, pp. 97–143.)

In contrast, student B writes admirably in his own voice but is led astray by his inability to transfer his own personal analogy (the airplane sitting in the hangar) to the problem of the baseball in midair. The microtheme's structure records the student's thinking process as he proceeds systematically from what he knows to what he is trying to learn. The middle paragraph shows a correct understanding of velocity and acceleration when applied to the simple example of the airplane in flight, and despite his misunderstanding by the end, the student may be only a few moments away from an "aha!" experience. A few probing questions from the instructor might make the concept snap into place for the student. By discussing microthemes such as this one, the instructor can review the concepts of acceleration and velocity while helping the class see where and how analogies can either be helpful or break down.

My point here is that short write-to-learn assignments, though not guaranteeing student learning, nevertheless provide a window into students' thinking that allows the instructor to monitor student progress, to readjust instruction, and to develop teaching strategies that reach different kinds of learners. (For a detailed account of how a mathematics professor analyzes and responds to learning problems revealed in student writing, see Keith, 1989, pp. 141–146.)

More Open Forms: Alternatives to the Thesis-Governed Paper

As discussed in Chapter Four, many teachers may be wary of thesis-governed writing, or weary of it, or simply more attracted to more personal forms of writing that privilege the subjective, creative, personal voice of the writer. There are many ways to assign formal, finished-product writing that offer variations from strictly closed-form, thesis-up-front prose: exploratory essays, reflection papers, personal narratives, myths, dialogues, letters, poems or short stories, magazine-style articles for popular audiences, advertisements, satires, parodies, and so forth. What follows are examples of alternative assignments.

Formal Exploratory Essays

An academically oriented alternative to thesis-based writing is an exploratory essay, which we might define as a *thesis-seeking* essay rather than a *thesis-supporting* essay. The assignment asks students to provide a chronological account of their thinking process while wrestling with a problem. It records the evolution of their ideas-in-flux (Ramage, Bean, and Johnson, 2009, pp. 175–208; Heilker, 1996; Spellmeyer, 1989; Zeiger, 1985). I often assign an exploratory essay as an intermediate stage in a research project leading ultimately to a thesis-governed final paper. Because the subject matter of the exploratory essay is *the student's thinking process* while doing research, the essay encourages and rewards critical thinking while giving teachers insights into the intellectual lives (and study habits) of their students. (An example of an exploratory assignment from nursing earlier in this chapter is "Assignment Option 5" on therapeutic touch, page 92; another example, from a Renaissance literature course, is in Chapter Thirteen, pages 247–249.)

Write a first-person, chronologically organized account of your thinking process as you explore possible solutions to a question or problem related to this course. Begin by describing what the question is, how and why you became interested in it, and why it is problematic for you (that is, why you can't answer it). Then, as you contemplate the problem and do research, narrate the evolving process of your thinking. Include three kinds of information for your reader: (1) external details of your search (coffee shop conversations, trips to the library, methods for finding sources—the narrative "story" of your search); (2) summaries of the new arguments/information you recovered along the way (summaries of arguments you read from the scholarly literature, new information from interviews, and so forth); and (3) your own internal mental wrestling to make sense of new material (what you were thinking about, how your ideas were evolving— reformulating the problem, changing your mind, experiencing confusion versus "aha!" moments). For this essay, it doesn't matter whether you reach a final position or solve the problem; your reader is interested in your process, not your final product. Make your exploratory essay an interesting intellectual detective story—something your readers will enjoy.

Another version of the exploratory paper is used by Berlinghoff (1989) in teaching mathematics. Berlinghoff asks each student to write a paper focusing "on the *process of solving* a particular problem" (p. 89, emphasis in original). He begins the course by teaching students a number of problem-solving tactics such as "check the definitions," "restate the problem," "draw a diagram," "argue by analogy," "solve a similar problem," and "reason backward from the desired conclusion." He then gives each student a challenging mathematical problem to try to solve and asks the student to write a paper about his or her process. "The student is asked to describe," Berlinghoff explains, "how he or she used these problem-solving tactics to attack a particular question. Thus, there is always something to write about, regardless of whether or not the student can 'solve' the problem. Even a dead end is worthwhile, provided the path to it can be described. Moreover, by paying careful attention to the problem-solving tactics (because they provide a guaranteed source of material for their papers), students often succeed in doing a lot more mathematics than they think they can" (p. 90).

Reflection Papers

A popular assignment for many teachers is a "reflection paper," sometimes called a "reader-response paper" or a "personal reaction paper." Although this genre seems to vary considerably in its meaning from teacher to teacher, in most cases it evokes writing that is more exploratory, tentative, and personal than the standard closed-form academic essay. Its essential nature is the exploration of the connections between course material and a person's individual life or psyche. Reflection papers are often assigned to elicit students' responses to complex, difficult, or troubling readings and invite the writer to "speak back" to the reading in a musing, questioning, and probing way (Qualley, 1997).

In a two- to three-page reflection essay, consider the following statement by Aristotle (*Ethics* II, 2) with respect to your own life:

"We are not studying in order to know what excellence is, but to become good, for otherwise there would be no profit in it . . . [We must therefore] consider the question of how we ought to act."

Are you studying in order to become good? Explain what you think Aristotle is getting at and then explore your own response. [Philosophy]

· · ·

Throughout this quarter we have looked at questions about the rights and obligations and the costs and benefits of being citizens of a civil society. Throughout our discussions about the social contract, the criminal justice system in the US, and panopticism on our city streets, we have returned again and again to questions of justice. *Your task is to write a self-reflective essay that narrates* **AND** *analyzes how your understanding of (or confusion about) justice has evolved as you encountered various theories of justice we have read this quarter* (Locke, Scarry, Williams, van den Haag, Reiman, Glover, and Foucault). Make sure that you are **specific** in your narrative (draw from **specific** journal entries and essays—quote from yourself!) and **specific** in your analysis (draw from at least three theorists we have read—quote from them!). In all cases, have fun with this and be real with yourself. [Adapted from freshman seminar assignment by Dr. Jennifer Schulz, Seattle University]

A Potpourri of Other Kinds of Alternative Formal Assignments

Many other kinds of assignments remain. What follows, in no particular order, is a potpourri of ten different kinds of alternative assignments. Each of these asks students to wrestle with a disciplinary problem or disciplinary ways of thinking, but in styles and genres different from closed-form, thesis-driven prose.

- A psychology professor asks his students to write a poem from the perspective of a schizophrenic. The teacher claims that students learn a great deal about schizophrenia in their attempt to walk in a schizophrenic's shoes. The best poems are moving and memorable (Gorman, Gorman, and Young, 1986).

- A religious studies professor asks students to write a dialogue:

  Write a dialogue between a believer (in God) and an unbeliever, in which the main issues that we have raised in class are debated. Each participant will be a spokesperson for a whole range of ideas and arguments, whatever serves to advance his or her basic position. As you write the dialogue, draw on the strongest ideas and arguments for each side that we have seen in this course. Wherever relevant, include your own responses or arguments. The point of this dialogue is not to have a clear victory for one side or the other; rather, the point is to engage the issues in an active and critical manner.

- A literature teacher has students rewrite the ending to a short story or retell a story from the perspective of a different narrator; a history teacher asks students to rewrite a historical narrative from a different point of view.

- A social psychologist requires students to interview someone who has a job, lifestyle, or worldview very different from the student's and then to write a "profile" of the person interviewed. The idea is for the student to encounter an "other" whose sphere of experience differs extensively from the student's.

- A women's studies professor asks students to create myths or parables to express their personal understanding or vision of the role of the feminine.

- A mathematics professor asks students to write their own "math autobiography" in which they reflect on their past math history and experiences. She reports getting very useful insights into the mathematical anxieties and learning problems of her students (as well as the causes of many of these problems).

- A history of religions professor asks students to write essays from the perspective of different persons—an exercise in decentering, seeing the world from a different context.

Write a brief letter back to Paul, as if you were a member of the Corinthian community, responding to his letter. You may choose any point of view you wish—arguing back from the point of view of a faction, repenting the error of your ways, or any other option you can think of.

- A sociologist teaching an environment course asks students to write personal narrative essays about their encounters with the natural world, taking as their models such nature writers as Loren Eiseley, David Quammen, Annie Dillard, and Lewis Thomas. In part, this course juxtaposes study of academic *articles* about nature and personal *essays* about nature. Students talk about what can and cannot be said in each genre.

- A teacher of a course called "Cyberspace and Digital Writing" asks students to create a multimodal argument. According to the assignment handout, this "text will be ten minutes in length composed with a computer software program that allows for multimodality (the inclusion of visuals, video, gestures, and/or sound to traditional literacy)" (Depew, 2009).

Conclusion: Writing Assignments in the Context of the Whole Course

Developing high-quality writing assignments is one of the best ways to improve students' writing. A good writing assignment also deepens students' engagement with course material, promotes critical thinking, and helps students learn the discipline's characteristic methods of inquiry, analysis, and argument. This chapter has tried to expand the notion of formal assignments beyond the conventional "term paper" and has shown how variations in rhetorical context for an assignment can promote different kinds of thinking. In addition to offering suggestions for designing effective assignment handouts (with interactive elements, meaning-constructing tasks, and clear expectations), it has provided examples of various kinds of assignments including closed-form, thesis governed assignments, writing-to-learn microthemes, and a variety of alternatives to thesis-governed prose.

The next chapter focuses on informal, low-stakes or nongraded writing aimed at helping students generate and explore ideas, deepen their thinking, and make personal connections between their courses and their lives.

Informal, Exploratory Writing Activities

Chapter Six focused on formal writing assignments calling for finished-product writing. This chapter focuses on unfinished, exploratory writing. A justification for exploratory writing, based on research into the writing processes of expert writers (where personal behind-the-scenes writing serves as a seedbed for ideas) and on studies showing its effectiveness for enhancing learning for students, has been provided in Chapters Two and Four. Among composition scholars, exploratory writing is associated with *expressive writing*, the term used by Britton in his influential work summarized in Chapter Four (Britton and others, 1975). Many teachers across the curriculum, however, prefer terms such as *informal writing, unstructured writing, personal writing, low-stakes writing, freewriting, journaling, brainstorm writing, think writing*, or simply *nongraded writing*.

Whatever term we choose, what we mean is the kind of exploratory, thinking-on-paper writing we do to discover, develop, and clarify our own ideas. Exploratory writing is typically loosely structured and tentative, moving off in unanticipated directions as new ideas, complications, and questions strike the writer in the process of thinking and creating. Examples of exploratory writing include journals, notebooks, thinking pieces, marginal notes in books, nonstop freewrites, reading logs, diaries, daybooks, letters to colleagues, electronic postings, notes dashed off on napkins, early drafts of essays, and what physicist James Van Allen, author of more than

270 scientific papers, calls "memoranda to myself": "The mere process of writing," explains Van Allen, "is one of the most powerful tools we have for clarifying our own thinking. I seldom get to the level of a publishable manuscript without a great deal of self torture and at least three drafts. My desk is littered with rejected attempts as I proceed. But there is a reward. I am never so clear about a matter as when I have just finished writing about it. The writing process itself produces that clarity. Indeed, I often write memoranda to myself solely for the purpose of clearing up my own thinking" (quoted in Barry, 1989, p. 9). Van Allen's point is that the process of writing drives thinking. Sometimes exploratory writing gets transformed into a finished product. More often, as in Van Allen's "memoranda," exploratory writing is an end in itself. College students typically do not realize the value of exploratory writing and are not given nearly enough opportunities for doing it. Consequently, they do not get enough practice at the kind of thinking and learning that such writing can stimulate.

Why I Find Exploratory Writing Valuable

From my more than forty years of college teaching, I have concluded that my single most valuable teaching strategy for promoting critical thinking is to require regular exploratory writing in response to disciplinary problems that I provide. (I call these assignments "thinking pieces." I explain my approach in more detail as this chapter progresses—always recognizing that there are many other ways to assign exploratory writing.) Here are six reasons why I cannot imagine teaching a class without an exploratory writing component:

○ *My thinking piece assignments continually present students with higher-order critical thinking problems.* They help me create a questioning, problem-posing environment for the course; they immerse students in complexity without being threatening.

○ *They change the way students approach course readings.* My tasks encourage students to read for meaning. They have to summarize an assigned reading's argument and then "speak back" to it, promoting an exploratory stance. Thinking pieces help students read texts both with and against the grain.

○ *They create higher levels of class preparation and richer discussions.* Having completed a thinking piece on a subject matter problem, students come to class ready to discuss it. They want to find out what others said in their thinking pieces and are ready to hear different points of view.

During lull moments in a discussion I can ask a student what he or she wrote for the day's thinking piece. The thinking pieces plant seeds that germinate later. (Ideas first explored in thinking pieces often get developed in formal papers.)

○ *Thinking pieces are enjoyable to read.* I can read them quickly, often just skimming them, looking for insights and signs of life—or I can read very carefully a random sampling of thinking pieces. Because I'm not reading for error or for coaching revision, I can forget the "red pencil" role and read for ideas only. Often the thinking pieces are lively with voice and personality.

○ *They help me get to know my students better.* I learn characteristic ways that different students think and study. I learn about their backgrounds and values and get insights into how I might engage them more fully or coach them more effectively. Also, thinking pieces give students a safe and easy way to disclose personal problems that may be affecting their studying or class performance.

○ *They help me assess learning problems on the spot.* For me, thinking pieces provide immediate formative assessment, giving me a constant reading of students' learning-in-progress. I can see where students are misunderstanding my lectures, not looking adequately at contradictory evidence or alternative views, or not appreciating nuance or complexity. They give me a chance to reexplain concepts based on student confusion. In short, they help me monitor the progress of student learning.

For an example of some of my own thinking piece assignments, see Exhibit 7.2, My Own Method of Explaining and Assigning Exploratory Writing, on page 130.

Common Objections to Exploratory Writing

I've just given my own testimonial for exploratory writing. Similar testimonials are evident throughout the WAC literature. Often teachers become believers in exploratory writing when they experience it firsthand in writing-across-the-curriculum workshops (see Stewart, Myers, and Cully, 2010; Drabick, Weisberg, Paul, and Bubier, 2007; Weimer, 2002; Abbott, Bartelt, Fishman, and Honda, 1992; Belanoff, Elbow, and Fontaine, 1991; Fulwiler, 1987a, 1987b; Young and Fulwiler, 1986; Fulwiler and Young, 1982; Freisinger, 1980).

Nevertheless, despite extensive empirical and testimonial evidence in support of exploratory writing, many of my colleagues remain unconvinced that it is worth the bother. Let's begin, then, by examining some of the objections that faculty raise against assigning exploratory writing in their classrooms.

Requiring Exploratory Writing Will Take Too Much of My Time

Many of my colleagues associate exploratory writing with stacks of student journals (if submitted in hard copy) or zillions of posts in a bulletin board drop box. But there are many ways to control the timing of exploratory writing submissions and to limit the amount you read. Requiring exploratory writing takes a lot of teacher time only if the teacher feels compelled to read everything students write—which is equivalent, I would argue, to a piano teacher's listening to tapes of students' home practice sessions. Ideally, requiring exploratory writing should require *no* teacher time, because exploratory writing is writing for oneself with the intention of stimulating creativity or deepening and focusing thought. Students should do it for the same reasons professional writers do—for the intrinsic satisfaction. In reality, though, most students need some teacher supervision to remain motivated, and teachers need to read some of their students' exploratory writing in order to coach their thinking processes. The trick is to read *some* of it, not *all* of it. Also, many teachers like to read students' exploratory pieces—such pieces are often lively and interesting, and they connect teachers deeply with their students as persons and learners. This chapter gives hints for cutting down teacher time: some of the strategies in this chapter require almost no teacher time; other strategies allow plenty of flexibility in the teacher time required.

Students Regard Exploratory Writing as Busywork

A more compelling objection to exploratory writing is that students regard it as busywork. Despite the value of exploratory writing proclaimed in the published literature, there will always be students who will see it as a waste of time. Whenever I assign thinking pieces, for example, I find that about 10 to 20 percent of my students never seem to warm up to them.

To some extent, a lack of enjoyment of exploratory writing may be related to learning styles (Jensen and DiTiberio, 1989; see also my discussion of learning styles in Chapter Four, pages 62–65). Some students are closure oriented and dislike the open-ended, seemingly goalless nature of writing for oneself. Another cause of student resistance—if the exploratory writing is ungraded—may be students' grade orientation rather than learning orientation. Janzow and Eison (1990) report that 25 to 38 percent of students said that "written assignments (for example, homework and projects) that are not graded are a waste of time" (p. 96). Still another cause may be a teacher's failure to integrate exploratory writing effectively into the course so that it seems purposeful. But the most important cause, I would argue, is that many students have not yet learned to pose the kinds of self-sponsored questions or problems that drive true inquiry. Students who still view knowledge as "right answers" rather than arguments are not used to the kind of dialogic thinking that exploratory writing facilitates. In short, they see no need for exploratory writing because they see no need to explore.

From my perspective, then, the best response to this objection is not to abandon exploratory writing but to help students see its value. This chapter offers many suggestions for doing so. Here, though, let me offer two key strategies for getting students to become personally invested in exploratory writing.

First, try to incorporate students' exploratory writing directly into the texture of your course. Wherever possible, use their exploratory writing to stimulate class discussions or help them explore ideas for formal essays or exams. Many teachers open class with a question that students have explored the night before in a bulletin board posting or thinking piece. Some teachers have students share ideas from their exploratory writing in small groups. Others collect exploratory writing from a random selection of students each day as a way to check on students' learning and to guide thinking. Particularly effective is to use exploratory writing tasks to help students generate ideas for an upcoming formal paper. (See how I use this strategy in Chapter Thirteen, page 249.) The point here is to help students appreciate exploratory writing as a purposeful part of the class.

Second, let them know that exploratory writing is something that expert writers do; it is not simply an exercise for students. Students often get interested in exploratory writing when they see their teachers use it to think through ideas. Whenever possible, teachers should freewrite with their students during in-class writing sessions. Teachers can also model the process by bringing their own exploratory writing to class and sharing it with students.

Exploratory Writing Is Junk Writing That Promotes Bad Writing Habits

Because exploratory writing is generally done without concern for organization, sentence structure, spelling, or mechanics, some instructors feel that this kind of writing simply encourages students to practice all the bad habits they already have.

This objection—that you should not encourage sloppiness—appears reasonable enough on the surface. However, it seems based on a faulty analogy between writing and some sphere of human behavior where sloppiness is a moral error (housekeeping? auto mechanics?) rather than a developmental stage in a process. Exploratory writing is often inchoate because the writer has to sort through tangled strands of ideas that need to be written out and reflected on before they can be untangled and organized. Worrying about spelling, grammar, and structure when you are trying to discover and clarify ideas can shut down any writer's creative energy. Exploratory writing is messy because thought is messy. Rather than junk writing, then, a better analogy for exploratory writing might be an architect's sketchbook of possible designs for a project or even a fertile patch of land sprouting with seeds.

Of course, students should not confuse rapid exploratory writing with the rapid writing they must produce in essay exams where hierarchical structure and formal coherence are important. I always explain to students that the brainstorming strategies for exploratory writing should not be used in an exam setting. Exploratory writing is *thesis-seeking*, whereas exam writing is *thesis-supporting*.

Logistics, Media, and Methods for Assigning Exploratory Writing

When I first started assigning exploratory writing in the late 1970s, its default form was the pen and paper journal, usually composed in a spiral notebook and submitted periodically during the term (leading to the "taking home a stack of journals" syndrome). Today, exploratory writing is most often submitted digitally to a class bulletin board, blog site, or the instructor's drop box (although I still ask for students to submit my thinking pieces on one-page hard copy). However, many different ways of assigning exploratory writing are available. Before designing one's own approach to exploratory writing, teachers may want to consider the following variables:

○ *What name or label should I use?* Many teachers call exploratory writing "low stakes writing" to reduce students' anxiety about it and to emphasize its function as a safe space to explore ideas. When done in class, it is often called "in-class freewriting" unless the instructor has in mind a specific genre of freewriting such as the "minute paper" or the "muddiest point" paper (see pages 132–133 later in this chapter). For out-of-class exploratory writing, the default name may still be "journal" or "electronic journal," but many other names are also popular, such as "thinking pieces," "thought letters," "reflections," "response papers," "blogs," "reading logs," "memos to oneself," "explorations," "meditations," "electronic postings," and so forth.

○ *When and how often is exploratory writing collected?* Teachers generally have four choices: (1) not collecting it at all—common practice for in-class freewriting unless the instructor wishes to look at random selections to check on student understanding; (2) collected in batches periodically during the term—common practice for journals or for portfolios of pieces submitted by the whole class at once; (3) collected individually piece-by-piece at selected points in the course (in recent years I have assigned one-page, hard copy "thinking pieces," which I collect at the end of class and return the next class period); and (4) listening in periodically to on-line blogs, postings, or threaded discussions.

○ *Who reads the exploratory writing?* The primary issue here is whether exploratory writing goes just to the instructor or is shared with classmates, who respond to each others' writing. Usually, pieces submitted on paper are read only by the instructor, unless students share ideas from them in small groups in class. Many teachers, however, ask students to post their exploratory writing to a course bulletin board that supports threaded discussions. Students are then assigned to read each others' pieces and respond to selected ones, creating an extended on-line conversation.

○ *How are they graded?* I offer suggestions for grading exploratory writing at the end of this chapter.

Explaining Exploratory Writing to Students

Today, most students are familiar with exploratory writing as a way of learning, having been taught about freewriting or idea mapping in their high school or college writing courses. Many have kept journals or posted exploratory pieces to electronic bulletin boards for courses outside of English. However, because teachers have a wide range of expectations about exploratory writing and have different goals for incorporating it into their courses, it is a good idea to explain to students what you expect when you assign exploratory writing. Exhibit 7.1 is a student handout on "guided journals" that a psychology professor and I developed for an introductory psychology course. I include it here both as an example of

EXHIBIT 7.1

Explanation of Exploratory Writing for Students

As part of the requirements for this course, you will keep a guided journal in which you will explore your responses to a daily question or problem that we will give you. The purpose of the journal is not (at least directly) to improve your writing skills but to stimulate thinking about issues, questions, and problems raised by your study of psychology. For the most part, you will be rewarded for the process of thinking, rather than for the end product itself. The kind of writing you will be doing is called "exploratory" or "expressive" writing—that is, writing that lets you "think out loud on paper" without having to worry whether your writing is effective for readers. Therefore, such features of formal writing as organization, correct sentence structure, neatness, and spelling won't matter in your journal. This is writing primarily for yourself or for a friendly "inside" reader who wants to follow your stream of thinking without judging your writing by formal standards.

Exploratory writing of this type can help many students become more productive and more focused thinkers. Research has shown that the regular habit of exploratory writing can deepen students' thinking about their course subjects by helping them see that an academic field is an arena for wonder, inquiry, and controversy rather than simply a new body of information. This way of looking at an academic field can make college more interesting, even exciting. The more you see yourself in this course asking questions and questioning answers, the more you will be thinking like a real psychologist.

How do I write a journal entry? We want you to employ a technique that composition teachers call *focused freewriting*. When you freewrite, you keep your fingers moving all the time (whether at a keyboard or with pen and paper) for several minutes at a stretch. Write steadily without being concerned about spelling, organization, or grammar. If your mind suddenly dries up, just write *relax* or another key word over and over again until a new thought springs into your mind. In regular freewriting, your mind can wander freely from topic to topic. In focused freewriting, however, you need to keep your entire entry focused on the assigned question or problem. Your purpose is to explore your responses to the question as fully as possible within the set time period.

Here is an example of a ten-minute focused freewrite on the question "Do you have any fears, phobias, or anxieties that might be explained by classical conditioning?"

Let's see, do I have any fears or phobias? Maybe I should start out by just trying to see what fears and phobias I have. I am afraid of moths. I am a male and to be afraid of moths is to be laughed at. My girlfriend once laughed at me for about an hour it seems because a moth got into our car and I had to stop and get out because it flapped around in front of my face. I get kind of creepy right now just thinking about the flapping wings. It is the sound the moth makes that scares me. I wonder why I am afraid of moths. I haven't really thought about that before. Is that the result of classical conditioning? I can't remember a time when I first became afraid of moths. Let's see right now I just thought about how I am not really afraid of snakes but I used to be and that I can relate that to classical conditioning but I still want to think about moths. I'll come back. relax relax okay back to moths. Let's see, if this were caused by classical conditioning I would have to have had at one time a natural fear that wasn't a phobia—maybe like being afraid of being crushed by some giant flapping thing. Then I would have had to have had that natural fear be associated with something else (the moth). In Pavlov's dog the natural response was salivating and the natural stimulus was seeing the

(Continued)

food—these were unconditioned responses and stimuli. Then the dog began associating the food with hearing the bell (conditioned response). I don't think that applies to my fear of moths. At least I can't think of anytime I learned to associate moths with something that should have naturally aroused my fear. Maybe my fear of moths can be better explained by some other theory of neurosis like Freud's psychoanalytic theory. Maybe a moth stands for something deep in my dream life. Even as I write this, I feel my fear of moths growing. This is so stupid. How could I possibly be afraid of moths when . . . (time is up).

As you can see, this writer just followed the stream of his thought, which is a quite different technique from what you may be used to—that is, thinking first and then recording later what you thought.

How long is a journal entry? In general, we want each entry to be at least one single-spaced page (12-point font, normal margins). We expect that you can write such a page in ten to fifteen minutes of freewriting.

Do I get automatic credit just for doing the entries? The syllabus specifies "quality" entries, yet it is a knotty problem to explain what we mean by "quality." You definitely will not be judged on things like spelling, organization, and grammar. But we will be looking for evidence that you are thinking seriously about psychology. Many of the entries will ask you to apply concepts explained in the text or in lectures. Your entries should show that you are wrestling with these concepts and have done your reading and studying before attempting your journal entries. Don't write about operant conditioning until you have studied that concept in your text. The student who wrote the freewrite on classical conditioning clearly has read the text and has tried to understand the concepts.

Unlike an essay examination, however, a journal entry doesn't require a well-organized argument; instead, it gives you the freedom to make mistakes. Writing in the journal helps you learn the concepts themselves, and if you get concepts mixed up, that is often OK. The journal should show evidence of trying, evidence that you are studying, thinking, seeing implications, and making connections. The best journal entries will be interesting for someone else to read because they will show a mind truly struggling with ideas . . .

[The handout continues by explaining methods of submitting the guided journals for this particular course—teachers have many options including electronic submission, posting to bulletin boards, paper versions submitted periodically, and so forth.]

Some Examples of Psychology Journal Tasks

Task 2. Suppose you are a parent who goes to a child psychologist for advice on how to get your ten-year-old child to practice the piano. The child rushes out of the room screaming every time you insist that he practice. What different advice would you get if the child psychologist were a behaviorist, a psychoanalyst, or a humanistic psychologist? Which "school" of psychology might you prefer as a parent and why?

Task 10. Suppose you had a theory that laboratory rats fed a steady diet of beer and hot dogs could learn to find their way through a maze faster than rats fed a steady diet of squash, spinach, and broccoli. How would you design a scientific experiment to test this hypothesis? In your discussion, use the terms *experimental group, control group, independent variable,* and *dependent variable.*

Task 29. Read the mind-body problem on in your textbook. Then explore your response to this question: "What is the difference between a human mind and a computer?"

one attempt to explain exploratory writing to students and as a further explanation to professors who may be fuzzy about the whole concept of expressive or exploratory writing. At the end of the handout, I include several examples of guided-journal tasks that we developed for the course. (In this particular course, a student's course points for the journal depended on the number of journal entries completed each week.) Many teachers have adapted this handout to their own courses, which have ranged from history to nursing to mechanical engineering. Generally, teachers provide their own course-related examples of freewriting and set up a grading scheme and submission methods that fit their course plan and technology preferences.

For another example of how exploratory writing might be assigned in class, see Exhibit 7.2, which shows a page from one of my own syllabi, in this case for a course in Shakespeare.

Using Blogs or Electronic Discussion Boards with Threaded Responses

Whereas journals or thinking pieces are often submitted just to the teacher, many instructors like to use blogs or electronic discussion boards for exploratory writing so that students can read each other's postings and initiate threaded discussions. Instead of a paper-and-pen journal or thinking piece submitted to the teacher, C. J. Bonk and K. Zhang (2008, pp. 71–73, 92–95) suggest that students create course-linked blogs in which they respond to teacher-designed tasks or initiate their own reflections and explorations of course material. To ensure student-to-student interaction, they advise teachers to assign bloggers to small teams of "critical friends" or "web buddies" who will read and respond regularly to each other's blogs. Occasionally students are asked to write reflections about what they have learned from their blogging experience.

Other teachers like to initiate asynchronous discussion forums or live chat. Students might be asked to post an exploratory piece to the discussion board each week and then respond to three or four postings from classmates. Or the teacher might initiate each threaded sequence by posting a "question of the week" on the bulletin board. A typical discussion forum assignment is described by Garrison and Vaughan (2008, pp. 129–132). Students are asked to read a course-related article that provokes multiple perspectives. Students are then required to post to the online discussion forum their own synopsis of the article along with an interpretive response reflecting their own perspective. Students must then read and respond to at least two other students' postings and offer evidence that "supports or

---

EXHIBIT 7.2

My Own Method of Explaining and Assigning Exploratory Writing

Explanation of "Thinking Pieces" from Syllabus for a Shakespeare Course

Sequence of exploratory "thinking pieces" (10%): As part of your homework on many class days, you will be asked to produce an informal, one-page, typed, single-spaced exploratory response to a question I provide. Bring these "thinking pieces" to class, where they will be collected each day. To receive a 4 or 5 on a thinking piece, it must address the assigned question; show that you have done the required reading; reveal interesting, engaged thinking; and be at least one single-spaced page long. You can drop any two thinking pieces; no late thinking pieces accepted (if you miss class you can email your thinking piece to me ahead of time). At the end of the quarter, an average of 4.3 or higher equals an A; 4.3–4.0 = A-; 3.9–3.5 = B; lower than 3.5 = C or lower.

Excerpts from Daily Schedule

Monday, April 9: PREPARATION FOR CLASS: Read *Midsummer Night's Dream:* Thinking piece #4: When we say "fall in love" and "fall asleep," we use the same metaphor of "fall." What is the significance of the metaphor "fall"? How is romantic love a "falling" experience? (Why don't we say "fall in friendship"?) Is there any connection between falling asleep and falling in love? IN CLASS: **Quiz on *Midsummer Night's Dream*.** Discussion of the play.

Monday, April 23 (Happy Birthday to William Shakespeare): Thinking piece #8: Imagine Touchstone and Rosalind both being asked to respond to the following assertion by Charles Reich from the 1960s pop culture classic *The Greening of America*: "Young people today insist upon prolonging the period of youth, education, and growth. They stay uncommitted . . . open toward the future. . . . Personal relationships are entered into without commitment to the future; a marriage legally binding for the life of the couple is inconsistent with the likelihood of growth and change." How might Touchstone and Rosalind respond differently to the values expressed in the quotation from Reich? IN CLASS: Discussion of *As You Like It*.

Wednesday, April 25: PREPARATION FOR CLASS: Read the article by Peter B. Erickson in our edition of *As You Like It*. Thinking Piece #9: Peter Erickson argues that Rosalind is liberated in the forest but loses that liberation when she becomes a wife. "*As You Like It* is primarily a defensive action against female power rather than a celebration of it." To what extent do you agree or disagree with Erickson's argument? IN CLASS: Continued discussion of *As You Like It*.

---

challenges the other students' interpretations" (p. 130). If a student's perspective is challenged, the student is asked to respond, trying either to refute the challenge or to "concede that the posting has compelled reconsideration of his or her original position" (p. 130). The authors provide a suggested scoring guide for grading participation in the online forum (p. 131).

The advantages of online discussion groups have been noted since the advent of e-mail in the 1990s. Meacham (1994) reported use of an e-mail network in a large lecture class in developmental psychology and multiculturalism. One student evaluated the experience as follows:

I found the computer list to be a wonderful learning experience for me. I am not very good at speaking out in large groups of people. I found it comforting to be able to voice my opinions to others in the class via e-mail . . . Many times, I feel lost in a class the size of ours. But the computer list seemed to keep my interest going on the issues discussed in class (p. 38).

Assigning electronic discussion tasks has now been facilitated by courseware such as WebCT, ANGEL, Blackboard, and others. For advice on online uses of exploratory writing, see Garrison and Vaughan (2008), Bonk and Zhang (2008), Brookfield and Preskill (2005), Bates and Poole (2003), Palloff and Pratt (2003), and Kirk and Orr (2003).

Twenty-Two Ideas for Incorporating Exploratory Writing into a Course

There are many ways to assign and use exploratory writing in a course. This section offers twenty-two suggestions for bringing the benefits of exploratory writing into the classroom. I use the term "exploratory writing" in its broadest sense to mean any kind of informal writing done without revision primarily to help a writer generate, extend, deepen, and clarify thinking.

I invite readers to skim the following options, looking for those most apt to fit their course goals and teaching style. I have tried to chunk them into the following categories:

- In-class writing (1–4)

- Out-of-class journals, thinking pieces, blogs, or electronic bulletin board postings (5–10)

- Tasks to deepen students' responses to course readings (11–14)

- Change-of-pace creativity exercises (15–17)

- Invention tasks for formal assignments (18–19)

- Low-stakes "shaped exercises" to practice thesis-governed writing (20–22). (Of these last three, I especially recommend option 21 as one of my personal favorites. I use it frequently in class.)

In-Class Writing

Perhaps the easiest way to use exploratory writing is to set aside five minutes or so during a class period for silent, uninterrupted writing in response to a thinking or learning task. Students can write at their desks while the teacher writes at the chalkboard or on a keyboard, with the projector turned either on or off as the teacher desires. (Teachers who are willing to write with their students are powerful role models.) Here are four suggestions for using in-class writing.

1. *Writing at the Beginning of Class to Probe a Subject.* Give students a question that reviews previous material or stimulates interest in what's coming. Review tasks can be open-ended and exploratory ("What questions do you want to ask about last night's readings?") or precise and specific ("What does it mean when we say that a certain market is 'efficient'?"). Or use a question to prime the pump for the day's discussion ("How does Plato's allegory of the cave make you look at knowledge in a new way?"). In-class writing gives students a chance to gather and focus their thoughts and, when shared, gives the teacher an opportunity to see students' thinking processes. Teachers can ask one or two students to read their responses, or they can collect a random sampling of responses to read after class. Since students are always eager to hear what the teacher has written, you might occasionally share your own in-class writing.

2. *Writing During Class to Refocus a Lagging Discussion or Cool Off a Heated One.* When students run out of things to say or when the discussion gets so heated that everyone wants to talk at once, suspend the discussion and ask for several minutes of writing.

3. *Writing During Class to Ask Questions or Express Confusion.* When lecturing on tough material, stop for a few minutes and ask students to respond to a writing prompt like this: "If you have understood my lecture so far, summarize my main points in your own words. If you are currently confused about something, please explain to me what is puzzling you; ask me the questions you need answered." You will find it an illuminating check on your teaching to collect a representative sample of responses to see how well students are understanding your presentations.

4. *Writing at the End of Class to Sum Up a Lecture or Discussion.* Give students several minutes at the end of class to sum up the day's lecture or discussion and to prepare questions to ask at the beginning of the next class period. (Some teachers take roll by having students write out a question during the last two minutes of class and submit it on a signed slip of paper.) A popular version of this strategy is the "minute paper" as reported by Angelo and Cross (1993, pp. 148–153). At the end of class, the professor asks two questions: (1) "What is the most significant thing you learned today?" and (2) "What question is uppermost in your mind at the conclusion of this class session?" In another variation, the professor asks, "What

is the muddiest point in the material I have just covered?" (Tobias, 1989, pp. 53–54).

Out-of-Class Journals, Thinking Pieces, Blogs, or Discussion Forum Postings

Out-of-class exploratory writing can be assigned in a variety of ways, from totally open-ended methods to highly guided ones. Teachers need to find an approach that best fits their own teaching style, their own course goals, and their own preference for having exploratory writing submitted only to the teacher or posted to a bulletin board to initiate threaded whole class discussions.

5. *Open-Ended Tasks.* Here you ask students to write a certain number of pages per week or a certain length of time per week about any aspect of the course. This approach leaves students free to write about the course in any number of ways. Students might choose to summarize lectures, to explain why a textbook is difficult to understand, to disagree with a point made by someone in class, to raise questions, to apply some aspect of the course to personal experience, to make connections between different strands of the course, to express excitement at seeing new ideas, or for any other purpose. The journal or collection of thinking pieces or blogs becomes a kind of record of the student's intellectual journey through the course. This is perhaps the most common way to assign journals and is widely reported in the writing-across-the-curriculum literature. An excellent description of the benefits of this kind of journal, from the perspective of a physics teacher, is provided by Grumbacher (1987):

> *I began my research on what happens when students write in physics class not knowing what I would find. I discovered that:*
>
> 1. *the best problem solvers in physics are students who are able to relate the theories of physics to experiences in their lives;*
>
> 2. *[journal] writing helps students find the connections between experience and theory;*
>
> 3. *students will do more work than is required if they are seeking answers to questions they initiate;*
>
> 4. *keeping learning logs on a regular basis encourages students to initiate such questions;*
>
> 5. *students need many opportunities to play with the ideas of physics; they need time to work with a concept in a number of different contexts before rushing on to new information . . .*

My students use writing and their logs the way real scientists have always used writing and journals: to clarify their thinking, to explore the ideas of science, to search for connections between theory and practice, and to ask questions [p. 328].

6. *Semistructured Tasks.* Although they give students nearly as much freedom as the open-ended approach, semistructured tasks provide guidance in helping writers think of things to say. For example, some teachers ask students to begin each entry by summarizing an important idea the student has learned since the previous entry, either from class or from reading, and then to respond to one or more additional questions such as these:

- What confused you in today's class or today's readings?
- How does your own personal experience relate to what you studied today?
- What effect is this course having on your personal life, your beliefs, your values, your previous understanding of things?
- How does what we have been studying recently relate to your other courses or to other parts of this course?

Many teachers develop their own sets of generic questions, appropriate to their disciplines, to guide students' journal entries. An example is a series of twenty-three "writing probes" developed by Kenyon (1989) to help mathematics students use journal writing to clarify their mathematical thinking. Here are some examples of these probes:

- What does that equation say in plain English?
- Why did you write that equation?
- Why are you stuck?
- What other information do you need to get unstuck?
- What makes this problem difficult?
- What were you thinking about when you did step X [p. 82]?

7. *Guided Tasks.* The guided task approach asks students to respond to subject-specific questions developed by the instructor, thus importing an active learning dimension into study time. Instead of saying, "Tomorrow, read Chapter Ten," the instructor can say, "For tomorrow do an exploratory piece in response to this question. Before you can do so, you'll need

to read Chapter Ten." Earlier in this chapter I presented examples of guided tasks from an introductory psychology course and from my own Shakespeare course. What follows are two additional examples of guided tasks from a religious studies course and a physics course.

- How have you seen religious beliefs function both to enhance and to restrict the spiritual growth of an individual? [Religious studies]
- Describe the concept of momentum to your kid brother. [Physics]

There is some debate among composition researchers about the different effects of the open-ended versus guided approaches. The open-ended strategy gives students more freedom to ask their own questions, pursue their own issues, and do their own pondering. However, guided tasks may be more effective at helping students explore problems directly related to the teacher's learning goals for the course (MacDonald and Cooper, 1992; these researchers use the terms *academic journal* and *dialogic journal* versus my terms *guided tasks* and *open-ended* or *semistructured tasks*).

8. *Double-Entry Notebooks.* The double-entry notebook, popularized by Berthoff (1987) and widely adopted across the curriculum, requires students first to reflect on course material and then later to reflect on their own reflections. It is thus also called a "dialectical notebook" or "dialogue journal." On right-hand pages of a standard spiral notebook (or the right columns of a word-processed page using the column/table function) students are asked to make copious lecture and reading notes, based on the theory that putting course material into one's own words enhances learning. Then, on the left-hand pages (or columns), students are to create an interactive commentary on the material—posing questions, raising doubts, making connections, seeing opposing views, linking course material with personal experience, expressing confusion, and so forth. In a variation on the double-entry notebook, students use the right-hand pages or columns to respond to course material in the manner of open-ended journals. Several days later, however, they are to reread their journals and on the left-hand pages or columns comment on their previous comments. Students often find themselves in dialogue with their own ideas, amazed on a Friday how they could have felt a certain way the previous Monday.

9. *Contemporary Issues Journals.* Here the teacher wants students to relate the course to contemporary issues and problems. The teacher asks students to read current newspapers or online news sites and blogs and to write about how course material applies to current affairs. Especially useful for social science and ethics courses, as well as for all professional

majors, this kind of journal usually generates considerable student interest by revealing the relevance of the course to life outside the academy.

10. *Exam Preparation Journals.* This method provides strong intrinsic motivation for exploratory writing and uses course exams to drive a maximum amount of learning. To use the method, the teacher, early in the course, gives out a list of essay questions from which midterm and final exam questions will be drawn. Students are instructed to devote a section of their journals to each question. Then students gradually work out answers to the questions as course material builds and develops. Some teachers allow students to use their preparation journals during the exams. While the exam is in progress, teachers can quickly look at each student's work and give course bonus points, if so desired, to students who have done a conscientious job of responding to each question.

Reading Journals or Reading Logs

Another use of exploratory writing is to focus specifically on course readings so that the writing helps students comprehend and respond to reading material. These strategies are all explained in Chapter Nine, Helping Students Read Difficult Texts.

11. *Marginal notes or focused reading notes.* See Chapter Nine page 177.

12. *Reading logs or summary/response notebooks.* See Chapter Nine, pages 176 and 177.

13. *Student responses to reading guides.* See Chapter Nine, pages 174–176.

14. *Imagined interviews with the author.* See Chapter Nine, page 179.

Creativity Exercises

For a change of pace in their use of exploratory writing, teachers can assign creativity exercises and use them as the basis for class discussion or group sharing. These exercises, which are usually fun for students, stretch language and thinking skills in valuable ways.

15. *Writing Dialogues.* Ask students to write imaginary "meeting of the mind" dialogues between people with opposing views (Kant and Mill on the use of torture to prevent terrorism; Jesus and the Grand Inquisitor on freedom; Copernicus and Ptolemy on the retrogression of the planets). Often these assignments make good out-of-class group projects for active learning wherein study teams of three or four students can write the dialogue together.

16. *Writing Bio-Poems.* A bio-poem uses a formulaic structure to create a poem expressing what the writer sees as significant or meaningful dimensions of a subject's life. In some settings, students might write bio-poems about themselves to help build community among classmates. But the method is particularly effective for helping students see the personal dimensions of important figures studied in a course. Thus students could write bio-poems of Plato, Caesar, Galileo, Frankenstein's monster, Rosa Parks, Harvey Milk, Osama bin Laden, or Simone de Beauvoir. Or students could interview a homeless person, an elderly person in a nursing home, or a Parkinson's disease patient and create a bio-poem that lets us enter that person's life. The formula for a bio-poem is as follows (Gere, 1985):

- Line 1: First name
- Line 2: Four traits that describe character
- Line 3: Relative of (brother of, sister of, and so on)
- Line 4: Lover of (list three things or people)
- Line 5: Who feels (three items)
- Line 6: Who needs (three items)
- Line 7: Who fears (three items)
- Line 8: Who gives (three items)
- Line 9: Who would like to (three items)
- Line 10: Resident of
- Line 11: Last name [p. 222]*

Here is a bio-poem written for a philosophy course (Yoshida, 1985) on Dostoyevsky's Grand Inquisitor.

Inquisitor,
Cynical, bold, all knowing, and fearless.
Friend of no one, peer of few.
Lover of self, wisdom, and unconquerable knowledge.
Who feels neither pity nor compassion nor the love of God.
Who needs no man, save for himself.
Who fears the kiss that warms his heart.

And the coming tide which will not retreat.
Who radiates cold shafts of broken glass
And who fits all mankind with collar and chain.
Who would like to see the deceivers burned
And Christ to be humbled before him.
Resident of ages past,
"The Grand Inquisitor" [p. 124].

17. *Metaphor Games, Extended Analogies.* Metaphoric or analogic thinking looks at X from the perspective of Y. It can make the familiar strange or the strange familiar. In my writing classes, I ask students to construct their own metaphors for the writing process, and afterward we compare the insights arising from each other's metaphors. "Writing an essay is like (pulling teeth? having a baby? swimming? building a model airplane? baking a cake? growing a garden? enduring torture?)." This game can be extended to comparative analogies: "Journal writing is like _____, but formal essay writing is like _____." Because analogic thinking is ubiquitous, it is an easy matter to create metaphoric or analogic games for courses in any discipline. Here are just a few examples: "Baroque music is like _____, but Romantic music is like _____." "The difference between Aquinas's view of the human person and Kierkegaard's view is like the difference between _____ and _____." "Napoleon is to the French Revolution as _____ is to _____." More freewheeling teachers might push metaphor games to playful limits with metaphoric questions such as these: "How would a comic book cover change as you go from Freud's view of the personality to Foucault's?" "If T. S. Eliot and Walt Whitman were car designers, what would be the differences in their cars?"

Students almost always enjoy metaphor games, which open up complex questions about language, reality, and thought. Finding the apt metaphor can be a wonderful exercise in clarifying a concept. But as the fallacy of false analogy reminds us, metaphors also obscure and distort. Thus, analogy games can lead to interesting class discussions about the role of language in shaping what we know. (For further discussion of metaphoric games, see Elbow, 1981.)

Invention Tasks for Formal Assignments

Besides in-class freewrites, various kinds of journals or thinking pieces, and occasional creativity games, exploratory writing can be used to generate ideas for formal papers. The desire to do well on the paper helps motivate student effort with the exploratory tasks.

18. *Tasks for Scaffolding a Major Assignment.* In this approach, the exploratory tasks all serve as scaffolding for a major paper. Students see how doing the tasks will help them think of ideas for the paper. The instructor, meanwhile, needs only to read the formal paper; he or she can give "process credit" to the student simply for doing the tasks. Here, for example, is how Hammond (1991) designed focused freewriting exercises to help students think deeply about a poem before writing an interpretive essay.

Freewrite on [poem's title] (5 minutes). Given this title, what do you think the poem may be about? What associations does it raise for you? What might draw you toward this poem or get in the way of your reading it?

Putting the text aside, list all the images you remember. Circle three significant images you will write about . . . Describe the first image (5 minutes). State what it means to you (3 minutes). . . . [questions continue] [p. 78]

Her tasks continue, causing the student to consider carefully all the details of a poem before arriving at a thesis. She sums up the advantages of this approach as follows: "An advantage of focused freewriting over first-draft writing is that it prolongs and structures the exploratory stage, whereas draft writing tends to push for closure. Foreshortening the analytical process is one of the most fundamental problems of undergraduates . . . and this procedure above all helps avert this premature closure" (p. 72).

Similar kinds of focused freewriting tasks can be designed for almost any kind of formal writing assignment. Exhibit 7.3 is a generic set of tasks for any kind of argumentative or persuasive essay addressing a controversial issue.

19. *Rapid First Drafts.* Another excellent means of using exploratory writing is to assign students to write first drafts for five or six essays but select only one or two for revision into formal, finished products (Belanoff and Dickson, 1991). By creating a number of assignments on which students have to write drafts, the teacher can ensure representative coverage of main course concepts. Students' abandoned drafts constitute the exploratory writing for the course. The revised essays plus the drafts of the unrevised essays are submitted in a portfolio toward the end of the term.

EXHIBIT 7.3

Eight Exploration Tasks for an Argument Addressing an Issue

1. Write out the issue your argument will address. Then write out your tentative answer to your issue-question. This will be your beginning thesis statement or claim.

2. Why is this issue controversial? Who are the stakeholders in the controversy? Why don't they agree? (For example, is there not enough evidence to resolve the issue? Is the current evidence ambiguous or contradictory? Are definitions in dispute? Do the parties disagree about basic values, assumptions, or beliefs?)

3. What personal interest do you have in this issue? What personal experiences do you have with it? How does the issue affect you?

4. Who is the audience that you need to persuade? What values, beliefs, and assumptions cause them to take positions different from yours? What evidence do they use to support their positions?

5. Through idea-mapping or freewriting, begin planning your own argument. What are the main reasons and evidence you will use to support your position? As you generate reasons and evidence, you are likely to discover gaps in your knowledge. Where could your argument be bolstered by additional data such as statistics, examples, and expert testimony? Where and how will you do the research to fill these gaps?

6. Role-playing your readers, imagine the counterarguments that your audience might make. Where does your claim threaten their beliefs, discount their own values, or otherwise cast them as losers rather than winners?

7. How can you respond to these objections and counterarguments? Take them one by one and brainstorm possible responses.

8. Finally, explore again why this issue is important. What are its broader implications and consequences? Why does it matter?

Low-Stakes "Shaped Exercises" to Practice Thesis-Governed Writing

For teachers who want the benefits of low-stakes write-to-learn activities but want students to practice thesis-governed rather than exploratory writing, an excellent option is to assign shaped writing exercises, including practice essay exams, thesis statement writing, and paragraphs shaped by templates.

20. *Practice Essay Exams.* Occasionally throughout the term, the teacher gives students an essay exam question due in class the next day (the student is instructed to do the writing at home, setting a watch to simulate exam conditions). The teacher collects the practice exams, checks them off in a grade book, and then reads a random sampling (every student's practice exam gets chosen occasionally throughout the term). The teacher then makes duplicates of an A exam for class discussion or writes one under the same timed conditions set for students. Discussion of the exam constitutes

review of course material as well as explanation of how to write essay exams. Teachers who want to try this method might turn to Chapter Twelve, which explains how to teach students to begin their essays with a one-sentence thesis that summarizes the writer's answer to the whole question. The importance of this summarizing skill leads to the following exercise.

21. *Thesis Statement Writing.* One of my favorite write-to-learn assignments asks students to write just one sentence. The trick, however, is that the sentence must be a thesis statement, which I define for students as a one-sentence summary of an essay's argument. The advantage of thesis statement assignments is the amount of leverage they provide—a lot of thinking packed into one sentence of writing. Students are often amazed at the fullness of the ideas that can be concentrated into a good generalization through effective use of embedded clauses. For example:

Question. "According to Robert Heilman, what is the difference between a tragedy and a disaster?"

Brief thesis. According to Heilman, a disaster is caused by an accident or outside force, whereas a tragedy is caused by the hero's wrong choice.

Elaborated thesis. For Robert Heilman, both disasters and tragedies bring about suffering or death; a disaster, however, is caused by an accident or outside force, so that the hero's physical suffering is not accompanied by guilt, whereas a tragedy is caused by the hero's wrong choice, leading to an agonizing discovery of personal responsibility, consequence, and spiritual suffering.

For instructors interested in teaching thesis-governed academic writing, I know of no single exercise that does a better job of teaching students how thesis statements work or that gives better practice at creating the governing abstractions that are the key to academic writing. See Chapter Ten, pages 190–191 (the "thesis-proposing strategy") for further explanation of this write-to-learn activity as a small group exercise.

22. *Paragraph Templates.* Templates give students an organizational pattern that guides their thinking about content. Students must come up with the needed generalizations and supporting data to flesh out the prescribed form. These are excellent assignments for teaching hierarchical structure. Here are some examples:

- To figure out how long it will take a small steel marble to roll down an inclined plane, you need to have, at a minimum, the following pieces of information. First, you need to know . . . Second, you need to know . . . [Third, . . . Fourth, . . .] *Note:* New learners might think that you need to know certain information that you actually do *not* need to know.

- Although some people think that wind power is . . . , I argue that. . . . [thesis statement, then support].

- The current tax structure is unfair to poor people for several reasons. First, . . . Second, . . . [Third, . . . Fourth, . . .]

As in practice exams, feedback for these assignments can come through discussion of strong paragraphs.

Evaluating Exploratory Writing

Throughout this chapter, I have referred to exploratory writing as informal and low-stakes. Although exploratory writing shouldn't be graded using the criteria for formal essays, it can be graded on the basis of either students' time on task (quantity of writing produced) or students' engagement and complexity of thinking (quality of the thought content)—or both.

Using a Check/Plus/Minus System or Simple Numeric Scale

In evaluating exploratory writing, many teachers use a check system or a simple scale. Here are examples:

Check/Plus/Minus Scale

Check: Indicates the piece meets your expectations for length (or time on task) and for engagement.

Plus: Indicates a strongly engaged, especially high-quality exploration.

Minus: Indicates that piece is too short or too superficial.

Five-Point Scale

Score of 5: Meets or exceeds required length (or time on task); strongly engaged, high-quality exploration.

Score of 4: Meets or exceeds required length; meets teacher's expectations for engagement.

Score of 3: High-quality exploration, but too short *or* meets required length or time on task but is too superficial.

Score of 2 or 1: Too short and too superficial.

Most teachers translate the check system or the scale into a letter grade on the basis of some formula: For the check system, a given number of checks equals a C; a certain combination of checks and pluses equals a B; a better combination of checks and pluses equals an A. For the number system, the total points earned translate into a letter grade.

What constitutes high-quality thinking varies from context to context. What I look for is evidence of dialogic thinking—seeing complexities, finding cruxes and puzzles, confronting inadequate explanations—so that I reward students for wading into the complexity of an issue. Teachers generally report that it is easy to distinguish insightful from superficial pieces of exploratory writing. The key question is not "How well written is this piece?" but "To what extent does this piece reveal engaged thinking about this topic?" I reward the process of thought rather than the product.

Weighing Exploratory Writing into the Course Grade

Once you have determined how you will translate minuses, checks, and pluses into a letter grade, your next decision is how much to weight the exploratory writing in computing the total course grade. There are numerous approaches here, ranging from negative penalties for failure to do assigned exploratory exercises to various kinds of positive incentives. Most teachers count the exploratory writing as some percentage of the course grade. How much to weight this grade is, of course, a knotty question. Too much weight leads to grade inflation (as most students get high scores for exploratory writing); too little provides insufficient motivation. I generally count exploratory writing as 10 to 15 percent of the course grade and allow myself to grade harder on tests and final papers as compensation for grading easier on the exploratory pieces.

Managing the Workload

Teachers who fear that requiring exploratory writing will increase their workloads inordinately should realize that many options are available, including some that take almost no instructor time. As the following list reveals, there are plenty of ways to use exploratory writing while still keeping your workload manageable.

Teacher Time Required for Exploratory Writing

No Out-of-Class Time

- Uncollected in-class freewriting (options 1–4)
- Exploratory tasks as "invention" for a formal essay (option 18)

- Exam preparation journals (option 10)
- Marginal notations in texts (option 11)

Minimal Time

- Thesis statement writing (option 21)
- Occasionally collected in-class freewriting (options 1–4)
- Pass/fail journals or thinking pieces (quantity only—options 5–10)
- Exam preparation journals if teacher gives bonus grade for quality (option 10)
- Practice exams (option 20—time used mainly for writing model answers if students do not provide them; after first course, however, teacher has a portfolio of answers to reuse)
- Abandoned drafts in the select-your-best-draft method (option 19)

Moderate Time

- Journals or thinking pieces read for quality (ways to cut down on time: skim entries or read selected entries only, either chosen randomly by teacher or preselected by student)
- Following conversations on class electronic bulletin boards if teacher judges quality of contributions (if the teacher just counts the contributions, the time demands are slight)

Most Time

Exploratory writing read and responded to thoroughly (many teachers report enough pleasure in reading journals/thinking pieces or bulletin board contributions that they compensate for their time by cutting down on other required writing, letting exploratory writing substitute for an essay exam or an additional formal paper)

Conclusion: Engaging Ideas Through Exploratory Writing

The evidence from both research and instructor testimony seems irrefutable: exploratory writing, focusing on the process rather than the product of thinking, deepens most students' engagement with course material while enhancing learning and developing critical thinking. Many teachers who try exploratory writing in their courses testify that they would never go back to their old way of teaching. The payoff of exploratory writing is students' enhanced preparation for class, richer class discussions, and better final-product writing. From in-class freewrites to reflective thought letters to extended bulletin board discussions, exploratory writing can help most students become more active and engaged learners.

Coaching Students as Learners, Thinkers, and Writers

8

Designing Tasks to Promote Active Thinking and Learning

The chapters in Part Two offer ways to incorporate formal and informal writing assignments into a course. Part Three now focuses on the broader goals of promoting active learning and critical thinking across the curriculum as well as accelerating students' growth as inquirers and researchers within their majors. Throughout Part Three, I emphasize the teacher's role as a coach (the metaphor for the critical thinking teacher used by Mortimer Adler, 1984), or—if one prefers the metaphor used by the Johnson brothers in their many works on cooperative learning—as a "guide on the side" rather than a "sage on the stage" (see Johnson, Johnson, and Smith, 1991, p. 81). In adopting this role, the teacher presents students with critical thinking problems, gives students supervised practice at addressing them, and coaches their performance by critiquing their solutions, providing helpful intervention and advice, and modeling critical thinking themselves. Although writing assignments are excellent means for promoting critical thinking and constructing a learner-centered pedagogy, other teaching strategies also play crucial roles. (For perspectives on learner-centered pedagogy, see Brookfield, 2006; Brookfield and Preskill, 2005; Fink, 2003; Weimer, 2002; Huba and Freed, 2000; Leamnson, 1999; Meyers and Jones, 1993; Goodenough, 1991; Bonwell and Eison, 1991; Bateman, 1990; Dillon, 1988; Kurfiss, 1988; and Hillocks, 1986.)

The chapters in Part Three offer strategies for coaching students as learners, thinkers, and writers. The present chapter focuses on the design of problem-based critical thinking tasks. Subsequent chapters focus on helping students read difficult texts (Chapter Nine); on classroom teaching methods to promote active learning, including using small groups (Chapter Ten); and bringing more critical thinking into lectures and discussion (Chapter Eleven); on enhancing learning and critical thinking in essay exams (Chapter Twelve); and on designing and sequencing assignments to teach undergraduate research (Chapter Thirteen).

This present chapter offers ten strategies for designing critical thinking tasks. Its underlying rationale comes from Kurfiss's summary of course features that characterize successful instruction in critical thinking. (I referred to Kurfiss's research in Chapters One and Two. Her complete list of eight features is on page 5.) My purpose for this chapter can be clarified by repeating features 2, 4, and 5 from Kurfiss's list:

2. *Problems, questions, or issues are the point of entry into the subject and a source of motivation for sustained inquiry.*

4. *Courses are assignment centered rather than text and lecture centered. Goals, methods, and evaluation emphasize using content rather than simply acquiring it.*

5. *Students are required to formulate and justify their ideas in writing or other appropriate modes [Kurfiss, 1988, p. 88].*

The teaching of critical thinking is thus rooted in the teacher's design of critical thinking tasks that present students with "problems, questions, or issues." These tasks require students to apply course concepts to new problems and to justify their ideas by making claims and creating arguments. This chapter provides a heuristic that can help teachers create a wealth of problems for critical thinking. Once created, a critical thinking task can be used in a variety of ways:

- As an exploratory writing task (in-class freewrite, "question of the day" journal task, thinking piece, and so forth—see Chapter Seven)

- As a formal writing assignment (a microtheme or a longer formal paper—see Chapter Six)

- As a question to foster engaged reading (Chapter Nine)

- As an essay exam question (Chapter Twelve) or a question for a practice exam (Chapter Seven)

- As a small group problem-solving task (Chapter Ten) or as an opening question for whole-class discussion or in-class debate (Chapter Eleven)

The goal in designing critical thinking problems is to convert students from passive to active learners who apply course concepts to new problems, learning how to gather and analyze data, prepare hypotheses, consider alternative views, and formulate arguments. The rest of this chapter offers practical suggestions for creating short, focused problems for students to think about.

Ten Strategies for Designing Critical Thinking Tasks

The design of critical thinking tasks gives professors great flexibility in incorporating critical thinking activities into their courses, in that the tasks can be used either as homework assignments (exploratory writing, microthemes, study group projects) or as questions for in-class discussions or small group tasks. The following are ten strategies for designing critical thinking tasks, each followed by one or more examples.

1. Tasks Linking Course Concepts to Students' Personal Experience or Previously Existing Knowledge

Tasks in this category are especially good for engaging students' interest in a problem or a concept before it is addressed formally in class or in readings. These tasks also help students assimilate new concepts by connecting the concepts to personal experiences. As cognitive research has shown (Zull, 2002; Bransford, Brown, and Cocking, 2000; Norman, 1980), to assimilate a new concept, learners must link it back to a structure of known material, determining how a new concept is both similar to and different from what the learner already knows. The more that unfamiliar material can be linked to the familiar ground of personal experience and already existing knowledge, the easier it is to learn.

Think of examples out of your own personal experience to illustrate the uses of vector algebra. You might consider such experiences as swimming across a river with a steady current, walking down an up escalator, crossing the wake while water-skiing, cutting diagonally across a vacant lot while friends walk around the lot, or watching a car trying to beat a moving train to a railroad crossing. Use one or more of these experiences to explain to a friend the kinds of problems that vector algebra tries to solve. Use both words and diagrams. [Mathematics]

• • •

Describe times in your own life when you have experienced role strain and role conflict. What are the key differences between these terms, and why is the distinction useful? [Sociology]

(Continued)

. . .

What are your current views toward what it means to live a full life? What specific things do you have to attain and work for in order to live as full a life as possible? [The instructor assigns this task near the beginning of the course; students reread their explorations at the end of the course to measure some of the changes in their thinking as a result of the course.] [Philosophy]

2. Explanation of Course Concepts to New Learners

One of the easiest ways to design critical thinking tasks is to ask students to explain course concepts to a new learner. This task gives students a teacher's role, making them search for ways to tie the course concept into the knowledge base of the hypothetical reader. It thus creates a purposeful rhetorical context wherein the writer writes to an audience for a reason. Because the stipulated audience knows less about the subject than the writer, the task helps students escape the student-to-examiner role that Britton finds debilitating for writers (Britton and others, 1975).

Explain to your mother why water stays in a pail when swung in a vertical circle around your head [Jensen, 1987, p. 331]. [Physics]

. . .

Write a procedure for finding the number m modulo n that a fifth grader could understand [Keith, 1989, p. 140]. [Mathematics]

. . .

Using layperson's language, explain to a new diabetic what is meant by the glycemic index of foods and why knowing about the glycemic index will help the diabetic maintain good blood sugar levels. [Nursing/nutrition science]

3. Thesis Support Assignments

As discussed in Chapter Six, one of the best ways to teach thesis-governed writing is to give students a controversial thesis to defend or attack. The assignment reinforces for students a view of knowledge as tentative and dialogic, with divergent interpretations of reality competing for allegiance. Given the assignment's concern for reasons and evidence, coupled with a demand that the writer or speaker attend to opposing views, it requires a high level of critical thinking. Thesis support tasks make excellent microtheme, practice exam, or short essay assignments. They also make good "believing and doubting" exploratory tasks (see page 176) or collaborative learning exercises in which groups are asked to develop arguments for and against the thesis. (For additional examples of thesis-support assignments, see Chapter Six, pages 107–108.)

People suffering from schizophrenia or manic-depressive disorder should/should not be forced to take their medication. [Nursing/medical ethics]

· · ·

An electric dipole is placed above an infinitely conducting plane. The dipole does/does not feel a net force or a torque. Explain [Mullin, 1989, p. 208]. [Physics course in electricity and magnetism]

· · ·

After all of Hamlet's shilly-shallying, Fortinbras is just what Denmark needs. Support or attack. [Literature]

· · ·

Read the accompanying handout on how historians evaluate the credibility and reliability of primary documents. Based on the criteria set forth in the handout, determine whether Pericles's Funeral Oration is/is not reliable evidence. [History]

---

4. Problem-Posing Assignments

With this strategy, instead of giving students the thesis, as in strategy 3, you give students the question, which they have to try to answer through thesis-governed writing or to contemplate through exploratory writing or small group problem solving. Often the assignment specifies an audience also—a person other than the teacher who either poses the question or needs the answer. Most teachers can get a ready supply of these questions by sorting through old essay exams, which often make excellent small group tasks or write-to-learn tasks for journals, practice exams, or microthemes. Often the questions can be incorporated into humorous stories or problem situations that make the assignment more fun.

An hourglass is being weighed on a sensitive balance, first when sand is dropping in a steady stream from the upper to lower part and then again when the upper part is empty. Are the two weights the same or not? Write an explanation supporting your answer to this question. Write to a fellow student who is arguing for what you think is the wrong answer. [Physics]

· · ·

(Continued)

Your thirteen-year-old brother mailed you a cartoon showing a picture of Frank and Ernest taking a number from the dispenser at an ice-cream parlor. The number they draw is $\sqrt{-1}$. Ernest has a puzzled look on his face. Your brother is taking a pre-algebra class and is familiar with the idea of square roots such as $\sqrt{4} = 2$ and $\sqrt{81} = 9$. He also knows how to do arithmetic with positive and negative integers. However, he does not understand the cartoon and wants you to explain it to him. Prepare a written explanation for your brother that builds on his current mathematics background. [Mathematics]

• • •

You are an accountant in the tax department of Kubiak, Kartcher, and Elway, certified public accountants. Saturday morning, you are in Winchell's Donuts, as usual. Just as you finish reading the comics and start on your second apple fritter, a gentleman sits down beside you. He introduces himself as Fred O. McDonald, a farmer from up in the valley. He says he recognizes you as "that CPA who frequents the donut shop." Fred has a problem and asks tax advice from you. Here is Fred's problem:

Last Tuesday, farmer McDonald planned to remove stumps from a pasture. So he drove out to the pasture, lit a stick of dynamite, and tossed it near the base of a stump. Fred's playful dog, Boomer, saw his master throw the "stick" and scampered to fetch it. Boomer picked up the stick. Fred yelled at the dog. Boomer, thinking he was going to be punished, ran under Fred's pickup truck. Boomer dropped the dynamite stick. The dog escaped harm just as the truck was totally destroyed by the blast. Fred wonders if he can deduct the loss of the truck for tax purposes.

Write a letter to Fred O. McDonald to answer his question. [Accounting]

5. Data-Provided Assignments

In a sense, this strategy is the flip side of the thesis-provided assignment in strategy 3. In the earlier strategy, the teacher provides the thesis; students must discover reasons and evidence to support it or attack it. In this strategy, the teacher provides the data; students must determine what thesis or hypothesis the data might support. This strategy is particularly useful in the sciences for teaching students how to write the "findings" and "discussion" sections of scientific reports. The teacher can explain the research question and methodology for an experiment and then give students the researchers' experimental findings displayed in terms of graphs, tables, or charts. Students can then be asked, first, to write the "findings" section of the report and then the "discussion" section. The strategy can also be used in a variety of ways to teach students how to use statistical data in arguments.

Examine the attached unsorted data about Mary Smith, a stroke patient who is soon to be transferred from an acute-care facility to a convalescent center. [The accompanying data include admitting information, history and physical data, progress notes, nursing notes, and a social service report.] Based on these data, write a discharge summary for Mary Smith. Your audience is the nursing supervisor of the convalescent facility, and your purpose is to help the convalescent center provide the patient with optimal continuity of care [adapted from Pinkava and Haviland, 1984, p. 271]. [Nursing]

. . .

To what extent do the attached economic data support the hypothesis "Social service spending is inversely related to economic growth"? First, create a scattergram as a visual test of the hypothesis. Then formulate a verbal argument analyzing whether the data do or do not support the hypothesis. [Economics]

6. Template Assignments

Template assignments are analogous to those old dance lessons for which the instructor pasted footsteps on the floor. A template assignment provides a slot for an opening thesis statement or topic sentence along with an organizational frame that students have to flesh out with appropriate generalizations and supporting data. Students have to dance their way through the paragraph or essay, but the assignment shows them where to put their feet. Often the template provides specific transition words or other organizational cues. Students report that such assignments help them learn a lot about organizational strategies. More importantly, they see how structure can stimulate invention in that they must generate ideas and arguments to fill the open slots in the template. (For use of template assignments as exploratory writing tasks, see Chapter Seven, pages 141–142; for their use as collaborative learning tasks, see Chapter Ten, page 191.)

In the last act of *Hamlet,* Hamlet seems to have changed in several ways. First, Hamlet [development] . . . Second, Hamlet [development] . . . [Third, . . . Fourth, . . .] [Literature]

. . .

Based on yesterday's discussion, our class hasn't resolved the question of _____. Several of my classmates argued that _____. I agree with them that _____. However, they are mistaken when they _____. In contrast, I argue that _____.

. . .

Socrates and the Sophists differed in their beliefs about truth. On the one hand, Socrates argued that [development] . . . The Sophists, on the other hand, argued that [development] . . . [Philosophy]

7. Assignments Requiring Role-Playing of Unfamiliar Perspectives or Imagining "What If" Situations

Role-playing unfamiliar or disorienting perspectives or imagining "what if" situations makes an excellent critical thinking exercise. Piagetians have shown that a major block to critical thinking is egocentrism—that is, a person's inability to imagine alternative views. According to Flavell (1963), an egocentric thinker, in the Piagetian sense, "sees the world from a single point of view only—his own—but without knowledge of the existence of [other] viewpoints or perspectives and . . . without awareness that he is the prisoner of his own" (p. 60). Tasks requiring role-playing or "what if" thinking encourage what Piaget calls decentering—getting students outside of the assumptions of their own worldview. By asking students to adopt an unfamiliar perspective or a "what if" situation, we stretch their thinking in productive ways.

Look at this prehistoric cave painting [attached reproduction shows a speared deer-like animal]. Imagine that you are the Ice Age artist who created the animal painting on the cave wall. What could have motivated you to create such a painting? [Art history]

. . .

Hobbes said that we are obliged to obey the state only so long as it guarantees our security. How would he react to compulsory military service in time of war [Maimon and others, 1981, p. 201]? [History, philosophy]

. . .

Assume that space scientists, working with sports clothing manufacturers, have developed a superflexible space suit that allows athletes to run and jump freely on extraterrestrial soil. As an all-world sports promoter, your uncle, Squeebly Rickets, decides to schedule an exhibition baseball game on the moon. One of his first tasks is to provide instructions for laying out the baseball diamond and outfield fences. But then he begins to wonder, How will the lack of an atmosphere and the greatly reduced gravitational force affect the game? For help, he turns to you as an expert in physics. [Physics]

. . .

Suppose experiments showed that the Coulomb law for point charges q_1 and q_2 were actually

$$F = \frac{q_1 q_2}{4\pi\varepsilon_0 r^2}(1 + r/\lambda)\exp(-r/\lambda)$$

where λ is a new constant of nature that is extremely large. (It turns out that λ depends on the mass of the photon m_γ with $\lambda = \infty$ for $m_\gamma = 0$.) Superposition still holds. Describe qualitatively how you would go about reformulating electrostatics. Quote results if you are able to, but mainly just indicate what procedures you would follow [Mullin, 1989, p. 207]. [Electricity and magnetism]

8. Summaries or Abstracts of Articles or Course Lectures

Writing summaries or précis of articles or lectures is a superb way to develop reading and listening skills, to practice decentering, and to develop the skills of precision, clarity, and succinctness (Bean, 1986). In composing a summary, the writer must determine the hierarchical structure of the original article, retaining without distortion the logical sequence of its general statements while eliminating its specific details. Summary writers must also suspend their own views on a subject to articulate fairly what is often an unfamiliar or even unsettling view in the article being summarized.

Teachers can assign summaries of various lengths. Perhaps the most common length is 200 to 250 words, but Angelo and Cross (1993) report successful use of one-sentence summaries in immunology, fundamentals of nursing, and physics for technicians (pp. 183–187). In another variation, Barry (1989, p. 24) reports good results assigning a "25-word précis"—a one-sentence abstract that must be exactly twenty-five words long. By requiring *exactly* twenty-five words, the assignment forces students through considerable revision, in which they must play with syntax and question the value of every word.

To promote careful listening and note-taking skills, some professors ask students to write summaries of their lectures. Chemistry professor Richard Steiner (1982) reported that having students write daily summaries of his lectures resulted in significantly improved test scores: "I decided that an effective way to utilize writing assignments as a way to promote understanding was to require written summaries of my organic chemistry lectures. Students were instructed to discuss briefly (one page) in writing the key points and relationships in each lecture . . . [The collected data]

Write a 200- to 250-word summary of Kenneth Galbraith's paper, "The Theory of Countervailing Power," which attempts to provide a theory that describes and accounts for the distribution of power. Your summary should accurately convey the content of the paper. It should be comprehensive and balanced with clear sentence structure and good transitions. [Political science]

• • •

Write a four-sentence summary of the attached scientific paper, followed by four questions. Your first four sentences make up a four-sentence summary of the scientific article—one sentence for each section of the paper. Recall that the *Introduction* states the question addressed in the study and explains why the question is important, *Methods* tells how the question was answered, *Results* shows the outcome of the experiment, and *Discussion* analyzes the results and suggests the impact of the new knowledge. Your second four sentences are four questions raised in your mind by the article. [Biology] indicate that the writing assignments directly contributed to student understanding" (p. 1044). Furthermore, by reading selected summaries after each day's lectures, Steiner was able to monitor places where students were having difficulty and adjust his lectures accordingly. (For further discussion of summary writing, see Chapter Nine, page 178. See also Cohen and Spencer, 1993, who describe an advanced economics course in which the initial writing assignments—aimed at teaching economic argumentation—are a sequence of abstracts of significant professional articles in economics.)

9. Dialogues or Argumentative Scripts

These assignments allow students to role-play opposing views without having to commit themselves to a final thesis. The freedom from traditional thesis-governed form, as well as the necessity to role-play each of the opposing views in the conversation, often stimulates more complex thinking than traditional argumentative papers, in which students often try to reach closure too quickly. By preventing closure, this format promotes in-depth exploration. The dialogue strategy is also recommended by Angelo and Cross (1993) as a useful strategy for formative assessment of critical thinking. According to Angelo and Cross, "Invented Dialogues provide rich information on students' ability to capture the essence of other people's personalities and styles of expression—as well as on their understanding of theories, controversies, and opinions of others. This technique provides a challenging way to assess—and to develop—students' skills at creatively synthesizing, adapting, and even extrapolating beyond the material they have studied" (p. 203).

Write a short dialogue (two to three pages) between a neo-elitist power theorist and a pluralist. First, take the role of the neo-elitist (be an intellectual son or daughter of Ganson) and explain to this poor, unenlightened pluralist the meaning and importance of the concepts of predecision politics and the mobilization of bias. Respond to this radical fluff in the role of a Yalie pluralist. Continue the dialogue by alternating roles; be sure to respond in the role of one theorist to the arguments raised by the other. [Political science]

• • •

For the design application we have been studying, your design team has proposed four alternative solutions: conventional steel roller bearings, ceramic bearings, air bearings, and magnetic bearings. As a team, write a dialogue in which each team member argues the case for one of the alternative solutions and shows weaknesses in the other solutions. [Mechanical engineering]

• • •

You suddenly fall into a weird time warp and find yourself in a tavern with Aristotle, Hegel, Arthur Miller, and literary critic Robert Heilman, all of whom have distinctive views on what constitutes a tragedy. They are arguing vociferously about Miller's *Death of a Salesman:* Is it a tragedy? Luckily, you have just studied Miller's play in your literature class and have strong feelings yourself on this matter. Write a mini-play in which you, Aristotle, Hegel, Miller, and Heilman express views on this question. [Literature]

10. Cases and Simulations

Case studies have long been a staple of instruction in law, medicine, and business. Long cases often require the writing of elaborate scenarios and the assembly of extensive packets of data. For this reason, many instructors use cases already published in textbooks, either directly or adapted to their own needs. It is possible, however, to create your own short cases adapted from recent news stories, campus events, or developments in your professional field. Good cases generally tell a real or believable story, raise thought-provoking issues based on conflict, lack an obvious or clear-cut right answer, and demand a decision reached through critical thinking and analysis. Because students can be asked to assume the role of someone inside the case writing to another person within the case, case assignments provide a realistic sense of purpose and audience as well as an exigency for writing. (For examples of cases used to stimulate critical thinking, see Davis, 2009; Carrithers and Bean, 2008; Carlson and Schodt, 1995; Barnes, Christensen, and Hansen, 1994; Boehrer and Linsky, 1990; and Di Gaetani, 1989).

Mr. X, a patient at City Hospital, suffers from kidney failure and requires periodic and fairly frequent dialysis, which is funded by the government. He is one of a number of patients who use the dialysis machine, and there are many other similarly afflicted individuals who are on a waiting list for the use of the machine. Mr. X finds dialysis quite painful and sometimes says that he would rather just forget the treatment and let the disease run its natural course. Lately he has begun to miss some of his treatments and has been failing to control his diet properly. He has even become abusive with the hospital staff who operate the dialysis machine. His wife is quite worried about him, especially since his behavior has changed toward her and their five children. Mr. X continues his erratic routine, sometimes taking his treatment quietly, sometimes taking it but abusing the staff, sometimes failing to take it at all. Suddenly, he begins to miss all his treatments. Two weeks later, he is rushed to the hospital in a coma. He must have immediate dialysis if he is to survive. Should the hospital perform the dialysis, or should Mr. X be allowed to die?

Initial roles. An ethicist taking a utilitarian position; an ethicist taking a deontological position; Mr. X's wife; a staff member; a representative of the people on the waiting list for the dialysis machine; a member of the Hemlock Society; members of the hospital board that will decide the case.

Conducting the simulation. Students discuss the case, taking their assigned roles.

Writing assignment. After hearing all the arguments presented by characters in the role-play, assume that you are a member of a hospital ethics team who must soon present its recommendation to the hospital board, which will decide the case. Write a three- to four-page argument supporting your position on the issue.

Conclusion: Strategies for Designing Critical Thinking Tasks

As a review of the ideas covered in this chapter, here is a list of possible strategies for designing critical thinking tasks for your courses. As suggested, these tasks can then be used in a variety of ways: in-class free-writes, at-home guided-journal tasks or thinking pieces, practice exams, microthemes, multidraft formal essays, small group collaborative tasks, or tasks for whole-class discussions or simulations.

- Think of tasks that would let students link concepts in your course to their personal experiences or prior knowledge.

- Ask students to teach difficult concepts in your course to a new learner.

- Think of controversial theses in your field (for thesis support assignments or believer-versus-doubter exercises).

- Think of problems, puzzles, or questions you could ask students to address.

- Give students raw data (such as lists, graphs, or tables) and ask them to write an argument or analysis based on the data.

- Design templates that will guide your students through a thinking process that you value. The templates create a frame of "slots" and transitions that students have to flesh out with generalizations and supporting details.

- Have students role-play unfamiliar points of view (imagine X from the perspective of Y) or "what if" situations.

- Select important articles in your field, and ask students to write summaries or abstracts of them. (Or ask students to write summaries of your lectures.)

- Think of a controversy in your field, and ask students to write a dialogue between characters with different points of view.

- Develop cases by writing scenarios that place students in realistic situations relevant to your discipline, where they must reach a decision to resolve a conflict.

9

Helping Students Read Difficult Texts

Whenever teachers discuss problems with student writing or critical thinking, they inevitably turn also to problems of student reading. Just as speaking and listening skills are intertwined, so too are writing and reading skills. Many of today's students are inexperienced readers, overwhelmed by the density of their college textbooks and baffled by the strangeness and complexity of primary sources and by their unfamiliarity with academic discourse. Armed with a yellow highlighter but with no apparent strategy for using it and hampered by lack of knowledge of how skilled readers actually go about reading, our students often feel overwhelmed by college reading assignments. The aim of this chapter is to suggest ways that we can help students become stronger readers, empowered by the strategies that we ourselves use when we encounter difficult texts.

Causes of Students' Reading Difficulties

Before we can help students improve their reading skills, we need to look more closely at the causes of their reading difficulties. Our students have, of course, learned to read in the sense of achieving basic literacy. Except for an occasional student with a reading disability, college students do not need to be taught reading in this ordinary sense. Rather, they need to be taught to read powerfully. In the words of a sociology professor collaborating with a reading theorist (Roberts and Roberts, 2008), students need to become "deep readers," who focus on meaning, as opposed to "surface readers," who focus on facts and information. Drawing on cognitive research in reading, Judith and Keith Roberts (2008) explain that deep reading is processed in "'semantic memory' (rooted in meaning) as opposed to 'episodic memory' (tied to a specific joke, gesture, episode, or mnemonic to aid recall)" (p. 126). Deep readers, they claim, interact with texts, devoting psychological energy to the task:

> *A good reader forms visual images to represent the content being read, connects to emotions, recalls settings and events that are similar to those presented in the reading, predicts what will happen next, asks questions, and thinks about the use of language. One of the most important steps, however, is to connect the manuscript [they] are reading with what [they] already know and to attach the facts, ideas, concepts, or perspectives to that known material [p. 126].*

The question we face as educators is how to teach and foster this kind of "deep reading." In this section I identify eleven contributing causes of students' reading difficulties.

1. A School Culture That Rewards Surface Reading

Roberts and Roberts (2008) make a powerful case that our current school culture, which allows savvy students to get decent grades for minimal effort, cultivates surface reading. They argue that the prolific use of quizzes and other kinds of objective tests encourages "surface learning based in . . . short-term memorization for a day or two . . . rather than deep learning that is transformative of one's perspective and involves long-term comprehension" (p. 127). Moreover, they argue, many students don't value a course's "big ideas" because deep learning isn't needed for cumulating a high GPA. (They cite evidence that nearly half of college students spend less than ten hours per week on out-of-class study, including time for writing papers and studying for exams.) Students like multiple choice tests, the authors say, because most objective testing allows students "to skim material a few days before an examination looking for the kinds of facts, definitions, concepts, and other specific information that the particular instructor tends to stress in examinations" (p. 129). When students apply a cost/benefit analysis, they see, quite rationally, that deep reading "may be an *unwise* use of valuable time if there are no adverse consequences" (p. 129). In short, unless we as teachers evaluate student performance at the levels of analysis, synthesis, and evaluation, "reading at that deeper level will not occur" (p. 129). (For an in-depth critique of school cultures that promote surface learning, see Weimer, 2002.)

2. Students' Resistance to the Time-on-Task Required for Deep Reading

Roberts and Roberts rightly identify students' desire to avoid the deep reading process, which involves substantial time-on-task. When experts read difficult texts, they read slowly and reread often. They struggle with the text to make it comprehensible. They hold confusing passages in mental suspension, having faith that later parts of the text may clarify earlier parts. They "nutshell" passages as they proceed, often writing gist statements in the margins. They read a difficult text a second and a third time, considering first readings as approximations or rough drafts. They interact with the text by asking questions, expressing disagreements, linking the text with other readings or with personal experience.

But resistance to deep reading may involve more than an unwillingness to spend the time. Students may actually misunderstand the reading process. They may believe that experts are speed readers who don't need to struggle. Therefore students assume that their own reading difficulties must stem from their lack of expertise, which makes the text "too hard for them." Consequently, they don't allot the study time needed to read a text deeply.

3. Teachers' Willingness to Lecture over Reading Material

Once students believe that a text is too hard for them, they assume that it is the teacher's job to explain the text to them. Since teachers regularly do so, the students' reading difficulty initiates a vicious circle: Teachers, frustrated by their students' poor reading comprehension, decide to lecture over the assigned texts ("I have to lecture on this material because students are such poor readers"). Meanwhile, teachers' lectures deprive students of the very practice and challenge they need to grow as readers ("I don't have to struggle with this text because the teacher will explain it in class").

4. Failure to Adjust Reading Strategies for Different Purposes

Inexperienced readers are also unaware of how a skilled reader's reading process will vary extensively, depending on the reader's purpose. Sternberg (1987) argues that college students—facing enormous amounts of reading—must learn to distinguish among different reading purposes and adjust their reading speed accordingly. Some reading tasks require only skimming for gist, while others require the closest scrutiny of detail. Sternberg gave people a reading comprehension test consisting of four passages, each of which was to be read for a different purpose—one for gist, one for main ideas, one for detail, and one for inference and application. He discovered that good readers varied their reading speed appropriately, spending the most time with passages they were to read for detail, inference, and application. Poor readers, in contrast, read all four passages at the same speed. As Sternberg puts it, poor readers "do not discriminate in their reading time as a function of reading purpose" (p. 186). The lesson here is that we need to help students learn when to read fast and when to read slowly. Not every text requires deep reading.

5. Difficulty in Adjusting Reading Strategies to Different Genres

Besides adjusting reading strategy to purpose, students need to learn to adjust reading strategy to genre. Students tend to read all texts as if they were textbooks—linearly from first to last page—looking for facts and information that can be highlighted with a yellow marker. Their tendency to get either lost or bored results partly from their unfamiliarity with the text's genre and the function of that genre within a discourse system. Learning the rhetorical function of different genres takes considerable practice as well as knowledge of a discipline's ways of conducting inquiry and making arguments. Inexperienced readers do not understand, for example, that the author of a peer-reviewed scholarly article joins a conversation of other scholars and tries to stake out a position that offers something new. At a more specific level, they don't understand that an empirical research study in the social or physical sciences requires a different reading strategy from that of a theoretical/interpretive article in the humanities. These genre problems are compounded further when students are assigned challenging primary texts from the Great Books tradition (reading Plato or Darwin, Nietzsche or Sartre, or an archived historical document) or asked to write research papers drawing on contemporary popular culture genres such as op-ed pieces, newspaper articles, trade journals, blogs, or websites.

6. Difficulty in Perceiving the Structure of an Argument as They Read

Unlike experts, inexperienced readers are less apt to chunk complex material into discrete parts with describable functions. They do not say to themselves, for example, "This part is giving evidence for a new reason," "This part maps out an upcoming section," or "This part summarizes an opposing view." Their often indiscriminate, almost random use of the yellow highlighter suggests that they are not representing the text in their minds as a hierarchical structure. To use a metaphor popular among composition instructors, these students are taking an ant's-eye view of the text—crawling through it word by word—rather than a bird's-eye view, seeing the overall structure by attending to mapping statements, section headings, paragraph topic sentences, and so forth.

7. Difficulty in Reconstructing the Text's Original Rhetorical Context

Inexperienced readers often do not see what conversation a text belongs to—what exigency sparked the piece of writing, what question the writer was pondering, what points of view the writer was pushing against, what audience the writer was imagining, what change the writer hoped to bring about in the audience's beliefs or actions—why, in short, the writer put pen to paper or fingers to keyboard. They have difficulty perceiving a real author writing for a real reason out of a real historical moment. Also, inexperienced readers often fail to appreciate the political biases of different magazines and newspapers or the theoretical biases of different academic journals and presses. These problems are closely related to the following one.

8. Difficulty Seeing Themselves in Conversation with the Author

Possibly because they regard texts as sources of inert information rather than as arguments intended to change their view of something, inexperienced readers often do not interact with the texts they read. They don't ask how they, as readers in a particular moment in time, are similar to or different from the author's intended audience. They don't realize that texts have designs upon them and that they need to decide, through their own critical thinking, whether to succumb to or resist the text's power.

9. Difficulty in Assimilating the Unfamiliar

Developmental psychologists have long noted the "cognitive egocentrism" of new college students who have trouble walking in the shoes of persons with unfamiliar views and values (Kurfiss, 1988; Flavell, 1963). No matter what the author really means, students translate those meanings into ideas that they are comfortable with. Thus, to many of our students, a philosophic Idealist is someone with impractical ideas, whereas a Realist is praiseworthy for being levelheaded. The more unfamiliar or more threatening a new idea is, the more students transform it into something from their own psychological neighborhoods. The insight of cognitive psychology here is that these problems are related neither to stupidity nor to intellectual laziness. To use language from brain research, learners must build new concepts upon neural structures already in their brains, and sometimes older structures need to be dismantled before new ones can be built (Zull, 2002).

10. Lack of the "Cultural Literacy" Assumed by the Text's Author

In the jargon of reading theorists, students do not have access to the cultural codes of the text—background information, allusions, common knowledge that the author assumed that the reading audience would know. Knowledge of cultural codes is often essential to making meaning of the text. (See Willingham, 2009, pp. 25–52, for a review of cognitive research on reading comprehension and background knowledge.) So significant is this cause that E. D. Hirsch has tried to create a national movement promoting "cultural literacy," lack of which he claims is a prime source of students' reading difficulties in college (Hirsch, 2006; Hirsch, 1988; Hirsch, Kett, and Trefil, 1987).

11. Difficulties with Vocabulary and Syntax

Inadequate vocabulary hampers the reading comprehension of many students. Using a dictionary helps considerably, but often students do not appreciate how context affects word meanings, nor do they have a good ear for irony or humor. Moreover, the texts they read often contain technical terms, terms used in unusual ways, terms requiring extensive contextual knowledge, or terms that have undergone meaning changes over time. Additionally, students have difficulty tracking complex sentence structures. Although students may be skilled enough reading syntactically simple texts, they often have trouble with the sentence structure of primary sources or scholarly articles. When they are asked to read a complex sentence aloud, their errors in inflection reveal their difficulty in chunking grammatical units; they have trouble isolating main clauses, distinguishing them from attached and embedded subordinate clauses and phrases.

Suggested Strategies for Helping Students Become Better Readers

Having examined these various causes, we recognize that reading skills, like writing skills, develop slowly over time as students develop better study habits, as they move upward intellectually on William Perry's developmental scale, as their vocabularies expand, as they grow in cultural literacy, as they increase their repertoire of reading strategies, and as they move from novice toward expert within their majors. Although we cannot teach reading directly, we can create learning environments that nurture reading growth. What follows are numerous suggestions for creating such an environment.

Develop a Course Design, Assignments, and Grading Methods That Require and Reward Deep Reading

If we want to address the causes of students' reading difficulties, we must try to change academic cultures that reward surface learning. The key is to change the homework dimension of a course to require reading for meaning. Increasing the homework demands does not necessarily mean adding more readings to a course (indeed, perhaps we'll need to assign fewer), but to develop homework tasks that require deep rather than surface processing. The last section of this chapter shows different kinds of possible homework tasks that promote deep reading. The more teachers can build these tasks into the homework dimension of a course, the more students will have to take responsibility for reading for meaning.

In the pedagogical literature, sociologist David Yamane (2006) provides a powerful example of a teacher who no longer needs to lecture over readings because he has changed the homework dimension of his course. Yamane developed a series of "course preparation assignments (CPAs)" which require students to come to class already prepared for an opening small group task. Completing the CPA requires understanding of the day's readings. Here are extracts from one of his example CPAs:

Objective [for the day's class]: To describe and analyze the causes of racial inequality in the contemporary United States

  Background: Consider the following data from the U. S. Census Bureau [attaches statistics on median family income for Whites versus Blacks]

  Assignment:

1. Read Chapter 12 of the textbook on racial inequality to familiarize yourself with its forms, causes, and consequences.

2. Generate at least five *testable hypotheses* you believe might account for the differences in income given above. In other words, the differences in income are your *dependent variables*. What are the *independent variables?* (247–248)

On this day, Yamane's students come to class having carefully read Chapter Twelve (necessary in order to do the CPA) and ready to share their testable hypotheses. Whereas in an earlier teaching life, Yamane might have lectured over Chapter Twelve, he has now upped the ante, pushing students to use their understanding of the reading to address a problem that teaches sociological thinking. (For another example of a teacher's changing the homework dimension of a course to promote reading for understanding, see the story of history professor John R. Breihan in Walvoord and McCarthy, 1990.)

Changing course design to promote deep reading may depend on our taking actions like the following.

Not Using Quizzes to Motivate Reading

Although there are occasions where reading quizzes may be appropriate, Roberts and Roberts (2008) make a persuasive case that quizzes tend to promote surface rather than deep reading. Quizzes encourage students to extract "right answers" from a text rather than to engage with the text's ideas, and they don't invite students to bring their own critical thinking to bear on a text's argument or to enter into conversation with a text's author.

Not Lecturing Over Readings

Lecturing over readings initiates the vicious reading cycle mentioned earlier: Teachers explain readings in class because students are poor readers; meanwhile, students read poorly because teachers explain the readings in class. Of course, teachers still need to help students with difficult portions of a reading, clarify confusions, and so forth. But teachers should send the signal that becoming an engaged reader is part of a student's homework component of a course.

Making Students Responsible for Texts Not Covered in Class

This strategy signals to students that all learning in a course does not have to be mediated through the instructor. Not only does this strategy allow instructors to include content material without feeling rushed to lecture over it—or even to discuss it in class—but it also sends a powerful message about the importance of reading for lifelong learning. When students know they will be tested on material not explained in class, they are forced to a deeper level of struggle.

Empower Students by Helping Them See Why Texts Are Difficult

I've found that students often gain confidence and hope if I say in class something as simple as this: "Of course, you are going to struggle with this reading. You aren't its intended audience. I'm going to be happy if you understand 50 percent of it. There are passages in it that I don't fully understand myself." When an economics colleague at my university asks his undergraduates to read Federal Reserve publications, he says, "Hey, you're running with the big dogs here. These pubs are aimed at Ph.D. economists" (see Robertson, Peterson, and Bean, 2007).

My point is that without encouragement from the teacher, students often feel incompetent, even stupid, when they fail to understand a text. Simply knowing that they aren't members of the text's intended audience—that they don't possess the background knowledge, cultural codes, and genre awareness needed for complete understanding—gives them a way of proceeding. If you can get students to say, "I had trouble with this text because I'm an outsider" rather than "I had trouble with this text because I'm a poor reader," you will have provided powerful help. (See my attempt to make this point in Exhibit 9.2, my reading guide for a first-year seminar.)

Explain to Students How Your Own Reading Process Varies

Students appreciate learning how their professors read and study. You might take some class time to discuss with students your own reading processes. One approach is to create research scenarios to help students see how and why your reading strategies vary according to purpose and genre. When you do your own research, for example, when do you skim texts? When do you read for gist but not for detail? When do you read carefully? Under what circumstances do you take notes on a text or write in the margins? What different kinds of genres do you read for your research? (In some disciplines primary data come from laboratory and field research—the task of reading may be primarily reserved for the review of the literature section of an article. In other disciplines primary data come from texts themselves, ranging from literary works to archived historical documents to political blogs.) When you read a primary source text—say, a philosopher reading Hegel or a new media specialist reading fan literature on a website—how do your reading practices differ from when you read a scholarly article in your field? When you read a complex theoretical article, how much do you reread and why? When in your reading are you influenced by the credentials of an author? How much does the prestige level of a scholarly journal or the political bias of a magazine or newspaper affect the way you read a text? The fifteen or twenty minutes it takes for such discussions can sometimes have a powerful influence on students' reading strategies.

Show Students Your Own Note-Taking and Responding Process

Just as it helps students to see a skilled writer's rough drafts, it helps them to see a skilled reader's marked-up text, marginal notations, and note-taking system. Bring in a book or article full of your own marginal notes and underlinings, along with entries you made in your note system. Show them what sorts of things you write in the margins. Explain what you underline and why. If your reading is part of a scholarly project, show them how you take notes and how you distinguish between what the author is saying and your own reflections on the material.

Help Students Get the Dictionary Habit

Students should keep a dictionary in the room where they study. They need to learn strategies that work for them when they encounter unfamiliar words. One strategy is to make small ticks in the margins next to words they are unsure of and to look them up later when they come to an appropriate resting place in the text. After they have looked up a word, they can briefly review the parts of the text in which it occurred before tackling the next portion.

Teach Students "What It Says" and "What It Does"

A helpful way to teach students to understand structural function in a text is to show them how to write "what it says" and "what it does" statements for each paragraph (Ramage, Bean, and Johnson, 2009; Bean, Chappell, and Gillam, 2011; Bruffee, 1993). A "what it says" statement is a summary of the paragraph's content—the paragraph's stated or implied topic sentence. A "what it does" statement describes the paragraph's purpose or function within the essay: for example, "Provides evidence for the author's first main reason," "Summarizes an opposing view," "Provides statistical data to support a point," or "Uses an analogy to clarify the idea in the previous paragraph." Here are examples for the paragraph you are now reading:

Says: Instructors can teach students about structure by having them write "what it says" and "what it does" statements.

Does: Gives another strategy for helping students become better readers.

Asking students to write out "what it says" and "what it does" statements for each paragraph in a scholarly article in your field will ensure not only careful reading of the article but also increased awareness of structure. Exhibit 9.1 shows one of my "Says/Does" assignments for a first-year seminar on the nature/nurture controversy in gender identity. I

EXHIBIT 9.1

Low-Stakes Assignment for a First-Year Seminar on Nature/Nurture Controversy in Gender Identity

Making Says /Does Statements to Promote Reading for Meaning

For Monday's class we will discuss psychologist Steven Pinker's argument in support of Lawrence Summers' controversial speech about why so few women hold tenured positions in math, physics, and engineering at top research universities. As models, I have made says/does statements for the first five paragraphs. As preparation for the discussion, make says/does statements for the remaining paragraphs in Pinker's article. Bring your says/does statements to class, where I will collect them.

Para	Says	Does
1	Since the 1970s the proportion of women in many scientific fields has increased significantly, and it would be morally wrong and hurtful to science to turn back the clock.	Introduces the subject of gender difference and presents author's assurance that he respects and values women scientists
2	Although Summers was not trying to turn back the clock, many prominent scientists and engineers protested vehemently against his speech.	Makes transition to Summers' case and lists examples of negative reaction against Summers
3	Summers never claimed that women have inferior math abilities; rather, he attributed women's underrepresentation in science and engineering to three factors: possible discrimination; possible biological gender differences; and women's reluctance to sacrifice family and child-rearing to time-intensive jobs.	Rejects the popular press's misrepresentation of Summers by summarizing Summers' actual argument
4	Anyone who has seen men talking about gadgets can understand why women might not be attracted to engineering; however, we must turn to science to help us determine to what extent gender differences are biological.	Supports the reasonableness of Summers' argument and asserts importance of using science to help determine whether gender differences are biological or cultural
5	The negative consequences of overestimating discrimination against women include falsely charging innocent people of sexism, proposing harmful remedies such as quota systems, and diverting attention from university policies on timing of tenure that hurt women during the childbearing years.	Shows the negative consequences of overestimating discrimination against women as the cause of women's underrepresentation in science and engineering

YOU DO THE REST.

composed the says/does statements for the first five paragraphs of an article and asked students to do the same for the rest of the article.

Awaken Students' Curiosity About Upcoming Readings

Students' reading comprehension increases if they are already engaged with the problem that a reading addresses or are otherwise interested in the subject matter. The trick is to arouse students' interest in a text before they read it so that they are already participating in the conversation that the text belongs to. For example, prior to assigning Plato's *Crito,* the teacher could present the following problem:

In the *Crito,* Socrates has been sentenced to death and waits for his execution. The state, perhaps embarrassed by its decision to kill Socrates, has made it easy for him to escape from prison. In this dialogue, Socrates's friend Crito urges Socrates to escape and go into exile. Socrates argues that he should stay in prison and accept execution. Try to predict the arguments that both Crito and Socrates will make. Give at least three good reasons for escaping and three good reasons for staying and dying.

Having role-played the dialogue in advance (as either an at-home thinking piece or an in-class group task), students will be interested in comparing Plato's actual arguments to the ones they predicted.

Show That All Texts Reflect the Author's Frame of Reference

Students often become more interested in scholarly works, even textbooks, when they realize that all authors necessarily distort their subjects, thereby opening up their work to interrogation and analysis. No textbook or scholarly work can give readers the "whole truth" about subject X, only the author's version of the truth—a version necessarily framed by the author's own selectivity, emphasis, and writing style. Teachers can awaken interest in these issues by comparing the coverage of subject X from competing textbooks or other scholarly works and by having students explore the differences between them. An excellent example of this strategy is provided by Swartz (1987), who contrasts two anthropological analyses of the role of women in the !Kung society in the African Kalahari. One anthropologist implies that !Kung women live a life of second-class drudgery, whereas the second anthropologist, observing the same data, casts !Kung women as "a self-contained people with a high sense of self-esteem" (p. 114). Class discussion of the differences in two accounts of the same subject helps students better understand the concepts of point of view, frame of reference, and authorial bias. Once students realize that all texts filter reality by privileging some aspects of X while censoring others, they tend to read more actively, more alert to point of view and to the persuasive power (and distortion) of metaphor, style, and narrative arrangement.

Show Students the Importance of Knowing Cultural Codes

Many students do not realize that a passage from a text can be baffling not because the reader is unskilled but because he or she does not know its cultural codes. An author assumes that readers have a certain background knowledge. If that knowledge is absent, the reader can quickly get lost.

To illustrate the importance of cultural codes to students, I have developed the following strategy. I project several cartoons on a screen and ask why persons new to U.S. culture might not see what's funny. One of my favorites is an old *Far Side* cartoon showing a group of partying dogs hoisting drinks inside a doghouse. One dog is speaking to another; the caption says, "Oh, hey! Fantastic party, Tricksy! Fantastic! . . . Say, do you mind telling me which way to the yard?" Understanding this cartoon requires a surprising amount of cultural knowledge:

That dogs in middle-class America frequently live in doghouses (and often have names like "Tricksy")

That at middle-class parties, people stand around holding drinks

That bathrooms are often hard to find in middle-class homes, so guests have to ask the host discreetly where they are located

That middle-class homes have backyards

That dogs relieve themselves in the yard

Written texts require similar kinds of background knowledge. After discussing a few cartoons, I distribute a brief news article from the Cold War era, requiring reconstruction of cultural context. The article refers to NATO, to Reagan and Gorbachev, to ballistic and antiballistic missiles, to neo-isolationism, and to the way that America's nuclear arms threw the Marxist-Leninist engine of history off its tracks. Few of my students know what NATO is, understand the difference between ballistic and guided missiles, or appreciate the historical events and American attitudes that are packed into the term *neo-isolationism*. Fewer still can explain the "engine of history" metaphor. A discussion of this article quickly clarifies for students how knowledge of cultural codes facilitates comprehension of a reading. One way to help students reconstruct a text's cultural codes is to create reading guides, as described later in this chapter.

Help Students See That All Texts Are Trying to Change Their View

This strategy relates closely to the preceding one. Students tend to see texts as conveyers of inert information rather than as rhetorically purposeful messages aimed at effecting some change in the reader's view of the subject. If students become more aware that texts are trying to change their views in some way, they can interrogate texts more actively, trying to decide what to accept and what to doubt. A useful exercise to help students appreciate the rhetorical nature of a text is to ask them to freewrite responses to the following trigger questions:

1. Before I read this text, the author assumed that I believed . . . [fill in].

2. After I finished reading this text, the author wanted me to believe . . . [fill in].

3. The author was/was not successful in changing my view. How so? Why or why not?

Create "Reading Guides"

Teachers can assist students by preparing "reading guides" that steer them through particularly difficult readings. Typically, these guides define key terms with special disciplinary meanings, fill in needed cultural knowledge, explain the rhetorical context of the reading, illuminate the rhetorical purpose of genre conventions, and ask critical questions for students to consider as they progress through the text. By requiring students to write their responses to several of the guide questions, teachers can use exploratory writing to encourage reflection. Exhibit 9.2 shows a reading guide I

EXHIBIT 9.2

Reading Guide for a Scientific Article for a First-Year Seminar on Nature/Nurture Controversy in Gender Identity

Reading Guide

Rebecca Knickmeyer, Simon Baron-Cohen, Peter Raggatt, and Kevin Taylor. "Foetal Testosterone, Social Relationships, and Restricted Interests in Children." *Journal of Child Psychology and Psychiatry*, 2005, *46*(2), 198–210.

 Background: This article can't be fully understood by nonspecialists (you and me) because we aren't its intended audience. The authors are writing for clinical biochemists and experimental psychologists who do their research on gendered behaviors. As nonexpert readers, we can't understand either the biochemistry or the complex methods of statistical analysis. However, we can understand the main gist of their research. This short reading guide will help you understand the article's big picture and offer strategies for reading any complex scientific article.

1. Look at the six-column reference list at the end. These articles have been closely read by the researchers and constitute the current state of knowledge that the researchers want to add to. Much of the introduction reviews the important ideas of these articles, identifying what is currently known and still unknown. Each of the articles in this huge list is explicitly mentioned in the article.

2. Read the title of the article and the abstract. The title lets us know that this article attempts to measure the effect of fetal testosterone on two variables: social relationships and restricted interests in children. The abstract gives you a big picture overview of the whole article.

3. Read the introduction—pages 198–200—trying to understand the basic gist of each paragraph. This introduction reviews the previous research literature (hence all the bibliographic references in parentheses) and explains the general theory behind their research. *Question 1: If you could read one of the research studies reviewed in the introduction, which would it be and why?*

4. Basically, the researchers are going to correlate the amount of fetal testosterone in each mother's amniotic fluid (taken when the child was in utero) with each mother's answers for her child on the Children's Communication Checklist (CCC) when the child was four years old. Read carefully the research hypothesis at the top of page 201, left column (last sentence in introduction). *Question 2: Restate the hypothesis in ordinary rather than scientific language. Make the hypothesis understandable to your kid brother.*

5. Under METHODS (starting on page 201) read the first two sections: *participants* and *Outcome Variable: the Children's Communication Checklist*. Look carefully at Table 1, which gives sample items from the Children's Communication Checklist. The range indicates the possible highest and lowest scores for each part of the checklist. The impairment column shows the score below which the child shows an abnormal or "impaired" score. The sample items column gives examples of questions on the CCC for each part. *Question 3: Based on these sample items, what do you think is meant by "restricted interests"? How are restricted interests related to autism?*

6. Skim the rest of METHODS and all of RESULTS. Focus only on what you can understand; don't worry about what you don't understand. These sections are aimed at insiders with expert knowledge of experimental design and statistical methods. Note: I probably can't understand any more than you can and perhaps less than some of you majoring in science.

7. Read carefully the DISCUSSION section on pages 205–206 to see the scientists' discussion of whether their data supported their initial hypotheses. *Question 4: Based on this study, how would a baby exposed to high levels of fetal testosterone differ in behavior from a baby exposed to lower levels of testosterone, regardless of whether the baby was male or female? In general, how did boys differ from girls with regard to social relationships and restricted interests?*

8. Here are two statements from the DISCUSSION section:

   - "[Our research] indicates that in both boys and girls, higher fT levels are associated with poorer quality of social relationships" (205).

   - "[Our research] indicates that in both boys and girls, higher fT levels are associated with more restricted interests" (205).

   For each of these results, draw a line graph showing the indicated relationship. (You don't need to plot the exact coordinates, just the general shape of the curve.) Label the axes for clarity to an outside reader and then create a title for your graph that explains what the graph shows. Before drawing your graph, consider these questions:

   - What goes on the x axis? What is the unit of measurement?

   - What goes on the y axis? What is the unit of measurement?

prepared for my first-year seminar on the nature/nurture controversy in gender identity. I wanted students to read a complete scientific paper bearing on the biology/culture question. Additionally, I wanted to assure students that it was okay to understand only, say, 20 percent of the article and to recognize why the other 80 percent was accessible only to experts.

Teach Students to Play the "Believing and Doubting Game"

The "believing and doubting game" (Elbow, 1973, 1986) teaches students the reader's double role of being simultaneously open to texts and skeptical of them. When playing the believing game, students try to listen empathically by walking in the author's shoes, mentally joining the author's culture, seeing the world through the author's eyes. By stretching students toward new ways of seeing, the believing game helps students overcome their natural resistance to ideas and views different from their own. In contrast, the doubting game asks readers to play devil's advocate, raising objections to the writer's argument, looking for its weaknesses, refusing to be taken in by the text's rhetorical force. To help students practice believing and doubting, the instructor can design exploratory writing tasks, in-class debates, or small group tasks that can encourage students to see both strengths and weaknesses in any author's stance.

Elbow's believing and doubting game is similar to what Paul (1987) calls "dialogical thinking" or "strong sense critical thinking." For Paul, the crucial habit that strong sense critical thinkers must develop is the active disposition to seek out views different from their own: "If we do not have informed proponents of opposing points of view available, we have to reconstruct the arguments ourselves. We must enter into the opposing points of view on our own and frame the dialogical exchange ourselves" (p. 129). Thus, according to Paul, students must be taught "to argue for and against each and every important point of view and each basic belief or conclusion that they are to take seriously" (p. 140). (For an application of methodological belief and doubt to a political science course, see Freie, 1987; see also "Pro and Con Grid" in Angelo and Cross, 1993, pp. 168–171.)

To apply this strategy to the teaching of reading, instructors need to emphasize that scholarly articles and other assigned readings are voices in a conversation that students need to join. For students, writing in the margins or otherwise responding to texts will begin to make sense when they see their responsibility to imagine and consider alternative points of view and thus to evaluate an author's thesis, reasons, and evidence.

Developing Assignments That Require Students to Interact with Texts

To conclude this chapter, let's consider ways that teachers can use informal or formal writing assignments to help students become more active and thoughtful readers. When assigned as homework, brief write-to-learn tasks can have a powerful effect on the quality of students' reading. Some of the following strategies are cross-referenced in Chapter Seven as widely used methods of assigning exploratory writing.

Marginal Notes Approach

Many teachers report success simply from forbidding students the use of underlining or yellow highlighters. Instead, they insist on copious marginal notations on the borders of the text itself. (If students plan to resell their texts or are reading library books, they can take marginal notes on separate pages keyed to the book page.) "Every time you feel the urge to highlight or underline something," the teacher can advise, "write out in the margins why you wanted to underline it. Why is that passage important? Is it a major new point in the argument? A significant piece of support? A summary of the opposition? A particularly strong or particularly weak point?" The teacher can then exhort the students: "Use the margins to summarize the text, ask questions, give assent, protest vehemently—don't just color the pages." The goal here is to get students to carry on lively dialogue with the author in the margins. The instructor can occasionally start class discussions by asking a student to read his or her marginal notations next to a certain passage.

Reading Logs

Like an open-ended journal, a reading log requires that students write regularly about what they are reading but gives them freedom in choosing what to say. Students can summarize the text, connect it to personal experience, argue with it, imitate it, analyze it, or evaluate it. Often teachers are interested in how a reading affects students on the personal level. They therefore encourage personal response in the reading log. Readers can describe their emotional, intellectual, or philosophical responses to the text and call into consciousness the hidden memories and associations the text triggers. The reader answers questions such as "What does this text mean to me?" and "What effect does this text have on my values, my beliefs, my way of looking at the world?" You can ask students to make these responses regularly in their reading log or occasionally in a more formal reflection paper.

Exploratory Writing Prompted by Teacher-Posed Questions

Another effective technique is to devise critical thinking questions that require students to respond thoughtfully to a text and then to build these into the course as part of a reading guide or a guided journal. (The guided journal is explained in Chapter Seven, pages 126–129 and 134–135.) By providing questions for students to respond to, you can get students to focus on points in the readings you find particularly important. You can often begin class discussions by having one or two students read their responses to one of your questions. Here is an example of a "thinking piece" task I posed in my first-year seminar on nature/nurture controversy in gender identity. (This was the first homework task of the seminar.)

Thinking Piece #1: Read Lawrence Summers' speech addressing the question of why there aren't more female professors in math, science, and engineering at Harvard. Summarize Summers' three possible explanations for the underrepresentation of women; then explore your reactions to Summers' speech based on your own critical thinking and experiences. [This should be a one-page, single-spaced thinking piece as explained in the syllabus.]

Summary Writing Approach

If one prefers a low-stakes microtheme approach, as opposed to exploratory writing, a powerful way to promote reading skills is to ask students to write a summary of an assigned article (Bean, Drenk, and Lee, 1986; Bean, 1986). An assigned summary can be as short as one sentence or as long as a page; the typical length is 150–250 words. Summary writing requires that the reader separate main ideas from supporting details, thereby providing practice at finding the hierarchical structure of an article. Moreover, it requires that readers suspend their own egocentrism, leaving out their own ideas in order to listen carefully to the author. An added bonus for the teacher is that summaries—submitted as microthemes—are easy to grade quickly. (For an example of how an economics professor uses a series of summary assignments to teach argumentation in economics, see Cohen and Spencer, 1993. See also the discussion of summary writing in Chapter Eight, page 157.)

Summary/Response or Double-Entry Notebooks

A summary/response notebook (see also "double-entry notebooks" in Chapter Seven, page 135) is a slightly more structured version of a reading log. It requires students to make two opposing responses to a text: first to represent the text to themselves in their own words and then to respond to it. The following instructions are typical:

For each of the readings marked with an asterisk on the syllabus, you will write at least two pages in your notebooks. The first page will be a restatement of the text's argument in your own words. You can write a summary, make an outline, draw a flowchart or a diagram of the reading, or simply take careful notes. The purpose of this page is to help you understand as fully as possible the structure and details of the author's argument. This page should help you recall the article in some detail several weeks later. Your next page is to be your own personal reflections on or reactions to the article. Analyze it, illustrate it through your own experience, refute it, get mad at it, question it, believe it, doubt it, go beyond it. I will skim your notebooks looking for evidence of serious effort and engaged thought.

Imagined Interviews with the Author

A change-of-pace strategy is to ask students to write dialogues in which they interview the author or otherwise engage the author in arguments. (My inspiration for this strategy is Francoz, 1979.) The student asks the author tough questions and then has to role-play the author in answering the questions, forcing the student to adopt the author's values, beliefs, and world view. The student can also be urged to play devil's advocate by arguing against the author's position. Students generally enjoy the creativity afforded by this assignment, as well as the mind-stretching task of role-playing different views. Some teachers ask groups to conduct mock panel discussions in which one group member plays the author of the article and others play people with different views.

Graphic Organizers

For some students, representing a text visually is more powerful than representing it through marginal notations, traditional outlining, or even summary writing. Graphic organizers can take the form of flowcharts, concept maps, tree diagrams, sketches, or drawings. Roberts and Roberts (2008) give their students choices in how they want to represent their deep reading of a text (on a given day students might submit a summary, a page of notes, or even a song) but they particularly recommend graphic organizers. Exhibit 9.3 shows how one of my students in a Renaissance drama course represented an article on Jonson's *Volpone* (Marchitell, 1991).

Writing "Translations"

A final strategy is to ask students to "translate" a difficult passage into their own words (Gottschalk, 1984). According to Gottschalk, "Creating the translation can help the reader see why a passage is important, or

EXHIBIT 9.3

Student's Graphic Organizer for "Desire and Domination in *Volpone*"

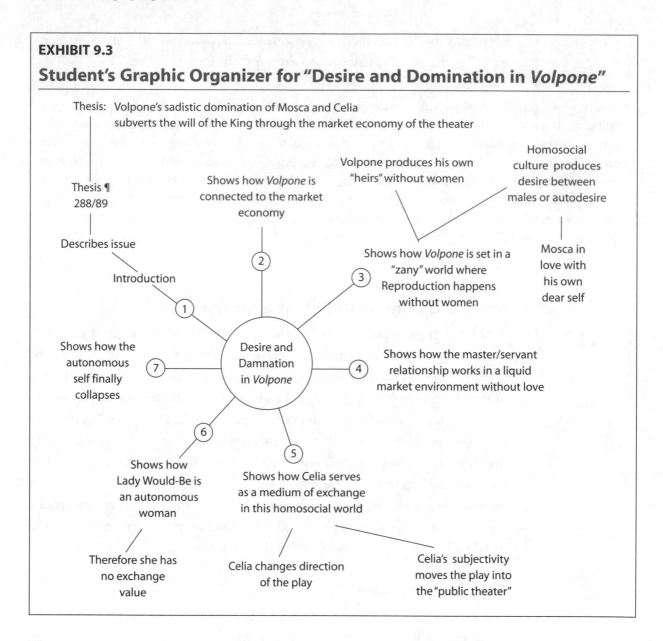

troublesome, and come to terms with its difficulties or significance" (p. 401). This is a particularly useful way for students to practice deciphering syntactically complex prose. The act of close paraphrasing also focuses students' attention on precise meanings of words.

Conclusion: Strategies Teachers Can Use to Help Students Become Better Readers

Exhibit 9.4 summarizes teaching strategies that address the reading problems discussed in this chapter.

EXHIBIT 9.4

Teaching Strategies

Students' Problem	Helping Strategy
Poor reading process	Show students your own reading process. Require marginal notes. Give tests on readings that you don't cover in class. Assign summary writing. Require students to freewrite in response to critical thinking problems about texts (reading logs, summary/response notebooks).
Failure to reconstruct arguments as they read	Assign summary writing. Have students make outlines, concept maps, flowcharts, or other diagrams of articles. Help students write "gist statements" in margins summarizing main points as reading progresses. Go through a sample text with students, writing "what it says" and "what it does" statements for each paragraph.
Failure to assimilate the unfamiliar; resistance to uncomfortable or disorienting views	Explain this phenomenon to students so that they can watch out for it; point out instances in class when students resist an unfamiliar or uncomfortable idea; draw analogies to other times when students have had to assimilate unfamiliar views. In lectures or discussions, draw contrasts between ordinary ways of looking at the subject and the author's surprising way. Emphasize the "believing" side of Elbow's "believing and doubting game."
Limited understanding of rhetorical context	Create reading guides that include information about the author and the rhetorical context of the reading. Through lectures or reading guides, set the stage for readings, especially primary materials. Train students to ask these questions: Who is this author? Who is the intended audience? What occasion prompted this writing? What is the author's purpose?
Failure to interact with the text	Use any of the response strategies recommended in this chapter—reading logs, summary/response notebooks, guided journals, marginal notations, reading guides.
Unfamiliarity with cultural codes	Create reading guides explaining cultural codes, allusions, historical events, and so forth. Show students the function of cultural codes by discussing the background knowledge needed to understand cartoons or jokes.
Unfamiliar vocabulary	Urge students to acquire the habit of using the dictionary. Create reading guides defining technical terms or words used in unusual ways.

(Continued)

Students' Problem	Helping Strategy
Difficulty with complex syntax	Have faith that practice helps. Refer students who have trouble decoding texts (perhaps they have a learning or reading disability) to a learning assistance center. Have students "translate" complex passages into their own words; also have students practice rewriting particularly long sentences into several shorter ones.
Failure to adapt to different kinds of discourse, genres, and purposes	Explain your own reading process: when you skim, when you read carefully, when you study a text in detail, and so forth. Explain how your own reading process varies when you encounter different genres of text: how to read a textbook versus a primary source, how to read a scientific paper, how to read a poem, and so forth.

10

Using Small Groups to Coach Thinking and Teach Disciplinary Argument

his chapter proposes that one of the best ways to coach critical thinking—and to promote the kind of productive talk that leads to thoughtful and elaborated writing—is a goal-directed use of small groups. Because the small group tasks recommended here usually require groups to produce a piece of writing—a brainstormed list, a thesis statement, a paragraph to be read aloud, an outline for an argument—these collaborative activities teach students how to make disciplinary arguments.

The suggestions in this chapter represent only one of many ways to use small groups in the classroom. MacGregor (1990) has identified at least six different root systems of the many intertwining vines that compose the collaborative learning movement: the experiential learning practices of Dewey, Piaget, and Vygotsky; the "cooperative learning" movement associated with David Johnson and Roger Johnson; the learning community movement, in which interdisciplinary teams of teachers become colearners with students in pursuing a many-faceted, multidisciplinary problem; the various disciplinary approaches to small groups, such as Kenneth Bruffee's work in rhetoric and composition or Uri Treisman's work with study groups in mathematics; and such problem-centered approaches as Harvard's case method. In addition to MacGregor's list, we should also add problem-based learning, often associated with the University of Delaware (Duch, Gron, and Allen, 2001).

The fruit from all these intertwining vines has been harvested by Barkley, Cross, and Major in their important synthesis *Collaborative Learning Techniques: A Handbook for College Faculty* (2005). This compendium of collaborative learning techniques (which they call CoLTs) provides a wealth of strategies for using small groups, ranging from the quick classroom use of unstructured "buzz groups" to elaborately planned use of structured teams whose members work cooperatively over multiple class sessions in purposeful stages designed by the instructor (see, for example, their discussion of "jigsaw," pp. 156–162).

The approach to collaborative learning taken in this chapter focuses on one of these many ways of using small groups—a way that I have found is particularly adept at integrating critical thinking, talking, and writing to help students learn to use the lens of a given discipline to ask questions and produce arguments. This approach integrates two pedagogies that have long influenced my own teaching: George Hillocks's "environmental mode" of teaching (1986, pp. 113–131) and Kenneth Bruffee's methods of collaborative learning using "consensus groups" (1983, 1984, 1993). Teachers who already use small groups undoubtedly will have developed methods and approaches somewhat different from those I describe here, but they may find this approach a useful addition to their repertoire. Other teachers may not have tried small groups, preferring to use class time for lecturing, leading whole-class discussions, or conducting other activities that involve the whole class rather than autonomous small groups. My goal in this chapter is to suggest small groups as another strategy for these teachers to consider.

The method I describe here might best be characterized as a goal-oriented use of small groups, aimed at giving students supervised practice in disciplinary thinking under the tutelage of the teacher as coach. This approach differs, for example, from what Barkley, Cross, and Major call "buzz groups," in which students exchange ideas in small groups without having to achieve consensus or give formal reports, or what Brookfield and Preskill (2005) call "circular response," in which each speaker begins by summarizing the views of a previous speaker in order to promote attentive listening and mutual respect. The method I describe has the specific goal of teaching question-asking and argument. It has a consistent and recurring rhythm:

1. The teacher presents a disciplinary problem requiring critical thinking (resulting in a claim with argument rather than a "right answer").

2. Students work together in small groups to reach consensus on a "best solution" to the problem.

3. In a plenary session, group recorders present their group's solutions and arguments.

4. As the reports unfold, the teacher coaches students' performance by pointing out strengths and weaknesses in the arguments, showing how the alternative claims emerging from groups often parallel on-going disciplinary debates, and otherwise offering constructive critiques.

5. At the end, the teacher may also explain how this problem would be (or has been) approached by experts.

The Advantages of a Goal-Oriented Use of Small Groups

According to Bruffee (1993), the pedagogical effectiveness of the consensus-group method was demonstrated in the late 1950s by Abercrombie's research in educating medical students at University Hospital in London. Abercrombie (1960) found that her students learned diagnostic skills more powerfully if they were placed in independent groups to address a diagnostic problem. The use of small groups did not lead simply to a pooling of knowledge, as if each student held one piece of the solution. Rather, collaborative learning promoted argumentation and consensus building: each student had to support a hypothesis with reasons and evidence in an attempt to sway the others. The improved thinking grew out of the practice of formulating hypotheses, arguing for their adequacy, and seeking a reasoned consensus that all group members could support.

The methods used by Abercrombie in medical training can be extended to classrooms in any discipline. By presenting small groups with critical thinking problems to wrestle with, teachers can create an environment of productive talk that leads to greatly enriched inquiry, analysis, and argument. The goal of each task is not to have small groups come up with the "right answer" but to come up with reasonable, supported answers that they will be asked to defend later in front of the whole class. On occasion, these answers will surprise the teacher with their sophistication and cogency; in my own field of literature, I often find that my view of a novel or a poem has been reshaped by the arguments of my students. Truly, the purported expert can become a colearner in such a setting.

There are several advantages of this goal-directed way of using small groups. First, this approach is particularly effective at helping students learn specific thinking strategies. Hillocks (1986) and Hillocks, Kahn, and Johannessen (1983) have shown that having students work independently in small groups on purposefully designed and sequenced tasks (what these researchers call the "environmental mode" of teaching) produces significantly higher levels of thinking—as measured by the degree of precision and elaboration in written arguments—than the lecture method, whole-class discussion methods, or nondirective group work.

A second advantage is that the method described here can be adapted to large lecture classes, even in lecture halls where students have to turn around in their seats to form groups. Whereas it is nearly impossible to lead a whole-class discussion in a room of two hundred students, it is entirely possible in a large class to give students a critical thinking task, have students work with their neighbors for ten minutes or so, and then ask representative groups to present and justify their solutions. I have personally made extensive use of small groups in classes of seventy-five students (students sat in five-person groups in a large open room), and I have observed group work conducted in large lecture halls. Thus this use of small groups can bring a powerful dimension of critical thinking and active learning to a lecture class. If a lecture transmits understanding of disciplinary subject matter, goal-oriented small groups can help students practice using this subject matter on problems requiring argument. Lectures and small groups together can help students learn both the conceptual and procedural knowledge of the discipline—both the discipline's subject matter knowledge and the discipline's ways of conducting inquiry and making arguments. (For more on using active learning methods in lecture settings, see Davis, 2009, and Bligh, 2000, pp. 251–290.)

Sequence of Activities for Using Small Groups During a Class Period

To work a small group activity smoothly into a class period, teachers might consider the following approach, which combines a small group session with a subsequent plenary session.

Designing the Task

A good small group task, like a good writing assignment, needs to be carefully designed. Good tasks present open-ended critical thinking problems that require "best solutions" justified with supporting arguments. Typical tasks ask students to reach consensus on a solution to a disciplinary problem; when consensus is impossible, students can also "agree to disagree," in which case final group reports will include majority and minority views with clarifying explanations of the causes of disagreement.

Many disciplinary problems can be used interchangeably either as small group tasks or as formal or informal writing assignments (for a heuristic for designing tasks, see Chapter Eight). Small group tasks can also be used in conjunction with a formal writing assignment to help students brainstorm ideas for an upcoming essay, discover and rehearse arguments, or critique rough drafts. In these cases, the small group tasks promote exploration of ideas needed for the essay. In all cases, a good small group task promotes controversy, has a product, can be accomplished in the specified time limit, and is directed toward a learning goal for the course. Further discussion of the design of small group tasks appears later in this chapter.

Forming Groups

There are many ways to form groups and much debate about the various benefits of permanent versus ad hoc groups, randomly assigned versus preplanned groups, homogenous versus heterogeneous groups, and so forth. My default method is to set up randomly assigned five-person groups, which I determine using a shuffled deck of 3x5 cards (the size of the deck determined by the size of the class); each card has a group number with one card in each group labeled "recorder." After I pass out the cards, I ask the "ones" to go to one part of the room, the "twos" to another part, and so on. In lecture settings, an alternative is having students in odd-numbered rows turn around to speak with classmates in even-numbered rows, forming small groups as best they can and choosing their own recorder.

In each group, the recorder's job is to take notes and to report the group's consensus solution at the plenary session. Therefore the recorder has to watch the clock and keep the group on task, directing the discussion toward the ideas he or she will need to make a good report. In essence, the recorder is both leader and secretary. (See the further discussion of forming groups and assigning roles later in this chapter.)

Assigning the Task

If possible, the task should be given to students in a handout or on a PowerPoint slide. The task should specify the question or problem to be addressed, the required group product, and the time limit. Times specified can be anywhere from a few minutes to a full class hour; however, if teachers want to integrate a complete cycle of activities into a fifty-minute class, they typically limit the small group activity to ten to fifteen minutes, thereby allowing time for group reporting and critiquing in a plenary session. To keep conversations focused and on task, groups should always be responsible for creating a product—usually a written product such as a thesis statement, list of pros and cons, idea map, outline of an argument, a drawing, a graph, or a group-composed paragraph. The point here is that conversations are generally more focused, elaborated, and sustained when each group has to "go public" with a product. For example, consider the differences between the following less effective and more effective tasks:

Less Effective

As a group, discuss your reaction to Plato's *Crito*.

More Effective

As a group, propose a list of three significant questions you would like to have the teacher address or the class discuss regarding Plato's *Crito*. Your initial list (which you will hand in to the instructor) should include at least six questions. Then reach consensus on what you consider your three best questions. Your recorder will write these questions on the board and will explain to the class why your group considers them pertinent, interesting, and significant. Time: 15 minutes.

Teachers might consider collecting and critiquing the written products during the first weeks of class as a way of signaling the importance they attach to group work.

Completing the Task

Once students understand the task, the teacher lets the students work on the problem independently. Some teachers believe it is best to leave the room entirely and not to return until it is time for the plenary session. This strategy signals to students their autonomy from the instructor and their responsibility for forming their own knowledge communities. Other teachers like to wander from group to group as a resource person or to eavesdrop from a corner of the room. What often surprises teachers is the amount of noise generated by the groups. My own experience suggests that despite the noise, it is best to keep all groups in the classroom rather than to allow some to go into the hall or into separate rooms. The loud hum in the room actually stimulates participation and draws groups closer together in tight circles.

Group Reporting

When the allotted time is up, recorders from each group report their group's solution to the class as a whole. (In large classes, the teacher usually asks only a representative sample of groups to report.) Although teachers vary in how they ask students to report, what works best for me is to insist on formal reports from groups: the recorder has to stand and present the group's consensus in an impromptu speech, thus practicing the kind of speaking skills that will be demanded on the job after college. The reports are not supposed to be "summaries of what the group talked about"—like minutes of a meeting—but actual persuasive presentations of the group's required product. (If group cannot reach consensus, I allow minority reports.) By putting pressure on recorders to make effective public speeches, I know the recorders will put pressure on groups to stay on task.

Plenary Discussion and Critiquing of Group Reports

As groups report, the teacher is challenged by the need to respond productively to group solutions, which are often confounding in their assortment of strong and weak ideas. Disagreement among the groups provides a wonderful occasion to stimulate further whole-class discussion of the problem. The instructor must help the class synthesize group reports by pointing out strengths and weaknesses while often praising and legitimizing views that are different from his or her own. The students are especially eager to hear the teacher's solution to the collaborative task. In giving it, the teacher not only represents the expert views of the disciplinary community (or one of the expert views) but becomes a powerful role model for the kind of arguing strategies that the discipline uses and values. But the teacher is now more vulnerable, more at risk, than in a lecture setting. After working independently, students are more confident in their own views. They become less passive, more active in raising questions, more challenging as audiences. For me, the class discussions that follow small group work are among the most stimulating, challenging, and satisfying of all my teaching experiences.

Relating the Task to the Learning Sequence

The best small group tasks are clearly related to some ongoing purpose that the teacher should make plain to students. Perhaps the task prepares students for a lecture that follows or focuses attention on key points or controversies in material just covered. Or perhaps the task requires students to sum up and synthesize readings and lectures or to become engaged in a new problem about to be explored in the course. Frequently, also, the task may be integrated with an upcoming formal writing assignment and allows students to talk through their ideas prior to writing. Because many students expect teachers to lecture, they will better accept collaborative work as "serious learning" if the teacher explains how the task relates to course goals. (For an extended example of a history teacher who successfully integrates small group tasks, writing assignments, and lectures into a semester-long course design, see "Arguing and Debating: Breihan's History Course" in Walvoord and McCarthy, 1990.)

Suggestions for Designing Productive Small Group Tasks

In my own approach to collaborative learning, I like to identify both a disciplinary content goal and a thinking or arguing goal for each task. Thus, for the *Crito* task described earlier, the teacher's content goal is to stimulate careful reading of *Crito*, to engage students in independent discussion of the text, and to see if students raise the same kinds of questions that have intrigued generations of commentators. (They often do.) The thinking skills goal is to increase students' ability to pose self-sponsored questions about a text and to determine what makes some questions better than others.

I find that in designing collaborative tasks, I rely extensively on the following strategies.

The Thesis-Proposing Strategy

In this approach, the instructor gives students a disciplinary problem framed as an open-ended question to which students must propose and justify a "best solution" answer. To keep students on task, I often ask groups to summarize their consensus solution in a one-sentence "thesis statement," which the recorder writes on a whiteboard, places on newsprint, or projects on a screen. Recorders then present justifying arguments supporting the thesis when they make their reports. If groups cannot reach consensus, I ask for a majority thesis and at least one minority thesis.

According to Fullinwider, three theories are frequently used to defend preferential hiring for both African Americans and women: compensatory justice, social utility, and distributive justice. Using one or more of these theories, address this question: To what extent is the legislature's proposed veterans preference law just? (Your thesis should summarize your argument.)

• • •

We have examined four alternative approaches to the design of a digital data-recording device for Company X's portable heart defibrillator. Which solution should be chosen and why?

• • •

In the text we've just read, the author quotes Peter Berger, an important American sociologist, to the effect that we are in "bondage" to society. Elsewhere that same author says, "In sum, society is the wall of our imprisonment in history." Your friend, I. M. Punker, rubs his hand through his orange hair, touches his nose ring, and says, "Nonsense. I am my own person, free to do whatever I want. I have already broken through the bondage of society." Which of these two views of human freedom does your group most agree with—Berger's or Punker's? Defend your choice with an argument that you must summarize in a thesis statement.

• • •

In what way, if any, is Jackson Pollock's *Autumn Rhythm* different from the results of a monkey throwing paint at a canvas? Your thesis should include one or more "because clauses" specifying your supporting reasons.

The Template Strategy

Using this strategy, the instructor gives students a template or mapping frame that forecasts the shape of a short essay but not the content. Students have to create content-specific point sentences to head each forecasted section and develop a supporting argument for each one. Often the instructor can include in the task a blank tree diagram or an outline indicating the slots that students' ideas must fit. This task requires not only that students generate ideas but also that they place these ideas within a clear structure. (For further examples of template questions, see Chapter Six, pages 141–142 and Chapter Eight, page 155.)

Based on the data about the "Acme Brewing Company" that you studied last night, what do you now think are the causes for this company's precipitous loss of market share? Place your solution into a frame that begins with the following sentence: "There are X [indicate a number] main causes for Acme's loss of market share. First, [state the cause and support it] ... Second, ... Third, ..." Continue with as many causes as your group determines.

· · ·

[Instructor provides a table giving chronological data about housing starts.] Your task is to create a graph telling the housing start story and then to write a paragraph that incorporates your graph. Begin your paragraph with this sentence: "The collapse of the economy in 2009 can be shown by the precipitous drop in housing starts beginning in...." Your paragraph must include a graph that tells the housing-start story. Be sure to label the graph properly, give it a figure number, and reference it in your text. Your paragraph must tell verbally the same story that the graph reveals visually.

The Question-Generating Strategy

This strategy is particularly effective for teaching the art of question asking in a discipline. After instruction in the kinds of questions asked by a particular discipline, the teacher breaks students into groups and has them brainstorm possible questions related to topics that he or she provides. After this phase, groups must then refine their lists into the two or three best questions and explain why each question is a particularly good one. (This is the strategy used in the earlier *Crito* example.)

Carefully observe this [poem, graph, statistical table, painting, advertisement]. What aspects of it puzzle you or intrigue you? As a group, pose three good questions that emerge from your observation of the item.

• • •

Now that you have studied the six levels of questions in Bloom's taxonomy, use the taxonomy to develop test questions about Chapter Six in your text. Ask at least two questions at each level of the taxonomy. Recorders should be prepared to explain why you think each question fits its respective level.

• • •

Scientists often pose research questions that have the following generic structure: "What is the effect of X on Y?" For example, "What is the effect of varying amounts of light on the growth of *Escherichia coli?*" or "What is the effect of an improved freshman advising system on students' retention rate between the freshman and sophomore years?" Using these examples as models, develop three good research questions that you could ask about each of the following topics: steroids, day-care centers, gangs, student test performance.

The Believing and Doubting Strategy

The "believing and doubting game," coined by Elbow (1973, 1986), asks students first to enter imaginatively into the possible truth of any statement, arguing in its favor (the believing game) and then to stand back from it, adopting a healthy skepticism (the doubting game). To use this strategy with small groups, the instructor gives students a controversial thesis and asks them to generate reasons and supporting arguments for and against the thesis. Angelo and Cross (1993, pp. 168–171) discuss a similar strategy using pro and con grids. (For a fuller discussion of the believing and doubting game, see Chapter Nine, page 176.)

The overriding religious view expressed in *Hamlet* is an existential atheism similar to Sartre's.

• • •

Baccalaureate engineering programs should be extended to five years.

• • •

The eighty-three-year-old stroke victim described in the case study should be informed of her daughter's diagnosis of terminal cancer.

The Evidence-Finding Strategy

The instructor's goal here is to have students use facts, figures, and other data or evidence to support a premise. In my own discipline of literature, this task often means finding textual detail from a poem, novel, or play that might be used to support an argument. In other disciplines, it might mean using primary evidence derived from library, laboratory, or field research. Such tasks teach students how experts in a field use discipline-appropriate evidence to support assertions.

Our design group recommends the choice of conventional steel bearings over air bearings for this application because the steel bearings will give comparable performance at a lower cost. Support this claim with the evidence needed to make it persuasive to both engineers and managers.

• • •

Although Hamlet claims to be putting on an antic disposition, at several places in the play he goes over the line and seems to lapse into genuine madness. What passages in the text could be used to support this assertion? How would you make the argument?

• • •

Your textbook describes typical kinds of problematic behaviors that children exhibit in kindergarten. You believe that a particularly unruly child—we'll call him Martin—would benefit emotionally from repeating kindergarten next year rather than entering first grade. Martin's parents are adamantly opposed to holding Martin back. What evidence might you use to help Martin's parents appreciate your advice on this issue? [Create your own hypothetical evidence for our hypothetical child, Martin—but make it plausible and realistic.]

Note that in working on an evidence-finding task, students often discover what teachers once struggled to learn themselves: that evidence is often selectively chosen, framed, and "interpreted." Conclusions supported by evidence can remain ambiguously open to further interpretation; a strong evidential case can often be made against the thesis as well as for it. Such ambiguity generally unsettles beginning college students, who expect the "experts" to know the right answer and who have not yet realized the extent to which arguments are not the same as proofs. (See the discussion of Perry's developmental theory in Chapter Two.) Teachers need to help students confront and endure such ambiguity, confident that doing so helps them move higher on Perry's scale of intellectual growth.

The Case Strategy

The use of small groups is particularly powerful in conjunction with cases that require analysis or decision making. Often small groups can be asked to make a decision at a key juncture in the case and to justify the decision with an argument. If the decision moment involves conflicting points of view from different stakeholders, each group can initially be assigned one of the stakeholder roles and asked to devise the best arguments it can from the assigned perspective. (For further discussion of cases, including an example, see Chapter Eight, page 159; see also Barkley, Cross, and Major, 2005, pp. 182–187, and Bligh, 2000, pp. 277–278.)

The Norming Session Strategy

This strategy, which is also discussed in Chapter Fifteen, helps students internalize the criteria by which the instructor will judge their formal essays. The instructor passes out three or four student essays from previous classes (with names removed) and lets students, in groups, rank the essays and develop arguments justifying their rankings. Later, in the plenary session, the instructor reveals his or her own rankings and initiates a general discussion of grading criteria for essays. Often teachers discover that students have erroneous notions about what teachers look for in a formal essay, particularly when they are learning the thinking processes and rhetorical conventions of new disciplines. For an excellent illustration of how a sociology professor conducts a collaborative norming session (complete with examples of student essays on the topic of ethnocentrism), see Bateman (1990, pp. 110–116). For a way to use norming sessions in a faculty development workshop, see Thaiss and Zawacki (2006, pp. 158–159).

The Peer Review Workshop Strategy

A common use of small groups in writing courses is the peer review workshop, in which students read and respond to each other's work in progress. The goal of these workshops is to use peer review to stimulate global revision of drafts to improve ideas, organization, development, and sentence structure. (Chapter Fifteen, pages 295–302, give detailed suggestions for using small groups for peer review. See also Barkley, Cross, and Major, 2005, pp. 251–255.)

The Metacognitive Reflection Strategy

Another effective use of small groups, discussed in detail by Bruffee (1993, p. 47), is to ask students to consider their own thinking and negotiating processes metacognitively. This strategy is especially useful when small groups produce solutions that strike you as off-base or just plain wrong. Our authoritarian impulse is to tell the groups that their answers are wrong and show them the right answer. Another approach, however, is to say that the class's solutions differ considerably from those of most experts in this field. A subsequent metacognitive task is to send students back into small groups to analyze the differences in reasoning processes between themselves and the experts. According to Bruffee, "The task is to examine the process of consensus making itself. How did the class arrive at its consensus? How do the students suppose that the larger community arrived at a consensus so different from their own? In what ways do those two processes differ?" (p. 47). The effect of this approach, in my experience, is to deepen students' understanding of how knowledge is created: instead of accepting (and perhaps just memorizing) the "right answer" based on the teacher's authority, students struggle to understand the principles of inquiry, analysis, and problem solving used by the experts to arrive at their views. They consider an answer not only a product but also the result of a process of disciplinary conversation.

The Group Paper Strategy

Another common practice is the group or collaborative paper in which teams of students work together to write one paper. This method is an attractive way of reducing the teacher's paper-grading load while giving students extensive practice at the kinds of group interactions common in professional life. Team writing or joint authorship is common in business and the sciences, so these disciplines are particularly well suited for group papers, but many humanities professors use the strategy also. Exhibit 10.1

EXHIBIT 10.1

Instructions for Group Project

You will be assigned to a group to argue, using empirical evidence, for or against one of the following statements:

   a. Capitalism provides fertile ground for the cultivation of virtue.

   b. Equality, justice, and a respect for rights are characteristics of the American economic system.

   c. A concern for ethics significantly undermines one's chances for success in a competitive market economy.

1. Consider material from Chapters Three and Four of your text as you begin to develop strategies for your argument. Also, be sure to define key terms in the proposition you are defending or refuting.

2. There will be no regular class on Thursday, [date]. You will have this time to use in whatever way your group judges best—for example, brainstorming, strategizing, or preliminary library research. Additional group meetings will have to be arranged by the groups themselves.

3. Each group will submit on Tuesday, [date], a formal essay presenting the best argument it can make for the position it has been assigned to argue. Who will be responsible for what tasks and how the essay will be written—for example, who will be responsible for its typing—are matters to be decided by the group.

4. Supporting arguments and evidence in the essays must be adequately and properly documented by means of footnotes or endnotes. Each essay must have a substantial bibliography—at least three good entries for each group member.

5. Each essay must run to at least five pages. The instructor is more interested in the quality of arguments than in the quantity of information.

6. The instructor will evaluate each group essay, and each person will evaluate the contribution of his or her group's members to the group effort. Individual grades will be based on both evaluations. (The instructor has each student fill out an evaluation sheet ranking the contributions each group member made to the group. The instructor then determines a grade for each individual, using a formula based on the group grade for the paper and the individual rankings provided by the groups.)

is a group assignment for a course in business ethics, from philosophy professor Kenneth Stikkers.

For further examples of collaborative writing assignments, including a sample peer evaluation sheet, see Lunsford and Ede (1990, pp. 251–258). Many other ideas for assigning and grading group projects—including strategies for discouraging freeloaders—can be found on the Web (search for "group writing" or "collaborative writing").

Making Small Groups Work

The substantial body of research on small group interaction and strategies for team building is too vast to be summarized here, but I can provide a few tips that may prove helpful in making small groups work.

What Is the Best Size for Groups?

Bruffee's review (1993, p. 32) of the research on small group dynamics indicates that the best size for classroom consensus groups is five students; six work almost as well. Groups larger than six are unwieldy and dilute the experience for participants. Groups of four tend to divide into pairs, and groups of three tend toward a pair and an outsider. In contrast to in-class consensus groups, long-range working groups (collaborating, say, to write a research report together) seem to function best when they are smaller—groups of three seem optimum. Smaller groups also work better for peer review sessions, in which dyads are often appropriate.

Should You Form Groups at Random or According to Some Distributive Scheme?

When forming permanent or semipermanent groups, some teachers like to ensure diversity—different learning styles, different aptitude or skill levels, different majors, different backgrounds, and so forth—so they wait to form permanent groups until they have gathered the appropriate data about their students. Others find that randomly formed groups work adequately. I personally tend toward randomly formed groups, except that I try to make them heterogeneous by gender in order to avoid all-male or all-female groups. I also mix nonnative speakers in with the rest of the class so that native students can experience multicultural perspectives and nonnative speakers can get practice conversing with native speakers.

How Do You Teach Groups to Work Well Together?

Students often need some initial instruction on why you think group work is valuable, what benefits they can expect to get from group activity, and how they can best learn to work together.

One approach is to give students tips on group interaction. I start by explaining Carl Rogers's theory of empathic listening (1961), which forbids person A from expressing disagreement with person B unless person A can accurately summarize person B's argument. I give students an exercise requiring careful listening, giving them practice in walking in someone else's shoes (Bean, 1986; see also Brookfield and Preskill's "circular response" strategy [2005, pp. 79–81]).

A teacher can also help students see how differences in learning style, gender, or ethnicity can explain some of the ways that various people behave in groups. For example, extroverts on the Myers-Briggs Type Indicator (MBTI) like to think through an issue by talking out their ideas with others and are therefore apt to be vocal and engaged in group discussions (Jensen and DiTiberio, 1989). Introverts, in contrast, like to think privately about an issue before talking about it and are often uncomfortable arguing in groups, although they listen carefully and take in what everyone is saying. Teachers can thus point out that quiet people in groups are often listening more carefully and thinking more deeply than their body language might indicate. Such persons, the instructor could explain, often have much to say but will be reluctant to say it until they are ready or until the group gently encourages them to contribute. To take another example, Myers-Briggs "judgers" reach decisions rapidly and are often impatient with an indecisive group that talks a problem to death. In contrast, MBTI "perceivers" resist early closure and want to talk through all possible points of view on an issue before reaching a decision. When students understand such differences in learning styles, they become more tolerant of classmates' behaviors that would otherwise annoy them. (For further discussion of learning styles, see Chapter Four, pages 62–65.)

Other differences worth discussing involve gender and culture. The class might discuss how the socialization of males in American culture tends to reward decision making based on abstract rigorously applied principles, whereas females tend to be more concerned with the interpersonal dimension of decision making (Belenky, Clinchy, Goldberger, and Tarule, 1986; Gilligan, 1982). At the cultural level, the teacher might explain that Americans often state their desires bluntly and assertively in ways that would seem rude in many Asian cultures, where the expression of desire would be masked in roundabout conversation. (For a detailed analysis of promoting discussions across cultural and gender differences see Brookfield and Preskill, 2005, Chapters Seven and Eight.)

Another approach for helping groups work well together is to explain to students the positive value of conflict. I explain that the creative dialectic of thesis-antithesis-synthesis works well only in an atmosphere of conflicting views. By showing students how conflict generates creative thinking, the teacher can help students welcome disagreements and see how a watered-down compromise that no one really likes is less valuable than a true synthesis that seems better than either of the original views.

To promote healthy conflict, the teacher can discuss *egothink* and *clonethink*. One kind of group dysfunction (egothink) occurs when members simply express their own opinions vociferously without trying to reach a higher level of understanding. The converse phenomenon (clonethink) occurs when the group quickly agrees with the first expressed view and decides that its task is over. Effective groups need to monitor their discussions, trying to steer a middle road between egothink and clonethink.

For a more elaborated and detailed discussion of forming groups, assigning roles, and helping groups perform optimally, see Barkley, Cross, and Major (2005); Brookfield and Preskill (2005); Bruffee (1993); D. W. Johnson and F. P. Johnson (1991); D. W. Johnson and R. T. Johnson (1991); Johnson, Johnson, and Smith (1991); Slavin (1990); Spear (1988); and Morton (1988).

The Controversy over Using Small Groups: Objections and Responses

Of course, not all teachers are as enthusiastic about small group work as I am. Many teachers choose not to use small groups in the classroom for pragmatic, pedagogical, or philosophical reasons. Before closing out this chapter, I would like to respond briefly to some of the objections that my colleagues have raised against using small groups. My purpose is not to be polemical but simply to clarify some of the issues in ways that might help professors decide what role, if any, small groups might play in their own teaching. (For a comprehensive literature review of the research on small group learning, see Barkley, Cross, and Major, 2005, pp. 3–26; for a meta-analysis of the effects of small group learning on undergraduates in science, mathematics, engineering, and technology, see Springer, Stanne, and Donovan, 1999.)

Using Small Groups Takes Minimal Teacher Preparation or Skill

Perhaps the most frequent objection made by my own colleagues is that using small groups seems like a lazy way of teaching, requiring little out-of-class effort or in-class teaching skill. Compared with the time and scholarship needed to prepare a good lecture, the preparation time for small group work seems minimal: put the students in groups, ask them a question, leave the room, and *voilà*, you're an innovative teacher.

In response, I must acknowledge that small group teaching looks easy—in fact, its practitioners can sometimes be observed wandering the halls while their students are working in groups. However, as with other modes of instruction, there are both well-prepared and ill-prepared users of small groups. The well-prepared teacher is hardly lazy: the use of small groups described here is a goal-directed form of teaching that places heavy emphasis on task sequencing and overall course design. Planning a good small group task demands articulation of course goals, identification of a particular goal to be addressed in the task, design of the task, and placement of the task within a sequence of learning activities, many of which include lectures and other kinds of class discussions. Thus the preparation time for using small groups can be extensive. In-class teaching skills come into play during group reports and plenary sessions, where the teacher integrates class discussion with short lectures that present the teacher's (or the discipline's) expert perspectives on the problem the groups have just addressed. (For a discussion of how a peer observer should evaluate a course taught through collaborative learning, see Wiener, 1986.)

Small Group Work Reduces the Amount of Productive Class Time Spent with the Teacher

Another objection is that small group work reduces classroom contact between student and professor. Students pay tuition to learn from professors, not from fellow students. At one workshop I shall never forget, a professor excoriated me: "Collaborative learning is unethical. I would be abdicating my professional responsibilities if I deprived students of time spent with me as teacher, especially when they are yet untrained to work independently." Behind this objection is the obvious fear that small groups leave the blind leading the blind.

In defense of small groups, however, I would argue that small group sessions are not really time away from the teacher (who has constructed the task and is observing behavior) any more than a scrimmage game at basketball practice is time away from the coach. In any discipline, the progress of new learners ought to be measured, at least partly, by what they can do independently of the teacher when faced with a new disciplinary problem requiring critical thinking. What we aim for is their ability, when confronting a new problem, to think and write like members of our discipline. Goal-directed small group work provides supervised practice in these skills.

What distinguishes this process from the blind leading the blind is the teacher's eventual entry into the conversation. The teacher's entry starts as a conversation between the teacher and group recorders, who must present a sustained argument in response to the problem posed in the collaborative task. Soon the conversation expands to include the whole class. Disagreements between teacher and students promote genuine discourse because the students, emboldened by group support, are not simply passive note takers. The teacher must play a complex, rhetorically savvy role, representing the discipline by bringing the best reasons to bear on his or her own claims. In hearing the teacher's response, students have access not only to the teacher's thinking and knowledge but also to the way arguments are structured and elaborated in the discipline. And in arguing back, in differing from the teacher's views, students move toward becoming autonomous thinkers who can join the conversation of the discipline.

Small Group Work Devalues Eccentricity and Teaches Social Conformity

Underlying many objections to group work is the belief that group consensus stifles creativity by forcing a leveling of talents. These objectors say that group work devalues the individuality of our potential artists, rebels, eccentrics, loners, and geniuses. From a Marxist perspective, collaborative learning is simply the latest example of how the colleges serve the needs of capitalists (Myers, 1986a). Today's business world no longer wants colleges to produce free-thinking individualists; it wants genial, cooperative team players. Thus collaborative learning becomes the new fad among educators at the same time that the fiercely independent, cigar-chewing boss is being replaced by the committee and the team.

These objectors are right in asserting that some students work better individually than in groups. But unless we reject completely the goal of preparing students for careers after college, it would be unfortunate indeed if these individualistic students had no experience whatever working in groups. Given that teamwork and committee work are essential parts of professional life in America, even our most eccentric geniuses can benefit from collaborative learning, which can serve as a learning laboratory for problems students will face throughout their lives.

The other element of this objection—that collaborative learning values consensus over difference—seems grounded in a false premise equating consensus with conformity. There is a qualitative difference between conformity—an easy and quick acquiescence to the first thesis produced by a group member—and a synthesis reached through dialectic conversation. In my own experience, group work does not suppress eccentric and individualistic ideas but in fact gives them a chance to be aired and tested in group conversation. Often creative insights come from shy persons who would never venture their ideas in front of the teacher and the whole class. What I observe in small groups is a lot of genuine exploration, elaboration, and shifting of ideas. Collaborative learning, far from promoting conformity, gives students opportunities to flex their own muscles, to push against the teacher, to test their own wings.

In this regard, it therefore seems impossible to avoid the political implications of collaborative learning, which does, I think, decenter the teacher. In a collaborative classroom, the teacher's arguments compete with arguments coming from various student groups. These arguments cannot simply be dismissed by an appeal to authority. The teacher must defend his or her views through the rules of reason. As a teaching method, collaborative learning is thus powerfully symbolic in conveying to students a view of academic life as rational dialogue rather than right answers dispensed by an authority.

Conclusion: Some Additional Advantages of Small Groups

I have argued in this chapter that using small groups in the classroom can be a powerful form of active learning, giving students the opportunity to practice disciplinary inquiry and argumentation under the tutelage of a teacher as coach. Hillocks (1986) and others have demonstrated the effectiveness of the method in producing measurable advances in the quality of thinking reflected in student writing. In addition, it gives students space to pursue their own lines of thought and test them against the thinking of their professors.

In closing, I would like to mention also the social advantages of collaborative learning—advantages that should not be lightly dismissed. Small group work can promote student interaction and friendships, help students develop leadership skills, and foster diversity. Students in a collaborative learning class get to know each other well. Groups sometimes meet outside of class for coffee or meals. Often group mates friend each other on Facebook or sign up together for classes in later terms. From a less rosy perspective, small-group work can also help students work tolerantly with persons they actively dislike. Additionally, small group work gives students practice at leadership, especially when they serve as recorders for a group discussion and must make a presentation to the whole class. Finally, collaborative learning takes advantage of the rich diversity of students at many of today's colleges and universities, allowing students to bring fascinating, varied, and often troubling life experiences to bear on issues related to the course. The opportunity to stimulate conversations of consequence among such diverse groups of people and to promote friendships among them is one of the joys of teaching through small groups.

11

Bringing More Critical Thinking into Lectures and Discussions

Chapter Ten focused on the use of small groups to promote critical thinking and disciplinary argument. This chapter looks at other strategies for promoting active learning in the classroom—particularly ways of using informal or formal writing tasks to bring more critical thinking into lectures and discussions. For teachers who wish to explore more deeply both the theory and practice of active learning in different kinds of class settings, I particularly recommend the following: Davis (2009); Heppner (2007); Brookfield (2006); Brookfield and Preskill (2005); Barkley, Cross, and Major (2005); Fink (2003); Weimer (2002); Stanley and Porter (2002); Bligh (2000); Bransford, Brown, and Cocking (2000); and Bonwell and Eison (1991).

Increasing Active Learning in Lecture Classes

Lecture courses, by nature, place students in a passive role. Lectures imply a transmission theory of knowledge in which students receive the ideas and information sent by the instructor. According to Bligh (2000), a well designed and delivered lecture can be "as effective as other methods for transmitting information" (p. 3). However, he shows that lectures "are not as effective as discussion for promoting thought [or changing attitudes]" (p. 3). His analysis of the problems of straight lecturing, based on his exhaustive study of the research literature, provides a must read for any teacher who lectures.

Happily, Bligh also offers productive advice on improving student learning in lecture courses. Drawing on research into attention span, motivation, and memory, he shows teachers how to design lectures that maximize the transmission of information while promoting "deep processing" of lecture content. In the last half of his book, he explains how to supplement lectures with active learning strategies that increase critical thinking and help transform attitude and values. In general, he advises teachers to punctuate their lectures with student-centered activities in which the instructor may give students a problem to solve at their seats, ask them to turn to neighbors for short "buzz group" discussions, and so forth. He also shows how to use technology to enhance active learning. (For other advice on how to improve lectures, see Davis, 2009; Heppner, 2007; and Stanley and Porter, 2002. For further critiques of the lecture method, see Weimer, 2002; Meyers and Jones, 1993; Johnson, Johnson, and Smith, 1991; and Bonwell and Eison, 1991. For alternatives to lecturing in large classes, see Prince and Felder, 2007; Prince, 2004; and Beichner and Saul, 2003. For illuminating insights linking lecture and discussion as complementary and liberating, see Brookfield and Preskill, 2005, pp. 44–48.)

In the rest of this section, I offer strategies for using informal or formal writing assignments to make students more active learners in lecture courses.

Develop Exploratory Writing Tasks Keyed to Your Lectures

The key here is to design tasks that cannot be completed unless the student pays close attention to the lectures. In this approach, the instructor designs low-stakes exploratory tasks (in-class freewrites or out-of-class thinking pieces or bulletin-board postings) that require students to use concepts or information from the lectures. For example, tasks can ask students to link lecture material to their own experiences, to apply lecture material in new contexts, to argue for or against certain propositions in the lectures, or to raise new questions.

Another use of exploratory writing is to engage students with a problem that the day's lecture will address or to activate prior learning and personal experience that will facilitate learning of new material. The teacher's goal here is to till the soil prior to planting the seeds in lecture. (See Chapter Seven, for an explanation of exploratory writing; see Chapter Eight for suggestions on the design of tasks.)

Break the Pace of a Lecture Using "Minute Papers"

The "minute paper," a term coined by Angelo and Cross (1993, pp. 148–153), allows the instructor to stop at an appropriate point in a lecture and ask students to freewrite for several minutes in response to a question. (Questions could range from "What is currently puzzling you?" to any kind of disciplinary problem connected to a current point in the lecture.) The instructor then asks one or two students to read their freewrites or collects a random sampling for reading after class. These freewrites serve as a means of intellectual communication between students and teacher and provide a window into students' thinking processes. Besides providing valuable feedback for the lecturer, the freewrites serve as a kind of seventh-inning stretch for students, refocusing their attention and increasing listening during the last part of the class period. (For an array of other strategies for "taking breaks" in lectures, see Heppner, 2007, Chapter Six.)

Ask Students to Write Summaries of One or More of Your Lectures

Another strategy for promoting better listening is to have students write one-page or one-paragraph summaries of your lectures. You can give students credit for submitting a summary and then read a random selection as a check on student understanding. Chemistry professor Richard Steiner (1982) reports two benefits from this process: students learned more from the lectures, and the instructor was able to make adjustments in his lectures based on his new awareness of problem areas. (For further discussion of summaries, see Chapter Eight, page 157, and Chapter Nine, page 178.)

Ask Students to Question Your Lectures

If appropriate to your discipline, at the beginning of a lecture or a series of lectures, introduce a major question or issue that your lectures will address, telling students that not all scholars in your discipline will agree with your views. Then give students a writing assignment in which they have to summarize your "answer" to the question and respond to it through analysis and further questioning. Perhaps they will even be persuaded to argue against your position. The point is to help students see your lectures as arguments rather than as mere information.

Design a Formal Writing Assignment Requiring Students to Integrate Lecture Material

Another good strategy is to develop a writing assignment that cannot be accomplished unless students have thoroughly understood the lecture material. One suggestion is to create an assignment that compares a point of view you have taken in a series of lectures with an alternative point of view they learn about through assigned readings or library research.

Deliver Narrative Lectures That Model the Thinking Process

Another way to promote critical thinking is to model it. Occasionally give a lecture that takes students through your own thinking process in addressing a problem or that summarizes the history of scholarship on a classic disciplinary problem. At the beginning of the lecture, pose the problem that puzzled you or your disciplinary community. Then, in detective story fashion, re-create for students the process of your thinking (or your discipline's collective thinking), complete with false starts, hunches that did not work out, frustrations, and excitement. (In effect, this is your own "lecture version" of the exploratory essay explained in Chapter Six, pages 116–117.) Because students are used to regarding their professors as repositories of received knowledge, they enjoy seeing a professor actively engaged as a critical thinker wrestling with a problem. For another view on how to make lectures model critical thinking, see Brookfield and Preskill (2005, pp. 44–48).

Increasing Active Learning in Discussion Classes

Whereas lecturing is often regarded as a passive form of instruction for students, most teachers think of discussion classes as active. However, discussion classes often fail to produce the kind of active learning desired. Particularly problematic are discussions in which the teacher simply tries to elicit correct answers or asks closed rather than open questions, leading students to "guess what the instructor is thinking."

Another problem with discussion classes, paradoxically, is that the teacher frequently monopolizes the talking. Brown and Atkins (1988) summarize research studies of discussion classes showing how often teachers, without realizing it, dominate the talk time; one study showed that teachers talked about 86 percent of the time, even though these teachers saw themselves as leading a discussion (p. 59). A related problem is that in many cases, the discussion is carried on by only a few students, while the majority (usually many more than the teacher realizes) listen passively. Even in discussions where there is lively give-and-take throughout the whole class, there often is not enough "space" for any one student to develop a point at length. A student is often cut off in mid-argument by the next person who wants to contribute. Indeed, as we all know from personal experience, participants in discussions often spend their time planning out the next point they want to contribute rather than listening actively to fellow participants.

An excellent resource for teachers interested in leading class discussions is the compendious advice offered in Brookfield and Preskill (2005). Their "tools and techniques" for leading discussions are grounded in philosophical hermeneutics (see, for example, their Chapter Fourteen on Habermas) and linked to the values of a democratic society. (A condensed version of the book's advice and method can be found in Brookfield, 2006.) In general, Brookfield and Preskill's advice emerges from their ongoing research in inquiry teaching, which addresses the kinds of questions to ask to initiate discussions, ways of responding to student contributions, techniques for keeping discussion on track and moving forward, and strategies for including all students in the conversation, often across gender, class, or ethnic difference. Skilled discussion leaders often move easily back and forth among lecture segments, whole class discussions, and small group work. For instructors interested in whole-class discussion techniques, in addition to the work of Brookfield and Brookfield and Preskill, I especially recommend Davis, 2009, as well as some classic older works such as Christensen, Garvin, and Sweet, 1991, and Bateman, 1990.

The following suggestions, which focus primarily on strategies that use writing, are intended to supplement the more comprehensive work on class discussions available in the previously cited sources.

Increase Wait Time by Using Freewriting

A simple strategy for improving class discussion is to increase your "wait time" after asking a question. Studies (including Rowe, 1987) have shown that many teachers, after asking a question, rarely wait more than a few seconds before initiating discussion (if hands go up) or giving prompts (if hands do not go up). One strategy is simply to wait in silence for fifteen or thirty seconds (or even a full minute) before calling on the first person. In many instances, an even better strategy is to let students freewrite for several minutes in response to your asking of an important question. You can then begin discussion by asking one or more students to read their opening freewrites. Shy students can often be drawn into the discussion if they are asked to read a freewrite.

Use Out-of-Class Exploratory Writing to Prime the Pump

You can prime the pump for class discussions by assigning questions in advance to be explored as homework in low-stakes thinking pieces. Then open class with questions that students have already been thinking about. By designing your course so that out-of-class exploratory writing is keyed to in-class discussion topics, you can greatly increase your class's readiness to engage in lively discussion. See Chapter Seven for advice on how to use exploratory writing.

During Heated Discussions, Consider Time-Outs to Let Students Freewrite Their Ideas

Sometimes discussions get so heated that more hands are in the air than you can call on. One way to promote thoughtful learning in such a situation is to stop for five minutes and have everyone freewrite the contribution he or she wants to make to the group. This method gives students the "space" to articulate their arguments without fear of being interrupted before they can get their own ideas clarified. Once the freewrites are completed, the instructor can resume the class discussion, perhaps by inviting several students to summarize their freewrites. If the heated discussion occurs near the end of class, you can ask students to continue by posting their discussions on a class bulletin board or e-mailing to a class listserv.

Have Students Generate the Questions to Be Discussed

Steffens (1989) reports a technique for increasing engagement with readings and for making students more active learners in class. When students have completed new assigned readings for his history seminars, he puts them in small groups to generate lists of questions raised by the readings. Each group has to reach consensus on one or two key questions group members would like the class to discuss. Once groups have reported their questions, the whole class works together to rank them. Steffens summarizes the benefits this way: "As the semester continued, students came to class with their favorite questions already in mind. As soon as they arrived, they sat with their groups and began working out the questions for the day . . . The wealth of questions helped to reinforce the intended impression that learning about the seventeenth century, or any other historical topic, can never be finished and over with. There is always more of interest to investigate" (p. 128). Brookfield and Preskill (2005) offer similar advice, often asking their students to post their potential class discussion questions on an electronic bulletin board or discussion group prior to class (pp. 67–68).

Stagger Due Dates for Short Formal Papers to Allow Daily Paper Presentations

In this strategy, the professor staggers due dates of short one- or two-page formal papers rather than having them due all at the same time. Through prior course design, the instructor gives different problem-based assignments to each student so that the papers due on any given day coincide with that day's discussion topic. At each class meeting, one or two papers are due, depending on the size of the class, the length of the term, and the number of required essays. Students come to class with enough photocopies of their essay for all their classmates, and each day's discussion is initiated by the arguments in the papers due that day. Some teachers then give students several additional days to revise their papers in light of the classroom critique and ensuing discussion. Teachers report that the pressure to "go public" forces students to do their best work and that the quality of the papers initiates excellent classroom discussion of the material. The paper load is easy for the instructor to handle because it involves grading only one or two papers each day—all of which have been critiqued in class at the draft stage several days earlier.

Have Students Complete a Weekly Critical Incident Questionnaire

Another valuable use of writing to promote discussions, recommended by Brookfield and Preskill (2005, pp. 48–50), is the "Critical Incident Questionnaire" (CIQ), a classroom assessment technique that helps students reflect on previous discussions and provides instructors with insights into how the class is going. Their CIQs always ask the same five questions:

1. At what moment in class this week were you most engaged as a learner?
2. At what moment in class this week were you most distanced as a learner?
3. What action that anyone in the room took this week did you find most affirming or helpful?
4. What action that anyone in the room took this week did you find must puzzling or confusing?
5. What surprised you most this week?

Brookfield and Preskill show how the teacher's reading of and responding to the anonymous CIQs can improve the democracy of the classroom and lead to enhanced student learning.

Early in the Course, Hold a Discussion about Discussions

Davis (2009, p. 98) recommends that teachers ask students to describe their own views about "an excellent class discussion." Calling on their own experiences, students often establish criteria for class discussions that match teachers' views: "an engaged, energetic class; well-prepared students; wide participation; respect for different opinions; thought-provoking questions; and thoughtful listeners." Brookfield and Preskill (2005) suggest a similar strategy by having students complete a series of whole class and small group tasks culminating in students' drafting a "charter for discussion." (See "Evolve Ground Rules for Conducting Discussions," pp. 52–56.)

Extend the Classroom by Initiating Online Discussion Forums

Chapter Seven (pages 129–131) discusses the use of blogs and online forums as excellent media for low-stakes exploratory writing. The electronic environment can also be used for online discussions, either through asynchronous posting to a discussion board or through real-time chat rooms. Many classroom teachers have applied strategies developed in online or blended courses to enhance the value of discussion in face-to-face settings. Brookfield and Preskill (2005) devote two chapters to online discussions, arguing that online discussions are "particularly well-suited for meaning-making" (p. 231). The authors explain strategies for creating online discussions that are "participatory, thoughtful, and disciplined" (p. 234). One of their strategies is to require "circular response," which asks participants to begin each of their posts with a reference to the observations and views of a previous course-mate's contribution so that the conversation builds on what others are saying. The best kinds of prompts, they argue, require students to respond knowledgeably to some part of course content but then to add their own views and experiences. As an example, they cite a prompt from an online course for practicing teachers:

> *How convincingly does Spring (2003) demonstrate that American schools from the past were intent on denying and even destroying the home cultures of their students, especially students from minority groups? Tell two brief stories about your own school or a school you know today: one that shows how the history Spring describes still affects us, and one that shows how things have changed [p. 238].*

One can imagine how online learners would enjoy reading their classmates' responses to this assignment, learning about each other's experiences while simultaneously thinking more deeply about an important course reading. The same strategies can be used in face-to-face classes, where an electronic forum extends opportunities for exchange of ideas. (For further discussion of online forums, see Garrison and Vaughan, 2008;

Bonk and Zhang, 2008; Bates and Poole, 2003; Palloff and Pratt, 2003; and Kirk and Orr, 2003.)

Conclusion: Engaging Ideas Through Active Learning

Through strategies that promote active learning, teachers hope to make students more engaged and inquisitive learners, more powerful thinkers, and better arguers. Outside the classroom, a good way to stimulate active learning is to assign exploratory or formal writing that presents students with critical thinking problems keyed to the reading and learning objectives of the course. In the classroom, active learning can be promoted both through small group work and through teaching strategies aimed at improving student engagement in lectures or whole-class discussions. Through a mixture of such methods, instructors hope to maximize students' intellectual growth.

12

Enhancing Learning and Critical Thinking in Essay Exams

Essay exams play an important yet problematic role in any writing-across-the-curriculum program. This chapter examines the pedagogical and theoretical problems posed by essay exams and then suggests ways that some of them may be overcome. It also describes strategies for helping students improve their ability to write essay exams.

The Importance of Essay Exams

Professors who value writing in their courses often take special pride in their use of essay exams rather than objective tests. These professors feel that essay exams, by requiring students to analyze and argue, can reveal students' mastery of subject matter in a way that objective tests cannot match. (Many specialists in measurement and assessment dispute this claim, as we shall see.) In addition, essay exam questions, unlike more narrowly focused out-of-class writing assignments, ask students to synthesize concepts and draw together various strands of course material. As a result, essay exams—more than out-of-class writing assignments—help students see the whole course in perspective and thus can be powerful tools for learning. Finally, essay exams help students learn to think and compose rapidly, providing apt preparation for professions that require working with documents under deadline conditions.

Why Essay Exams Are Problematic

Nevertheless, essay examinations pose problems for many educators, specifically for specialists in testing and measurement, who compare essay exams to objective tests, and for specialists in writing across the curriculum, who compare them to other kinds of formal and exploratory writing assignments. Let's look at the problems with essay exams from each of these perspectives.

The Measurement and Testing Perspective

For the most part, specialists in educational testing and measurement prefer objective tests over essay exams even when the instructor wishes to test at the upper levels of Bloom's taxonomy (1956) of education objectives. Jacobs and Chase (1992) cautiously endorse essay exams for testing higher cognitive skills but prefer a series of short ten-minute essays rather than one or two in-depth ones. The literature in this field generally takes a foundationalist, perhaps even positivist, view of knowledge, regarding a course's content as a body of objective testable material that students can learn at various levels of depth and subtlety. Based on this assumption (which many faculty who support essay exams will not grant—especially those with postmodern doubts about the objectivity of knowledge), assessment specialists believe that the extent of any individual student's learning can be measured by skillfully constructed objective items ranging from simple recall questions to questions measuring Bloom's upper levels of analysis, synthesis, and evaluation.

Although proponents of essay exams often claim that essays are more effective than objective tests at measuring a student's critical thinking about course material, assessment specialists claim that expertly designed multiple-choice items can do the same thing (Clegg and Cashin, 1986). Cashin (1987) identifies six limitations of essay exams, four of which are particularly relevant to this discussion. I summarize these as follows:

1. They can sample only limited content. Because essay exams involve so much writing time, they can "only sample a very small portion of the domain of content and skills to be learned." Consequently, students' scores reflect "the luck of the draw" rather than their "command of the entire domain" of what was taught (Cashin, 1987, p. 2).

2. They are not reliable. Research reveals that scores assigned to a given essay vary from scorer to scorer. Perhaps more disturbing, the same scorer will assign different grades to the same essay at different times.

3. Scores may be influenced by the scorer's impression of the student. Unlike scores on objective tests, the scores on essay exams often reflect the teacher's previous impressions of the student—the "halo effect."

4. Scores reflect factors not related to content knowledge. Scores on essay exams are influenced by the students' handwriting, grammatical and spelling skills, and other writing skills not directly related to course content.

As a consequence of these limitations, "especially with respect to reliability," Cashin recommends limiting the use of essay exams to only "learning outcomes that cannot be satisfactorily measured by 'objective' items" (p. 2). For Cashin, these situations may occur if the instructor specifically wants to emphasize writing or wants "to encourage students to explore attitudes more than testing for cognitive achievement" (p. 2). Even then he warns teachers to use essay exams only "when the instructor has more confidence in his or her ability as a critical reader than as an 'objective' test constructor" (p. 2).

The Writing-Across-the-Curriculum Perspective

Specialists in writing across the curriculum tend to bring to this issue different assumptions and concerns, focusing more on learning than on testing. Skeptical of the positivist metaphor of a course subject as a "body" or "domain" of material, the mastery of which can be measured empirically, these persons tend to locate subject matter knowledge in the ability to use course theories, concepts, and facts or data in meaning-making ways to produce arguments. From this perspective, essay exams are preferable to objective tests. The objection to essay exams from the writing-across-the-curriculum perspective is that they tend to replace other more effective kinds of writing assignments. Teachers have only so much time to devote to student writing. Teachers who grade lots of essay exams tend to reduce their requirements for other formal or exploratory writing assignments, which are generally more effective than essay exams both at teaching writing skills and at promoting learning and critical thinking. The effect is that writing as testing drives out writing as learning.

The reduced learning from essay exams results largely from the minimal time on task that they require. A midterm exam typically keeps students actively writing and thinking for fifty minutes or so, a final exam for two to four hours. In contrast, a guided journal could involve many more hours of active thinking during a term, as could a short formal essay that goes through multiple drafts. Thus the power of essay exam questions to stimulate synthetic thinking is diminished by the small amount of time students actually spend on the task.

A related problem is that essay exams send the wrong message about process. In-class essay exams, when submitted to teachers, are almost always unedited, unrevised first drafts. During the entire life cycle of an exam answer, its only reader is the teacher. (Students themselves almost never read their own exam answers—either before turning them in or after getting them back.) Therein lies the problem. As we saw in Chapter Two, the teaching of writing is largely the teaching of revision. In learning to revise, students learn first to become better readers of their early drafts—a process that leads to deepening and complicating of thought through discovery of weaknesses and gaps, attention to alternative views, subsequent reformulation of the logic and structure of the argument, and so forth. These powerful thinking activities associated with revision are lost in a timed exam setting.

Another problem—related to the reliability issue raised by specialists in testing and measurement—is that teachers are not consistent in what they look for on essay exams. (For an interesting survey of the literature on reliability in the scoring of essay exams, see Jacobs and Chase, 1992, pp. 106–109.) As students go from teacher to teacher, the criteria for exam answers shift mysteriously. Some teachers look for thesis-governed arguments, in which case much of what a student has learned in the course has to be omitted or reshaped to keep the essay focused on the proposition at hand. Other teachers reward "all about" exams in which students need to unload everything they know about topic X. Some teachers demand well-organized essays; others are willing to sift through confusing strings of material looking for required points that they check off in the margins. Some teachers want straight feedback of material from readings and lectures; other teachers want fresh insights that go beyond what was covered in class. My sense is that few students know what any one teacher really wants in an exam and that teachers vary so much in what they want that weaker students never get the hang of writing exams.

Finally, students are seldom taught how to write essay exams. This problem could be addressed if teachers shifted their emphasis from testing to learning. In such cases, students could be required to rewrite weak exams until they had achieved at least the B level. Teachers could work as coaches by showing students the kinds of "thinking moves" needed to write A-worthy answers. The payoff for this coaching would be students' rethinking the course material and learning the strategies of effective exam writing. In practice, however, students are rarely given much feedback on their exams; even more rarely are they allowed to rewrite an exam for a better grade.

How We Can Improve Our Use of Essay Exams

Despite these problems with essay exams, my own view—coming from the writing-across-the-curriculum perspective—is that essay exams are preferable to objective tests for examining students' ability to think critically about course material. Essay exams send the important pedagogical message that mastering a field means joining its discourse—that is, demonstrating one's ability to mount effective arguments in response to disciplinary problems. My own view, then, is that we should not eliminate essay exams but rather improve their effectiveness without letting them replace other kinds of writing assignments. Our goal would be twofold: to increase the amount of learning derived from essay exams and to increase students' ability to write serviceable prose under pressure. I believe we could improve our use of exams by taking four basic actions: (1) teaching students how to write essay exams, (2) building more opportunities for process into the exam setting, (3) improving the focus and clarity of our exam questions, and (4) establishing more consistent grading criteria and improving grading methods to improve reliability. Let's look at each in turn.

Teaching Students How to Write Exams

Particularly in lower-division courses, where students are still learning academic discourse, instructors need to teach students how to write essay exams. Exhortations such as "be clear" or "plan before you write" do not do much good. Fortunately, several genuinely helpful techniques can be implemented in most classrooms.

In-Class Norming Sessions

The teacher collects from a previous class four to six exams graded from A to C– or D. (It's best to have the exams typed to facilitate photocopying and to avoid the variable of difficult handwriting.) Students read the exams and, in small groups, rank them from best to worst, trying to determine what grades the teacher gave. After the groups have reported their consensus on grades, the teacher explains the grading of the essays and leads a discussion. Internalizing the criteria for A exams is a good start toward learning how to write them. Norming sessions are also salutary experiences for instructors, who are forced to articulate their criteria for good exam answers. Because the exams focus on course content, the norming session also serves as a review of course material. (See Chapter Ten, page 194; Chapter Fourteen, page 287; and Chapter Fifteen, page 292, for further discussion of norming sessions.)

Practice Exams

Many teachers have had good results giving students practice exams. Some teachers have their students write a twenty-minute essay in class under exam conditions and then ask selected students to read their exams aloud. Through class discussion, teachers can help students see what constitutes a strong exam. Another technique is to use practice exams as homework. You can reuse all your old exam questions by having students respond to one or two per week as homework under self-timed conditions. The teacher can treat these as exploratory writing and provide coaching through models feedback (see Chapter Fifteen, page 313). Not only does this technique improve exam writing, but it also promotes learning in a premium way. (For further discussion of practice exams, see Chapter Seven, pages 140–141.)

Teaching Students to Begin an Exam with a Thesis Statement

Another good way to teach exam writing is to show students how to begin their answers with a thesis statement opener, which can be defined as a one-sentence summary answer to the overall question. By opening with a thesis, students are forced to plan their answers in terms of both content and organization. The one-sentence thesis statement thus serves as both a summary and a map of the whole essay. Here are some examples:

Question: How does Darwin's theory of evolution threaten the Elizabethan notion of a great chain of being?
  Opening sentence: Darwin's theory of evolution threatens the Elizabethan notion of a great chain of being by challenging the idea that creatures are linked in an ascending order of hierarchies that reflect a divine purpose and intelligence at work in the universe. [Humanities]

Question: When the tablecloth was pulled from underneath the dishes, the dishes stayed on the table. Why?
  Opening sentence: The dishes remained on the table because the rapidly moving tablecloth did not give them much momentum, which is a product of both force and time [Kirkpatrick and Pittendrigh, 1984, p. 161]. [Physics]

(For additional discussion of thesis statement writing, see Chapter Seven.)

Group Thesis Statement Writing

As the examples just given suggest, teaching students to open with a thesis statement forces them to plan ahead and to conceptualize their whole response at once. This skill is so valuable, in fact, that teachers can have students practice writing thesis statements in small groups. An excellent way to review course material while teaching exam-writing skills is to give students practice exam questions in class and ask them in small groups to compose effective opening sentences for the answer. (See Chapter Ten, pages 190–191, for further discussion of this method.)

Showing Examples of A-Worthy Exams

After each exam, place copies of representative A-graded answers in the library or post to a class bulletin board (of course, remove the students' names and get their permission). Seeing what an A essay looks like is often better feedback for students than putting comments on the exams themselves.

Letting Students Revise an Exam

Occasionally a student can benefit greatly from the opportunity to rewrite a weak exam, particularly if the weakness stems from an unsuccessful strategy or approach as opposed to a lack of preparation or study. Often students improve remarkably following a bit of coaching in what constitutes a strong answer. Students are gratified by the experience of succeeding and may learn skills that can be transferred to other exams in other courses.

Building Opportunities for Process into the Exam Setting

A second major strategy for improving essay exams is to build opportunities for process into the exam setting. Although time normally cannot be provided for multiple drafts during an in-class exam, instructors can develop strategies for focusing students' studying prior to the exam so that they do considerable prewriting or invention ahead of time. What follows are several strategies that generally result in better exams and more focused learning.

Revealing Potential Exam Questions in Advance

One of the easiest techniques, employed by many professors, is to hand out a list of potential exam questions a week or so ahead of the exam. Diligent students are apt to prepare answers for all the questions, especially if they have been trained to begin an answer with a one-sentence summarizing thesis. On a review day, groups could be asked to create thesis statements for each of the answers. These thesis statements could then be compared and discussed in a plenary session. (It should be noted that many assessment specialists recommend against handing out questions in advance on the grounds that one may simply be testing "the students' ability to memorize someone else's thinking" [Cashin, 1987, p. 3]. Here again, the assessment community's emphasis is on testing rather than cooperative learning.)

Exam Preparation Notebook

A more formal elaboration of the strategy just described is to require (or allow) exam preparation notebooks. In this approach, teachers give out a list of fifteen or so possible final exam questions at the beginning of the term and ask students to dedicate a separate section of their notebooks to each question. Throughout the term, students enter ideas from readings, lectures, and discussions relevant to each of the questions and explore their thinking through expressive writing. (See Chapter Seven, page 136, for further discussion of this very effective technique.)

Crib Sheets

Another variation on the strategy of handing out potential questions in advance is allowing or even requiring a crib sheet for each question. Instead of simply hoping that students will prepare for the exam, you require that they bring to the examination session a crib sheet on a 3x5 card for each question. Writing as minutely as they wish, students can cram whatever information they want onto the note cards. Some students will put a thesis statement and an outline on the cards; others will put lists of supporting data. Students can use the crib sheets during the examination, and they must turn all of them in with their exams—including those for questions not asked. In lieu of requiring the crib sheets, teachers can simply allow their use. Most students will prepare them voluntarily in order to remain competitive on the exam. Although this method may seem to diminish the testing nature of an exam, it greatly enhances the power of exam questions to promote learning and critical thinking. It is an especially valuable strategy for problem-focused exam questions that do not have just one right answer but require extensive argument and support on the student's part.

Take-Home Exams

Among the most popular ways to allow process is to switch from in-class to take-home exams. However, the rules for take-home exams differ widely from instructor to instructor. Some teachers treat them like formal essays.

They urge students to revise extensively and encourage use of peer review and even help from writing centers. These teachers envision their students' spending as much time on the take-home as they would on a formal essay. Other teachers treat take-home exams as less pressured and more convenient versions of in-class examinations, to be done under the honor system fairly quickly and without help. These teachers expect minimally edited one-draft writing done in perhaps three or four hours instead of two. According to conversations I have had with students, the main objection they have to take-home exams is not knowing what the competition is doing or what the teacher expects. A part-time student who has cleared the decks for finals week might spend ten to fifteen hours on the exam. The harried full-time student with a job might have only three or four hours at maximum. The latter student might be justified in wondering whether the exam is fair. Teachers should be aware of these concerns and try to help students resolve them in advance. Each teacher should be particularly clear on the following issues:

1. Are multiple drafts expected? That is, will this be graded like a formal essay?

2. Is the exam open-book and open-notes, or is it closed-book on the honor system?

3. May the student get help from a writing center or learning center consultant or from fellow classmates?

4. How much time does the teacher intend students to spend?

5. How long should the exam be?

Jacobs and Chase (1992, pp. 126–127) recommend setting a page limit for a take-home exam and penalizing students for exceeding it.

Improving the Focus and Clarity of Exam Questions

A third broad strategy is for teachers to improve the focus and clarity of their exam questions. In Chapter Six, I argued that good writing on the student's part begins with good assignments on the teacher's part. Nowhere is this connection clearer than in an exam setting, where a student needs to start moving in the right direction within the first five minutes.

Research by composition scholars into effective prompts to assess writing proficiency has revealed connections between the kinds of writing tasks students are given and the quality of writing they produce fifty minutes later (for example, see Brossell, 1983). Although most of the findings are predictable, some findings seem counterintuitive, even surprising.

I list here key pieces of advice from this research because I believe that these findings can be translated from a writing proficiency setting to an essay exam setting in a content area.

Limit Choice

Although teachers often believe they are doing students a favor by giving many options among questions, giving choices may actually do more harm than good. The current practice for proficiency exams in composition is to give only one question but to make sure that it is an excellent one. Cashin (1987) agrees with this view, but from a measurement perspective. He advises teachers to "avoid optional questions" because "it is almost impossible to write several essay questions which are of equal difficulty . . . The result is that different students are taking tests of varying difficulty but you will grade these the same. This may penalize the 'better' students because they may choose the more difficult (challenging) questions and so will not score as well as students who choose the easier questions" (p. 3). (See also Jacobs and Chase, 1992, p. 113.)

Keep Each Question Short and Avoid Subquestions or Hints

In an attempt to stimulate ideas or guide thinking, teachers sometimes add a series of subquestions under the main question or otherwise provide hints about possible directions to take in the exam essay. But this extra "help" may be counterproductive. Students feel constrained to either answer each of the subquestions in turn or slavishly follow the suggested direction. It is better to ask your question and stop. (See Chapter Six, pages 104–105, for further discussion of the negative value of subquestions.)

Call for Thesis-Governed Writing and Avoid Tasks Phrased as Imperatives

Perhaps most surprising, students seem to do best when the task is stated either as a thesis that must be supported, modified, or refuted or as a single question, the answer to which will be the writer's thesis statement. Students do not do as well on tasks that are stated as imperatives using such verbs as *discuss, analyze, evaluate,* and *compare and contrast.* Imperative tasks tend to result in more aimless answers than tasks stated as a thesis or a focusing question. The use of imperatives is acceptable, however, if the imperative verb is sufficiently contextualized to avoid ambiguity and if the implied problem is clear. Exhibit 12.1 gives some example questions.

EXHIBIT 12.1

Framing Essay Exam Questions

Less Effective Questions	Improved Questions
Pick one of the following, and write an essay about it: (a) Gothic cathedrals; (b) Charlemagne; (c) the Black Death	"There is a connection between the world view of a culture and the kind of architecture it produces." To what extent does this quotation explain the differences between Romanesque and Gothic churches?
Discuss the use of pesticides in controlling mosquitoes.	What are the pros and cons of using pesticides to control mosquitoes?
Analyze the influence of Platonic thought on Christianity.	"The otherworldly focus of Christian fundamentalism owes more to Plato than to Jesus." Agree or disagree with this proposition.

Establishing More Consistent Grading Criteria and Improving Grading Methods

A final broad strategy is to develop grading criteria, explain them clearly to students, and then establish grading methods that apply those criteria reliably.

If we want students to become savvy exam writers, we need to explain the criteria we use in grading essay exams. How much do we reward intelligent generalizations, even if the supporting data are fuzzy, as opposed to regurgitation of data without much argument? Do we want the essay to read like finished writing, or do we scan it for the points we are looking for, checking them off with ticks in the margin? Do we penalize grammatical and spelling errors, or do we read past them? Chapter Fourteen shows teachers how to articulate their grading criteria and gives advice on developing rubrics. These can be developed for essay exam questions as well as for formal out-of-class essays.

One of the stickiest issues an instructor faces is what to do about exam answers that are riddled with sentence errors. Although I cannot presume to answer this question for others, I will offer my own (no doubt controversial) recommendations for dealing with sentence-level errors in an exam setting.

As explained in Chapters Two and Five, first-draft writing, even by highly skilled writers, often contains awkward sentence structures and mistakes in grammar and punctuation. The more difficult the subject matter, the more frequent the tangled sentences. My own belief is that in an exam setting, we must learn to live with these problems, whether produced by a native or nonnative speaker. Because students haven't time to revise, they are unable to find and correct the numerous errors that show up naturally in drafts. I therefore recommend reading demandingly at the macro level (thesis, organization, use of evidence) and forgivingly at the micro level (sentence structure, punctuation errors). We would all be happier, of course, if students could write error-free first drafts, but because this skill is not being tested in a content area exam, I recommend reading primarily for content.

I take the same position on spelling errors. In formal out-of-class essays (most students rely on spell-checkers to catch errors), poor spelling needs to be severely penalized. But a writer cannot worry about spelling during the act of composing itself. Teachers who insist on accurate spelling during timed writing—or even worse, teachers who tell students to bring dictionaries to the exam—are doing a disservice to struggling writers. While other writers are getting their ideas in order, the poor speller is thumbing through a dictionary. We do not know the neurological or environmental causes of poor spelling. We do know that it is not easily remedied. I treat poor spelling in a written exam the way I would treat the problems of a stutterer in an oral examination: with sympathy, patience, and forgiveness.

Once professors have established grading criteria for exam answers and have made their own separate peace with the sentence error dilemma, their final responsibility is to establish grading practices that increase reliability by minimizing the halo effect and other factors leading to overly impressionistic grading. Based on my own experiences, I recommend the following:

- Do not look at students' names when you read the exams. Have students write their names on the backs of the exams, or even better, ask students to identify their exams with a random four-digit number they choose on the spot. After you have graded all the exams, ask students to identify their numbers.

- Grade the exam one question at a time. Rather than read the whole exam of each student, grade all the responses to question 1, then all the responses to question 2, and so forth.

- Shuffle the exams after you complete each question so that you read them in a different order. Record scores in such a way that you do not know what a student received on question 1 when you grade question 2.

- If possible, read a random sample of exams rapidly before you make initial decisions about grades. Your goal here is to establish "anchor papers" that represent prototype A, B, and C grades. Then, when you come to a difficult essay, you can ask yourself, "Is this better or worse than my prototype B? How about my prototype C?"

The foregoing methods, all of which grew out of research in the evaluation of writing (White, 1994), help eliminate the halo effect and provide psychological assistance in eliminating extraneous factors.

Conclusion: Getting the Most from Essay Exams

Essay examinations are valuable writing assignments if the exams do not replace even more valuable formal or exploratory writing assignments. From a writing-across-the-curriculum perspective, problems with essay examinations arise primarily when teachers regard them as sufficient components of writing in a course. Once we recognize the problems posed by the exam setting—time constraints that prevent writing as process—we can take steps to improve our examination procedures so that students learn more course content from our exams while improving their skills at writing under pressure.

13

Designing and Sequencing Assignments to Teach Undergraduate Research

The research paper (or term paper) can be one of the most valuable assignments we give students. Research assignments flow from our desire that students become self-directed inquirers who can bring their own critical thinking to bear on interesting problems. But our students' research papers are often disappointing. Despite our admonitions that students should do their own thinking and analysis in research papers, many students regard a research paper as an informative pastiche or an "all about" report on a topic area. We all know students' tendency to manufacture a term paper by patching together passages closely paraphrased from their sources. There is something mechanistic about the way many of our students produce research papers, something disturbingly unlike the motivated inquiry and analysis that we value.

And yet many undergraduates pursue research with gusto. A number of years ago, I had the opportunity to attend a National Conference on Undergraduate Research (NCUR). I was impressed by the fascinating range of problems that undergraduates posed and by the quality of their research and critical thinking. Here are some titles of undergraduate papers presented at the 2008 NCUR conference at Salisbury University (NCUR, 2008; a CD is available from the NCUR website):

Reconstructing the Feminine in Cubist Theories of Space and Time (art history)

Differentiation in Synaptic Function: Are Drosophila Neuromuscular Junctions a Good Example? (biology)

Density Functional Theory Investigation of the Reaction Mechanism for Hydrogen Generation from Ethanol over a Palladium Catalyst (engineering)

Retention of Emergency Care Knowledge Among Nursing Students (nursing)

How English Proficiency Affects the Income of Hispanic Immigrants (economics)

Hair Color and Perceived Job Ability: Why Stereotypes Attached to Red-Haired Men and Women May Lead to Hiring Discrimination (management)

Destabilization of the Niger Delta Region of Nigeria: A Qualitative Examination of the Exploitation of the Minority Ethnic Groups by Foreign Oil Corporations (political science)

Racialization in Sports: Deconstructing Race in United States Swimming (sociology)

The question we face, then, is how to transform students from writers of uninspired, pseudo-academic research papers into engaged undergraduate researchers. What goes wrong when students regurgitate (or even plagiarize) sources in a term paper? What goes right when students become invested in academic inquiry, doing real undergraduate research? My goal in this chapter is to help us rethink how we teach research writing. The chapter begins with an analysis of the conceptual difficulties that research writing presents for undergraduates. I then move to the design of short research assignments that, for many courses, may be preferable substitutes for longer research papers. A third section, based on the principle of backward design, presents a variety of pedagogical strategies that can help teachers integrate research writing into a course. Particularly, teachers can design short scaffolding assignments early in the course to teach the research skills needed for a longer research paper due at the end. The last section focuses specifically on writing in the major, suggesting ways that a whole department might work together—this time employing the principle of backward design to the whole curriculum—to design sophomore and junior assignments that prepare students to produce capstone research papers as seniors. The payoff for the strategies suggested in this chapter is more satisfaction with our students' work, made possible by shorter, more manageable, and more purposeful research assignments.

Simultaneously, these strategies help alter the environmental conditions that breed plagiarism by enabling students to investigate research sources with a higher level of critical thinking and intentionality.

The Complexities of Research Writing

Writing a good research paper is more difficult than teachers may at first realize. In this section I examine these difficulties from three perspectives—students' misperceptions about the meaning of "research," faculty misperceptions about how students develop as researchers, and the actual difficulty of research subskills embedded in any research project.

Students' Misperceptions About Research—and the Ensuing Cycle of Cynicism

Students' traditional conception of the term paper may be rooted in school reports that call for informational "all about" writing rather than analysis or argument. (My prototype example from back in the day is an old junior high assignment—"Write a report on North Dakota"—that invited paraphrase from an encyclopedia.) Today's students go first to Google—with an early stop at Wikipedia—rather than to print encyclopedias, but their motivation is the same: to find a variety of informational sources that can be assembled into a kind of collage paper that meets the assignment's page limits and number of required sources.

This focus on information is motivated, in part, by a novice's misperception of what is meant by "research." According to one study, 87 percent of freshmen think of research as "going to the library and finding books and articles to use in my paper" (Ritter, 2005, p. 628). In other words, when students hear the word *research* they think of "going to a library" (or perhaps going to Google); they don't think of, say, observing organisms in pond scum, analyzing body language in a crowded elevator, or investigating longitudinal unemployment data for the last ten years in a certain region. Going to a library or library portal, in other words, is only part of what happens when many disciplinary professionals pursue research. The term "research paper" conveys to our students the going-to-the-library part but leaves out the critical inquiry part.

This conception of the term paper often creates a vicious cycle of cynicism among teachers and students. Cohen and Spencer (1993), writing about upper-division term papers in economics, complained that student papers were "mediocre, regurgitative, and uninspired." They report:

[At the end of the term] over half of the students never picked up their papers. That pile of uncollected papers was a sure sign of student alienation from their writing . . . When students were asked about the lack of coherent arguments in their writing, typical responses were: "How can you expect an undergraduate to say anything original?" or "How can I [the novice student] tell you [the expert instructor] anything you don't already know?" [p. 222].

Student alienation is perhaps exacerbated by faculty hysteria over plagiarism. As more and more faculty, in understandable frustration with student work, turn to the policing mechanisms of turnitin.com or other plagiarism-detection software, the term paper experience becomes increasingly unsatisfying—with faculty obsessed with student cheating and students frustrated by lack of understanding of what they are supposed to do.

The student comments from Cohen and Spencer—that they didn't have anything original to say—suggest that traditional research assignments often leave students feeling voiceless and powerless. Cohen and Spencer addressed this problem by switching from topic-centered assignments to problem- or thesis-centered assignments. According to Cohen (the economist in the coauthor pair): "The thesis-less papers that I had previously received in the form of explanations of other authors' positions . . . were, in fact, rational responses to my vague instructions 'explain and comment.' In their place, I substituted more argumentative instructions . . . " (p. 224). In his revised assignments, Cohen gives students disciplinary problems requiring an argumentative claim, thus giving purpose and direction to their research.

Misperceptions About Student Development as Researchers

Ironically, another obstacle to teaching undergraduate research is the prevailing faculty belief that students learn to write the "research paper" in first-year composition. The *research paper* is a fossilized school genre with only a loose resemblance to the actual genres of academic research. (When we professors talk about our own research, we might say that we are writing a *conference paper* or a *research article*, but not a *research paper* or a *term paper.*) The problem with the label is that it implies a stable, one-size-fits-all genre that students can learn in first-year composition and then transfer to any discipline. It leads to the assumption that because students are taught the research paper in Freshman English, teachers across the curriculum can now assign research papers in history, anthropology, or nursing.

But the research writing that students produce in first-year composition, although helpful in introducing students to academic research and use of sources, only loosely approximates the inquiry and argument that we value in our own disciplines. The research paper, as many scholars have shown, is a pseudo-academic genre—one scholar calls it a "mutt genre" (Wardle, 2009, p. 774)—that has different meanings to different teachers across the curriculum (Nowacek, 2009; Beaufort, 2007; Thaiss and Zawacki, 2006; Carroll, 2002; Larson, 1982). When teachers assign a research paper in a disciplinary course, then, they may mistakenly assume that the research skills introduced in first-year composition transfer directly to new contexts.

The process of moving from outsider to disciplinary insider or from novice to expert is neither simple nor linear. What we need is a description of this process that differs from the prevailing perception that students learn to write the research paper in first-year composition. A useful developmental model has been suggested by MacDonald (1994). Her four-stage schema is as follows:

MacDonald's Four-Stage Schema of Students' Development as Writers*

1. Nonacademic writing [what students bring from high school]

2. Generalized academic writing concerned with stating claims, offering evidence, respecting others' opinions, and learning how to write with authority [the goal of first-year composition]

3. Novice approximations of particular disciplinary ways of making knowledge [early courses in the major]

4. Expert, insider prose [advanced courses in the major] (p. 187)

Although MacDonald doesn't elaborate on this schema, its general sequence can be mapped onto the typical undergraduate curriculum. Within MacDonald's schema, stage 1 represents students' high school experience, in which they write primarily nonacademic or pseudo-academic prose such as personal essays or five-paragraph themes. Because American high schools typically don't demand or teach university-level critical argument, it is the goal of first-year composition course to teach "generalized academic writing" (stage 2)—writing that introduces students to academic discourse without trying to teach disciplinary ways of thinking and arguing. What MacDonald emphasizes, however, is that little of what students learn in first-year composition transfers directly into

---

* From MacDonald, S. P. *Professional and Academic Writing in the Humanities and Social Sciences.* Carbondale: Southern Illinois University Press, 1994. Used by permission of the publisher.

disciplinary courses. When students enter their chosen majors (stage 3), they essentially start over as writers—producing "novice approximations" of disciplinary discourse—because they haven't yet learned how the new discipline poses questions, analyzes evidence, applies theories, or produces arguments in conversation with other scholars. The last stage of MacDonald's schema describes students who eventually become acculturated into the discipline, learning to produce "expert insider prose" as defined appropriately by disciplinary faculty for undergraduates.

MacDonald's particular insight is the importance of stage 3—those early courses in the major where students are starting to learn how scholars in their field make new knowledge. If students don't reach the stage of "expert insider prose" in their majors—that is, if as seniors they are not thinking and writing like historians, chemists, psychologists, or nurses— the problem cannot be solved by better teaching of the "research paper" in first-year composition. Rather, the solution, as this chapter tries to suggest, is in the design of short, purposeful assignments at the "novice approximation" stage.

The Difficult Subskills of Research Writing

For a third perspective on why research writing is difficult for students, consider the complexity of subskills that novice research writers have to learn, especially when they are simply told to write a "research paper" without further guidance. I see at least seven of these subskills—all of them together revealing that good research writing is intellectually demanding and cognitively complex. Let's look at each in turn.

1. How to Ask Discipline-Appropriate Research Questions

Students generally don't see question asking as part of their role. (They are used to answering professors' questions but not generating their own.) To complicate the task, the nature of questions differs from discipline to discipline, and fields are often divided by theoretical or methodical differences that affect the way questions are framed. Instructors therefore must teach students how to pose their own discipline-appropriate questions that are interesting, significant, and pursuable at the undergraduate level.

2. How to Establish a Rhetorical Context (Audience, Genre, and Purpose)

Writers write to an audience for a purpose within a genre. When teachers design research problems for students, they can build into the assignment an audience, purpose, and genre (see the discussion of best practices in assignment design, including giving students a RAFT and a TIP, pages

98–100). When students choose their own research topics, however, establishing such a rhetorical context for themselves is a surprisingly difficult task. Are they addressing the teacher or someone else? Is their purpose to inform or persuade or what? What expectations will their targeted readers have about genre?

3. How to Find Sources

Although students are usually introduced to database searching in first-year composition, most students will be unsophisticated in their searching strategies and will know nothing about a discipline's specialized databases. Moreover, they will lack sophistication in evaluating sources for political or theoretical bias. Teaching students how to find and evaluate sources within a disciplinary field is often best accomplished when the instructor collaborates with a reference librarian specializing in the disciplinary area.

4. Why to Find Sources

As noted earlier, novice researchers often think that the purpose of sources is to provide information on a topic and that the majority of words in a research paper ought to be quotations or paraphrases from the sources. But if the researcher's task is to analyze or argue—with most of the words in the paper being the writer's own voice making his or her own case—the purpose of sources becomes less clear. A research source, for example, might provide a background fact, provide puzzling material for analysis, supply evidence to support a claim, or put forth an opposing view to push against. Later in this chapter I'll develop this problem in more detail and suggest a strategy for helping students recognize different functions of research sources (see discussion of Bizup's BEAM, pages 237–241).

5. How to Integrate Sources into the Paper

Equally difficult for students is figuring out what to do with their sources—when to quote versus when to paraphrase, to summarize, or simply to reference. In an effort to fill their pages with words, beginners often seem primarily interested in reproducing their sources through long block quotations or lengthy paraphrases, rather than using them purposefully within their own arguments.

6. How to Take Thoughtful Notes

Today's students resist taking research notes, preferring instead yellow highlighting on photocopies or downloaded printouts. By not taking notes, students avoid the active critical thinking that note taking demands: reflecting on the sources, deciding what is or is not important, writing summaries of arguments, or recording their own ideas through exploratory writing as they read a source.

7. How to Cite and Document Sources

Learning the proper formats for citing sources, though the least of concerns in the hierarchy of skills needed for research writing, is often the foremost concern for students. Judging from the number of students who come into my own institution's writing center to ask questions about bibliographic and citation formats, it is the concern they think teachers emphasize most. The wide variation in formats from discipline to discipline further complicates this problem.

Having suggested some of the problems behind the traditional term paper assignment, in the rest of this chapter I turn to practical suggestions for helping students become skilled undergraduate researchers. The next section focuses on the design of short meaning-constructing research assignments aimed at rooting research in authentic problems that give students a point of entry for their own voices.

Creating Short Meaning-Constructing Research Assignments

Before turning students loose to write long research papers on topics of their own choice, we can design short, meaning-constructing assignments aimed at teaching students to use research sources to make their own arguments. The key is to apply the principles of assignment design discussed in Chapter Six—designing meaning-constructing tasks that also provide a rhetorical context by specifying a role, audience, and genre.

Illustrations of Meaning-Constructing Research Assignments

A meaning-constructing research task asks students to bring their own critical thinking to bear on research sources within the context of an authentic problem demanding analysis and argument rather than mere information. To illustrate, let's return briefly to the thought exercise in Chapter Six on nursing assignments investigating therapeutic touch ("Considering the Effects of Small Variations in Assignment Design" pages 92–93). I reprint here the first three variations on a possible assignment:

Assignment Option 1

Write an eight- to ten-page research paper on therapeutic touch. Follow APA conventions for documentation.

. . .

Assignment Option 2

You are a staff nurse at a large urban hospital. Recently the hospital became embroiled in a major controversy when several nurses were discovered to be practicing TT on patients without the permission or knowledge of their supervisors or of attending physicians. The hospital governing board reprimanded the nurses and issued a general statement forbidding the practice of TT, which they called "non-scientific quackery." Research the professional literature on TT, looking especially for evidence-based studies. Then write a four- to five-page argument, addressed to the hospital governing board, supporting or attacking the board's decision to forbid the practice of TT. Support your position with reasons and evidence based on the professional literature.

. . .

Assignment Option 3

Assume that you and several colleagues seek grant funding to do a controlled research study on the efficacy of TT for reducing anxiety and pain in surgery patients. Research the current professional literature on TT and then write the "review of the literature" section of your grant proposal.

As I explained in Chapter Six, when I've given this exercise in workshops, teachers regularly agree that options 2 and 3 (which ask students to construct meanings) are more effective than simply assigning a research paper. All three of these options are research assignments, but options 2 and 3 provide both a problem and a rhetorical context. Option 2 asks students to write a policy argument to the hospital board while Option 3 asks for the literature review section of a grant proposal. (Before students could write the literature review, they would need to understand the function of this genre, which is to identify a significant gap in current knowledge about therapeutic touch as a prelude to proposing an empirical study to fill this gap.) Whereas option 1 is apt to lead to an "all about" informative paper, options 2 and 3 require the writer's engaged critical thinking in order to bring research findings to bear on authentic problems. Workshop participants agree that options 2 and 3 are apt to produce more engaged learning and growth than will option 1.

Modulating Difficulty Levels: Stepping Gradually into Research Waters

In designing problem-based research assignments, instructors can control both the difficulty of the research problem and the amount of research required. For example, for an early research assignment, the instructor might design a fairly easy research problem and supply all the research sources. A second short assignment might give a similar problem but send students to the library or a library portal to find their own sources. Here is a possible hierarchy of tasks based on the amount of independent research required:

- Instructor gives all students the same problem (set at appropriate levels of difficulty).
  - Provides all the sources (via a printed packet or course website)
  - Provides some of the sources and asks students to find one or two more on their own
  - Asks students to find all the sources (as in options 2 and 3 of the therapeutic touch assignment in nursing)
- Instructor asks students to choose their own topics (which they must convert into a research problem) and find their own sources.

Using easier tasks as scaffolding assignments, instructors can build different kinds of sequences into a single course. For example, an instructor might assign a major choose-your-own-topic research paper for the end of the term, but earlier in the term, as scaffolding, assign one or two skill-building assignments using sources supplied by the instructor. Conversely, instead of a long research paper, a teacher might give two shorter research assignments during a term, providing all the sources for the first assignment and then letting students find some or all of their own sources for the second. Between the first and second assignment, the teacher might arrange an instructional session with a reference librarian geared directly to the second assignment. In the next section, I illustrate this second option—two short research projects, the first of which uses teacher-supplied sources.

A Two-Assignment Sequence of Short Meaning-Constructing Research Tasks

In Exhibit 13.1, an economics professor at my university, Gareth Green, builds two short research assignments into his course. His goal is for students to apply course concepts and mathematical methods to public policy issues.

Several aspects of this assignment are noteworthy. First, the assignment provides both a meaning-constructing task and a rhetorical context. Second, it requires students to think intentionally about research sources while also applying to a new problem the skills of economic analysis they are learning in class. By providing the sources and adding the requirement for an annotated bibliography, the professor can assess students' thinking processes as they read the source material. Note that the assignment

EXHIBIT 13.1

Paper #1: Recommendation Memo

Background: You take an internship with the Seattle Department of Transportation (SDOT) as a research economist to help inform Elizabeth Canon, the director of SDOT, on the implications of Seattle's Community Parking Program. Like most cities, Seattle is dealing with large budget deficits, and city council members are interested in finding new sources of revenue. One option under consideration is to significantly raise parking meter fees.

 Your Task: Canon has asked you to write a two-page memo on whether to increase parking meter fees. The memo must summarize the pros and cons of your recommended position, giving both supporting and alternative views. Fortunately, another intern (who has since been let go for not following directions) has performed the background research and found the sources that follow. You need to review these sources, make calculations regarding the fee increase and potential revenue, determine your position, write a two-page memo, and develop a graph that helps support your position. Not all pros and cons are quantifiable. It is important that you give quantitative and qualitative information so Canon can justify her position. There are public organizations and city council members on both sides of this issue, so it is imperative that your work is complete so Canon is well prepared.

 Format: Canon prefers the following standard memo format:

1. A paragraph orienting Canon to the purpose of your memo and summarizing your recommended position

2. Bullet points giving reasons in support of your recommendation, based on your analysis, calculations, and relevant information from the sources provided

3. Bullet points giving reasons opposing your recommendation

4. A graph that you must develop to support your own position, which should be referred to in the bullet points (Canon loves to show graphs to the media, so clarity is critical)

5. An appendix with supporting calculations that are clearly described

6. An annotated bibliography, because Canon wants to know which sources you use, which you do not use, and why.

 Canon, who is not an economist, is *extremely* busy. All writing has to be clear, concise, and accurate. (Note: She probably will not read your appendix describing your calculations, but she may ask another economist—me!—to do so.) The maximum length for the memo is two pages (not counting the graph, the annotated bibliography, or the appendix showing your calculations).

 Provided Sources: [The assignment lists seven articles provided on the course website. Articles range from peer-reviewed articles on the pricing of parking spaces to newspaper articles.]

 Grading: The memo will be graded using the following rubric

Grade Rubric		
Category and Percent of Grade	**Score 3–0**	**Comments**
Summary Paragraph – 10% Stating purpose of the memo, why important, and your recommendation, clearly written for intended audience		
Pro Points – 20% A complete list, clearly stated, supported with your own analysis and references		
Con Points – 20% A complete list, clearly stated, supported with your own analysis and references		
Graph – 10% Informative, correctly labeled and referenced in text, connected to objective		
Analysis/Calculations – 20% Demonstrating appropriate methodology, supporting objective, clearly explained		
Annotated Bibliography – 10% High-quality sources, explanation of value for your argument, referenced in report if used		
Mechanics – 10% Grammatically correct and clear report, has effective document design, is typographically correct		
Total		

doesn't ask students to use all seven sources in the paper, but only those that serve the purpose of the recommendation memo. Research savvy, the assignment implies, includes rejecting sources, not just piling them up for a longer bibliography.

The professor's second assignment, due at the end of the term, again asks students to role-play being a tax consultant on a policy issue (this time they have to advise a legislator on whether to support a state sales tax on candy) but ups the ante by sending students to the library and the Web to find their own sources. To help students find their own sources, the professor schedules a class session with a reference librarian on appropriate databases and search strategies for finding relevant sources. Again, a required annotated bibliography allows the professor and the librarian to assess students' information literacy skills.

Designing Backward: Teaching Research Skills to Novices

In the previous section, I suggested principles for designing short meaning-constructing research assignments that can serve as scaffolding for longer papers. This section, based on the principle of backward design, offers strategies for explaining research to students and for developing and sequencing research assignments. These strategies can be applied either to individual courses or to a whole curriculum. At the course level, teachers can use scaffolding assignments early in the term to prepare students for a major research project at the end. At the department level, faculty colleagues can coordinate a whole curriculum by developing assignments early in the major that prepare students for capstone projects as seniors. (The last section of this chapter focuses on the departmental level.) What follows are a variety of strategies for getting the most engaged student learning out of your research assignments.

Stress the Asking of Research Questions

Asking important, problematic, and significant questions is the heart of engaged research. By teaching students the art of question asking, teachers can remind them of the difference between an "all about" paper and a paper focused on a problem. Moreover, we want students to understand that the answers to their research questions are not something they *find* lying inertly in their research sources, but something they *make* through their own critical thinking brought to bear on the sources (Bean and Iyer, 2009).

As students move from discipline to discipline, they need to learn the kinds of questions that scholars in a given discipline typically ask. Novices often don't know how to distinguish a good question from a naïve one. One teaching approach is to model question-asking by regularly posing well-framed questions for students to consider through exploratory writing, small group discussions, or class debates. Another strategy is to help students see how the teaching points in a lecture are connected to underlying questions (see Chapter Eleven, pages 202–205, for modeling critical thinking in a lecture). Still another approach is to develop taxonomies of disciplinary questions, often in the form of templates that help students see typical ways that disciplinary questions are framed. Exhibits 13.2 and 13.3 show examples of question templates in the empirical sciences and in literary theory.

Explain the Function of Research Sources

As noted earlier in this chapter, students often think of research as going to the library or the Web to find information on a topic. Most of the words in a research paper, they assume, will be quotations, paraphrases, or summaries of these sources. Once they realize that most of their words should present their own arguments in their own voices, they become confused about the purpose or function of their sources. They are like new chess

EXHIBIT 13.2

Asking Determinate Research Questions

Question Type	Explanation	Natural Science Example	Social Science Example
1. *Existence Questions*: "Does X exist in domain Y?"	Often researchers simply want to determine whether a given phenomenon occurs or exists within a given domain.	Do fragments of fungi exist in Precambrian sediments?	Do advertisements for computers appear in women's fashion magazines?
2. *Measurement Questions*: "How large/small/fast/much/many/bright is X?"	Here researchers want to measure the extent to which something occurs (percentages) or the degree or size of a phenomenon.	How hot is the surface of Venus?	What percentage of children's birthday cards currently displayed at local stores contain gender stereotyping?
3. *Comparison Questions*: "Is X greater/less than Y or different from Y?"	Researchers frequently want to study how two events, groups, or phenomena differ according to greater or less amounts of some measure.	Is radiation from Jupiter's moon greater in volcanic areas than in nonvolcanic areas?	Do humanities majors report fewer study hours per week than non-humanities majors?
4. *Correlation questions*: "If X varies, does Y vary?"	This is a more complex kind of comparison question in which researchers determine whether differences in X are accompanied by corresponding differences in Y.	Does the aggression level of male rats vary with testosterone levels in their blood?	Do students' evaluations of their teachers vary with the grades they expect to receive from the course?
5. *Experimental questions*: "Does a variation in X cause a variation in Y?"	Here researchers move beyond correlations to try to determine the direct causes of a certain phenomenon.	If male rats are forced into stress situations to compete for food, will the level of testosterone in their blood increase?	Will preschool children taken shopping after watching TV commercials for high-sugar cereals ask for such cereals at a higher rate than children in a control group who did not see the commercials?

Source: *Adapted from Ramage, Bean, and Johnson, 2009, p. 24.*

players learning the moves of the pieces without any sense of the game's overall goal or strategies.

To address this problem, Joseph Bizup (2008) has developed a useful schema that can help undergraduates understand different functions that a source might play in a research paper. Bizup refers to his schema by the

---

EXHIBIT 13.3

Excerpt from Handout on Asking Questions About Literary Texts from Critical Perspectives

---

Political Criticism (Marxist, Feminist, Queer Theory)

Political critics look at texts through the lens of oppressed or disenfranchised groups. They try to show how a given text reproduces or challenges oppressive ideologies.

- How does this text reflect the author's class, gender, ethnicity, or sexual orientation? What assumptions or biases does it treat as "natural" or "universal" as opposed to socially constructed?

- Who are the silenced or marginalized characters in this text? If these characters could speak, how would they tell the same narrative? Why doesn't the author let them speak? What points of view are silenced or suppressed in this text? What is conveniently left out?

- What is the ideological vision of this text? How does it support (or fight) a social order that the critic finds unjust? How does it idealize social conflicts out of existence?

Deconstruction

Deconstructive criticism is very difficult to explain briefly. In general, deconstructive critics focus on the undecidability of texts. No single meaning can be ascribed to a text, because language doesn't refer to any consistent reality outside the text. Language is simply an endless echoing of other language.

- What binaries or oppositions are set up by this text (male/female, master/servant, city/country, nature/culture, old/young, beautiful/ugly, chaste/lustful)? For each binary, how does the text create a hierarchical value system that privileges or marks as superior one pole of the binary while devaluing the other? How can this value system be revealed as socially constructed as opposed to "universal" or "natural"? How do certain gaps, lacunae, or problematic passages in the text work to deconstruct the text's primary binaries?

- How can the same passages in the text be read in opposing ways?

- How does any consistent reading or interpretation of the text depend on an interpretive frame that can be shown to be culturally constructed? How can the critic deconstruct this frame and thus undermine the reading?

- How does our attempt to interpret any text break down at certain key places in the text? Why do readers always have to leave out parts of a text that don't fit their interpretations?

---

acronym BEAM, which I summarize in Exhibit 13.4 using my own explanations and examples. In my experience, Bizup's schema has more explanatory power than the sometimes slippery distinctions among primary, secondary, and tertiary sources. Unlike the concepts "primary" or "secondary," which are defined in terms of "distance" or "steps removed" from the writer's subject, Bizup's terms refer to the actual function of the source within the writer's argument.

In Bizup's schema, the "B" stands for Background sources, which constitute what the writer intends as uncontested facts and shared ideas

EXHIBIT 13.4

Bizup's "BEAM"

Kind of Source	Explanation	Example from literature *How are we to regard Jane's marriage to Rochester—liberation or loss?*	Example from sociology *How does gender socialization impact college-age drinking behaviors and attitudes?*
B Background sources	Any source, assumed to be noncontroversial, used to provide context—what writer and reader can stipulate as shared facts and information.	Encyclopedia article on Evangelism. Biography of the Brontës. Books or articles on the history/culture of a literary period. [When functioning as background, these sources are intended to provide shared information, not to serve as contestable parts of the argument.]	Current statistics on college-level drinking. Shared knowledge about gender socialization. News anecdotes about college-age drinking. Current relevant cultural artifacts (ads, movies, music, and so on). [These sources would typically appear in the introduction to provide context for the research.]
E Exhibits or Evidence derived from exhibits	Documents, data, field/lab observations, visual images, or other artifacts/objects that the writer analyzes. Particulars from "exhibits" are often used as evidence within the writer's argument.	The text of *Jane Eyre*. Contemporary cultural documents and reviews. Quotations, paraphrases, or other textual citations from *Jane Eyre* or other exhibits used to support the writer's claims (evidence).	Field observations of gender differences in drinking behavior at a party. Audiotapes of focus group interviews (researchers must design the questions and code the transcripts). Results of questionnaire data.
A Argument sources	The conversation of critical views and relevant scholarship surrounding the writer's question. Constitutes the "they" in "They say/I say" (Graff and Birkenstein, 2009). Usually argument sources are other scholarly articles or papers.	Books or scholarly articles that have addressed the writer's critical problem in *Jane Eyre*. Argument sources create the critical conversation that the writer is joining. The writer's goal is to add something new or challenging to this conversation.	Scholarly articles and papers that address gender socialization as potentially related to college-age drinking. Summary of argument sources creates the literature review, which aims to show what is still unknown or unresolved.
M Method or Theory sources	References to the theories or methods the writer is employing (sometimes implicit but often explicit).	Specific references to critical theories or methods—feminism, post-colonialism, new historicism, and so forth. Paper may cite particular theorist such as Foucault, Edward Said, or Judith Butler.	Citations to competing sociological theorists or theories about gender socialization. Citation of scholars associated with particular research methodologies.

Source: *Adapted from Bizup, J., 2008, 72–86.*

that provide the context for a paper. Background information, which the writer assumes will be accepted by the reader without controversy, might come from encyclopedias, reference works, news sources, textbooks, canonical earlier research, or other trusted disciplinary sources of shared knowledge.

Bizup's remaining kinds of sources—Exhibits, Argument sources, and Method/Theory sources—make up the rhetorical heart of academic research. Exhibits are the actual data/phenomena/artifacts that the researcher is puzzling over—an unusual rock formation, data from a spectrometer, private letters from an obscure eighteenth-century public official, the text of *Hamlet.* Extracted material from exhibits often becomes evidence in support of the researcher's thesis. What confuses novice students is that in some disciplines researchers go to the library to find their exhibits, whereas in other disciplines researchers go to a laboratory or the field. Whereas a history major may do her exhibit research in a library, working with archival sources, a biology major may do exhibit research observing plant fungi in a meadow. Meanwhile a literature major may do exhibit research simply by sitting in a coffee shop rereading *Hamlet.* Students need to understand that in all these cases, researchers are *doing research* by studying exhibits, even though only some of the cases involve a library.

Bizup's next category is an Argument source—his designation for the work of other scholars or commentators with whom the researcher is arguing—that is, other scholars who have studied the researcher's same question. For argument sources, researchers almost always go to a library or a library portal. Their goal is to position themselves in the scholarly conversation surrounding the topic—previous and contemporary scholars with whom the writer agrees or disagrees or upon whose work the researcher builds. The student researcher may also need to learn that different disciplinary genres use argument sources in different ways. In science writing, the conversation of different voices is usually placed near the beginning of the research report in the "review of the literature" section. In literary criticism, however, a writer often carries on a running argument with other scholars throughout the essay.

Bizup's final category is Method or Theory sources—references to scholars whose methods or theories the researcher is following or evoking. Thus a philosopher might apply the ethical theories of Kant or Mill to an issue in genetic engineering, even though these thinkers never addressed that issue. Similarly, an economist might evoke Keynesian theory to propose a government response to new economic data, while in the humanities and social sciences, scholars might look at a cultural artifact or phenomenon through the lens of critical theorists such as Foucault or Irigaray. Likewise, in the physical sciences scholars often employ specific methodological approaches that need to be documented.

Bizup sums up the distinctions among his categories by using different verbs for each kind of source. Writers *rely* on background sources, *analyze* or *interpret* exhibits, *engage* argument sources, and *evoke* or *imply* method/ theory sources. In my experience, spending class time explaining Bizup's BEAM in the context of one's own research assignments helps students use sources more purposefully. It has the additional advantage of helping students understand differences between disciplines or subdisciplines— particularly the differences in the kinds of exhibits scholars analyze or in the theories and methods they employ. (For another testimony to the usefulness of Bizup's scheme, see Troutman, 2009.)

Consider Teaming with a Subject Matter Librarian

Another major task is to teach students how to unlock the resources of the library and the Web, including online searches of databases and disciplinary archives. Novice researchers also need to learn how material gets included in a particular database and how to evaluate sources for political or theoretical bias. As a general rule, generic library tours are not as effective as discipline-specific workshops occurring at a "need to know" time for students. Teachers can work in partnership with reference librarians to develop appropriate strategies for a particular course or discipline. (The pedagogical literature has many examples of librarian/subject teacher partnerships and other ways that librarians can work with faculty to teach and assess information literacy. I particularly recommend Bent and Stockdale, 2009, as well as a pioneering work in information literacy across the curriculum, Lutzker, 1988.)

Develop Scaffolding Assignments for Using Evidence in a Field (Bizup's "Exhibits")

In his study of teaching practices that enhance learning, Light (2001) notes that "a surprising number of undergraduates describe learning how to use evidence to resolve controversies in their field, whatever their field, as a breakthrough idea" (p. 122). Short assignments that teach students how to derive evidence from disciplinary "exhibits" can help demystify a discipline's methods of inquiry and analysis. Depending on the discipline, exhibits might include experimental data, field observations, patient intake interviews, historical documents, poems or paintings, cultural artifacts, census data, and so forth. Such assignments also teach disciplinary ways

---

EXHIBIT 13.5

Example Assignments: Evidence

1. In light of our discussions of Christianity in *Jane Eyre*, read the nineteenth-century document "The Pious Little Sunday Scholar" from the *Children's Friend*. Then write a short paper (no more than two pages) addressing this question: To what extent would the author of "The Pious Little Sunday Scholar" consider Jane Eyre a Christian? For evidence, draw on a close reading of "Pious Little Sunday Scholar" as well as textual detail from *Jane Eyre*.

. . .

2. Using the attached tables as data, write a paragraph that makes a claim about the pattern of immigrant labor into postwar Germany from 1955–1970. Within your paragraph, reference a graph of your own design that argues visually what your paragraph argues verbally. Give your graph a figure number and a title, and label the axes clearly.

---

of framing and displaying evidence including, depending on the discipline, the use of quotations or summaries, graphs or tables, and photographs or drawings. (See Exhibit 13.5 for examples.)

Short assignments based on exhibits can be particularly illuminating in courses that rely primarily on textbook reading. Textbooks typically present a discipline's accumulated knowledge, but often make invisible the field's actual knowledge-making practices. Students reading a textbook chapter learn what astronomers know about the conversion of matter to energy in a star, but they often aren't taken behind the scenes to watch astronomers puzzling over spectroscopic data from a telescope. By giving students interesting exhibits to analyze, instructors let students role-play disciplinary scholars at work.

Develop Scaffolding Assignments for Joining an Academic Conversation (Bizup's "Argument" Sources)

At the heart of critical thinking is the argumentative move that Graff and Birkenstein (2009) call "They say / I say"—the ability to push against a view that differs in some way from one's own. Students need to be able to summarize what others have said about a problem ("they say") and then to assert their own voice into the conversation ("I say"). One of the best ways to teach this skill is to ask students to summarize an argument in your field (such as a scholarly article or a passage from an article) and respond to it in ways that teach disciplinary thinking.

Most students will have been introduced to these skills in first-year composition, where they learn how to summarize a text and then to speak back to it by analyzing the text's rhetorical strategies or by asserting their own ideas in response to the text. (Specific suggestions for teaching summary/strong response are found in Chapter Nine, pages 178–179.) In addition to assignments built around a single text, teachers can design more complex assignments that ask students to summarize two or more texts and then analyze similarities and differences among their claims, their methods, their theoretical perspectives, or their uses of evidence. Such assignments can be expanded to teach the kinds of literature reviews typical of many disciplinary genres. Here are three commonly recurring kinds of literature reviews that can be easily adapted to undergraduate research assignments. Such assignments can serve as scaffolds, teaching students how to use argument sources in a longer research paper.

Literature Review Establishing a Controversy

Common in the humanities or in civic arguments, this kind of literature review establishes a controversy. The writer typically summarizes scholarly works that take competing points of view on a disciplinary problem and then stakes out a claim that supports one side in the controversy (but adds something new), takes a synthesis position, or reframes the debate. (See Exhibit 13.6 for examples.)

"State of the Art" Literature Review

A "state of the art" literature review is common in professional disciplines where experts apply their knowledge and skills to clients' problems. The writer's goal is to determine the current best thinking of experts on an

---

EXHIBIT 13.6

Example Assignments: Controversy

1. You are a literary scholar addressing the following problem: "How are we to regard Caliban in Shakespeare's *The Tempest*?" I have posted on our course website two articles that answer this question in different ways. Write the section of your introduction that sets up this controversy through summary of the opposing views. Devote 150–200 words to each article. *Note:* I'm not asking you to have your own thesis—just summarize the controversy.

· · ·

2. Some states are considering legalizing marijuana and then taxing it as a source of state revenue. There are obviously qualitative arguments over whether this policy would be wise (ethical questions, social consequences), but for this paper I want you to focus only on quantitative arguments: Would legalizing and taxing marijuana significantly increase total state revenues? Your task is to write a brief literature review (no more than two pages) that summarizes the debate over this issue among economists and other finance and tax policy experts. Use as sources the two articles I have placed on our course website, but also find on your own one additional peer-reviewed article for a total of three articles. Do not take a position on this issue. Just summarize the controversy, showing the causes of disagreement.

EXHIBIT 13.7

Example Assignments: "State of the Art"

1. What does the current peer-reviewed literature say about the value of insulin pumps in managing Type I diabetes? Imagine as your audience a college-educated Type I diabetic contemplating switching from injections to a pump.

· · ·

2. Your research team has been asked to investigate how our university disposes of used computers, monitors, and other electronic equipment and to determine whether this method is environmentally sound. Write the review of the literature section of your report. Your aim is to show the current thinking about best environmental practices for disposing of used computers and monitors.

---

issue or question, often as part of a proposal to solve a problem. In this role, the writer researches cutting-edge knowledge on some contemporary problem and then reports what the experts currently think (see Exhibit 13.7). The writer's larger purpose is to apply this knowledge to a current problem (or help the targeted audience apply this knowledge).

"Gap in Knowledge" Literature Review

Common in the social and physical sciences, a "gap in knowledge" literature review shows what is known and not known about an empirical problem, often as part of the introduction to a scientific paper or grant proposal aimed at filling the gap through new research (see Exhibit 13.8).

Reverse-Engineer Your Course by Designing the Last Assignment First

So far I have discussed how short scaffolding assignments can help students learn how to incorporate research sources into their own arguments.

EXHIBIT 13.8

Example Assignments: "Gap in Knowledge"

1. Here are four experimental reports on the efficacy of different brushing methods (duration of brushing, brushing techniques, use of hand versus electric brushes) for removing plaque-forming bacteria from teeth and gums. Using these articles, write a brief literature review that explains what is known and not known about the most effective methods of brushing. (In class, we'll discuss possible experiments that might be the next step in research.)

· · ·

2. You are investigating the effect of sleep deprivation on cognitive function. Using the peer-reviewed articles I have supplied and finding at least three more on your own, write a literature review for a possible grant proposal to fund further research. Your goal is to highlight a gap in current knowledge about the effect of sleep deprivation on cognitive function.

In this section I turn to assignment design and sequencing within a whole course. In some courses, teachers might decide that one or more short assignments using sources can take the place of a longer research paper. In other courses, the instructor might prefer a substantial choose-your-own-topic research paper at the end of the term. In such a case, my advice is to design this last assignment first. Doing so can help instructors design earlier scaffolding assignments to teach skills needed for the final project or help students generate ideas for it.

I'll illustrate this process with one of my own courses. Exhibit 13.9 shows how I reverse-engineered a writing-intensive course in Renaissance literature—a course that had as one of its goals the teaching of research writing in literary studies. (For a departmental rationale for this course, see Bean and Iyer, 2009.) I'll first describe the "backward design" sequencing of assignments and then explain each assignment in more detail.

In the far right column of the table is the final assignment for the course, in which students had to pose their own interpretive question about a literary text and develop their own argument in conversation with other critics. Approximately three weeks before the final research paper is due, I require an exploratory essay, which is a personal narrative of each student's research and thinking process. (An alternative is an annotated bibliography due well before the final paper.) Near the middle of the term, students submit a prospectus, which guides them toward a problem-thesis structure and helps me identify students who need extra help. Still earlier in the term I assign a "mini-guided-research paper"—a scaffolding assignment that students can revise for a higher grade. Finally, as a means of generating ideas and modeling literary problems, I assign regular thinking pieces throughout the term. All the writing done earlier in the course thus serves as scaffolding for the final paper.

It should be noted that an instructor can assign this much writing only in a relatively small, writing-intensive course. For most courses the amount of writing could be pared down considerably. However, simply assigning a research paper at the end of the term without one or two scaffolding assignments along the way invites disappointment.

In the rest of this section I explain my scaffolding assignments in more detail.

Thinking Pieces

My regular use of thinking pieces follows strategies I describe in Chapter Seven. I use the thinking pieces to model question-asking strategies, to help students generate their own ideas, and to plant seeds for class discussions and small group tasks.

EXHIBIT 13.9
Example of a "Backward Designed" Assignment Sequence

Beginning of term ——————————————→ End of term

		Major Research Project		
Frequently Assigned Low-Stakes "Thinking Pieces" Along with In-Class Discussions and Small Group Tasks	**Skill-Building Research Assignment on *Paradise Lost***	**Prospectus for Major Researched Literary Paper**	**Exploratory Essay**	**Major Researched Literary Paper**
Thinking Piece #2: One of the most heated early debates on Hamlet—when critics focused on character—was why Hamlet delays. Try entering this debate. What is your theory on why Hamlet doesn't swoop to his revenge as he promises? *Thinking Piece #7:* The poet William Blake once said that Milton was "of the devil's party without knowing it." To what extent does Milton cast Satan as a heroic figure in Books I and II of *Paradise Lost?* *Thinking Piece #10:* Play the believing and doubting game with the following thesis: Milton's view of Eve is misogynistic.	See the assignment and rubric on p. 247 asking students to argue whether Milton's view of Eve is misogynistic and incorporating the views of one argument source (Gilbert and Gubar). Students can revise this paper for a new grade.	Submit a one-page (single-spaced) prospectus that describes the interpretive problem or question that you plan to address. Explain why you are personally interested in and invested in this question. Show how the problem or question is rooted in your chosen literary text. Show why the question is both problematic and significant.	Write an exploratory essay in which you narrate in first-person chronological order the evolution of your thinking as you reread your chosen text(s) and investigate what other scholars have said about your interpretive problem. In your paper, summarize the arguments of at least three scholars and explore your responses. At the end of your paper, you may or may not have found the thesis for your final argument. *Note:* An alternative assignment is an annotated bibliography.	Write an eight- to twelve-page literary argument addressing a significant question related to any of the texts we have read this term. The introduction to your paper should pose the question or problem that your paper will address and engage your reader's interest in it. Within your paper, you must join in conversation with other scholars who have addressed your interpretive problem. Your proposed answer to this question (summarized in a single sentence) will serve as the thesis statement for your paper. Imagine this paper will be delivered at an undergraduate research conference. Assume that your audience has *not* read this assignment and will attend your conference session because your title hooked their interest.

Mini-Guided-Research Paper

This scaffolding assignment, which students can revise and resubmit for better grades, teaches students the moves they will need for the larger research project due at the end of the term (see Exhibit 13.10). This "mini-guided-research paper" helps students learn to work with both an exhibit and an argument source (to use Bizup's terms from pages 237–241). Students must defend their own view of Eve's role in *Paradise Lost*, using literary evidence shrewdly. They also have to summarize another critic's view accurately and integrate it into their own argument. Finally, the assignment teaches MLA manuscript form and documentation style, so that the peculiarities of MLA become more second nature when they write the major paper that follows. Because all students in the class are working on the same assignment, class time can be devoted to classroom debates about the role of Eve in *Paradise Lost* and to skills needed for research writing within the literature major.

Prospectus

Requiring a prospectus gets students started early while emphasizing the problem/thesis structure of academic papers. Here are the questions I ask for my own course in literary studies. The questions can be adjusted to fit the demands and conventions of other disciplines.

Questions to Address in Your Prospectus

- What interpretive problem or question do you intend to address? Explain the problem, showing how it arises from your chosen text.

- What makes your problem problematic? What disagreements among scholars, gaps in knowledge, or complexities or inconsistencies in the literary text characterize the problem?

- What's at stake in addressing this problem? Why is it significant? To whom does it matter? How will solving it advance the conversation? How does your small problem connect to some larger problem?

- In addition to your chosen literary text, do you envision using any other exhibits (primary sources) such as other literary texts, contemporary historical documents, and so forth?

- Attach a preliminary bibliography of peer-reviewed scholarly articles or books that seem relevant to your interpretive problem. Some of these may serve as argument sources in your final paper (the network of other voices in the conversation that you are joining).

Such a prospectus moves students from a topic focus to a problem focus. Because the prospectuses will vary in quality, they can help the

EXHIBIT 13.10

Was Milton a Misogynist?

Situation: Renaissance misogynist writers typically tell the Adam and Eve story to justify patriarchy and warn men about women's seductive and deceitful nature. You wonder whether Milton in *Paradise Lost* has similarly misogynistic views of Eve. To extend your thinking, you have read "Milton's Bogey: Patriarchal Poetry and Women Readers" from Sandra Gilbert's and Susan Gubar's classic feminist study of nineteenth-century women novelists, *The Mad Woman in the Attic*.

    Your Task: Write a three- to four-page paper (double-spaced) that provides your argument in response to the question *"Does* Paradise Lost *reproduce the misogynist view of Eve frequently encountered in Renaissance anti-feminist discourse?"* Besides presenting your own well-supported position on this question, your essay must be in conversation with Gilbert and Gubar's views about Milton's misogyny in *Paradise Lost*.

    Follow the manuscript conventions of the Modern Language Association (MLA). Your essay will be graded on the criteria shown in the following rubric.

Title and Introduction

Criteria	10 9 8	7 6 5 4	3 2 1 0
Has a good title Presents and develops the problem of interpreting Eve Briefly summarizes a view being "pushed against" Ends with contestable thesis	Meets all criteria at high level; clear	Meets some criteria; uneven; less clear	Meets few criteria; unclear

Overall Quality of Ideas, Argument, Effective Evidence

Criteria	30 27 24	21 18 15 12	9 6 3 0
Has well-supported argument that anticipates reader's objections Uses "textually dense" evidence from *PL* (references to specifics including brief quotations, summaries of scenes, and so on) Has strong insights; shows clear wrestling with complexity	Meets all criteria at high level; clear	Meets some criteria; uneven; less clear; less precise use of evidence	Meets few criteria; unclear

Integration of Gilbert and Gubar

Criteria	10 9 8	7 6 5 4	3 2 1 0
Accurately summarizes Gilbert and Gubar's arguments about Eve and misogyny in *PL* Integrates summary smoothly into writer's argument Uses G and G effectively either as an opposing view, as support for the writer's own argument, or in other ways	Meets all criteria at high level; clear	Meets some criteria; uneven; less clear	Meets few criteria; unclear

Organization, Development, Sentence Clarity and Grace

Criteria	10 9 8	7 6 5 4	3 2 1 0
Has clear, easy-to-follow structure (reader doesn't get lost) Has sufficient development Follows old/new contract; has unified, coherent paragraph with good transitions Has clear, graceful, grammatically correct sentences	Meets all criteria at high level; clear	Meets some criteria; uneven; less clear	Meets few criteria; unclear

MLA conventions

Criteria	5	4 3 2	1 0
Looks like a professional paper in literary studies Follows MLA conventions for citation and documentation Follows MLA formatting for Works Cited and page design	Meets all criteria at high level	Meets some criteria; uneven; some deviation	Meets few criteria

Penalty for Editing Errors

+5 0 −2	−4 −6 −8	−10 −15 −20
Flawless paper (+5) or an occasional but minor error Strong professional ethos	Some distracting noise via spelling, punctuation, or apostrophe errors or occasional grammar mistakes (subject-verb agreement; fragments; nonparallel constructions); writer seems careless	Paper seriously marred by editing errors or grammatical mistakes; professional "ethos" of writer is destroyed by errors

teacher identify which students need early assistance. Also, the preliminary bibliography reveals something about students' research skills and their professionalism in following disciplinary formats for bibliographic entries.

Exploratory Essay

My favorite way to promote inquiry and combat plagiarism is to assign an exploratory essay due several weeks before the final research project. The exploratory essay is a first-person narrative account of the student's research process, tracing the evolution of his or her thinking. It requires that students keep their research problem open, delay closure, and hence explore their issues in depth. I enjoy reading these exploratory essays, which combine the genre of annotated bibliography with that of narrative reflection. (For a more detailed description of exploratory essays, see Chapter Six, pages 116–117. Note that the fifth hypothetical nursing assignment on therapeutic touch—pages 92–93—is an exploratory essay.) An alternative to the exploratory essay is simply an annotated bibliography.

Help Students Understand Why Their Readers Need Good Titles and Introductions

When students are turned loose to write a major research paper on topics of their own choice, they need to learn rhetorical strategies that make their work understandable and effective for new readers. Of particular importance are titles and introductions. (I typically ask students to imagine that they are presenting their papers at an undergraduate research conference where attendees choose sessions on the basis of a paper's title.) The quality of research papers often improves when students think about their readers' needs. Let's look first at introductions and then at titles.

Explaining the "Moves" in an Academic Introduction

Although disciplinary genres vary in many ways, most academic introductions follow some variation of a problem-thesis-blueprint structure. Novice writers can benefit from learning these three basic moves:

1. *Begin by explaining the problem you paper will address:* The writer's goal is to hook the reader's interest in the problem being examined, showing why the problem is problematic and what is at stake in solving it. (What are the gaps, contradictions, or disagreements that keep the problem open? What benefits will come from solving the problem? How will solving this one small problem help us understand or approach a related but larger problem?) In many cases, this opening section sets up either counterviews that the writer intends to oppose or a gap in knowledge or understanding that the writer intends to fill.

2. *Present your paper's purpose or thesis:* After explaining the problem, writers sometimes state their thesis directly: "Whereas Jones says X, I am going to argue Y." At other times, writers may use a "purpose statement," delaying their thesis until later. "The purpose of this paper is to show the inconsistencies of Jones's approach and to offer a possible way to resolve them."

3. *Provide an overview or blueprint of your paper.* The final move in a typical introduction gives the reader an overview of the whole paper, either by providing a brief summary of its argument or by forecasting its structure through a blueprint statement ("First, I will show . . . ; the second part of the paper explores . . . ; finally, I show . . . ").

Of course, experienced writers can vary from this suggested three-part structure. Additionally, some genres mandate important variations. (The experimental report, for example, substitutes a hypothesis for a thesis statement and omits the blueprint because readers already know the sections that will follow: Methods, Results, Discussion.) However, these three prototypical moves recur with such frequency that novice research writers should practice them.

To illustrate these moves, I provide students with one or two examples of academic introductions. Here is one such example, a particularly succinct academic introduction from a professional journal in economics; it is followed by my explanatory commentary. (I have numbered the sentences to facilitate commentary.)

Money and Growth: An Alternative Approach

[1] An enormous body of literature, beginning with the work of James Tobin (1965) and Miguel Sidrauski (1967), assesses the effects of sustained price inflation on the equilibrium growth path in a neoclassical setting. [2] The issue of how sustained capital accumulation, in turn, affects money's role in an evolving system of payments has received far less attention. [3] Thus, this paper takes an alternative approach to studying the problem of money and growth by developing a model in which both sides of the money-growth relationship may be examined. [*Sentences 4–9 summarize the argument to be presented.*] [10] Taking an alternative approach to money and growth, therefore, reveals that the most striking effects run not from money to growth, but from growth to money.

—P. E. Ireland, *American Economic Review,* March 1994, p. 47.

• • •

Sentence 1 provides background on a general problem and refers briefly to the academic conversation this article will join. Sentence 2 states the narrower problem this article will address; the actual question is implied:"How does sustained capital accumulation affect money's role in an evolving system of payments?" Sentence 2 also hints briefly at why this issue is significant: it has received little attention and thus promises to contribute to understanding. Sentence 3 presents a purpose statement indicating that the article will address the problem of growth and money by developing a model. Sentences 4–9 provide an overview of the whole article by summarizing its argument. Sentence 10 states the argument's thesis.

Once students appreciate the typical structure of introductions—the problem at the beginning and the thesis or purpose with blueprint at the end—they will better understand that their own research papers should follow a similar structure.

Explaining Titles

Once students understand the rhetorical function of introductions, they can understand the similar function of titles. Without guidance, students often write titles like "Paper #2" or "The Economy." But if you tell them that a good title replicates in miniature the problem-thesis function of the introduction, they will see how their titles should hook into their readers' already existing interest in a question or problem while also providing a nutshell hint of what's new. To help students compose effective titles for their own research papers, I point out three of the most common conventions for academic titles:

1. *State your question.* Some academic titles simply state the question that the body of the paper will address, thus implying that the paper will present a new answer ("Does Inhibition Decrease Overstimulation in Neural Networks?").

2. *Summarize your thesis or purpose.* Some academic titles summarize the paper's thesis or purpose, thus implying the preceding question ("The Relationship Between Client and Therapist Expectation of Improvement and Psychotherapy Outcome").

3. *Create a two-part title with a colon.* Some (perhaps most) academic titles use a two-part structure separated by a colon. The most common approach is to present key words from the question or problem to the left of the colon and key words from the thesis to the right ("Money and Growth: An Alternative Approach"). Another common pattern is to start with an interest-arousing "mystery phrase" that may not become clear until the reader reads the whole paper. Following the colon, the writer usually summarizes the article's problem, thesis, or purpose ("The Great White Out: A Triangulative Examination of the Exclusion of Blacks from Big Business").

After explaining these conventions for titles, I have students write tentative titles for their own research papers using each of the conventions. This exercise, which forces students to nutshell the whole of their arguments, often helps students discover a better focus for their drafts in progress.

Provide Models

A final strategy for helping students improve their research papers is to create a file of model papers from your past courses. Attach to each one an explanation of why you admire the paper, pointing out features you particularly like. If possible, include the prospectus and all the drafts of one of the papers. You can put this file on library reserve or post the papers on your class website.

Departmental Collaboration to Teach Undergraduate Research in the Major

At the beginning of this chapter, I mentioned my admiration for students presenting at the National Conference on Undergraduate Research (see the representative list of titles on pages 224–225). These students crossed the threshold from outsiders to "insiders," producing at an appropriate undergraduate level what MacDonald (1994) has called "expert insider prose." To me, their work embodies one of our aspirations as teachers—our hope that our advanced majors are learning to think and write like historians, economists, chemists, nurses, engineers, or literary critics and that upon graduation they will be able to transfer these disciplinary skills into their chosen professions. (Wanting our students to produce expert insider prose does not mean that we are grooming them all for graduate school. The skills needed for research writing—problem-posing, systematic gathering of data, analysis, consideration of alternative views, and responsible use of evidence to support a claim—are valued in any kind of career.) Moreover, I surmise that as students cross the threshold from outsider to insider, they also cross the threshold from superficial learning motivated by grades to deep learning motivated by engagement with questions. Their transformation entails an awakening—even, perhaps, a falling in love.

My goal in this final section is to use a novice/expert framework to explore the knowledge and skills that students must acquire to think and write as disciplinary insiders and then to suggest how departmental faculty can design a coherent curriculum that teaches and reinforces these skills sequentially. The key is to integrate into early and middle courses in the major the instructional modules and scaffolding assignments that prepare students for capstone projects in their senior year. On my own campus, we have used the national mandate for assessment to create departmental communities committed to these tasks of curricular design (Bean, Carrithers, and Earenfight, 2005).

Skills and Knowledge Needed for Expert Insider Prose

As we saw earlier in this chapter, the process of moving from novice to expert writer is neither simple nor linear. However, many of our students make this journey. The skills and knowledge needed for expert insider prose have been helpfully identified in a taxonomy developed by Anne Beaufort (2007, p. 19). Exhibit 13.11 provides my own expanded adaptation of Beaufort's taxonomy, to which I have added some of my own elements. (Particularly, I have added information literacy—a needed knowledge that

EXHIBIT 13.11

Skills/Knowledge Needed to Produce Expert Insider Prose in a Discipline

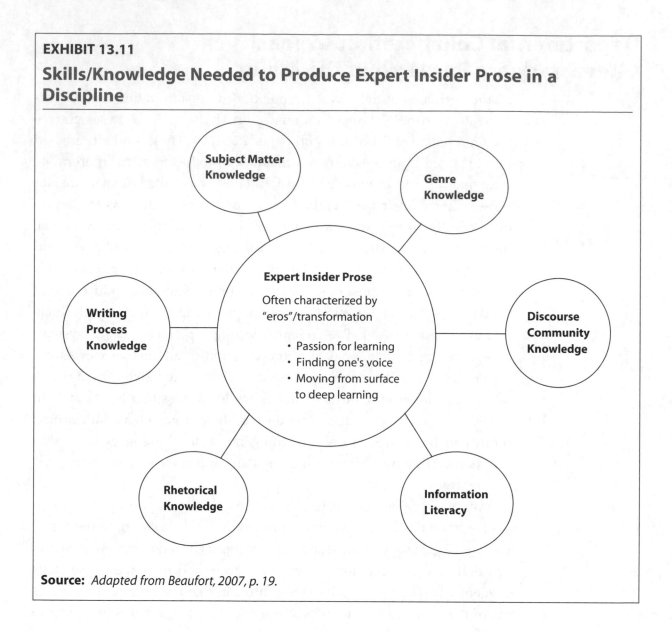

Source: *Adapted from Beaufort, 2007, p. 19.*

Beaufort implies but subsumes under other skills—and I have placed "eros" at the center of the diagram to express my own view of students' "awakening" into what we might call a love for the discipline.) Exhibit 13.11 thus aims to give readers a quick overview of ideas that Beaufort develops at greater length throughout her study.

As shown in the exhibit, "expert insider prose" requires students to develop at least six different kinds of knowledge or skills: subject matter knowledge, genre knowledge, discourse community knowledge, information literacy, rhetorical knowledge, and writing process knowledge. Some of these skills and kinds of knowledge can be introduced and practiced in first-year composition or in writing-intensive courses in a discipline. For example, almost any first-year writing course teaches writing process knowledge, entry-level information literacy, some rhetorical knowledge, and some introductory knowledge about different genres. The transfer of these skills and knowledges into later courses is facilitated by meaning-constructing assignments set within a rhetorical context (see earlier discussions of RAFT and TIP, pages 98–100).

However, some of these kinds of knowledge and skills can be learned only within the discipline itself. Of first-order importance is students' growth in subject matter knowledge, both conceptual and procedural. Willingham (2009), summarizing research in cognitive science, shows how expert thinking or behavior depends on an elaborate network of background knowledge, arranged in interconnected schemas and built into long-term memory. When confronted with a new problem, experts draw on this background knowledge, including similar problems they have faced in the past, flexibly chunking and combining facts, concepts, and procedures stored in memory. Willingham cites the "ten-year rule" (p. 139): it takes ten years of intense study and practice to become an expert in any field—to demonstrate what lies ahead for a novice entering a new domain of knowledge. Undergraduates obviously cannot be experts in this sense, but they can certainly be "experts-in-training," insiders rather than outsiders, persons who have begun their ten-year journey. Beaufort's taxonomy rightly shows the importance of disciplinary background knowledge, built up through a variety of courses in the major, as essential to expert insider prose.

Other kinds of knowledge are also acquirable only within the discipline itself, particularly discourse community knowledge and genre knowledge (I'll discuss genre knowledge in more detail shortly). In a sense, discourse community knowledge is the rhetorical equivalent of subject matter knowledge: one not only walks the walk of a disciplinary insider but also talks the talk. To enter a discourse community—to know a discipline's language—a person needs to know the discipline's specialized terminology, its evolving history, its competing theories and methods, its major scholars and works, its current questions and debates, and its other moves, motivations, and gestures that only insiders would recognize. Undergraduates, of course, can have only an entry-level sense of an expert's discourse community knowledge, but this entry-level sense can be enough to qualify for insider status.

At the center of my diagram, below the header "Expert Insider Prose," is the phrase "Often characterized by 'eros'/transformation." My intention here is to signal the importance of the affective domain as well as the cognitive in a student's journey. The movement from outsider to insider status is often marked by a movement from surface learning to deep learning and by an awakening interest in the field's questions and problems. Students start to discover their disciplinary "voices," their own agency as critical thinkers within a disciplinary conversation. This presence of engagement, passion, or enthusiasm among insider students has been documented by Thaiss and Zawacki (2006): "Students care deeply about how they can find room for their 'own ideas' and ways of expression within the intellectual and formal framework of the discipline" (p. 107). They develop a "passion for inquiry" (p. 140).

Teaching the Genres of Your Discipline

I devote a separate heading here to what Beaufort calls "genre knowledge." Because the conventional term paper is a pseudo-academic genre, students aiming for expert insider status need to present their research in one of the real genres of their discipline. Teachers can facilitate this process by building real genres into their assignments (see the discussion of RAFT, pages 98–100).

To help students gain genre knowledge in their disciplines, I have found helpful a scheme of "metadisciplines" and "metagenres" developed by Carter (2007). Exhibit 13.12 displays his scheme in a chart format using my own examples.

Carter shows how disciplines that are quite different in conceptual content have surprising similarities in the kinds of disciplinary work they do. Carter identifies four metadisciplines, which I label in Exhibit 13.12 as Problem Solving, Empirical Inquiry, Interpretive/Theoretical, and Performance. For example, professionals in business and engineering—despite the huge differences in their subject matter—often use their expertise to solve problems for targeted clients. Their prototypical metagenre is the practical proposal (see my template for this genre in Exhibit 13.13). In contrast, the physical and social sciences both focus on scientific inquiry aimed at advancing knowledge about the empirical world. Their shared metagenre is the empirical research report (Exhibit 13.14). The humanities generally focus on interpretation of cultural artifacts examined through the lens of various methods and theories. In Carter's terms, these disciplines conduct research by directly analyzing their chosen artifacts, by finding and examining archival or other sources that place their artifacts in an appropriate historical or cultural context, and by entering debates with other scholars. Their common metagenre (flexible in structure, without a fixed template) is the academic paper (journal article, conference paper) or academic book. Finally, the performance disciplines—dance, music, painting, creative writing, journalism—produce creative works or performances rather than academic papers. However, they share a common

EXHIBIT 13.12

Metadisciplines, Metagenres, Examples

Metadiscipline	Explanation	Typical Disciplines	Examples: Ways of Doing	Metagenre	Related Genres
Problem Solving	Disciplinary professionals use disciplinary knowledge and procedures to solve real-world problems for a targeted client.	Business, engineering, applied economics, agriculture, some subdisciplines in the social sciences	Finance professional proposes better way to forecast future value of a new product. Engineering team designs a lighter battery with a faster recharging time.	Practical proposal to solve a problem	• Recommendation memo • Technical report • Feasibility studies • White paper • Management plan • Technical documentation • Funding proposal
Empirical Inquiry	Researchers use disciplinary knowledge and procedures to advance empirical understanding of the world.	Physical and social sciences	Biologist studies energy transfer within cells. Psychologist studies effect of stress on test performance.	Experimental Research Report with IMRD structure (introduction, methods, results, discussion)	• Ethnography • Qualitative study • Technical description • Scientific article • Poster • Conference presentation • Research proposal
Interpretive/ Theoretical	Researchers interpret documents/artifacts/cultural phenomena through various theoretical lenses with expectations that problems will be continuously debated rather than "solved."	Humanities and interpretive disciplines within Fine Arts (such as art history)	Literary scholar uses New Historicist theory to interpret *Hamlet*. Historian uses archival documents and feminist theory to reinterpret medieval queenship.	Disciplinary journal article (no clear structural template)	• Conference paper • Conference presentation • Book chapter • Book • Edited collection
Performance	Ways of knowing result in performances.	Fine arts (such as dance, musical performance sculpture), journalism, multimedia production, creative writing	Sculptor mounts a studio exhibit. Journalist writes a feature article.	Reflection/ critique	• Program notes • Reviews • Portfolio

Source: *Adapted with my own modifications from Carter, 2007, 385–418.*

EXHIBIT 13.13

Structural Template for Practical Proposal

Letter of Transmittal

- Usually addressed to decision maker who has power to act on proposal
- Introduces writer
- Explains purpose and significance of proposal from perspective of targeted audience
- Briefly explains the proposal
- Briefly summarizes main reasons for acting, focused on values of audience

Exploration questions

- Is the targeted audience already aware of the problem?
- If not, how can I motivate engagement?
- How can I frame the problem, solution, and justification from the perspective of the audience?

Executive Summary (optional for short proposals)

- Summarizes the problem, proposed solution, and justification
- Provides quick overview for busy reader

Exploration questions

- How can I condense this proposal into a nutshell?
- How can I keep the focus on the main ideas while omitting details?

Description of Problem

- Describes and develops problematic situation
- Shows who is harmed by problem and why
- Gives problem "presence"
- Explains significance of problem—why it is worth solving

Exploration questions

- What is the problem? Explain it to someone who might not have seen or felt the problem.
- For whom is the problem a problem?
- How do these people experience the problem?
- How are they inconvenienced or harmed by the problem? (Give specific examples in order to make the problem real and vivid to the reader.)
- Who has the power to solve the problem?
- Why hasn't the problem been solved up to this point?

Description of Proposed Solution

- Describes the solution at an appropriate level of detail for audience; includes specifics and costs
- May include and reject alternative solutions or move this section to justification

Exploration questions

- What are possible ways this problem could be solved?
- Which solution seems the most feasible or practical or cost-effective?
- Create a specific proposal on how to solve the problem.

Justification of Proposed Solution

- Shows the benefits to be derived from the proposal
- Shows why benefits outweigh costs
- As appropriate, makes additional arguments based on principles (say, doing X is just) or on precedents (say, X has been done successfully elsewhere)

Exploration questions

- What are the probable benefits of acting on your proposal?
- What costs are associated with your proposal?
- Who will bear those costs?
- Why should this proposal be enacted? (Create the best possible argument for acting on the proposal.)
- Why is it better than alternative proposals?

EXHIBIT 13.14

Structural Template for Empirical Research Report (APA Style)

Title Page

- Gives title of paper and author's name; provides a "running head" that will subsequently appear before the page number in the upper right-hand corner

- Follows format of an APA title page and body of research report (see current APA manual)

Abstract

- Provides one-paragraph summary of whole paper (problem, methods, major findings, significance of study)

Introduction

- Explains the problem to be investigated

- Shows importance of the problem

- Reviews previous studies examining the same problem (a *literature review*) and points to conflicts in these studies or to unknowns meriting further investigation

- Poses the determinate research question(s) to be investigated

- Presents the researcher's hypothesis

Method

- Describes how the study was done (enabling future researchers to replicate the study exactly)

- Often has subheadings such as "participants," "materials," and "procedure"

- Often provides operative definitions of key concepts in the problem/hypothesis

Results

- Presents the researcher's findings or results

- Often displays findings in figures, charts, or graphs as well as describing them in words

- Usually does not present raw data or behind-the-scenes mathematics; data focuses on composite results

- Presents statistical analysis of data to show confidence levels and other advanced statistical implications or meanings

Discussion

- Presents researcher's analysis of the results

- Interprets and evaluates the collected data in terms of the original research question and hypothesis

- Speculates on causes and consequences of the findings

- Shows applications and practical or theoretical significance of the study

- Usually includes a section pointing out limitations and possible flaws in the study and suggests directions for future research

(Continued)

References

• Presents a bibliographic listing of cited sources

• Follows APA format (see current APA manual)

Appendices

• Provides a place to include questionnaires or other materials used in study

written metagenre—the reflection that aims to explore the artist's intentions and methods and offers a critique of the work or performance. (For a possible template, see Exhibit 13.15.)

Carter's work helps us appreciate the implications of what Thaiss and Zawacki (2006) call "compact" versus "diffuse" disciplines (pp. 14–16). In a compact discipline (typical examples might include literature departments, chemistry departments, and many psychology departments), department members tend to work in the same metagenre. In a diffuse discipline, however, department members are apt to work in different metagenres, complicating curricular design for undergraduates. For example, in a diffuse field like political science, some scholars do problem-solving aimed at public policy, others do empirical research, and still others do interpretive/theoretical work.

Whether a student majors in a compact or a diffuse discipline, Carter's taxonomy can help undergraduates make sense of the kinds of work done by scholars in their major field. By creating rhetorical contexts for their assignments, teachers can introduce students to their discipline's metagenre(s) as well as to the network of related genres that are particularly valuable for undergraduates.

Designing the Curriculum Backward

Working together, departmental faculty can design the curriculum backward to ensure that the skills and knowledge needed for expert insider prose are taught gradually and sequentially in key courses throughout the major. Backward design requires faculty members to give up some autonomy in key courses in favor of coordinated teamwork that may include at designated places in the curriculum communally designed assignments or community-designated assignment types—what Gerald Graff (2009) calls a dismantling of "courseocentrism" in favor of shared goals.

A typical place to begin is deciding what kind of research project might be required at the end of the undergraduate major, a project that would

EXHIBIT 13.15

Structural Template for Performance Reflection

The metagenre of "performance reflection" is more open, fluid, and subject to individual variation and creative voice than are the metagenres of proposal, experimental report, or academic paper in the humanities. The following template is suggestive of one way in which a performance reflection might be structured.

Overview of the performance project	• Set context by providing details about time and place of performances , shows, or exhibits • [Or] provide details about what is included in a portfolio, including your principles for selecting portfolio pieces.
What was I trying to do?	• Explain your intentions and goals for your work or performance: What were you trying to accomplish? • Situate your work within a context of other works: Whom were you trying to emulate or resist? What influences were you trying to follow or shake off? • Explain some of the decisions you made along the way. Why did you take one path rather than another? [Your purpose in this section is to help your reader understand your creative process and your behind-the-scenes thinking and decision making.]
How well did I succeed?	• Evaluate your own work—do a self-critique. • Explain the criteria you use to judge a performance in your medium or craft. • Explain the extent to which your work meets these criteria and show why.
What did I learn about my craft/medium/art form?	• Explain what you learned about your craft/medium/art form now that you have completed this project. • Show what you've learned about the demands of this craft and about the nature of the creative process.
What did I learn about myself?	• Explain what you have learned about yourself. • Connect your performance to your overall growth as an artist, performer, or learner. • Reflect on how your work connects to your overall education. How can you integrate your performance with your overall sense of purpose in life and goals for your future?

culminate in "expert insider prose." What counts as expert insider prose could range, depending on discipline, across a variety of genres and audiences:

- Academic or scholarly writing within the discipline (for example, a capstone paper suitable for presentation at an undergraduate research conference, whether in the sciences or the humanities)

- Professional workplace writing (proposals, reports, technical papers, or other disciplinary kinds of professional writing aimed at specific audiences)

- Civic or public argument on local or national issues related to the discipline

- Other kinds of writing or communication projects specific to a major or discipline (creative projects, websites, multimedia presentations, and so forth)

Ensuring that all students in the major have to produce such a paper or project for graduation requires faculty decisions about curriculum design. Some departments embed such papers in senior seminars or a senior capstone course. Others embed the papers in designated 400-level electives. Still others require such a paper as part of a senior portfolio. How to define expert insider prose—and how high to set the bar—is the responsibility of faculty who teach within the major.

Upstream from the senior project are courses earlier in the major charged with creating assignments and instructional modules that teach the skills that students will need as seniors. (Of course, not all courses in a curriculum need to focus on research papers or research writing. There should be plenty of room in a curriculum for assignments focused on goals other than undergraduate research.) Early scaffolding assignments in courses selected for the research-writing stream teach students how to frame disciplinary questions and work with the discipline's "exhibits" or exhibit sources. At least one early course needs to focus on information literacy, teaching the databases and specialized resources used by disciplinary insiders. Scaffolding assignments in such a course can teach students how to join conversations going on in the discipline's peer-reviewed literature. Throughout the curriculum, assignments with the features recommended in the NSSE/WPA best practices research—interactive elements, meaning-making tasks, and clear expectations and grading criteria (see pages 97–100)—will ensure that students practice using all the kinds of knowledges and skills in Beaufort's taxonomy.

Conclusion: Engaging Students in Research

Although first-year composition courses can teach the "research paper" in a generalized way, these skills don't transfer easily into research papers across the curriculum. When disciplinary faculty appreciate the complexity of academic research writing in general, and the specialized practices of their own disciplines in particular, they see why the skills required for undergraduate research need to be taught within the major. Although this chapter has focused primarily on pedagogical strategies for teaching undergraduate research, I have also had, I freely admit, a subgoal: I hope to spark faculty discussions about pedagogy that can inspire teachers to overcome "courseocentrism" in favor of departmental communities working together on a shared curriculum.

Reading, Commenting On, and Grading Student Writing

14

Using Rubrics to Develop and Apply Grading Criteria

art Three focused on a variety of strategies for promoting active learning and for coaching students as thinkers and writers. In Part Four, we turn to strategies for coaching the writing process and for commenting on and grading student papers. As teachers, our goal is to maximize the help we give students while keeping our own workloads manageable. Although assigning grades may be the last step of this process, planning your grading criteria at the outset (and communicating these criteria clearly to students) will enhance your ability to coach student writers and make your commenting on student papers more efficient and helpful.

Because of the importance of determining grading criteria at the time you create an assignment, Part Four begins with this present chapter, which offers advice on creating and using rubrics. Chapter Fifteen turns to timesaving strategies for coaching the writing process so that teachers don't become buried in paper grading. Finally, Chapter Sixteen focuses on ways to write revision-oriented marginal and end comments that guide students to make significant, global revisions of drafts.

At first it may seem that determining grading criteria is a straightforward matter—after all, "good writing is good writing." But the processes by which individuals make judgments about writing are surprisingly complex, and controversies concerning evaluation of writing are among the most heated in composition studies. I begin this chapter with a brief summary of this controversy. I then provide an overview of different kinds of rubrics, giving teachers options for finding an approach that is adaptable to their disciplinary goals and to their own teaching styles and evaluation practices. In the last sections of the chapter, I describe objections that some teachers make to rubrics, explain my own method for using rubrics, and offer suggestions on how teachers can find approaches to grading that work for them.

Controversies About Evaluation Criteria

Trying to decide the relative merits of a piece of writing can lead to a tangle of uncertainties. Because we teachers have little opportunity to discuss grading practices with colleagues, we often develop criteria that seem universal to us but may appear idiosyncratic or even eccentric to others. In fact, the first half-hour of a paper-grading workshop can be demoralizing even to the most dedicated proponents of writing across the curriculum. What do teachers actually want when they ask students to write?

Answering this question requires us to steer a middle ground between subjective and communal standards. Professional writing teachers grant that the assessment of writing, like the assessment of any art, involves subjective judgments. But the situation is not entirely relative either, for communal standards for good writing can be formulated, and readers with different tastes can be trained to assess writing samples with surprisingly high correlation. But the potential for wide disagreement about what constitutes good writing is a factor with which both students and teachers must contend.

The extent of this disagreement was illustrated by Paul Diederich (1974) in one of the most famous experiments in composition research. Diederich collected three hundred essays written by first-year students at three different universities and had them graded by fifty-three professionals in six different occupational fields. He asked each reader to place the essays in nine different piles in order of "general merit" and to write a brief comment explaining what he or she liked and disliked about each essay. Diederich reported these results: "Out of the 300 essays graded, 101 received every grade from 1–9; 94 percent received either seven, eight, or nine different grades; and no essay received less than five different grades" (p. 6).

However, Diederich discovered some order in this chaos. Through factor analysis, he identified five subgroups of readers who correlated highly with one another but not with readers in other subgroups. By analyzing the comments on the papers, Diederich concluded that each subgroup was consistently giving predominant weight to a single criterion of writing. Sixteen readers were putting main emphasis on quality of ideas; thirteen on sentence structure, usage, spelling, and punctuation; nine on organization and development; nine on creative wording or phrasing; and seven on liveliness or committed voice, a factor Diederich labeled "flavor and personality." (Diederich counted one reader in two categories; hence these numbers add up to fifty-four rather than fifty-three; see his book, pp. 6–10, for details.)

Diederich's research enabled him to develop procedures through which a diverse group of readers could be trained to increase the correlation of their grading. By setting descriptions for high, middle, and low achievement in each of his five criterion areas—ideas, organization, sentence structure, wording, and flavor—Diederich was able to train readers to balance their assessments over the five criteria. Since then, numerous researchers have refined or refocused Diederich's criteria and have developed strategies for training readers as evaluators and for displaying criteria to students in the form of rubrics (see, particularly, Walvoord and Anderson, 2009; White, 1994, 1992; and Cooper and Odell, 1977). Through participation in departmental or cross-disciplinary "norming sessions" individual instructors can be trained to reach high levels of agreement on grades, often coming to see their own idiosyncrasies in evaluating writing and appreciate more fully other teachers' ways of reading. This strand of grading practice—which might be called the "pro-rubric" strand—aims to minimize differences among readers in order to achieve interrater reliability in the application of communally determined criteria.

I say the "pro-rubric" stand because not everyone values rubrics, although there seems to be a consensus in favor of rubrics within most composition programs and WAC/WID programs. My experience also suggests that most teachers across the curriculum welcome rubrics, especially if they have the freedom to choose the kinds of rubrics that best fit their values and teaching styles. I'll explain the controversy over rubrics later in this chapter, but first let's look at the many different kinds of rubrics available.

An Overview of Different Kinds of Rubrics

Rubrics come in many different sizes, shapes, and flavors. The primary variations are the following:

- They can be analytic or holistic
- They can be generic or task-specific (sometimes called "primary trait")
- They can use different methods of describing performance levels
- They can have a grid or a non-grid design

Let's look at each in turn.

Analytic Versus Holistic

Evaluation criteria can be presented to students either analytically or holistically. The analytic method gives separate scores for each criterion—for example, ideas, organization, use of evidence, attention to alternative views, sentence structure—whereas the holistic method gives one score that reflects the reader's overall impression of the paper, considering all criteria at once. Many instructors prefer analytic scales because the breakdown of the grade into components, when combined with the instructor's written comments, conveys detailed information about the teacher's judgment of the essay. Many analytic scales weigh some criteria more heavily than others, depending on what the instructor wishes to emphasize. Thus you might allot twenty-five points for ideas, fifteen points for organization, and ten points for sentence structure. Some people object philosophically to analytic scoring on the grounds that writing cannot be analyzed into component parts. They argue that ideas can't really be separated from organization, or clarity of expression from clarity of thought. Such people often prefer holistic evaluation, which does not suggest that writing is a mixture of separable elements. Also, holistic grading is faster and so is often preferable when one's main concern is rapidity of scoring rather than providing detailed feedback. Exhibit 14.1 is an analytic rubric that gives separate scores for each criterion. Exhibit 14.2, designed for grading of summaries, is a holistic rubric that gives a single score for each summary.

Generic Versus Task-Specific

Both analytic and holistic rubrics can also be classified as generic (sometimes called "general description") or as task-specific (sometimes called "primary trait" rubrics). Generic rubrics follow one-size-fits-all designs, aimed for use across a variety of writing tasks. As much as possible they try to be universal. In contrast, task-specific rubrics are designed to fit an individual assignment or genre. Exhibit 14.1 illustrates a general description rubric. To a lesser degree, so does Exhibit 14.2, which identifies the generic traits of a good summary without reference to any particular article

EXHIBIT 14.1

Generic Writing Rubric Using Analytic Method

Author's Name _____   Title of Piece _____

	1 Does Not Meet	2 Partially Meets	3 Does Not Fully Meet	4 Meets	5 More Than Meets	6 Exceeds
Content/Ideas	Writing is extremely limited in communicating knowledge, with no central theme.	Writing is limited in communicating knowledge. Length is not adequate for development.	Writing does not clearly communicate knowledge. The reader is left with questions.	Writes related, quality paragraphs, with little or no details.	Writing is purposeful and focused. Piece contains some details.	Writing is confident and clearly focused. It holds the reader's attention. Relevant details enrich writing.
Organization	Writing is disorganized and underdeveloped with no transitions or closure.	Writing is brief and underdeveloped with very weak transitions and closure.	Writing is confused and loosely organized. Transitions are weak and closure is ineffective.	Uses correct writing format. Incorporates a coherent closure.	Writing includes a strong beginning, middle, and end, with some transitions and good closure.	Writing includes a strong beginning, middle, and end, with clear transitions and a focused closure.
Vocabulary/Word Choice	Careless or inaccurate word choice, which obscures meaning.	Language is trite, vague, or flat.	Shows some use of varied word choice.	Uses a variety of word choices to make writing interesting.	Purposeful use of word choice.	Effective and engaging use of word choice.
Voice	Writer's voice/point of view shows no sense of audience.	Writer's voice/point of view shows little sense of audience.	Writer's voice/point of view shows a vague sense of audience.	Writer uses voice/point of view. Writes with an understanding of a specific audience.	Writer has strong voice/point of view. Writing engages the audience.	Writes with a distinct, unique voice/point of view. Writing is skillfully adapted to the audience.
Sentence Fluency	Frequent run-ons or fragments, with no variety in sentence structure.	Many run-ons or fragments. Little variety in sentence structure.	Some run-ons or fragments. Limited variety in sentence structure.	Uses simple, compound, and complex sentences.	Frequently varied sentence structure.	Consistent variety of sentence structure throughout.
Conventions	Parts of speech show lack of agreement. Frequent errors in mechanics. Little or no evidence of spelling strategies.	Inconsistent agreement between parts of speech. Many errors in mechanics. Little evidence of spelling strategies.	Occasional errors in agreement between parts of speech. Some errors in mechanics. Some evidence of spelling strategies.	Maintains agreement between parts of speech. Few errors in mechanics. Applies basic grade-level spelling.	Consistent agreement between parts of speech. Uses correct punctuation, capitalization, and so on. Consistent use of spelling strategies.	Uses consistent agreement between parts of speech. No errors in mechanics. Creative and effective use of spelling strategies.

This rubric is provided by ReadWriteThink.org, a Thinkfinity website developed by the International Reading Association, the National Council of Teachers of English, and in partnership with the Verizon Foundation..

EXHIBIT 14.2

Generic Rubric for Summary Writing Using Holistic Method

Explanation: A summary should be directed toward imagined readers who have not read the article being summarized. The purpose of the summary is to give these persons a clear overview of the article's main points. The criteria for a summary are (1) accuracy of content, (2) comprehensiveness and balance, and (3) clarity, readability, and grammatical correctness.

Rubric

6 A 6 summary meets all the criteria. The writer understands the article thoroughly. The main points in the article appear in the summary with all main points proportionately developed (that is, the writer does not spend excessive time on one main point while neglecting other main points). The summary should be as comprehensive as possible and should read smoothly, with appropriate transitions between ideas. Sentences should be clear, without vagueness or ambiguity and without grammatical or mechanical errors.

5 A 5 summary should still be very good, but it can be weaker than a 6 summary in one area. It may have excellent accuracy and balance but show occasional problems in sentence structure or correctness. Or it may be clearly written but be somewhat unbalanced or less comprehensive than a 6 summary or show a minor misunderstanding of the article.

4 A score of 4 means good but not excellent. Typically, a 4 summary will reveal a generally accurate reading of the article, but it will be noticeably weaker in the quality of writing. Or it may be well written but cover only part of the essay.

3 A 3 summary must have strength in at least one area of competence, and it should still be good enough to convince the grader that the writer has understood the article fairly well. However, a 3 summary typically is not written well enough to convey an understanding of the article to someone who has not already read it. Typically, the sentence structure of a 3 summary is not sophisticated enough to convey the sense of hierarchy and subordination found in the essay.

2 A 2 summary is weak in all areas of competence, either because it is so poorly written that the reader cannot understand the content or because the content is inaccurate or seriously disorganized. However, a 2 essay convinces the grader that the writer has read the essay and is struggling to understand it.

1 A 1 summary fails to meet any of the areas of competence.

---

that the student has been assigned to summarize. In contrast, Exhibits 14.3 and 14.4 are task-specific rubrics, 14.3 for the genre of the practical proposal and 14.4 for an assignment requiring use of graphics. Note how particular details of the genre or the assignment appear in the rubrics, such as "Description of the Proposed Solution" in Exhibit 14.3 or "Quality of the Interrelationship between Graphics and Words" in Exhibit 14.4. Neither of these rubrics could be applied universally to a different genre or assignment.

EXHIBIT 14.3

Task-Specific Rubric for a Genre: Practical Proposal

Letter of Transmittal and Document Design	10 9 8	7 6 5 4	3 2 1 0
• Has an effective letter of transmittal (addressed to appropriate decision maker; serves as executive summary: briefly explains problem, describes proposed solution, and summarizes supporting reasons) • Has professional appearance; good document design with clear headings and appropriately labeled diagrams (if needed); conveys strong ethos	Meets all criteria at high level	Meets some criteria; uneven	Meets few criteria
Presentation of the Problem	10 9 8	7 6 5 4	3 2 1 0
• Clearly describes the problem without presupposing the solution • Gives problem "presence" (chooses appropriate methods for motivating reader to care about problem) • Adequately develops the problem (shows who is affected, what is at stake); anticipates objections of a skeptical reader who dismisses the problem	Meets all criteria at high level; clear and developed	Meets some criteria; uneven; occasionally thin; some lapses in clarity	Meets few criteria; often unclear or undeveloped
Description of the Proposed Solution	10 9 8	7 6 5 4	3 2 1 0
• Describes proposed solution clearly • Explains costs; pays attention to practical details; convinces reader that writer has done his or her homework • Solution is made to seem doable • If writer proposes a planning committee to develop details of solution, writer clearly points out the details of a successful solution	Meets all criteria at high level; clear, easy to follow	Meets some criteria; uneven or has some lapses in clarity or development	Meets few criteria; often unclear or undeveloped
Justification for Proposed Solution	10 9 8	7 6 5 4	3 2 1 0
• Strongly motivates reader to act on the proposal; designs justification section by imagining chief reasons for audience resistance • States clear, effective reasons in support of proposal • Supports reasons with effective evidence • Effectively ties into values and beliefs of audience	Meets all criteria at high level; clear, easy to follow	Meets some criteria; uneven or has some lapses in clarity or development	Meets few criteria; often unclear or undeveloped

(Continued)

Overall Clarity of Writing	10 9 8	7 6 5 4	3 2 1 0
• Follows reader-expectation theory (forecasting, mapping; old/new contract; strong organization with topic sentences at head of paragraphs) • Is clear, concise, adequately developed, and graceful • Avoids errors in grammar, punctuation, usage, or spelling	Meets all criteria at high level	Meets some criteria; uneven	Meets few criteria
Overall Effectiveness of Document	10 9 8	7 6 5 4	3 2 1 0
• Effectively accomplishes writer's purpose of calling attention to a problem, proposing a solution, and giving strong reasons for acting on the proposal • Will make a persuasive first impression on intended audience if sent in present form • Shows strong ethos—gives decision maker a favorable impression of the writer's professional motives, and good will	Ready to submit with only minor revisions/edits	Good potential but some/significant revision or editing still needed	Back to the drawing board

---

EXHIBIT 14.4

Task-Specific Rubric for an Assignment Requiring Graphics

The assignment: You are a technical writer for an environmental organization that advocates for a coherent national energy policy. Periodically this organization publishes one-page informational pieces aimed at the general public. (Typically, the organization buys newspaper space for the pieces, which are desktop published in a two-column format that wraps around one or more inserted visuals—see attached example.) You are asked to write one of these one-page informational pieces on some meaningful "story" related to energy production and consumption, as shown in Table 888, "Energy Supply and Disposition by Type of Fuel: 1960–2003" from the U.S. Census Bureau, *Statistical Abstract of the United States: 2006.* Your goal is to pull information from the table to raise public consciousness about an environmental problem. Make your piece camera-ready by using a two-column format in which text wraps around at least one rhetorically effective graphic.

Rubric for Graphics Assignment

Quality of content (tells a significant energy story)	10 9 8	7 6 5 4	3 2 1 0
Increases reader's understanding of an environmental problem related to energy Has a clear informative purpose aimed at raising consciousness Uses "new" or "surprising" information to change reader's original view about some aspect of energy production or consumption Shows significance of the issue Is clearly written and easy to follow	Meets all criteria at high level; clear and easy to follow	Meets some criteria; uneven or has some lapses in clarity or development	Meets few criteria; often unclear or undeveloped

Quality of graphics	10 9 8	7 6 5 4	3 2 1 0
Graphics are visually appealing and easy to read Graphics have effective titles that refer to all pertinent dimensions of the graphic (both axes, legends) Graphics have effective labels, legends Graphics are effectively referenced in text	Meets all criteria at high level; clear and developed	Meets some criteria; uneven; some lapses in clarity	Meets few criteria; often unclear or undeveloped
Quality of the interrelationship between graphics and words	10 9 8	7 6 5 4	3 2 1 0
Follows principle of independent redundancy (tells in words the same story told by the graphic) Chooses effective details from the graphic to highlight the graphic's message Is easy to follow—reader readily sees how graphic supports story and story supports graphic	Meets all criteria at high level; clear, easy to follow	Meets some criteria; uneven or has some lapses in clarity or development	Meets few criteria; often unclear or undeveloped
Has strong overall effectiveness (professional appearance, clarity, Impact)	10 9 8	7 6 5 4	3 2 1 0
Is camera-ready, formatted to look like the model example Effectively integrates graphics into the page design Is clear, well-organized, concise, adequately developed, and graceful Is well-edited, without errors in grammar, punctuation, usage, or spelling (see separate reduction for editing errors)	Meets all criteria at high level	Meets some criteria; uneven	Meets few criteria

Deductions for Rule-Based Errors in Grammar, Punctuation, Usage, or Spelling

Positive ethos		Annoying noise		Errors destroy ethos	
+5 0 −3		−5 −8 −10		12 −15	

Different Methods of Describing Performance Levels

Finally, analytic rubrics can differ in the way they specify levels of achievement for each criterion. The most common approach, illustrated in Exhibit 14.1, gradually "steps down" the descriptors from level to level (in this case, six levels) to indicate different degrees of performance or merit. Typical step-down language includes terms such as these:

always	usually	some of the time	rarely
fully	adequately	partially	minimally
high or broad	adequate	limited	very limited

Although this step-down approach with specific descriptors for each level seems to be the gold standard for analytic rubrics, teachers often find the production of step-down descriptors inordinately time-consuming. As a result, they may be reluctant to develop a new task-specific rubric for each assignment, preferring either to not use rubrics or to find a one-size-fits-all generic rubric. A workable solution to this problem is to use the simplified step-down approach shown in Exhibits 14.3 and 14.4. In these rubrics the traits for excellence for each criterion are listed in the left-hand column. The right-hand columns then use boilerplate descriptors for "stepping down" the performance:

Meets most criteria   Meets some criteria   Meets few criteria

To adapt the rubric to different assignments, a teacher merely needs to identify the traits to be evaluated (identified in the rows) and the criteria for strong performance (placed in the left column). For the right-hand columns, the teacher pastes in a boilerplate grid. In many cases, some of the traits and criteria descriptors—particularly for "sentence clarity" or "mechanics"—can stay the same for different assignments.

Grids Versus No Grids

Finally, some teachers want to explain their grading criteria to students but avoid the constraints of grids and specific descriptors that may seem overly positivist and prescriptive. One teacher's solution is the gridless rubric shown in Exhibit 14.5. Instead of specific descriptors for each criterion, this teacher simply presents each criterion as a question, leaving blank space in which to write brief comments explaining the student's numerical score for each criterion.

Controversies About Rubrics

I value rubrics, and I will shortly argue in favor of using rubrics tailored to individual assignments; however, before we proceed, it is worth summarizing the important controversies that have been provoked by the use of rubrics.

The Problem of the Universal Reader

In his important book *What We Really Value: Beyond Rubrics in Teaching and Assessing Writing* (2003), composition researcher Bob Broad raises philosophical and pedagogical objections to an underlying aim of many pro-

---

EXHIBIT 14.5

Analytic Rubric with Non-Grid Design: Argument Assignment

1. Does the introduction effectively present the issue and the thesis, while evoking reader interest? (10 points)

2. Are the ideas sufficiently complex? Are there good reasons in support of the thesis? Is the argument logical? (30 points)

3. Are opposing or alternative views adequately and fairly summarized? Are the responses to the opposing views effective? (20 points)

4. Is there appropriate and sufficient evidence? Is the argument well-developed, with appropriate details? (20 points)

5. Is the essay well organized into a unified whole? Are there good transitions? Do paragraphs have topic sentences? (20 points)

6. Is language style effective? Is language well chosen for the intended audience? Is the tone appropriate? (10 points)

7. Are sentences well constructed? Is the paper carefully edited? (20 points)

---

rubric advocates—the achievement of interrater reliability in the evaluation of writing. This aim, he argues, promotes the false notion of a "universal reader," trained to read in an unnatural way in order to apply negotiated criteria that do not, in any holistic or meaningful sense, belong to the actual reading practices of real readers. The message sent to students is that there are universally agreed-on standards for good writing, when in fact these standards are temporarily forged via norming sessions that cause individuals to read unnaturally. Moreover, the criteria set forth in typical rubrics are an oversimplification of what we really value, leaving out the subtleties and nuances valued by real readers.

Although rubrics can help assessors reduce a complex performance into a single grade, Broad argues that this practice hides an important reality that students must learn to negotiate: different readers read in different ways. (We teachers learn to negotiate this reality when an article submitted to a scholarly journal gets praised by one peer reviewer and slammed by another.) Consider, for example, the difference in the messages contained in the following two kinds of comments that we might hypothetically place on a student paper:

Comment 1: Although the ideas in this paper are often superb, showing lots of insights into the differences between Smith and Jones, the paper nevertheless has organizational problems that caused you to lose points. Grade = B

Comment 2: Readers who value organization are going to find your paper rough sledding. But those who work hard at filling in some of the gaps in your prose will be excited by superb ideas in this paper, particularly your insights into the differences between Smith and Jones.

Here Comment 1, based on a typical rubric, shows how losing points for organization causes the grade to be a B. Comment 2, in contrast, conveys the more rhetorically complex world of actual readers who read in different ways. Whereas Comment 1 shows how the writer lost points, Comment 2 shows how the writer lost certain readers. Comment 2 avoids sending the message that the paper's impact or worth can be reduced to a single grade.

The Problem of the Generic Rubric

Closely related to the problem of the universal reader is the problem of the generic rubric—the dream that a single one-size-fits-all rubric could be applied to a variety of writing contexts. For a typical example of a generic rubric, consider Exhibit 14.1, a "writing rubric" available on the websites of the National Council of Teachers of English and the International Reading Association. The criteria along the vertical axis of the rubric closely match the criteria established by factor analysis in Diederich's original research. Its seamless progression of performance categories across all the criteria lulls readers into believing that the rubric could be applied to any piece of writing.

What is masked by the rubric is the carnival of different reading practices produced by different disciplinary expectations and genres. The difficulties of establishing a generic rubric are made especially clear in the cross-disciplinary research of Thaiss and Zawacki (2006), who studied the criteria used by faculty across the disciplines in grading student writing. The authors discovered that teachers from any discipline tended to use the same universal language when discussing the kind of prose they valued ("good organization," "good ideas," "clarity," "absence of errors," and so forth). However, their interpretation of these terms was shaped by their different disciplinary practices so that what an art historian meant by "good organization" or "good ideas" might differ substantially from the meanings intended by a chemist, nurse, or political scientist. (See also Nowacek, 2009, for an analysis of how a literature teacher, a history teacher, and a religion teacher mean different things by "thesis statement." I discuss her research on pages 60–61) These researchers also emphasize the influence of subdisciplines in creating different reading practices among persons in the same broad disciplinary field. For example, subdisciplines within political science create their own characteristic expectations for effective writing: a normative policy proposal differs substantially from a theoretical argument in political philosophy, and both of these differ from an empirical study of voting practices in urban versus suburban districts in a given county. These examples show why a generic rubric can't accommodate the rhetorical contexts of different disciplines and genres. However, narrower rubrics, adapted specifically to a genre or to an individual assignment, may still be valuable.

The Problem of Implied Precision

Another problem with rubrics raised by some readers is their seeming claim to precision. It's one thing to say that a paper's organization is confusing or that the writer fails to identify underlying assumptions in one of the sources. It's another thing entirely to circle numbers showing the precise location of this paper on several different criterion categories—as if our minds had a set of grading meters that registered, say, 8 on the "organization" scale, 22 on the "ideas" scale, and 15 on the "effective use of evidence" scale. Although we might circle the numbers in a way that feels comfortably consistent and fair, we might also have little faith in the exactness implied by the scales. The powerful rhetorical effect of the rubric grid and its neat categories pushes us toward pretending an objectivity that does not match the complex mixture of likes and dislikes we feel toward any particular paper. For this reason, different readers react differently to different kinds of rubrics. A highly specified rubric with many different criteria categories and carefully spelled out performance gradations may appeal to one kind of reader and repel another. (For those repelled, a very simple rubric in a non-grid format—see Exhibit 14.5—might be a compromise.) In any case, we each need to make our own decisions about the kinds of rubrics that work for us, while at the same time providing students with a helpful and meaningful assessment of their work.

My Own Approach to Using Rubrics

I hope that the preceding overview of the kinds of rubrics and of the objections some users make to them will help individual teachers decide the role of rubrics in their own grading practices. In this section I explain my own personal (and perhaps idiosyncratic) way of using rubrics, which I offer as an example of how one teacher has tried to resolve some of the grading dilemmas raised by objections to rubrics.

My own approach is to design task-specific rubrics for each assignment and apply them using what I call a "left-brain, right-brain" method. I prefer task-specific rubrics because generic rubrics don't easily accommodate the subject matter and rhetorical contexts of my assignments and because task-specific rubrics give students more meaningful feedback about their performance. (I have been particularly influenced in my use of task-specific rubrics by the work of Walvoord and Anderson [2009], who call these rubrics "primary trait analysis scales.") To speed up the design of new rubrics, I use the simplified step-down approach shown in Exhibits 14.3 and 14.4, which allows me to boilerplate parts of the rubric using templates that I store on my hard drive. An example of one of my own rubrics adapted to a specific assignment is shown in Chapter Thirteen, pages 248–249.

My own method of using rubrics may at first seem counterintuitive. Because I want to avoid the impression that rubrics imply *precision*, I make sure that the numbers on my rubric grids do not represent either course points or percentage points (the numbers on my grids never add up to 100). Moreover, when I return graded papers to students, I always present the grade as a letter (B or C– for example), not as a rubric score. I explain to students that the circled numbers on the rubric represent a kind of "For Official Use Only" space often seen on bureaucratic forms. I then explain to students how I grade a paper. Here is my process:

- I quickly read over a small sample from the whole set of papers to get a sense of their range and to assess the kinds of problems likely to show up. I then begin reading and marking the papers one at a time.

- As I read a paper, I make marginal comments along the way (see Chapter Sixteen).

- I give the paper a holistic right-brain letter grade based on my head-and-gut feeling of where the paper falls on an A-to-F scale. I place this provisional grade very lightly in pencil in one corner of the paper (for example, "B–").

- I write my end comment on the strengths of the paper and the recommendations for revision (see Chapters Fifteen and Sixteen).

- I then staple a copy of the rubric to the paper and circle my number scores for each trait. But I don't add up the numbers at this time. (Later, the sum of the numbers will be my provisional left-brain score for the paper.)

- I then move on to the next paper.

When I have graded all the papers in this way, I then add up the numbers on each rubric so that each student's paper now has two provisional grades—a right-brain letter grade and a left-brain rubric number.

My next step is to compare the two grades by seeing how the high, middle, and low letter grades match up with high, middle, and low rubric scores. Usually the rankings correspond quite closely, but occasionally I will find mismatched anomalies needing reconciliation. For example, I might have given different letter grades (let's say an A– and a B) to two papers that ended up with the same rubric score (let's say a 61). To reconcile the scores, I reread both papers, making adjustments as needed. In my hypothetical case, I might note that other papers with rubric scores in the 61 range received an A–. So if I thought the B paper should actually receive an A–, I simply erase the provisional B and change the grade. Conversely, if I think it deserves a B, I fudge the numbers on the rubric to deduct some more points. Once I have reconciled the anomalous papers, I can determine ranges for each letter grade so that rubric scores and letter scores correspond. Thus, on my hypothetical example, I might say that 63 and above is an A; 60–62 is an A–; 57–59 is a B+; 49–58 is a B; and so forth. In a sense, the two sides of my brain negotiate the grade so that a numerical rubric score serves as a check on the holistic letter grade—a process quite different from letting the rubric scores determine the grade directly according to some algorithm.

Although this process might seem time-consuming, I believe it leads to fairer and more thoughtful grades because each paper receives a score from both a holistic and an analytic perspective. The occasional differences between the right-brain and left-brain scores invite me to reread anomalous papers in order to give the paper the fairest possible grade. (Typically in a batch of twenty-five papers I might have four or five anomalous papers.) In practice, the process isn't very time-consuming at all, and I rather enjoy comparing rubric scores to initial right-brain grades.

The payoffs for me in using this system are as follows:

- The combination of two provisional grades on each paper leads to more balanced and fair grading.

- This system means I don't have to abandon my holistic brain-and-gut awareness that a paper's value can't be reduced to the sum of its parts (my right-brain holistic score trumps the rubric).

- The descriptive criteria on the rubric, along with the circled scores for each trait, provide helpful feedback to students and allow me to write shorter marginal and end comments. I don't have to repeat in my comments the same information conveyed by the rubric.

- My explanation to students of how I grade papers lets me privilege my holistic right-brain judgment and de-emphasizes the rubric numbers. I almost never have students challenge the numbers or ask "Why did I lose points in this category?"

- My rubric scores on a paper make my revision conferences with students more efficient because the circled scores for each trait indicate at a glance the main problem areas in the paper.

- Finally, by analyzing the distribution of rubric scores for each trait among the set of papers ("ideas," "attention to alternative views," "use of evidence," "organization," and so forth), I can identify general patterns of strength and weakness in student performance and develop ideas for improving instruction next time.

Deciding on an Approach to Grading That Works for You

This concluding section illustrates the range of options available to teachers in developing task-specific rubrics, suggests strategies for conducting a departmental "norming session," and ends with some comments about setting standards for grades.

Finding What Works for You—From Simple to Elaborate Rubrics

As my overview of the range of options has shown, teachers differ substantially in the kinds of rubrics and grading practices that work for them. Some teachers simply can't warm up to scaled rubrics with descriptors and grids. They are often happy, however, with a gridless rubric of the kind shown in Exhibit 14.5. Other teachers prefer simple rubrics that provide students with only a few high-level messages. As an example of a very simple rubric, consider Exhibit 14.6, which was developed by an English professor for an assignment on Joseph Conrad's *The Secret Sharer.* The task-specific rubric, which she gives to students at the time she passes out the assignment, reinforces key features she expects in students' essays and also serves as a guided checklist for peer reviews.

Another kind of simple rubric—often preferred by teachers who combine short assignments with models feedback—is a six-point holistic

EXHIBIT 14.6

Simple Rubric for an Introductory Literature Course Scoring Guide for Assignment on *The Secret Sharer*

Your essay is supposed to provide a supported answer to the following question:

How has the experience with Leggatt changed the captain so that what he is at the end of the story is different from what he was at the beginning?

In order to do well on this paper, you need to do these things:

1. Have your own clear answer to this question.

2. Support your answer with strong arguments and textual details.

3. Make your essay clear enough for a reader to understand with one reading.

Criterion 1. Does your essay have a thesis statement at the end of the first paragraph that answers the question regarding changes in the captain?

No thesis or unclear thesis   Clear thesis

2	4	6	8	10

Criterion 2. Is your thesis supported with strong argumentation and use of significant details taken from the story?

Weak argument and/or lack of details as support   Strong argument and good details as support

2	4	6	8	10

Criterion 3. Is your paper easy for a reader to follow?

Paragraphing and transitions

2	4	6	8	10

Clear sentences

2	4	6	8	10

Accurate mechanics: grammar, spelling, punctuation, neatness

2	4	6	8	10

Source: Used by permission of Dr. Dolores Johnson.

scale such as that shown in Exhibit 14.7. This rubric was used for grading the physics microthemes discussed in Chapter Six (pages 113–115). For a discussion of models feedback, see Chapter Fifteen, pages 313–314).

In contrast, other teachers prefer highly detailed rubrics. Exhibit 14.8, developed by two chemistry professors who team-designed a sophomore organic chemistry course, is an elaborate rubric for grading the final experimental reports submitted by students at the end of the year. (For a description of this course, which eliminated "lab reports" in favor of teaching the real genre of a scientific paper, see Alaimo, Bean, Langenhan, and Nichols, 2009.)

EXHIBIT 14.7

Holistic Scale for Grading Physics Microthemes.

6, 5 Microthemes in this category will show a confident understanding of the physics concepts and will explain those concepts clearly to the intended audience. A 6 theme will be clearlywritten throughout; will contain almost no errors in spelling, punctuation, or grammar; and will have enough development to provide a truly helpful explanation to learners. A 5 theme will still be successful in teaching the physics concepts to the intended audience but may have more errors or somewhat less development than a 6. The key to microthemes in the 6, 5 category is that they must show a correct understanding of the physics and explain the concept clearly to a new learner.

4, 3 Microthemes in this category will reveal to the instructor that the writer probably understands the physics concepts, but lack of clarity in the writing or lack of fully developed explanations means that the microtheme would not teach the concept to new learners. Microthemes in the 4, 3 category are usually "you know what I mean" essays: someone who already understands the concepts can tell that the writer probably does, too, but someone who does not already understand the concepts would not learn anything from the explanation. This category is also appropriate for clearly written essays that have minor misunderstandings of the physics concepts or for accurate essays full of sentence-level errors.

2, 1 These microthemes will be unsuccessful either because the writer fails to understand the physics concepts, because the number of errors is so high that the instructor cannot determine how much the writer understands, or because the explanations lack even minimum development. Give a score of 2 or 1 if the writer misunderstands the physics, even if the essay is otherwise well written. Also give a score of 2 or 1 to essays so poorly written that the reader can't understand them.

EXHIBIT 14.8

Elaborate Rubric for a Scientific Paper in Chemistry

Introduction

General background and theory

8 7 6	5 4 3	2 1 0
Adequately sets the stage for the specific context and relevance of the experimental aim. Background information and theory are concise and correct.	Inadequately sets the stage for the specific context and relevance of the experimental aim. Background information and theory are somewhat broad, wordy, or partly incorrect.	Does not set the stage for the specific context and relevance of the experimental aim. Background information and theory are too broad or wordy and incorrect.

Specific context and relevance

8 7 6	5 4 3	2 1 0
Describes why the study is important in the context of the known literature. Naturally leads the reader to the scientific aim. Context is concise and correctly described.	Context is only partly described. Organization confuses link between context and scientific aim. Context is incorrectly described in some places or wordy.	Does not describe why the study is important in the context of the known literature. Does not lead the reader to the scientific aim. Context is incorrectly described and too wordy.

Scientific aim

4 3	2	1 0
Clear statement of the scientific aim. Reader is sure of the scientific questions being asked. Aim is understood correctly by the author.	Refers generally to scientific goals without focusing on specific scientific questions. Aim is only partly understood by the author.	Unclear, very general, vague. Includes educational objectives. Aim is misunderstood by the author.

Experimental Procedures

Is the description complete and concise?

10 8	6 4	2 0
Procedure contains enough information that it is reproducible (through the text or by appropriate referencing). Procedure conveys only necessary and relevant information.	Procedure is missing some critical information required for fully evaluating or reproducing the experiment. Procedure is wordy in some sections. Contains some unnecessary or irrelevant information.	Procedure is so vague that readers cannot begin to evaluate or reproduce the experiment. Procedure is verbose and contains large quantities of unnecessary or irrelevant information.

Data/Results

Text

10 8	6 4	2 0
Text is complete and concise. Data interpretation not included.	Text is wordy or incomplete in some sections.	Text is missing or contains large amounts of incorrect or irrelevant information.

Data choice, data processing, figures

5 4	3 2	1 0
Contain all data that support or contradict the arguments made in the discussion. Contain no irrelevant or redundant data. Data are processed correctly.	Missing some critical data or contain irrelevant or redundant data. Data are processed incorrectly in some places.	Missing most critical data or contain large amount of irrelevant or redundant data. Data are processed incorrectly in most places.

Data/figures presented in a logical, organized, professionally formatted fashion

5 4	3 2	1 0
Presentation choice (table, graph, or figure) enhances understanding. Appropriate legends and captions are included. Data format is correct.	Presentation confuses understanding of information. Legends and captions are unspecific or difficult to follow. Data format is mostly correct.	Presentation choice makes understanding the data impossible. Legends or captions are missing. Data are improperly formatted.

Discussion

Is discussion persuasive?

10 8	6 4	2 0
Effectively uses data to address scientific aim. Key data are interpreted correctly. Deeply thought-out argument that logically leads to conclusions.	Relationship between data and scientific aim sometimes muddled. Key data are not always interpreted correctly. Uses some important data. Argument is sometimes weak.	Does not effectively use data to address scientific aim. Key data are interpreted incorrectly. Fails to use the key data. Argument is weak or nonexistent.

(Continued)

Is discussion complete?

10 8	6 4	2 0
All data and error that support or contradict the conclusions are discussed.	All data and error that support or contradict the conclusions are partially discussed.	All data and error that support or contradict the conclusions are poorly discussed.

Restatement of aim

2	1	0
Scientific aim is restated clearly without using the same language found in the introduction.	Scientific aim is restated clearly by copy/paste from the introduction.	Scientific aim is not restated clearly.

Summary of key experimental findings

8 7 6	5 4 3	2 1 0
Summary is clear, concise, complete, and correct.	Summary is unclear, verbose, incomplete, and/or incorrect in a few places.	Summary is unclear, verbose, incomplete, and incorrect in most places.

References

Are references appropriate?

5 4	3 2	1 0
Reference sources are appropriate for a scientific paper. Number and variety of references indicate that the author has a high level of understanding of the subject.	Some reference sources are not appropriate for a scientific paper. Number and variety of references indicate that the author has a moderate understanding of the subject.	Reference sources are inappropriate for a scientific paper. Small number of references indicate that the author has little understanding of the subject.

Are references formatted properly?

5 4	3 2	1 0
References properly cited in text and formatted correctly.	References not properly cited in the text but formatted correctly.	References are improperly cited in the text and formatted incorrectly.

Overall Writing Style

Is the writing style appropriate for the audience?

5 4	3 2	1 0
Sounds like a professional chemist—clear, concise, persuasive.	Sounds like a good chemistry student—somewhat clear, concise, persuasive.	Sounds like a chemistry student new to scientific writing—unclear, verbose, unpersuasive

Writing mechanics

5 4	3 2	1 0
Grammar, punctuation, usage, and spelling enhance paper quality.	A few mechanical errors, but does not distract reader too greatly.	Many mechanical errors severely distract from meaning of paper.

Source: Alaimo, Bean, Langenhan, and Nichols. Originally published in WAC *Journal 20 (November) 2009 and used courtesy of WAC Journal.*

Conducting a Group Norming Session

A good way to improve one's grading practices is to join a conversation with colleagues about what constitutes excellent, good, satisfactory, and poor papers. My favorite approach is a strategy recommended by Thaiss and Zawacki (2006, pp. 158–159), which I summarize here.

A facilitator preselects four sample papers written in response to an assignment within your discipline. (If the group is cross-disciplinary, the sample papers might come from a composition course or a core/gen-ed course.) The facilitator should select papers that exhibit a range of proficiency but that are close enough in quality so that participants, in making distinctions among the papers, must articulate and apply their criteria. The process begins with a discussion of two of the papers: participants are asked to judge which is better and why. As participants make their cases for one or the other of the papers, the facilitator lists on the board each criterion mentioned in the discussion. The group then reads the remaining two essays, once again exchanging views on which of the two is better. (If this discussion elicits new criteria not previously mentioned, the facilitator adds them to the cumulative list.) Finally, the group rates all four papers against each other. To end the exercise, Thaiss and Zawacki recommend a concluding step: the facilitator points to each of the criteria mentioned in the discussions and asks participants to vote, by a show of hands, which they consider "important." Because some criteria will drop out for lack of support, the criteria remaining on the list represent a consensus.

Participating in a norming session such as this can increase instructors' communal confidence in their grading practices. At first, participants may feel disoriented, even dismayed, to realize that their judgments of a paper are not shared by colleagues. But discussion soon reveals that differences among readers occur because readers are applying different criteria. Confidence returns once participants recognize that a paper's "grade" is a contestable claim rather than a Platonic essence—that judgments must be supported by criterion-based arguments. Participants appreciate that, with some adjustments of reading strategies, criteria can be shared and explained to students through rubrics. Moreover, each participant's criteria may expand and become more subtle and nuanced as his or her reading practice is influenced by those of colleagues. For other approaches to conducting group norming sessions, see White (1992), who provides a detailed description of a large-scale norming session along with sample student essays and reader-developed scoring criteria. See also Bateman's discussion of scoring a set of sociology essays dealing with ethnocentrism (1990, pp. 110–116).

Determining Grades

It is one thing to say that one essay is stronger than another. It is quite another thing to decide whether the stronger paper merits an A or a B or something else. Assigning a final grade to a piece of writing always poses a dilemma, and I can offer no easy advice. Teachers who worry about grade inflation argue that high grades should be given only to truly excellent papers that meet the "superior" standards set on a benchmarked rubric. Teachers who worry that low grades can affect students' psyche, motivation, scholarship eligibility, or career options—or who fear that low grades may influence student evaluations of their teachers—are often satisfied with a lower bar. The knottiest question of all is determining what we mean by a "high" grade and a "low" grade. In my day a C was an OK/satisfactory grade, but to many students now it is a low or very low grade, Is a B+ a high grade or an OK grade? (Politically, if faculty members want to engage the grade inflation debate, benchmarked rubrics can be very helpful. Teachers can first try to agree where papers fall on the rubric. Then a separate discussion can determine how letter grades should be keyed to the rubric scores.)

No matter where you draw the line for a certain grade, it is best to strive for as much consistency and fairness as possible. In grading essay exams or short papers, many teachers develop schemes for not knowing who the authors are until the papers are graded. (One method is to have students identify their papers with a randomly chosen number and to disclose their code number only after the papers are graded; another is to have students put their names on the back of the last page.) Not knowing who wrote which essay eliminates any halo effect that might bias the grade.

To avoid grading on the curve, some teachers like to establish criteria for grading that are as objective and as consistent as possible. Although this is no easy task, Exhibit 14.9, written several decades ago by Cornell University English professor Harry Shaw (1984), shows how one professor makes his decision. It is as good a guide as any I know.

Conclusion: The Role of Rubrics in Coaching the Writing Process

The aim of this chapter is to help instructors articulate their expectations for papers early on and to determine their grading standards in advance of an assignment. If instructors attach a rubric to their assignment handouts, this advanced information about grading criteria helps them coach student writers more efficiently (see Chapter Fifteen) and write more

---

EXHIBIT 14.9

How I Assign Letter Grades

In grading "thesis papers" I ask myself the following set of questions:

1. Does the paper have a thesis?

2. Does the thesis address itself to an appropriate question or topic?

3. Is the paper free from long stretches of quotations and summaries that exist only for their own sakes and remain unanalyzed?

4. Can the writer produce complete sentences?

5. Is the paper free from basic grammatical errors?

   If the answer to any of these questions is "no," I give the paper some kind of C. If the answer to most of the questions is "no," its grade will be even lower.

   For papers which have emerged unscathed thus far, I add the following questions:

6. How thoughtful is the paper? Does it show real originality?

7. How adequate is the thesis? Does it respond to its question or topic in a full and interesting way? Does it have an appropriate degree of complexity?

8. How well organized is the paper? Does it stick to the point? Does every paragraph contain a clear topic sentence? If not, is another kind of organizing principle at work? Are the transitions well made? Does it have a real conclusion, not simply a stopping place?

9. Is the style efficient, not wordy or unclear?

10. Does the writing betray any special elegance?

11. Above all, can I hear a lively, intelligent, interesting human voice speaking to me (or to another audience, if that's what the writer intends) as I read the paper?

    Depending on my answers to such questions, I give the paper some kind of A or some kind of B [pp. 149–150].

---

helpful, encouraging, and revision-oriented comments on drafts or final papers (see Chapter Sixteen). This chapter has explored various kinds of rubrics and various ways of using rubrics to determine a grade for a paper. While rubrics can help teachers arrive at more consistent and fairer grades, they do not remove the subjective element from grading or reduce paper grading to a positivist activity. Used in conjunction with a well-designed assignment, they go a long way toward making your expectations clear to students and helping them revise their papers to achieve the kind of work you look forward to reading.

15

Coaching the Writing Process and Handling the Paper Load

College professors are busy people. This chapter assumes that you have a heavy teaching load, many committee responsibilities, obligations for scholarship and professional development, and hope for a meaningful life outside of work. Because you have only limited time to spend on student writing, the goal of this chapter is help you spend that time as efficiently as possible. Whereas the previous chapter focused on developing rubrics for grading student work, this chapter gives you ten timesaving strategies for coaching students as they work on one of your assignments. These strategies will help your students produce their best work, while keeping your paper-grading load manageable.

The general theory behind these strategies is to accomplish the following:

- Get students on the right track early in the writing process before serious problems begin cropping up in drafts.

- Take advantage of the "summarizable" nature of closed-form thesis-governed writing.

- Enlist other students in the class (or writing center consultants) as first readers of drafts.

- Make efficient use of student conferences.

- Develop timesaving methods for marking and grading student essays.

Some of the following strategies, though moderately time-intensive the first time you try them (for example, developing task-specific rubrics), produce materials that can be reused for years. Taken all together, the following ten strategies will help you promote your students' growth as writers and thinkers without burying you in endless stacks of papers.

1. Design Good Assignments

One of the best ways to save time is to consider carefully the kinds of writing assignments you give. Much of the writing you assign can be behind-the-scenes exploratory writing, which can be integrated into a class in a variety of ways and often requires only moderate teacher time or even none at all. (See Chapter Seven for ways to use exploratory writing.) When assigning formal papers, you will start your students on the right track if you follow the best practices for assignment design explained in Chapter Six. See especially the discussion of the NSSE/WPA research on writing assignments that promote deep learning (page 97) and the suggestions for giving your students a RAFT and TIP (pages 98–100). Also the advice in Chapter Six and Chapter Thirteen on dejveloping the last assignment first and using earlier assignments to scaffold the last assignment can help students work on their own toward better final papers (pages 96 and 241–250).

You can also save time by assigning one or two short papers rather than a long one. Also consider not assigning a generic research paper or term paper—a pseudo-academic school genre—in favor of developing more compact research assignments that teach disciplinary ways of using evidence and making arguments (see Chapter Thirteen). A short paper employing cognitive leverage—a lot of student thinking packed into a small amount of writing—can often produce more student learning than a traditional research paper. Also, consider giving all students the same problem-based assignment rather than letting them choose their own topics (see the discussion of historian Marc McLeod's assignment in Chapter Six, pages 100–104). Still another technique is to assign a sequence of microthemes that are graded using "models feedback" (Bean, Drenk, and Lee, 1986). See Chapter Six for a discussion of microthemes (pages 111–115); models feedback is described later in this chapter on pages 313–314.

Well-designed assignments up front prevent problems later on. They help students get started early and make progress on their own; they also provide firm starting ground for writing center consultations. If an assignment is vague or unfocused, students may barrage you with questions or submit papers that don't do what you intended. When you distribute the assignment in class, also include your grading rubric and allow plenty of time for questions. If possible, you might also consider providing an example of an A paper on an analogous assignment from a previous class. This is also a good opportunity to stress the value of multiple drafts. Consider asking students to submit, with their final papers, all their earlier rough drafts, notes, and doodles (a good defense against plagiarism as well as a way to stress the value of process).

2. Clarify Your Grading Criteria

The more clearly you define your criteria at the outset, the better the final products you will receive. The more students get a feel for what you are looking for, the more help they can give one another during peer review sessions. Here are two effective ways to clarify criteria:

Develop Task-Specific Rubrics

Chapter Fourteen gives advice on designing rubrics for an assignment. In most cases, the best rubrics are task-specific, with criteria statements geared specifically to the assigned task.

Hold an In-Class Norming Session

A particularly effective learning strategy is an in-class norming session in which students work in groups to reach consensus on the relative ranking of four or five student essays, preselected by the instructor from former student work and written for a similar assignment. After student groups have "graded" the papers, the instructor leads class discussion with the aim of clarifying his or her criteria and explaining the grades that he or she would give. (See Chapters Ten and Fourteen for procedural advice on how to conduct a norming session [pages 194 and 287]).

3. Build in Exploratory Writing or Class Discussion to Help Students Generate Ideas

The more students can brainstorm for ideas early on, the more detailed and complex their papers will become. Chapter Seven provides many ideas for building exploratory writing into a course. Exploratory talking is also powerful. If a writing assignment is directly linked to key concepts in the course, class time spent generating ideas for the assignment will not detract from course content. Here are some suggestions for stimulating rich talk about ideas.

Collaborative Small Group Tasks

When all students in the class are given the same assignment (say, to support or attack a given thesis or to respond to the same problematic question), collaborative groups could be asked to develop a series of reasons supporting and opposing the thesis or to create possible solutions to the assigned question. Later in the hour, the instructor could lead a discussion about the kinds of evidence and argumentation needed to support various theses. This kind of exploratory talk helps students expand their own thinking, rehearse their own arguments, and get a sense of alternative points of view.

An alternative is to have the whole class work together on a related topic; then, outside of class, they can apply the same thinking processes to their own topics.

Paired Interviews

Another useful strategy, especially if students are working on different topics, is to have students interview each other about their work in progress. Place students in pairs (or groups of three) and ask them to talk through their ideas with their partners. I guide the discussion by giving interviewers Paired Interview Questions to ask (Exhibit 15.1).

During these discussions, I ask writers not to look at their drafts or notes. I do not want them reading what they have already written, but rather reformulating their ideas conversationally in this new context. I generally require each student to hold the floor for ten to fifteen minutes of active talking; the interviewer's job is to keep the talker on task by asking probing questions or playing devil's advocate.

EXHIBIT 15.1

Paired Interview Questions

1. What problem or question is your paper going to address?

2. Why is this question controversial or otherwise problematic? Why is it significant? Show me what makes this a good question to address.

3. What is your one-sentence answer to this question? (If the writer doesn't have a good thesis statement yet, go on to the next question and then come back to this one. Perhaps you can help the writer figure out a thesis.)

4. Talk me through your whole argument or at least explain your ideas so far. (As you interview your writer, get him or her to do most of the talking; however, you can respond to the writer by offering suggestions, bringing up additional ideas, playing devil's advocate, and so forth.)

4. Have Students Submit Something Early in the Writing Process

I personally dislike reading students' rough drafts (I allow rewrites instead), yet I find it valuable to check in on their progress early in the writing process. Rather than asking for drafts, teachers can ask students to submit something else early on—something that can be read quickly and that helps identify students who need extra guidance.

Before offering some suggestions on what to ask for, let me suggest what you should *not* ask for: outlines. Although teachers have traditionally required students to submit outlines in advance, both research and theory show that requiring outlines is not as effective as teachers imagine. First, asking for outlines early on distorts the composing process of many writers who discover and clarify their ideas in the act of writing. As discussed in Chapter Two, the "think first, then write" model implied by early outlines seriously undervalues drafting as a discovery process. The tradition of requiring outlines is perhaps a holdover from the days of "all about" informational reports ("Write a report on a famous mathematician of your choice"). It is relatively easy to make a preliminary outline of an "all about" report because the outliner, like the writer of an encyclopedia article, merely divides up a large topic area into chunks with headings. In contrast, the parts of a thesis-governed paper that lend themselves to an outline often cannot be discovered until complex meanings are worked out through composing and revising.

Another disadvantage of requiring outlines is that the word *outline* carries unfortunate baggage for many students—their memories of teachers who treated outlines as finished products, with their own peculiar rules about placement of periods, hierarchies of numerals and letters, and so forth. Once graded down for getting a period in the wrong place, a student will forever after think of outlines as foes, not friends. Finally, research in cognitive psychology suggests that the traditional outline may not be as powerful an organizing tool as the more visual tree diagram (see the discussion of tree diagrams later in this chapter).

Rather than asking for outlines, then, teachers might consider asking for one or more of the following items.

A Prospectus

For long writing projects (such as researched disciplinary arguments) for which students select their own topics, students can submit a prospectus in which they describe the problem they will address and the direction they intend to take. (For a more detailed description of what to ask for in a prospectus, see Chapter Thirteen, page 247.) An effectively designed prospectus assignment can guide students toward a problem-thesis structure and steer them away from "and then" or "all about" writing.

Two Sentences: Question and Thesis

For shorter papers, students can be asked to submit two sentences: a one-sentence question that summarizes the problem the paper addresses and a one-sentence thesis statement that summarizes the writer's argument in response to the question. These two sentences can reveal a surprising number of problems in students' drafts, enabling teachers to identify students who need extra help. I require these two-sentence summaries for all of my short formal essay assignments. I can read and respond to thirty of them in less than an hour, dividing them into three piles: a "looks good" pile, a "promising but here's a quick suggestion" pile, and a "come see me in my office" pile.

Abstracts

An alternative to asking for question/thesis summaries is to ask students for 100- to 200-word abstracts of their drafts. Writing abstracts is a classic exercise for developing reading skills, especially the ability to distinguish main ideas from subordinate material (see Chapter Eight, page 157 and Chapter Nine, page 178). The act of summarizing one's own argument helps writers clarify their own thinking and often reveals organizational and conceptual problems that prompt revision. By asking writers to submit abstracts of their drafts, rather than the drafts themselves, teachers cut down on their own reading load while assigning a salutary exercise for students.

5. Have Students Conduct Peer Reviews of Drafts

Another timesaving strategy is to have students review each other's drafts. Of course, peer reviews sometimes have disappointing results. Unless the teacher structures the sessions and trains students in what to do, peer reviewers may offer eccentric, superficial, or otherwise unhelpful—or even bad—advice. A successful peer review process should benefit both the reviewer and the writer and lead to genuine substantial revision. The good news is that there are ways to make peer reviews work effectively, whether through in-class workshop sessions or through out-of-class strategies whereby peers exchange and review papers on-line. Additionally, recent developments in computer-assisted strategies for peer reviews, although controversial, have been praised by some teachers. (See later discussion of Calibrated Peer Review [CPR] and Scaffolded Writing and Rewriting in the Discipline [SWoRD™].) Let's look at each of these strategies in turn.

In-Class Peer Review Workshops

For conducting in-class workshops, teachers must decide which philosophy of peer review best fits their teaching style: response-centered reviews or advice-centered reviews (a full explanation of the differences follows shortly). Both types have their characteristic strengths, and each approach probably works best with certain kinds of students or writing tasks. However, they require teachers to structure the review sessions differently.

Second, a teacher must decide the process for exchanging drafts. Some teachers prefer that writers read their drafts out loud to the peer reviewers—the experience of hearing one's language read aloud helps writers discover problem areas. (The read-aloud approach works only for short papers.) Other teachers ask students to bring copies of their drafts to class to enable silent reading. Still others have students exchange and read each other's drafts prior to class in order to make class time more efficient.

Response-Centered Reviews (face to face)

This process-oriented, nonintrusive approach shown in Exhibit 15.2 places maximum responsibility on the writer for making decisions about what to change in a draft. In this method, no one gives the writer advice. Respondents simply describe their reactions to the piece. Often the writer receives contradictory messages: one reader might like a given passage, while another dislikes it. Thus the group sends the writer equivocal, ambiguous messages that reflect the truth about how real readers respond to real writing, leaving the writer responsible for deciding what to do. (For more detailed advice on conducting response-centered peer reviews, see Spear, 1988, and Elbow and Belanoff, 1989.)

Response-Centered Reviews (guided by teacher-prepared peer-review sheets)

In this approach, students exchange drafts before class and do the reviews as homework, following the instructions on a peer-review sheet prepared by the teacher. (If possible, teachers should structure the exchanges so that each student conducts two reviews and receives two reviews.) Peer reviewers then meet with writers in class to discuss their reviews. When designing questions or prompts for the peer-review sheets, teachers should consider a strategy advocated by Nilson (2003), who shows that prompts

EXHIBIT 15.2

Classroom Procedure for Response-Centered Reviews

1. Divide the class into groups of four or five.

2. The writer reads the draft out loud (or provides photocopies for group members to read silently).

3. Group members are given several minutes to take notes on their responses. (I ask listeners to divide a sheet of paper into three columns headed +, –, and ?. In the + column, they note aspects of the draft that worked well. In the – column, they note problem areas and any negative reactions, such as disagreement with ideas. In the ? column, they note questions that occurred while listening, such as places that need clarification or more development.)

4. Each group member, in turn, explains to the writer what he or she found effective or ineffective, what parts were clear or confusing, and so forth. Group members do not give advice; they simply describe their personal responses to the draft as written.

5. The writer takes notes during each response but does not enter into a discussion. (The writer listens, without trying to defend the piece or explain "what I meant.")

6. After each group member has responded to a writer's essay, the next group member reads his or her essay. The cycle continues.

EXHIBIT 15.3

Judgment Versus Descriptive Questions for Peer Reviews

Judgment Questions	Descriptive Questions
Does the paper have a thesis statement? Is the thesis clear?	In just one or two sentences, state what position you think the writer is taking. Place stars around the sentence that you think presents the thesis.
Is the paper clearly organized?	On the back of this sheet, make an outline of the paper.
Does the writer use evidence effectively to support the argument?	List the kinds of evidence used to support the writer's argument. Which pieces of evidence do you think are the strongest? Which are the weakest?
Is the paper clearly written throughout?	Highlight (in color) any passages that you had to read more than once to understand what the writer was saying.
How persuasive is the argument?	After reading the paper, do you agree or disagree with the writer's position? Why or why not?

calling for descriptions of (and reactions to) specific features of a draft are more effective than prompts calling for evaluations, opinions, or judgments. I illustrate her advice in Exhibit 15.3, which contrasts "judgment questions" and "descriptive questions":

Nilson's analysis shows how prompts calling for description and reaction elicit more time on task from the peer reviewers and produce more useful information for the writer. For example, if peer reviewers describe the draft in quite different ways (stating the writer's argument differently, making different outlines), these differences help writers figure out clearer ways to keep readers on the same track. Because the peer reviewers are invited to respond personally to the writer's argument—explaining whether they agree or disagree with the writer's position—they engage the writer and reviewers in a peer conversation about ideas—a benefit that may help writers strengthen their arguments, address alternative views, or even change their views.

Advice-Centered Reviews

This approach is more product-oriented and more directive: peer reviewers collaborate to give advice to the writer. This method works best when students have internalized criteria for an assignment through norming sessions or teacher-provided rubrics. Exhibit 15.4 is a recommended process for an advice-centered peer review.

Because advice-centered reviews take quite a bit longer than response-centered reviews, I usually ask writers to supply copies of their drafts to their peer reviewers the night before class so that the reviewers can read the drafts carefully ahead of time. Because the reviews are collaboratively written by two students, they are usually well considered and thoughtful. Of course, the writer should take the reviews as advisory only and make his or her own decisions about how much of the advice to use.

EXHIBIT 15.4

Classroom Procedure for Advice-Centered Reviews

1. Divide the class into pairs, and have each pair exchange drafts with another pair. (If the class has an odd number of students, I have a pair of students exchange with a single student whom I consider a strong writer.)

2. The two students in each pair collaborate to compose a jointly written review of the two drafts they have received. I ask pairs to create a written review of each draft, guided by the rubric. To sum up their reviews, I ask reviewers to do the following:

   a. Write out at least two things that you think are particularly strong about this draft.

   b. Identify two or three aspects of the draft that are currently weak, problematic, or ineffective.

   c. Make two or three directive statements recommending the most important changes that the writer should make in the next draft.

3. The pairs then return the drafts to the original writers, along with their collaboratively written reviews. If time remains, the two pairs can meet jointly to discuss their reviews.

Out-of-Class Electronic Peer Review

Many teachers prefer that students do their peer reviews outside of class time. Many online strategies are available to assist with this process including some recently developed online peer-review systems developed particularly for large classes.

Exchanges on Course Discussion Boards

An easy way to set up out-of-class peer reviews is to have students exchange drafts via a class discussion board. Depending on the technology available, students should be able to upload their papers to a dropbox, access each other's papers, and conduct paper-less reviews by posting comments on each other's drafts. Teachers can provide specific instructions about what to include in the peer reviews.

The next two strategies—Calibrated Peer Review and Scaffolded Writing and Rewriting in the Disciplines—have attracted much attention among some teachers. It is difficult at this time to know whether these strategies will have staying power, but their application of technology to the problem of peer review is ingenious and their goals thought-provoking.

Calibrated Peer Review

Calibrated Peer Review (CPR) is a free web-based program, originally designed for large introductory science courses, that allows students to peer review classmate's drafts in a guided learning environment (Chapman and Fiore, 2001; A. A. Russell, 2004; Reynolds and Moskovitz, 2008; Gunersel, Simpson, Aufderheide, and Wang, 2008).

To use CPR, an instructor needs to register on the CPR website and follow the instructions. The instructor first creates an assignment, along with a set of scaled or yes/no peer review questions. The instructor must also provide three calibration essays: an exemplar model and two middling or weak models chosen to display characteristic problems in content or style. The instructor's "grading" of these three calibration essays is stored in the system.

Students upload their essays to the system, which then sends each writer three anonymous, randomly chosen student essays to review. However, before students can do the peer reviews, they must pass a "calibration test" based on their reviews of the three calibration essays provided by the instructor. Once students have passed the calibration test, they score their assigned peer essays. They are then prompted to score their own essay using the same rubric. Finally, students receive the review results from their peers.

The CPR website provides helpful information about the system, along with lists of institutions using the program and links to reviews of its effectiveness. The host website also contains a bank of open-source assignments from a variety of disciplines that instructors are free to use. (See Reynolds and Moskovitz [2008] for a warning that not all the assignments in the assignment bank are designed to promote higher-order thinking and writing skills.) According to A. A. Russell (2004), studies at three different universities in chemistry, biology, and economics have shown that "students taught using CPR assignments perform approximately 10% better on traditional course exams than students taught through traditional lecture and text-book methods" (p. 2). Gunersel, Simpson, Aufderheide, and Wang (2008) also argue that CPR also improves writing skills.

Before I comment on CPR, I must register a caveat: I have never used the system myself, but have heard anecdotal comments from others, some extolling its benefits and others rejecting it after unsuccessful trials. As a means of promoting criteria-focused peer review, this system seems to have remarkable strengths. Teachers are able to use their own assignments and rubrics (although some teachers complain about the extent of revision needed to fit the parameters of the software). The system also encourages students to look objectively at their own drafts. If the system were used to promote revision and if the revised essays were subsequently submitted to the instructor or TA's for further commentary and grading, my views would be quite favorable.

However, I am troubled by CPR's potential to increase the distance between students and instructors and to promote alienation from writing as meaningful work. The system seems to encourage a teacherless process in which instructors never read the student essays at all, but simply use the peer-review scores to determine grades on the assignment. In this teacherless system, student work is treated as a final product to be scored rather than as a draft to be revised. Defenders of CPR might say that the purpose of the assignments is to promote writing-to-learn rather than to teach global revision. The payoff comes in increased understanding of subject matter content as measured in exams. Moreover, because assignments often ask writers to explain a concept to a classmate, classmates provide a more authentic audience than the teacher, who already knows the concept. So I am caught in a dilemma. CPR in service of global revision or writing to learn has remarkable potential. But something of deep importance may be lost when teachers no longer read student work. The absence of a teacher as a mentoring reader creates a system whereby writing and peer review become an arbitrary exercise done only for a grade. Perhaps a compromise is possible, wherein the teacher reads representative samples of student work and discusses features of strong and weak performances in class using the procedure I have called "models feedback" for microthemes (see pages 313–314).

Multiple Peer Reviews Through SWoRD

In contrast to Calibrated Peer Review, Scaffolded Writing and Rewriting in the Discipline (SWoRD) is designed specifically to encourage global revision of drafts, but it also has the potential to become a teacherless system. Developed by a research team in cognitive psychology at the University of Pittsburgh, SWoRD is a "web-based reciprocal peer review system [that] supports writing practice, particularly for large content courses in which writing is considered critical but not feasibly included" (Cho and Schunn, 2007, p. 409).

SWoRD (currently a free system available through the SWoRD website at the University of Pittsburgh) guides students through several phases of review, including one phase in which writers rate their peer reviewers. The five-phase process is as follows:

1. Students upload an anonymous first draft of their essays to SWoRD, which randomly assigns each student six peer essays to review (the instructor can change the defaults).

2. Students download their assigned peers' drafts and score them using a teacher-provided rubric. Teachers can also choose the system's default rubric using a 7-point scale (from 1 = "disastrous" to 7 = "excellent") across three dimensions: "flow," "logic," and "insight." SWoRD also provides space for written commentary, with instructions on how to write helpful comments. An algorithm then computes a weighted mean peer-review score for each paper, making statistical adjustments to lessen the effect of outlier reviewers. All the reviews and algorithmically computed scores are returned to the original writer.

3. Students revise their drafts, prompted by insights from the peer reviews, and upload them to the system. During revision, students are asked to reflect on the helpfulness of the reviews in general and to identify reviews that were most helpful.

4. Each writer provides a "back review" for each reviewer, explaining the helpfulness of each reviewer's written feedback on a scale of 1 ("not helpful") to 7 ("very helpful"). Reviewers then receive their back reviews from all the writers whose drafts they have peer reviewed (see an example in Cho and Schunn, 2007, p. 415).

5. In phase 5, the final cycle, peer reviewers read and review the final drafts of each writer, again scoring them on the same 7-point scale. Phase 5 thus allows reviewers to see (and appreciate) the kinds of revisions made as a result of the first reviews.

What teachers receive from this system, then, is a final set of papers that have been substantially revised as a result of feedback from six peers. The instructor also has statistical information about each student both as a writer (the adjusted peer review mean score on the student's draft and on the final paper) and as a peer reviewer (the "helpfulness" score computed from the back reviews). The system thus provides incentive for each student to provide helpful peer reviews and to revise substantially. The developers of SWoRD have conducted a number of empirical studies of the effectiveness of the system for improving student writing (see particularly Patchan, Charney, and Schunn, 2009). These studies support the value of peer review in encouraging revision, showing that students learn as much by doing the reviews as by receiving them.

The researchers have also demonstrated that the weighted mean score of peer reviewers correlates closely with scores provided by experts. Some teachers therefore use the weighted peer review mean scores on the final peer reviews to determine a student's grade on the essay (similar to the teacherless use of scores made possible by the Calibrated Peer Review system). However, Christian Schunn, one of the developers of the system, told me that "the most common use of SWoRD is a hybrid mode in which peers give feedback on first drafts and then instructors (or teaching assistants) grade/comment upon second drafts." According to Schunn, the system has been especially popular among teachers of relatively small classes (ten to thirty students) in which "teachers use SWoRD to provide students with more feedback and more revision opportunities rather than to replace teacher feedback." When used in this way, SWoRD seems to have remarkable potential for promoting multiple drafts and global revision.

6. Refer Students to Your Institution's Writing Center

Writing centers, whether staffed by professional tutors or student peers, are rich resources for both faculty and students. (If your institution does not have one, lobby for one.) Most contemporary writing centers help students at any stage of their writing—clarifying an assignment, brainstorming for ideas, overcoming writer's block, producing a first draft, or making substantive revisions in a draft with the aim of deepening, complicating, and clarifying ideas, improving organization, strengthening use of evidence, and polishing style and mechanics. However, sometimes writing centers are underused because faculty and students think of them only as places for last-minute "fixes" or as extra resources for weak writers. They are in fact intended for all writers, including graduate students, and in some ways they create for writers the kind of writers' communities that professional writers establish for themselves.

For faculty, writing centers can offer helpful suggestions for improving the clarity of their writing assignment handouts. You can ask tutors to read your assignments before you hand them out, helping you spot places where students are likely to become stuck. (Tutors are particularly astute readers of assignment handouts because they see so many students struggling with unclear, complex, overly difficult, or hard-to-comprehend instructions from professors.) Because writing center sessions almost always begin with a discussion of the teacher's assignment, asking someone in your writing center to preview your assignment with you can not only improve the assignment but also help tutors work more efficiently with your students.

Students themselves are often surprised at how helpful a writing center session can be. In general, tutors are terrific listeners and readers who engage student writers in in-depth conversation about the ideas in a paper. My friend Carol Haviland, writing center director at California State University at San Bernardino, with whom I often discuss writing center work, gave me this description of a tutor-writer conversation:

> *I overheard a student and her eight-year-old leaving the writing center after her conference:*
> *Son:*   *"Mom, I thought you said that this was a writing center."*
> *Mother: "It is."*
> *Son:*   *"Well, it sounds more like a talking center to me."*

I love this anecdote because it expresses the rich connection between writing and talking. Through productive talk, tutors help students figure out assignments, generate ideas and questions, locate resources, and situate themselves within disciplinary discourses. They also help students edit and proofread, but they do not function as an editing service (much to some students' dismay). Rather than correct all the errors in a paper, tutors pick out one or two characteristic kinds of errors and help students learn the syntactical and grammatical principles that help advance their ability to find their own errors.

It is important for both faculty and students to remember that "going to a writing center" does not guarantee an improved paper or higher grade. Tutors don't rewrite or correct the papers. However, if students are willing to invest time after a conference to revise their drafts, they are apt to experience what composition teachers call "re-visioning" (seeing again): they are often inspired to revise substantially as a response to an engaged discussion of a draft-in-progress with an experienced interested reader.

If you are unsure of what happens at your college's or university's writing center, call or e-mail its director (many of whom are faculty colleagues), check out its website, or even stop by for a firsthand look. In most cases, you will find directors and tutors engaged in rich, highly invested discussions of writing. Writing center directors also are often able and willing to support you and your students in other ways. For example, Larry Nichols, the writing center director at my own institution, will send undergraduate peer tutors to a professor's class to help facilitate a draft workshop, to demonstrate what happens in a writing center conference, or to role-play how a tutor might plan a thinking, researching, and writing strategy in response to a course assignment. Such class visits from the writing center will also introduce students to a campus resource they can use throughout their college careers.

7. Make One-on-One Writing Conferences as Efficient as Possible

The art of conferring with students on their writing requires good listening skills supplemented with the ability to provide timely, appropriate guidance. This section offers some advice on how to conduct an individual writing conference.

Distinguish Between Early, Higher-Order Concerns and Later, Lower-Order Concerns

Conferences are most productive if you help students concentrate first on the early concerns of ideas, organization, and overall logic and development (higher-order concerns) as opposed to the later concerns of style, grammar, and mechanics (lower-order concerns). The lower-order concerns are *lower* not because they are unimportant but because they cannot be efficiently attended to until the higher-order concerns have been resolved. Early in the process, too much emphasis on style and grammatical correctness can lead not only to writer's block but also to the shutting down of the connection between drafting and thinking. It is counterproductive to spend time editing a paragraph that might actually need to be dismantled and reconceptualized. Conferences should focus primarily on helping students create good, idea-rich arguments and wrestle them into a structure that works.

Start the Conference by Setting an Agenda

Conferences work best when students are encouraged to do most of the talking—rehearsing their papers' arguments while the teacher listens and coaches. Too often, though, conferences become dominated by teacher talk. Try to avoid the tendency to tell students what to say in their papers. Although you might picture an "ideal essay" in response to your assignment, very few students are going to produce what you yourself would write. Conferences should be primarily listening sessions, where the instructor asks questions and the student does 80 to 90 percent of the talking. Most students have never experienced a teacher's actually being interested in their ideas. Engaging them in genuine conversation, showing real interest in their work, respecting their ideas—these are enormous favors to a novice writer.

To establish a supportive listening tone at the beginning of a conference, the instructor can work with the student to set a mutual agenda. Exhibit 15.5 suggests a sequence of stages for starting the conference.

EXHIBIT 15.5

Stages for Starting the Conference

Instructor	Student
Ask the student to explain the assignment. How would you summarize the assignment in your own words? Are there any parts of the assignment that you are fuzzy on?	Student reveals how well he or she understands the assignment.
Find out the student's expectations for the conference. How do you like your paper so far? What kind of help do you need from this conference?	Instructor learns something of the student's own assessment of the paper and attitude toward it. Instructor gets some sense of what kind of help the student wants.
Get the student to discuss his or her draft and writing process. How much work have you put into this draft? How far are you in the writing process? How much more time are you willing to put into the paper?	Student begins to feel comfortable talking; instructor gets a better sense of the student and the paper as well as of the student's own unvoiced problems with the paper. Instructor gets insights into the student's writing process.
Read the draft silently while giving the student the following task: write out your thesis and main points, then write down the main problems you see with your draft.	Student writes in response to the writing prompt. Student must take responsibility for making an initial assessment of the draft.

EXHIBIT 15.6

Stages for Setting the Agenda

Instructor	Student
Begin with positive comments. I really like this part [be specific]. You do a good job here.	Student, who sits in agony waiting to hear what you will say about the paper, receives reinforcement.
Inform the student honestly of your own assessment. You are definitely on the right track here. You do a great job with Jones. But there are some places where I got lost, and sometimes you include summaries of information without analysis. I've marked a few passages where I can't see your point.	Student gets a sense of your assessment right away. Student does not have to guess what you are thinking. Student sees strengths in the draft but gets a sense of the kinds of problems you think should be worked on.
Reassure the student that it is common to have such problems with rough drafts. It's normal in a first draft to wander from the thesis. This happens to me all the time. That's why I have to go through so many drafts.	Student sees writing as a process, starts to see comments less as criticism and more as guidelines for improvement. Student feels less "dumb" and gains confidence in the value of revision.
Collaborate with the student to set an agenda for the conference. Choose a limited number of problems to work on. You don't have to solve every problem for your next draft. Should we just work on clarifying your thesis and getting your argument better organized?	In response to your initial suggestion, student might say, "But I'd also like to see more clearly what you mean by analysis rather than just summary." Student becomes involved in deciding what to work on. Instructor and student have a plan for how to spend the rest of the conference.

As you read the draft, take mental notes that will help you focus the conference later. One suggestion is to place symbols in the margins of the draft such as + (things that are well done), * (problem areas), and ? (things you want to ask questions about). (I usually ask the student's permission before writing on the draft.) From your marginal symbols, you can see the positive elements that you want to reinforce as well as problem areas and places to ask questions about. Decide the two or three most important things to work on, beginning with the early "big picture" or higher-order concerns first. Exhibit 15.6 shows how the conference might resume.

Develop a Repertoire of Conferencing Strategies

After you have read the draft and set an agenda, you begin the actual conference. How you conduct the conference depends on where the student is in the writing process. Some students need help at the very highest levels—finding a thesis and a basic plan for an argument. Others might have a good overall plan but lots of confusing places along the way. In conducting a conference, you may wish to try one or more of the following strategies, tailored to each individual case.

If Ideas Are Thin

- Make an idea map to brainstorm for more ideas (explained later in this chapter).

- Play devil's advocate to deepen and complicate the ideas.

- Help the writer add more examples, better details, more supporting data or arguments.

If the Reader Gets Lost

- Have the student talk through the ideas to clear up confusing spots.

- Help the student sharpen the thesis by seeing it as the writer's answer to a controversial or problematic question (get the student to articulate the question that the thesis "answers").

- Make an outline or a tree diagram to help with organization (explained later in this chapter).

- Help the writer clarify the focus by asking him or her to complete these starter phrases:

  "My purpose in this paper is ..."

  "My purpose in this section/paragraph is ..."

  "Before reading my paper, the reader will have this view of my topic: ...; after reading my paper, my reader will have this different view of my topic: ..."

- Show the student where you get confused or miscued in reading the draft ("I started getting lost here because I couldn't see why you were giving me this information," or "I thought you were going to say X, but then you said Y").

- Show the student how to write transitions between major sections or between paragraphs.

If You Can Understand the Sentences but Cannot See the Point
Help the writer articulate meaning by asking "so what" questions: "I can understand what you are saying here, but I don't quite understand why you are saying it. I read all these facts, and I say, 'So what?' What do these facts have to do with your thesis?" (This helps the writer bring the point to the surface. You can then help the writer formulate topic sentences for paragraphs.)

Throughout the conference, try to make "readerly" rather than "writerly" comments—that is, describe your mental experience in trying to read the draft rather than telling the writer how to fix it. For example, say, "I had trouble seeing the point of this paragraph," rather than, "Begin with a topic sentence." This approach helps writers see that their purpose in revising is to make the reader's job easier rather than to follow "English teacher rules." When the student clarifies the point that he or she is trying to make in the paragraph, you can then say, "Write that sentence at the head of the paragraph! It will then be a useful topic sentence for the reader."

In conducting conferences, I often take notes on my computer, turning the screen so that the student can see it with me. As the student talks, I key in the student's ideas. At the end of the conference, I print out the notes as a record of the conference. Sometimes the students and I work together to create either an idea map or a tree diagram. The next two sections explain these strategies.

Use an Idea Map for Brainstorming

Idea maps (sometimes called *mind maps* or *concept maps*) work best early in the writing process as a tool for generating ideas. To help a student writer make an idea map, you draw a circle in the center of the page and write a triggering word or phrase in the circle (usually a broad topic area, a question, or a thesis). Then, as the writer talks, you record his or her ideas on branches and subbranches that extend from the circle. As long as the writer pursues one train of thought, you keep recording the ideas on subbranches off the main branch. But as soon as that chain of ideas runs dry, you lead the writer to a new starting point and begin a new branch. Exhibit 15.7 shows an idea map that a student and I made for an assignment to evaluate arguments by Carl Cohen and Peter Singer for and against the use of animals in medical research.

As Exhibit 15.7 illustrates, an idea map records a writer's emerging ideas in a visual format; notations are arranged randomly around the initial hub but hierarchically off each branch. This half-random, half-hierarchical pattern stimulates productive thinking, for it invites the writer to elaborate previously recorded ideas (by adding new subbranches off an existing branch) or to begin a new train of thought (by adding a new branch). The idea map thus stimulates open-ended brainstorming while simultaneously helping the writer discover the beginnings of an organizational structure. My goal is to have the student leave my office with idea map in hand, along with my cheery exhortation to write a draft.

Use a Tree Diagram to Help with Structure

After generating an idea map, a student needs to develop the ideas further by writing a rough draft. At this point, most writers need some sort of plan, but how elaborate or detailed that plan is varies considerably from writer to writer. Some writers need to plan extensively before they can write; others need to write extensively before they can plan. But somewhere along the way, whether at the first-draft stage or much later in the process, writers need to concentrate on the shape of their arguments. At

EXHIBIT 15.7

An Idea Map

Is speciesism really the same as racism/sexism?

Do I really accept his notion of speciesism?

Am I really being prejudiced if I believe humans are more valuable than dogs?

Does the pain of all animals and humans really count equally?

What bothers me about Singer?

I can accept not using animals for cosmetic research but not for medical research.

I am bothered (why?) by his statement that there is no trait possessed by a human infant that an animal doesn't possess in greater degree.

What do I like about Cohen?

Do animals have rights? Cohen versus Singer

What do I like about Singer?

His argument that pain of humans outweighs pain of animals appeals to me.

He justifies medical research using a consequence argument.

Singer has really made me think a lot about being a vegetarian.

Singer apprecintes the pain and suffering of animals.

Persuades me

If we apply the kinds of consequence arguments that Cohen uses to eating meat, we would have to become vegetarians.

Factory farming

Medical experiments

Animals do not have "rights" because they are not moral creatures.

But as Singer says, animals have "interests"

I am confused!

Better health

Feed the world

Help stop greenhouse effect

Animal fats and cancer, etc.

More efficient to grow grains for humans than feed cows!

Cutting down tropical rain forest is driven by need to graze cattle

What don't I like about Cohen?

He seems to be able to overlook the pain of animals.

I like Cohen when I think of these issues in the abstract, but when I think of Singer's vivid descriptions of animal pain, I get confused again.

this point, I recommend the power of tree diagrams over traditional outlines.

A tree diagram differs from an outline in that headings and subheadings are indicated through spatial locations rather than through a system of letters and numerals. Exhibit 15.8 (produced by the same student who brainstormed the idea map in Exhibit 15.7) shows a tree diagram of an evaluative essay comparing two arguments on animal rights. The writer's thesis is shown at the top of the tree, with supporting arguments displayed vertically on branches beneath the thesis.

Although the traditional outline may be the more familiar way to represent an argument's structure, tree diagrams are often a more powerful device for planning and shaping. Their visual nature makes it easy to see at a glance both the skeletal structure of an argument and its sequential parts. Tree diagrams can also be powerful aids to invention because you can put question marks anywhere on a tree to hold a space open for ideas that you have not thought of yet. For example, early in his planning stages, the writer of the animal rights paper wrote a preliminary tree diagram with a branch that looked like Exhibit 15.9.

Using question marks as place markers allows the writer to visualize a large-scale structure for the paper while holding a slot open for parts of the argument still to be "discovered." The fluid, evolving nature of the tree diagram (see Exhibit 15.8), in which branches can be added or moved around, makes it a particularly valuable planning tool for writers.

When Working on Sentence Concerns, Focus on One or Two Paragraphs

Having helped a writer find ideas and get them focused, organized, and developed, the teacher has done the lion's share of the work of coaching writing. Many students, of course, will have additional problems with grammar, sentence structure, and mechanics or with sentence styles that are wooden, verbose, awkward, or choppy. If you have the time and the inclination to work with students on these matters, consider helping to edit one or two paragraphs and then asking the student to scrutinize the rest of the draft in the same way. It is important that you do not become the student's editor or proofreader. Writers need to learn how to find and fix their own grammatical and stylistic problems. (That is why I also suggest not circling or marking errors when you grade papers—see Chapter Five and also Chapter Sixteen, pages 330–331, where I suggest strategies for making students find and fix their own errors.)

EXHIBIT 15.8
A Tree Diagram

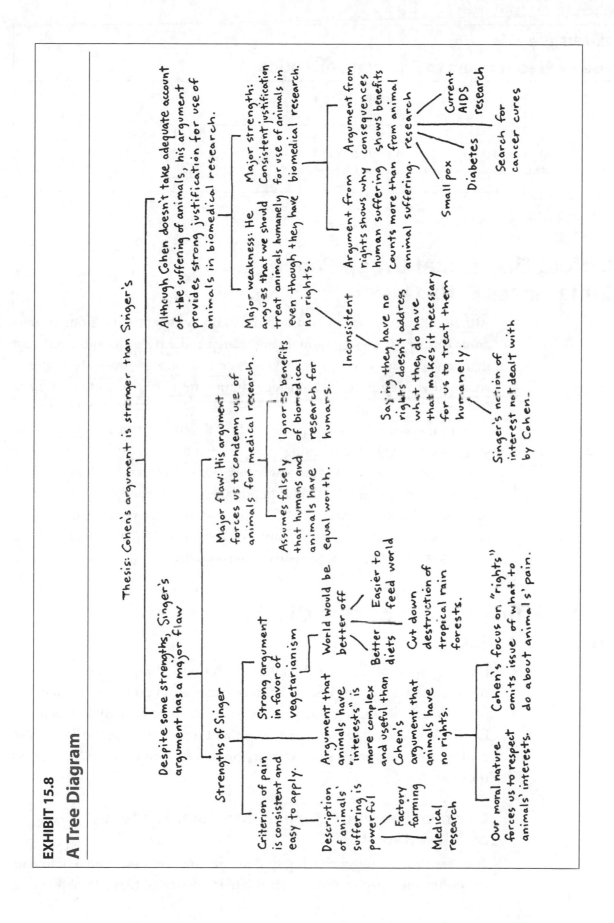

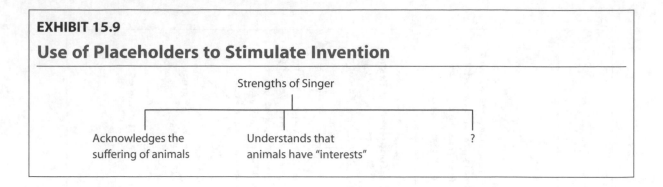

EXHIBIT 15.9

Use of Placeholders to Stimulate Invention

Strengths of Singer

Acknowledges the   Understands that   ?
suffering of animals   animals have "interests"

8. Hold Occasional Group Paper Conferences Early On

Although teachers usually work individually with students, group conferences can sometimes be more lively, more productive, and more efficient
than one-on-one conferences. Whenever a group of students shares a
common writing problem, consider inviting four or five students at once
for a group conference.

Group conferences are particularly valuable at the idea-generating
stage of writing. While listening to the teacher help student A find a focusing question for a paper topic, students B, C, and D start thinking of ideas
for their own papers. But more importantly, students B, C, and D often
come up with great ideas for A. The back-and-forth dynamics of a group
conference, in which the participants collaborate to help one another, make
them especially useful at the early stages of writing.

9. Use Efficient Methods for Giving Written Feedback

Perhaps the most traditional way to coach the writing process is to place
comments on students' essays. Because commenting on papers is a major
part of teaching writing, Chapter Sixteen is devoted entirely to this topic.
However, a few suggestions about commenting are appropriate here. I also
explain two alternatives to written comments: "models feedback" and
rubrics.

Comment on Drafts Rather Than Final Products, or Allow Rewrites

The best strategy for improving student writing is to place your comments
not on finished papers but on typed late-stage drafts. (An alternative is to

permit rewrites of papers so that you treat "final versions" as if they were drafts in progress.) The purpose of the comments is to provide advice on how the draft needs to be revised. Composition research suggests that unless students do something with the teacher's comments—by making the suggested revisions—the teacher's commenting time is largely wasted. Comments, in other words, do not transfer well to later papers; they need to be applied directly to the work in progress.

My own personal strategy is not to read drafts but to permit rewrites (except for papers due at the end of the term). This method allows me to comment on papers as if they were drafts in progress and yet assign a grade as if they were finished products. Students who are satisfied with their grades do not rewrite (thus cutting down on the number of resubmissions I receive). I have settled on this method—imperfect as it is—because it has been more effective for me than commenting on drafts. The quality of writing I initially receive is higher (students, not wanting to rewrite, try to turn in their best work on the first try), and for some students, the desire to improve their grades motivates serious revision. Whichever method you choose, the point of your commentary is to stimulate and guide revision.

Make Limited, Focused Comments and Avoid Marking Errors

Rather than commenting on everything wrong with the draft so that the student is overwhelmed with suggestions, consider limiting your comments to the major changes you would like to see in the next revision, focusing first on the higher-order concerns of ideas, organization, development, and clarity. See Chapter Sixteen for a detailed discussion of how to write revision-oriented comments on student essays. I also suggest that you do not circle errors or rewrite sentences, following instead the principles of minimal marking discussed in Chapter Five (pages 82–84) and Chapter Sixteen (pages 330–331).

Use Models Feedback on Short Assignments

When students write microthemes or other short essays in response to the same assignment, consider using "models feedback." With models feedback, you do not make any comments on the papers; consequently, you can grade them very rapidly (often taking no more than a minute or two per paper). You provide feedback through in-class discussion of selected essays. If you find a good A response in your set of papers, duplicate it for the class or project it on screen. If not, write your own A-worthy microtheme as a model. The models feedback comes from a discussion of what constitutes an A response as well as a discussion of typical problem areas found in weaker papers. This discussion accomplishes two purposes: it clarifies for students the writing and thinking skills exhibited in strong papers, and it reviews and clarifies recent course material (the content part of your assignment). Often students say they learn more about writing from models feedback than from traditional comments on papers.

Use a Rubric

Rubrics are discussed in detail in Chapter Fourteen. Briefly, they allow you to score separate features of a piece of writing according to criteria and levels of performance. Although rubrics cannot provide as much information as individual comments, they are more informative than a single grade by itself. They are particularly useful when your workload prevents detailed commentary on papers.

10. Put Minimal Comments on Finished Products

If you have been willing to comment on rough drafts or if you accept rewrites, switch your role at the end of the process from that of coach to that of judge. You need not feel obligated to write on the finished-product version of a paper at all. Simply attach a rubric based on your evaluation criteria and give the paper a grade. Students always appreciate a brief end comment about your reaction to the paper or your justification for a score in a certain area, but you need not feel obligated to make extended comments. This saves time particularly with papers due at the end of a term, when students will not be revising their work.

Conclusion: A Review of Timesaving Strategies

The traditional way to coach writing—making copious, red-penciled comments on finished student products—is almost universally regarded by composition specialists as an inefficient use of teacher energy. The comments seldom lead to improvement in student writing, and the thought of grading stacks of depressingly bad student essays discourages teachers from assigning writing. This chapter suggests ten different strategies for coaching writing, aimed at improving the quality of final products while reducing the amount of commenting time teachers need to devote to papers. Here is a nutshell review of the ten strategies discussed in this chapter.

1. Design good assignments.

   - Consider using low-stakes exploratory writing as a way of deepening learning and engagement.

   - Consider the value of short assignments, including microthemes.

   - Consider giving the whole class the same problem-based assignment (rather than having them choose their own topics).

   - For formal assignments, create assignment handouts that provide a rhetorical context (RAFT) and engage students with a problem (TIP) (see pages 98–100 for details).

   - For formal assignments, follow the NSSE/WPA "best practices" criteria of "interactive elements," "meaning-making task," and "clarity of goals and criteria" (see pages 97–98 for details).

2. Clarify your grading criteria.

   - Create task-specific rubrics.

   - Hold an in-class norming session (see Chapter Ten, page 194).

3. Build in exploratory writing or class discussion to help students generate ideas.

   - Develop exploratory writing tasks that help students generate ideas for a formal paper.

   - Create a small group brainstorming task.

   - Have students work in pairs to interview one another.

4. Have students submit something to you early in the writing process.

   - Consider asking for a prospectus, a question/thesis summary, or an abstract (but not an outline—see page 294).

   - Use these to identify students who need extra help.

5. Have students be the first readers of each other's drafts.

   - Require peer reviews (either response-centered or advice-centered).

   - To preserve class time, consider online out-of-class peer reviews.

6. Refer students to your institution's writing center.

   - Recognize the value of writing centers for all writers, not just weak writers.

   - Stress the usefulness of writing centers at all stages of the writing process.

- Consider asking the writing center to review your assignment handout.

7. Make one-on-one conferences as efficient as possible.

- Focus first on early higher-order concerns (ideas, focus, organization and development).

- Begin each conference by setting an agenda.

- Develop a repertoire of conferencing strategies.

- Consider using idea maps and tree diagrams to help students generate and organize ideas.

8. Consider holding group conferences early in the writing process.

9. Use efficient methods for giving feedback on papers.

- Comment on late drafts rather than final products (or allow rewrites).

- Make revision-oriented comments, focusing first on higher-order concerns.

- For microthemes, use models feedback in lieu of traditional comments.

- When time is at a premium (or on final products that won't be revised), use a rubric instead of making comments.

10. Put minimal comments on finished products that will not be revised.

16

Writing Comments on Students' Papers

Perhaps nothing involves us so directly in the messiness of teaching writing as our attempts to comment on our students' essays. Whenever I conduct workshops in the marking and grading of student writing, I like to quote a sentence from William Zinsser's *Writing to Learn* (1988): "The writing teacher's ministry is not just to the words but to the person who wrote the words" (p. 48). I value this quotation because all of us as teachers, late at night, having read whole stacks of student essays, sometimes forget the human being who wrote the words that currently frustrate us. We become harsh or sarcastic. We let our irritation show on the page. Even though we know how we ourselves feel when we ask a colleague to read one of our drafts (apologetic and vulnerable), we sometimes forget these feelings when we comment on students' papers. Sometimes we do not treat students' work in progress with the same sensitivity that we bring to our colleagues' work.

The best kind of commentary enhances the writer's feeling of dignity. The worst kind can be experienced as dehumanizing and insulting—often to the bewilderment of the teacher, whose intentions were kindly but whose techniques ignored the personal dimension of writing.

Imagine, for a moment, a beginning tennis class in which we ask George to give his first performance. In skill category 1, serving the tennis ball, poor George whacks the ball sideways into the fence. Here is the instructor's feedback: "You didn't hold the racquet properly, you didn't toss the ball in the correct plane, you threw it too high, you didn't cock your wrist properly, and you looked awkward. Moreover, you hit the ball with the frame instead of the strings. Weren't you paying attention when I explained how to do it? I am going to have to place you in remedial tennis!"

Although we are far too enlightened (and kind) to teach tennis this way, the analogy is uncomfortably apt for the traditional way that writing teachers have taught writing. Ignoring the power of positive reinforcement, writing teachers have red-penciled students' errors with puritanical fervor. These teachers have of course aimed for the right goals—they want to produce skillful and joyful writers, just as the tennis instructor wants to produce skillful and joyful tennis players. But the techniques have been misguided.

Students' Responses to Teachers' Comments

Part of the problem is that our comments on students' papers are necessarily short and therefore cryptic. We know what we mean, and we know the tone that we intend to convey. Often, however, students are bewildered by our comments, and they sometimes read into them a tone and a meaning entirely different from our intentions.

The extent to which students misread teachers' comments is revealed in Spandel and Stiggins's study (1990), in which the investigators interviewed students about their reactions to teachers' comments on their papers. Students were asked to describe their reactions to specific marginal comments that teachers placed on their essays—either what they thought the comments meant or how the comments made them feel (pp. 85–87). When a teacher wrote, "Needs to be more concise," students reacted this way:

> *Confusing. I need to know what the teacher means specifically.*
> *This is an obvious comment.*
> *I'm not Einstein. I can't get every point right.*
> *I muffed.*
> *I thought you wanted details and support.*
> *This frustrates me!*
> *Define "concise."*
> *Vague, vague.*

When a teacher wrote, "Be more specific," students reacted this way:

You *be more specific.*
I'm frustrated.
I tried and it didn't pay off.
It's going to be too long then.
I feel mad—it really doesn't matter.
I try, but I don't know every fact.

When a teacher wrote, "You haven't really thought this through," students reacted this way:

That is a mean reply.
I guess I blew it!
I'm upset.
That makes me madder than you can imagine!
How do you know what I thought?

When a teacher wrote, "Try harder!" students reacted this way:

I did try!
You're a stupid jerk.
Maybe I am trying as hard as I can.
I feel like kicking the teacher.
Baloney! You don't know how hard I tried.
This kind of comment makes me feel really bad and I'm frustrated!

The conclusions of this study are worth quoting:

Negative comments, however well intentioned they are, tend to make students feel bewildered, hurt, or angry. They stifle further attempts at writing. It would seem on the face of it that one good way to help a budding writer would be to point out what he or she is doing wrong, but, in fact, it usually doesn't help; it hurts. Sometimes it hurts a lot.

What does help, however, is to point out what the writer is doing well. Positive comments build confidence and make the writer want to try again. However, there's a trick to writing good positive comments. They must be truthful, and they must be very specific [p. 87].

Spandel and Stiggins's insights accord with current brain research, which reveals the importance of emotions to learning. Zull (2002) shows that positive emotions enhance cognition. In a section entitled "The Amygdala and the Teacher," Zull explains that "when we want to help someone learn, we should be aware that our learner will be quickly and subconsciously monitoring the situation through her amygdala [the primitive "fear center" or "danger center" of the brain]" (p. 59). Zull's point is that fear, anxiety, or anger blocks meaningful learning, which is associated with pleasure. To promote meaningful learning, Zull argues, teachers should build on student successes, evoking feelings of hope and confidence rather than failure—the same point made by Spandel and Stiggins.

In a similar vein, composition researchers have explored the effect of direct versus "mitigating" comments on student papers. Mitigating comments frame criticism in a positive way in order to buffer students' anger or mitigate feelings of inadequacy (Treglia, 2009; Weaver, 2006). In a study of marketing majors at a large Midwestern university, Smith (2008) showed students the following two examples of possible end comments for a paper—one presenting critical statements directly, with no attempt at mitigation, and the other including positive as well as negative statements:

> [Direct criticism—no mitigation]: *Your paper has not fulfilled all of the assignment requirements because it is missing a conclusion discussing whether you are a good match for the company you researched. The writing needs proofreading, and several source citations are missing in the text of the paper. The paper could use more research on your employer.*
>
> [Mitigated criticism—positive and negative elements]: *Your paper's introduction was really excellent, as was your detailed information on salaries and the career path for this position. The stages of the recruitment process were well-covered and gave good direction. Your paper hasn't fulfilled all of the assignment requirements because it is missing a conclusion discussing whether you are a good match for the company you researched. The writing needs proofreading, and several source citations are missing in the text of the paper. The paper could use more research on your employer [p. 330].*

The students in Smith's study overwhelmingly preferred the mitigated version that mixed positive and negative elements. One person called the unmitigated end comment "mean"; another said it "only gives the bad and makes the student feel like a failure." Still another said, "If I were a student who was going to rewrite this paper, I probably wouldn't bother because the evaluation the professor wrote made it sound like he/she didn't like it at all" (p. 328).

To improve our techniques for commenting on our students' papers, then, we need to remember our purpose, which is not to point out everything wrong with the paper but to facilitate improvement. When marking and grading papers, we should keep in mind that we have two quite distinct roles to play, depending on where our students are in the writing process. At the drafting stage, our role is coach. Our goal is to provide useful instruction, good advice, and warm encouragement. At the end of the writing process, when students submit final copy, our role is judge. At this stage, we uphold the standards of our profession, giving out high marks only to those essays that meet the criteria we have set. It is possible, of course, to do both simultaneously. In the marketing study mentioned in the previous paragraph, Smith (2008) shows that the most effective method of grading written products is to combine mitigated commentary (marginal and end comments that stress positive elements while also identifying weaknesses) with rubric scores revealing the teacher's criteria-based judgments.

The Purpose of Commenting: To Coach Revision

When we comment on papers, the role we should play is that of a coach providing guidance for revision, for it is in the act of revising that our students learn most deeply what they want to say and what their readers need for ease of comprehension. Revising doesn't mean just editing; it means "re-visioning"—rethinking, reconceptualizing, "seeing again." It is through the hard work of revising that students learn how experienced writers really compose.

As mentioned briefly in Chapter Fifteen, you can best ensure that your comments will stimulate revision if you place your comments on a late-stage rough draft or if you allow rewrites. If you comment on drafts, you'll probably need to do so at least a week before students are to submit their finished papers. When using this strategy, I prefer to comment only on late-stage drafts, after the writers have gone through peer review.

The second strategy, which is my favorite method, is to allow rewrites after I return the "finished" papers. Because not all students will choose to rewrite, this method is less time-consuming for me, and the quality of the writing I initially receive is higher. By allowing rewrites, I can gear all my comments toward revision yet also feel comfortable applying rigorous grading standards, because I know that students can rewrite. Moreover, the opportunity to improve less-than-hoped-for grades inspires many students toward serious revision.

From a teacher's standpoint, commenting to prompt revision, as opposed to justifying a grade or pointing out errors, may also change one's whole orientation toward reading student writing. (Recall the difference between the revision-oriented and the editing-oriented commentary on the student paragraph in Chapter Five, pages 83–84.) You begin looking for the *promise* of a draft rather than its mistakes. You begin seeing yourself as *responding to* rather than *correcting* a set of papers. You think of limiting your comments to the two or three things that the writer should work on for the next draft rather than commenting copiously on everything. You think of reading for ideas rather than for errors. In short, you think of coaching rather than judging.

General Strategy for Commenting on Drafts: A Hierarchy of Questions

Commenting effectively on drafts requires a consistent philosophy and a plan. Because your purpose is to stimulate meaningful revision, your best strategy is to limit your commentary to a few problems that you want the student to tackle when preparing the next draft. It thus helps to establish a hierarchy of concerns, descending from higher-order issues (ideas, organization, development, and overall clarity) to lower-order issues (sentence correctness, style, mechanics, spelling, and so forth). What follows is a sequence of questions arranged in descending order of concern. My recommendation is to limit your comments to only two or three of the questions and to proceed to lower-order concerns only after a draft is reasonably successful at the higher levels.

As you read through the following discussion, you may find it useful to have at hand one or two student papers that you are currently marking and to try out my suggestions, perhaps comparing them to your current practice. These questions assume an assignment calling for thesis-based academic writing. They also assume that your students are reasonably competent writers. Sometimes teachers across the curriculum encounter what writing teachers call "basic writers" or "developmental writers," many of whom have severe problems producing grammatically coherent text. If you have such students in your class, I suggest that you seek advice from a writing professional such as the director of your writing center or the director of first-year composition on your campus.

Does the Draft Follow the Assignment?

If the draft doesn't follow the assignment, there is no purpose in commenting further. Tell the writer that the draft is on the wrong track and that he or she needs to start over by rereading the assignment carefully and perhaps seeking help from you. I generally return such a draft unmarked and ungraded.

Does the Draft Address a Problem/Question? Does It Have a Thesis?

Once you see that a draft addresses the assignment, look next at its overall focus. Can you tell where the draft is headed? Does it wrestle with a real question or issue? Does the draft have a thesis? Is it stated at a place appropriate to the assigned genre and the reader's expectations?

Drafts exhibiting problems at this level may have no discernible problem-thesis structure; other drafts may have a thesis, but one that is not stated explicitly or is buried deep in the body of the paper, forcing you to wander about lost before finally seeing what the writer intends. Frequently drafts become clearer at the end than they were at the beginning—evidence that the writer has clarified his or her thinking during the act of composing. To use the language of Flower (1979), such a draft is "writer-based" rather than "reader-based"; that is, the draft follows the order of the writer's discovery process rather than a revised order that meets the reader's needs. Thus drafts that become clear only in the conclusion need to be revised globally. In some cases, you may wish to guide the writer toward a prototypical academic introduction that explains the problem to be addressed, states the thesis, and gives a brief overview of the whole argument. (See the discussion of academic introductions in Chapter Thirteen, pages 250–252.) Composing such an introduction forces the writer to imagine the argument from the reader's perspective. Typical end comments addressing thesis and focus include these:

> *Serena, although I can see good ideas along the way, I can't find a thesis in this draft, nor is it clear what problem or question you are addressing. Please see me for help.*
>
> *Diego, in the beginning you really captured your reader's interest, but then I started to get lost. By the end of the paper your argument became clear again. For the next draft, help your reader out by moving your thesis up to the end of the introduction. Also, the reader might need a preview map of your argument.*

What Is the Overall Quality of the Writer's Ideas/Argument?

If a paper has a thesis that addresses a problem, you are ready to look at the quality of the argument itself. What are the strengths and weaknesses of the writer's ideas? How effective are the supporting reasons and evidence? Are the ideas developed with sufficient complexity, subtlety, and insight? Is there adequate awareness of and attention to opposing views? The following are possible marginal comments for addressing these concerns:

Interesting idea!

Nice comparison of X to Y here.

Good point—I hadn't thought of it in quite this way.

Expand and explain; could you give an example?

Aren't you overlooking X's point of view here?

I don't see how you got from X to Y. Argument is confusing.

This is too much a rehash of X. Move from summarizing to analyzing.

You have covered X well but haven't addressed Y or Z.

You need to anticipate and respond to opposing views here.

What's your evidence for this assertion?

Is the Draft Effectively Organized?

As writers, we all struggle with organization, often rethinking our first-draft structure significantly as we revise. Student writers have even greater problems with organization—not only with creating a logical and coherent structure but also with signaling that structure to readers.

To size up the organization of a student's draft, consider questions like these:

- Do the title and introduction orient the reader to the draft's purpose and forecast where the paper is going?

- Could the reader easily outline the draft or write a summary of the argument?

- Can the reader tell the purpose or function of each paragraph?

- If you get temporarily lost, does the overall argument start getting clearer at the end (a sure sign that the writer is clarifying his or her ideas as she writes)?

- Are paragraphs unified and coherent? (Common problems include paragraphs that are short and choppy, that have no topic sentences, or that change direction midstream.)

- Do some parts of the draft need more development, especially with details and evidence?

- Are there parts that should be added or deleted? Are there parts that should be shifted or moved around?

- What's missing from the draft?

What follows are some commenting strategies that may help writers improve their structure as they revise.

Use Marginal Comments to Note Where You Get Lost or Confused

A first rule of commenting is simply to tell students where you get confused. Consider "readerly" marginal notes such as the following:

> *Whoa, you lost me.*
>
> *How does this part relate to what you said on the previous page?*
>
> *Can you clarify your point in the section that I have bracketed?*
>
> *Your readers need a transition here.*
>
> *These short, choppy paragraphs make it hard to tell what your main points are.*
>
> *This paragraph wanders. What's its central idea?*
>
> *You seem to be making several points here without developing them. Break into separate paragraphs and develop each?*
>
> *Your introduction made me think you would do X next, but this is about Y.*
>
> *You're bouncing all over. I need a road map of where we have been and where we are going.*

Comment on the Title and Introduction

Readers pick up important clues about structure from the title and the introduction. Good titles often "nutshell" the writer's argument (see discussion of titles in Chapter Thirteen, pages 251–252). Good introductions serve the same purpose. They should engage the reader's attention and, in most academic writing, set forth the problem or question that the essay will address. Typically, the writer's thesis comes at the end of the introduction (see discussion of introductions in Chapter Thirteen, pages 250–251). To help students understand why writers need to orient readers early on, I make it a regular practice to comment on titles and introductions. I praise strong titles and ask the student to revise weak ones. If the introduction sets up the problem well or has a good thesis, I praise it. If it doesn't, this weakness becomes the primary focus of my end comment. In many academic papers, writers also need to provide a mapping passage that forecasts the structure of the paper. Asking students to add a forecasting passage can encourage them to solve structural problems as they revise.

Comment on Topic Sentences and Transitions

When I help colleagues revise their article or book drafts for publication, I find that my most frequent comments focus on topic sentences of paragraphs. Drafts can often be improved dramatically if the opening sentence of key paragraphs better states the writer's point. (Often a paragraph or a whole section needs to be revised once the topic sentence is clarified.) Also, transitions between paragraphs may need to be added or improved, either through use of transition words ("next," "therefore," "on the other hand," "moreover") or through backward-looking summaries and forward-looking forecasting ("In the previous section I have argued [X], but now a new question arises: Y"). I regularly praise good topic sentences or transitions as well as call attention to problem areas. My hope is that when I point out paragraphs without topic sentences or transitions, students can see models of "the right way" in their own drafts.

As an example of the kinds of paragraph-level revisions one hopes to promote, Exhibit 16.1 shows how a student in a first-year seminar revised a section of a draft in response to teacher commentary.

Does the Draft Effectively Manage Old and New Information?

Cognitive psychology has shown that humans store new concepts in long-term memory by linking them to existing concepts. In other words, new information becomes meaningful only if it can be linked to old information (Willingham, 2009; Zull, 2002). Cognitive research applied to reading reveals that readers process information in a text by linking each new sentence to the meanings developed so far in those parts of the text already read (Colomb and Williams, 1985; Gopen and Swan, 1990). For prose to be cohesive (and hence easily understood), most of the sentences need to follow the "old/new contract": Old information comes at the beginning of a sentence—linking back to what has gone before—while new information comes later, often in the predicate, after the sentence has linked to the old. Once the reader assimilates a sentence's new information, that new information becomes old information, integrated into the unfolding meaning of the text. When writers consistently break this contract by beginning sentences with new information, the reader gets lost ("Hold on," says the reader. "I'm confused. You're dropping in stuff out of nowhere.") I illustrate this principle for students with the thought exercise in Exhibit 16.2.

Most students agree that Version 2 follows the old/new contract and is therefore easier to understand quickly. Each sentence opens with something old—either a repeated word from the previous sentence or a summarizing synonym for something earlier (for example, in sentence three "principle" stands for "old/new contract"). It is possible to understand Version 1, but it takes more "reader energy" to do so because it is harder to figure out how each sentence relates to the previous one.

EXHIBIT 16.1

Student Revision of a Draft in Response to Teacher Commentary

A problem is that nuclear power plants aren't safe. The Three Mile Island accident in 1979 and the disastrous Chernobyl meltdown in 1986 are examples of lack of safety.

Confusing. I thought you were supporting nuclear power.

An editorial in the *Los Angeles Times* describes how a July 2007 magnitude 6.8 earthquake in Japan caused an indefinite shut down of a major nuclear plant and caused radioactive leaks into the air and the ocean ("No to Nukes").

Is this whole section a summary of opposing views?

While considering external shocks, opponents also want to remind us that nuclear plants are considered attractive terrorist targets, which raises the risk associated with nuclear technology. They point out that weapons proliferation is another problem. This is due to the fact that the process of reprocessing spent fuel requires the separation of plutonium from other materials to create new fuels (Editorial from the Los Angeles Times, 413).

Good transition — here you clarify that you are summarizing opponents.

Too many short paragraphs make it hard to follow your ideas.

Plutonium by itself is an excellent bomb material, which is probably the reason why 200 kilograms and 30 kilograms have gone missing in Japan and Britain respectively (Editorial from the Los Angeles Times, 413) This is of great importance considering the fact that the bomb dropped on Nagasaki only contained six kilograms of Plutonium.

What does "this" stand for?

Student's Revised Paragraph

One of the reasons that people oppose nuclear power is their belief that it is unsafe. Opponents regularly cite the Three Mile Island accident in 1979 and the disastrous Chernobyl meltdown in 1986. A list of smaller nuclear accidents is provided by an editorial from the *Los Angeles Times,* which describes how a July 2007 magnitude 6.8 earthquake in Japan caused an indefinite shut down of a major nuclear plant and caused radioactive leaks into the air and the ocean ("No to Nukes"). Opponents also argue that nuclear plants are attractive terrorist targets. A properly placed explosive could spew radioactive material over densely populated areas. Nuclear power plants also provide opportunities for terrorists to steal plutonium for making their own nuclear weapons. According to the same *Los Angeles Times* editorial, 200 kilograms of plutonium have been reported missing in Japan and 30 kilograms in Britain. This number may seem small unless we consider that fact that the bomb dropped on Nagasaki contained only six kilograms of plutonium. These worries about safety and terrorism keep many people from considering the benefits of nuclear power.

When I give this example in class, I also show students how the old/new contract can clarify connections between paragraphs as well as between sentences. I ask them to reread the opening sentence of Version 2 ("Another principle for writing clear closed-form prose is the old/new contract") and then predict what the preceding paragraph was about. They see that the previous paragraph must have also concerned a principle for

---

EXHIBIT 16.2

Thought Exercise on the Old/New Contract

What follows are two explanations of the "old/new contract," taken from Ramage, Bean, and Johnson, 2009, p. 477. One of these explanations follows the principle of old-before-new and the other doesn't. Which one follows the old/new contract? Why?

Version 1

The old/new contract is another principle for writing clear closed-form prose. Beginning your sentences with something old—something that links back to what has gone before—and then ending your sentence with new information that advances the argument is what the old/new contract asks writers to do. An effect called *coherence*, which is closely related to *unity*, is created by following this principle. Whereas the clear relationship between the topic sentence and the body of the paragraph, between the parts and the whole, is what *unity* refers to, the clear relationship between one sentence and the next is what *coherence* relates to.

Version 2

Another principle for writing clear closed-form prose is the old/new contract. The old/new contract asks writers to begin sentences with something old—something that links back to what has gone before—and then to end sentences with new information that advances the argument. Following this principle creates an effect called *coherence*, which is closely related to unity. Whereas *unity* refers to the clear relationship between the body of a paragraph and its topic sentence, between the parts and the whole, *coherence* refers to the clear relationship between one sentence and the next, between part and part.

---

writing clear closed-form prose, but something other than the old/new contract. Perhaps the previous paragraph had a topic sentence like this: "One principle for writing clear closed-form prose is to state a paragraph's point at the beginning of the paragraph." The opening sentence of the next paragraph can then begin with a backward reference ("Another principle of writing clear closed-form prose"—something old) and then conclude with the new information ("is the old/new contract"). Once stated, the phrase "the old/new contract" shifts from new information to old information. The rest of the sentences in the paragraph can now begin with a reference to "old/new contract."

The old/new contract also has explanatory power at the macro level. For example, it explains why a thesis statement typically comes at the *end* of the introduction. The thesis is the *new information* presented in the paper. The *old information* is the question that the thesis addresses. Before encountering the thesis, the reader must first understand the question, which hooks into something the reader is already interested in. The opening parts of a thesis-governed essay therefore typically begin with the question to be addressed rather than with the thesis.

EXHIBIT 16.3

Student Revision to Fix Problems with Old/New (O/N) Contract

Another argument against nuclear power is that plants are too expensive to build. But this argument is flawed.▼On March 28, 1979, Three Mile Island (TMI) Nuclear Station suffered a meltdown. It was the worst accident in commercial nuclear power operation in the United States. During its investigation of TMI the Presidential Commission became highly critical of the U.S. Nuclear Regulatory Commission (NRC), which responded by generating hundreds of new safety regulations. These regulations forced utility companies to modify reactors during construction. Since all the changes had to be made on half-completed plants, the cost of design time, material, and personnel had to be very large.▼The standards set by the NRC would not be acceptable to a utility company. ▼All reactors now being built had been ordered before 1973.▼With all the experience gained by research here in the U.S. and overseas, the licensing process can be cut in half without reducing the safety of the plant. A faster approval rate could lower the cost of the construction of a plant because it eliminates all the delays and cost overruns.	*O/N* *Confusing string of O/N*

Student's Revised Paragraph

One argument against nuclear power plants is that they are too expensive to build. But this argument is flawed because a major cause of the expense is not the cost of the power plants themselves but the tangle of regulations that builders must adhere to. These tangled regulations grew out of reforms following the March 28, 1979, meltdown of the Three Mile Island Nuclear Station. During its investigation of Three Mile Island, the Presidential Commission became highly critical of the U.S. Nuclear Regulatory Commission (NRC), which responded by generating hundreds of new safety regulations. These regulations forced utility companies to modify reactors during construction. Since all the changes had to be made on half-completed plants, the cost of design time, material, and personnel had to be very large. However, the NRC regulations are not so costly if they are applied to new designs rather than modification of old designs. With all the experience gained by research here in the U.S. and overseas, the licensing process for constructing new-design reactors can be cut in half without reducing the safety of the plant. A faster approval rate could lower the cost of the construction of a plant because it eliminates all the delays and cost overruns.

Research has shown that violation of the old/new contract is a frequent cause of confusion in drafts (Colomb and Williams, 1985). I find that it takes about fifteen minutes to explain the old/new contract to students, and after that I can use this concept to make helpful marginal comments in a text (I use the abbreviation "O/N"). Exhibit 16.3 shows how the student writer arguing for nuclear power revised a paragraph to fill in gaps caused by violations of the old/new contract. (For further explanation of the old/new contract, see Ramage, Bean, and Johnson, 2009.)

Is the Draft Free of Errors in Grammar, Punctuation, and Spelling?

Although I have called grammatical errors, misspellings, and punctuation mistakes "lower-order concerns" from the perspective of the writing process, they can be high-level concerns for readers. Finished work marred by these errors greatly annoys teachers and may have disastrous consequences in the work world—professional embarrassment, loss of ethos, or even failure to be hired or promoted. (See my discussion of Beason, 2001, and Hairston, 1981, in Chapter Five, pages 80–81.) What teachers should do about these errors, particularly teachers across the curriculum who are not writing teachers, remains a knotty problem. If teachers circle all the errors in students' papers or serve as a line editor by making corrections, they significantly compound their workload and in most cases don't help their students improve. In Chapter Five I argue for an approach to error that places maximum responsibility on students for learning to edit their own work. This philosophy follows Haswell's practice of "minimal marking" (1983), in which teachers don't mark student errors but require them to find and correct their own errors. The teacher tells a student that his or her paper is marred by sentence errors and that the student's grade will be either reduced or unrecorded until most of the errors are found and corrected. (Haswell places a check in the margin of lines where errors occur.)

The beauty of this policy, from a teacher's perspective, is that abandoning the role of proofreader and line editor saves substantial marking time (although it adds time required to look at rewrites). More importantly, it trains students to develop new editing habits for eliminating their own careless errors. The policy goal is to encourage students to edit their drafts with a reader's eye, to use a grammar handbook, and to keep lists of their characteristic errors. Students with severe sentence-level difficulties may even be motivated to take another writing course or to seek tutorial help. The point, in any case, is to make students responsible for their own editing. (See Chapter Five for a full discussion of this complex and politically charged matter.)

When I recommend "minimal marking," therefore, I am not advocating being soft on error. On the contrary, I am arguing that students' errors should be noted emphatically and that some stick-and-carrot strategy should be applied to motivate students to find and fix them. My own strategy is to write an end comment like this:

Sally, no grade yet because your paper is marred by sentence level errors. Your ideas are worth more careful editing. Please find and correct errors and resubmit.

How high I raise the grade depends on how successful the student is in reducing the number of sentence errors. To speed rereading of corrections, I follow Haswell's practice of placing a check in the margins of lines that have errors so that I need to reread only those lines to determine whether the error was corrected. If a sentence is grammatically incomprehensible, I mark it with a comment such as "garbled" or "tangled syntax."

Another approach is to line edit one or two paragraphs and then ask the student to do the same for the rest of the draft. If you line edit, however, be careful to distinguish rule-based mistakes from stylistic choices. When you cross something out, for example, students often do not know if what they did was "wrong" or just stylistically unpolished. (The next section deals with stylistic, as opposed to grammatical, problems.)

A final strategy for helping students with sentence errors is to note characteristic patterns of errors. Shaughnessy (1977) demonstrated that what often looks like a dozen errors in a student's draft may really be one error repeated a dozen times. If you can help a student learn a rule or a principle, you can often clear up many mistakes in one swoop. Sometimes teaching a principle is a simple matter (explaining the difference between *it's* and *its*); at other times it is more complex (explaining what is meant by a comma splice). Even if you do not explain the rule or principle, helping students recognize a repeated pattern of error is a real service. Here is a typical end-comment:

> *Sam, you have lots of sentence errors here, but many of them are of two types: (1) apostrophe errors—you tend to use apostrophes with plurals rather than possessives and (2) comma splices (remember those from English class?).*

Is the Draft Free of Stylistic Problems?

What distinguishes stylistic problems from grammar errors is that stylistic problems are rhetorical, between-sentence concerns rather than concerns of correctness. Errors in grammar are violations of the rule-based conventions that govern pronoun cases, subject-verb agreement, dangling modifiers, parallelism, sentence completeness, capitalization, and so forth. In contrast, stylistic problems involve rhetorical choices—matters of clarity and grace rather than right or wrong. Wordiness, choppiness, weak verbs, or excessive use of the passive voice are problems of rhetoric or style, not grammatical errors.

Students often need advice on achieving the right level of formality and voice in a paper (depending on genre and audience) or on understanding when technical language or the passive voice is or is not appropriate. In addition, every teacher has pet peeves about style, so you might as well make yours known to students and note them on drafts when they start to annoy you. Here are my own personal top three annoyances. (I invite readers to make their own "top three" lists.)

Wordiness. Even though I am not always able to practice what I preach, I prefer a succinct, plain style unclogged by deadwood or circumlocutions. I urge students to cut and prune their drafts to achieve economy and tightness. Here's an example:

> ***Original Version:*** *As a result of the labor policies established by Bismarck, the working-class people in Germany were convinced that revolution was unnecessary for the attainment of their goals and purposes.*

> ***Improved Version:*** *Bismarck's labor policies convinced the German working class that revolution was unnecessary.*

Lazy use of "this" as a pronoun. Some writers try to create coherence between sentences by using *this* as a pronoun to link backward. Sometimes the "this" stands for a noun in the preceding sentence, but more often it is meant to stand for a whole idea. No grammatical rule actually forbids using *this* as an all-purpose pronoun (although some handbooks call the practice "broad reference" and frown on it), but its overuse can lead to gracelessness, reduced coherence, and outright ambiguity. Here is an example:

> ***Original Version:*** *As a little girl, I liked to play with mechanical games and toys, but this was not supported by my parents. Fortunately, a woman math teacher in high school saw that I was good at this and advised me to major in engineering. But this turned out to be even more difficult than I imagined.*

> ***Improved Version:*** *As a little girl, I liked to play with mechanical games and toys, but my parents didn't support such "boylike behavior." Fortunately, a woman math teacher in high school noticed my talent in math and physics and advised me to major in engineering—advice that turned out to be even more difficult to follow than I had imagined.*

Choppy sentences—excessive coordination. Experienced writers vary the length and structure of their sentences to emphasize main ideas, placing subordinate ideas in subordinate phrases or clauses. In contrast, beginning writers often string together a sequence of short sentences—or simply join them with coordinating conjunctions such as *and, or, so,* or *but*. Excessive coordination creates a choppy effect that fails to distinguish between more important and less important material. By occasionally marking excessive coordination on a draft, you can help students learn to combine sentences by subordinating subordinate ideas.

> *Original version:* I am a student at Sycamore College, and I am enclosing a proposal that concerns a problem with courses. During lectures many students use laptops. These students aren't taking notes. They are surfing the web or answering e-mail or checking Facebook. This usage makes it hard for other students to concentrate. The quality of learning goes down. The university should forbid use of laptops in classrooms.

> *Improved version:* As a Sycamore College student, I am enclosing a proposal to forbid the use of laptops in lecture courses as a way of improving student learning. My proposal notes the frequency with which students use laptops during lectures to surf the web, answer e-mail, or check Facebook rather than to take notes. Because this behavior makes it hard for other students to concentrate, the best solution is to forbid laptops.

To help students overcome my top three peeves, I sometimes line-edit early examples of each problem and then ask the writer to do the same sort of thing throughout. I also draw a box around every "this" as pronoun.

Suggestions for Writing End Comments That Encourage Revision

On the last page of a student's paper, teachers typically write an end comment, accompanied by the paper's grade. If they think of the end comment as a justification of the grade, the end comment tends to emphasize the bad features of the paper ("Here are the problems with the paper that caused me to give you a C"). But if teachers think of the end comment as guiding revision, it can become more affirmative. A draft that is unsuccessful as a final product may still be an excellent draft in terms of its potential. I like to tell students that a draft is to a finished product as a caterpillar is to a butterfly: all that's missing is the metamorphosis.

In writing end comments, I try to imagine the butterfly while critiquing the caterpillar. The purpose of the end comment is not to justify the current grade but to help writers make the kinds of revisions that will move the draft toward excellence. The strategy I recommend is to follow a three-step template: (1) strengths, (2) summary of a limited number of problems, and

(3) recommendations for revision. In all cases, try to be as specific as possible. Here are some examples of end comments that follow this template:

> *Shanita, you have a good draft here that should be easy to improve. You present a strong thesis that* The Tempest *supports the colonial project, and you often use textual detail effectively for support. However, your introduction is hard to follow because you state your thesis before the reader quite sees what conversation you are joining. A second problem is that some of your discussions of Caliban aren't clearly connected to your thesis about the play's political work. (See my marginal notes.) Finally, you don't address counterarguments. Many of your classmates think that* The Tempest *opposes colonialism.*
>
> *To improve this draft:*
>
> - *In your introduction, explain the question before you state your thesis.*
> - *Keep your discussion of Caliban focused on the colonial project by showing why you think Shakespeare's presentation of Caliban is similar to Hakluyt's view of natives in America.*
> - *Anticipate the objections of those classmates who have a different view of Caliban.*
> - *Respond to my marginal comments.*

• • •

> *Paula, This is an excellent draft, perhaps one revision away from an A. I like very much your discussion of Diem's leadership and the rise of dissent in Vietnam. You set your ideas clearly and with strong evidence.*
>
> *However, I got lost in a few places, which I noted in the marginal comments. It would also help your reader if you mapped out your purpose and structure more clearly in the introduction. Finally, in the middle of the paper, you need to expand and clarify your discussion of Vietnamese attitudes toward American soldiers. I wasn't quite sure what your point was in that whole section. Again, check my marginal comments to see where I got confused. Good job. I'm looking forward to your revision.*

Conclusion: A Review of General Principles

The following list summarizes the main principles of commentary discussed in this chapter.

General Procedures

1. Comment first on ideas and organization: encourage students to solve higher-order problems before turning to lower-order problems.

2. Whenever possible, make positive comments. Praise strong points.

3. Try to write an end comment that reveals your interest in the student's ideas. Begin the end comment with an emphasis on good points and then move to specific recommendations for improvement.

4. Avoid overcommenting. Particularly avoid emphasizing lower-order concerns until you are satisfied with higher-order concerns. If a draft requires major revision at the level of ideas and organization, it is premature to worry about sentence errors.

5. As you read the essay, indicate your reaction to specific passages. Particularly comment on the ideas, raising queries and making suggestions on how the argument could be improved. Praise parts that you like.

6. Resist the urge to circle misspellings, punctuation errors, and so forth. Research suggests that students will improve more quickly if they are required to find and correct their own errors.

Marking for Ideas

7. The end comment should summarize your assessment of the strengths and weaknesses of the writer's ideas. Challenge writers to deepen and complicate their thought at a level appropriate to their intellectual development.

Marking for Organization

8. Use marginal comments to indicate places where structure becomes confusing.

9. Praise good titles, good thesis statements, good transitions, and so forth.

Marking for Sentence Structure

10. Although I recommend against marking or circling sentence errors, you might consider placing checks in the margins where they occur. When you return the papers, either withhold a grade or lower the grade until students who made substantial numbers of errors have reedited their work. Most students should be able to find and fix a majority of their errors. Students with severe sentence-level problems may need to seek personal tutoring.

11. Note places where sentence-level problems cause genuine confusion (as opposed to annoyance). Marginal comments such as "Tangled sentence" or "This passage is garbled" help the writer see where problems occur.

Some Further Principles

12. Try to make comments as legible and as straightforward as possible. As anyone who has looked at papers graded by a colleague knows, teachers' comments can be difficult to decipher. Teacher comments are often unintentional examples of first-draft writing—clear to the writer but cryptic and baffling to others.

13. Whenever possible, use one-on-one conferences instead of commenting on papers. Perhaps my most frequent end comment is this: "You're making real progress. Please see me so that I can help you move to the next stage." An invitation for personal help is particularly useful when the student's problems involve higher-order concerns.

14. Finally, think of your commentary as personal correspondence with the student, something that makes your own thinking visible and permanent. Try to invest in your commentary the tone of a supportive coach—someone interested in the student as a person and in the improvement of the student's powers as a writer and thinker.

In sum, when students know an instructor's criteria for a final product and when they have opportunities to revise their work with the guiding help of the instructor's comments on drafts, the quality of their final work will noticeably improve. It is satisfying indeed to see how well many undergraduates can write when they are engaged in their projects and develop their ideas through multiple drafts. The point, then, of assigning writing across the curriculum is to engage students in the process of inquiry and active learning. When teachers give students good problems to think about—and involve them actively in the process of solving these problems—they are deepening students' engagement with the subject matter, promoting their intellectual growth, and increasing the pleasure of learning for both students and teachers.

References

Abbott, M. M., Bartell, P. W., Fishman, S. M., and Honda, C. "Interchange: A Conversation Among the Disciplines." In A. Herrington and C. Moran (eds.), *Writing, Teaching, and Learning in the Disciplines*. New York: Modern Language Association, 1992.

Abercrombie, M.L.J. *The Anatomy of Judgment: Concerning the Processes of Perception, Communication, and Reasoning*. London: Hutchinson, 1960.

Adler, M. *The Paideia Program: An Educational Syllabus*. New York: Macmillan, 1984.

Alaimo, P. J., Bean, J. C., Langenhan, J., and Nichols, L. "Eliminating Lab Reports: A Rhetorical Approach for Teaching the Scientific Paper in Sophomore Organic Chemistry." *WAC Journal 20*, 2009 (November): 17–32.

Alexander, P. A. "The Development of Expertise: The Journey from Application to Proficiency." *Educational Researcher*, 2003, *32*(8), 10–14.

Anderson, P., Anson, C., Gonyea, B., and Paine, C. Using results from the Consortium for the Study of Writing in College. Webinar handout. *National Survey of Student Engagement*, 2009. Retrieved April 26, 2010, from http://nsse.iub.edu/webinars/TuesdaysWithNSSE/2009_09_22_UsingResults CSWC/Webinar%20Handout%20from%20WPA%202009.pdf

Angelo, T. A., and Cross, K. P. *Classroom Assessment Techniques: A Handbook for College Teachers*. (2nd ed.) San Francisco: Jossey-Bass, 1993.

Baikie, K., and Wilhelm, K. "Emotional and Physical Benefits of Expressive Writing." *Advances in Psychiatric Treatment*, 2005, *11*, 338–346. http://apt.rcpsych.org/

Bain, K. *What the Best College Teachers Do*. Cambridge: Harvard University Press, 2004.

Barkley, E. F., Cross, K. P., and Major, C. H. *Collaborative Learning Techniques: A Handbook for College Faculty*. San Francisco: Jossey-Bass, 2005.

Barnes, L. B., Christensen, C. R., and Hansen, A. J. *Teaching and the Case Method: Text, Cases, and Readings*. (3rd ed.) Boston: Harvard Business School Press, 1994.

Barry, L. *The Busy Prof's Travel Guide to Writing Across the Curriculum*. La Grande: Eastern Oregon State College, 1989.

Bartholomae, D. "The Study of Error." *College Composition and Communication*, 1980, *31*(3), 253–269.

Bartholomae, D. "Inventing the University." In M. Rose (ed.), *When a Writer Can't Write: Studies in Writer's Block and Other Composing Process Problems*. New York: Guilford Press, 1985.

Bateman, W. L. *Open to Question: The Art of Teaching and Learning by Inquiry*. San Francisco: Jossey-Bass, 1990.

Bates, A. W., and Poole, G. *Effective Teaching with Technology in Higher Education: Foundations for Success*. San Francisco: Jossey-Bass, 2003.

Bawarshi, A. *Genre: The Invention of the Writer*. Logan, Utah: Utah State University Press, 2003.

Bazerman, C. "What Written Knowledge Does: Three Examples of Academic Discourse." *Philosophy of the Social Sciences*, 1981, *11*, 361–387.

Bazerman, C. "Codifying the Social Scientific Style: The APA Publication Manual as a Behaviorist Rhetoric." In J. Nelson, A. Megill, and D. McCloskey (eds.), *The Rhetoric of the Human Sciences: Language and Argument in Scholarship and Public Affairs*. Madison: University of Wisconsin Press, 1987.

Bazerman, C. *Shaping Written Knowledge: The Genre and Activity of the Experimental Article in Science*. Madison: University of Wisconsin Press, 1988.

Bazerman, C., Little, J., Bethel, L., Chavkin, T., Foutquette, D., and Garufis, J. *Reference Guide to Writing Across the Curriculum*. West Lafayette, Ind.: Parlor Press, 2005.

Beach, R. "Self-Evaluation Strategies of Extensive Revisers and Non-Revisers." *College Composition and Communication*, 1976, 27(2), 160–164.

Bean, J. C. "Summary Writing, Rogerian Listening, and Dialectic Thinking." *College Composition and Communication*, 1986, *37*(3), 343–346.

Bean, J. C., Carrithers, D., and Earenfight, T. "Transforming WAC Through a Discourse-Based Approach to University Outcomes Assessment." *WAC Journal: Writing Across the Curriculum*, 2005, *16*, 5–21.

Bean, J. C., Chappell, V., and Gillam, A. *Reading Rhetorically*. (3rd ed.) New York: Longman, 2011.

Bean, J. C., Drenk, D., and Lee, F. D. "Microtheme Strategies for Developing Cognitive Skills." In C. W. Griffin (ed.), *Teaching Writing in All Disciplines*. New Directions for Teaching and Learning, no. 12. San Francisco: Jossey-Bass, 1986.

Bean, J. C., and Iyer, N. "'I Couldn't Find an Article That Answered My Question': Teaching the Construction of Meaning in Undergraduate Literary Research." In K. A. Johnson and S. R. Harris (eds.), *Teaching Literary Research*. Chicago: Association of College and Research Libraries, 2009.

Beason, L. "Ethos and Error: How Business People React to Errors." *College Composition and Communication*, 2001, 53(1), 33–64.

Beaufort, A. *College Writing and Beyond: A New Framework for University Writing Instruction*. Logan, Utah: Utah State University Press, 2007.

Beichner, R. J., and Saul, J. M. "Introduction to the SCALE-UP (Student-Centered Activities for Large Enrollment Undergraduate Programs) Project." Paper submitted to the Proceedings of the International School of Physics "Enrico Fermi," Varenna, Italy, July 2003.

Belanoff, P., and Dickson, M. (eds.). *Portfolios: Process and Product*. Portsmouth, N.H.: Boynton/Cook, 1991.

Belanoff, P., Elbow, P., and Fontaine, S. I. (eds.). *Nothing Begins with N: New Investigations of Freewriting*. Carbondale: Southern Illinois University Press, 1991.

Belenky, M. F., Clinchy, B. M., Goldberger, N. R., and Tarule, J. M. *Women's Ways of Knowing: The Development of Self, Voice, and Mind*. New York: Basic Books, 1986.

Bent, M., and Stockdale, E. "Integrating Information Literacy as a Habit of Learning—Assessing the Impact of a Golden Thread of IL in the Curriculum." *Journal of Information Literacy*, 2009, 3(1), 43–50.

Berlinghoff, W. P. "Locally Original Mathematics Through Writing." In P. Connolly and T. Vilardi (eds.), *Writing to Learn Mathematics and Science*. New York: Teachers College Press, 1989.

Berthoff, A. "Dialectical Notebooks and the Audit of Meaning." In T. Fulwiler (ed.), *The Journal Book*. Portsmouth, N.H.: Boynton/Cook, 1987.

Bizup, J. "BEAM: A Rhetorical Vocabulary for Teaching Research-Based Writing." *Rhetoric Review*, 2008, 27(1), 72–86.

Blaauw-Hara, M. "Why Our Students Need Instruction in Grammar, and How We Should Go About It." *Teaching English in Two-Year College*, 2006, 34(2), 165–178.

Blaauw-Hara, M. "Mapping the Frontier: A Survey of Twenty Years of Grammar Articles in *TETYC*." *Teaching English in the Two-Year College*, 2007, 35(1), 30–40.

Bligh, D. A. *What's the Use of Lectures?* San Francisco: Jossey-Bass, 2000.

Bloom, B. S. (ed.). *Taxonomy of Educational Objectives*. Vol. 1: *Cognitive Domain*. New York: McKay, 1956.

Boehrer, J., and Linsky, M. "Teaching with Cases: Learning to Question." In M. D. Svinicki (ed.), *The Changing Face of College Teaching*. New Directions for Teaching and Learning, no. 42. San Francisco: Jossey-Bass, 1990.

Bonk, C. J., and Zhang, K. *Empowering Online Learning: 100+ Activities for Reading, Reflecting, Displaying, and Doing.* San Francisco: Jossey-Bass, 2008.

Bonwell, C., and Eison, J. *Active Learning: Creating Excitement in the Classroom.* ASHE-ERIC Higher Education Report No. 1. Washington, D.C.: ERIC Clearinghouse on Higher Education and the Association for the Study of Higher Education, 1991.

Booth, W., Colomb, G., and Williams, J. *The Craft of Research.* (3rd ed.) University of Chicago Press, 2008.

Braddock, R., Lloyd-Jones, R., and Schoer, L. *Research in Written Composition.* Urbana, Ill.: National Council of Teachers of English, 1963.

Bradford, A. N. "Cognitive Immaturity and Remedial College Writers." In J. N. Hays, P. A. Roth, J. R. Ramsey, and R. D. Foulke (eds.), *The Writer's Mind: Writing as a Mode of Thinking.* Urbana, Ill.: National Council of Teachers of English, 1983.

Bransford, J. D., Brown, A. L., and Cocking, R. R. (eds). *How People Learn: Brain, Mind, Experience, and School.* Expanded edition. Committee on Developments in the Science of Learning. Washington, D.C.: National Academy Press, 2000.

Bridwell-Bowles, L. "Discourse and Diversity: Experimental Writing Within the Academy." *College Composition and Communication*, 1992, *43*(3), 349–368.

Britton, J., and others. *The Development of Writing Abilities (11–18).* London: Macmillan, 1975.

Broad, B. *What We Really Value: Beyond Rubrics in Teaching and Assessing Writing.* Logan: Utah State University Press, 2003.

Brookfield, S. D. *Developing Critical Thinkers: Challenging Adults to Explore Alternative Ways of Thinking and Acting.* San Francisco: Jossey-Bass, 1987.

Brookfield, S. D. *The Skillful Teacher: On Technique, Trust, and Responsiveness in the Classroom.* (2nd ed.) San Francisco: Jossey-Bass, 2006.

Brookfield, S. D., and Preskill, S. *Discussion as a Way of Teaching: Tools and Techniques for Democratic Classrooms.* (2nd ed.) San Francisco: Jossey-Bass, 2005.

Brossell, G. "Rhetorical Specification in Essay Examination Topics." *College English*, 1983, *45*(2), 165–173.

Brown, G., and Atkins, M. *Effective Teaching in Higher Education.* London: Methuen, 1988.

Bruffee, K. A. "Writing and Reading as Social or Collaborative Acts." In J. N. Hays, P. A. Roth, J. R. Ramsey, and R. D. Foulke (eds.), *The Writer's Mind: Writing as a Mode of Thinking.* Urbana, Ill.: National Council of Teachers of English, 1983.

Bruffee, K. A. "Collaborative Learning and the 'Conversation of Mankind.'" *College English*, 1984, *46*(6), 635–652.

Bruffee, K. A. *Collaborative Learning: Higher Education, Interdependence, and the Authority of Knowledge.* Baltimore, Md.: Johns Hopkins University Press, 1993.

Bruffee, K. A. *A Short Course in Writing: Composition, Collaborative Writing, and Constructive Reading.* (4th ed.). New York: Longman, 1993.

Carlson, J. A., and Schodt, D. W. "Beyond the Lecture: Case Teaching and the Learning of Economic Theory." *Journal of Economic Education*, 1995, 26(1), 17–28.

Carmichael, S. "A Declaration of War." In M. Goodman (ed.), *The Movement Toward a New America: The Beginnings of a Long Revolution.* Philadelphia: Pilgrim Press/Knopf, 1970. (Originally published 1968.)

Carrithers, D., and Bean, J. C. "Using a Client Memo to Assess Critical Thinking of Finance Majors." *Business Communication Quarterly*, 2008, 71(1) (March), 10–26.

Carrithers, D., Bean, J. C., and Ling, T. "Messy Problems and Lay Audiences: Teaching Critical Thinking Within the Finance Curriculum." *Business Communication Quarterly*, 2008, 71(2) (June), 152–170.

Carroll, L. A. *Rehearsing New Roles: How College Students Develop as Writers.* Carbondale: Southern Illinois University Press, 2002.

Carter, M. "Ways of Knowing, Doing, and Writing in the Disciplines." *College Composition and Communication*, 2007, 58(3), 385–418.

Cashin, W. *Improving Essay Tests.* IDEA Paper No. 17. Manhattan: Kansas State University Center for Faculty Evaluation and Development, 1987.

Chapman, O. L., and Fiore, M. A. "The White Paper: A Description of CPR." *Calibrated Peer Review*, 2001. http://cpr.molscie.ucla.edu

Cho, K., and Schunn, C. D. "Scaffolded Writing and Rewriting in the Discipline: A Web-Based Reciprocal Peer Review System." *Computers and Education*, 2007, 48, 409–426.

Christensen, C. R., Garvin, D. A., and Sweet, A. (eds.). *Education for Judgment: The Artistry of Discussion Leadership.* Boston: Harvard Business School Press, 1991.

Clegg, V., and Cashin, W. *Improving Multiple-Choice Tests.* IDEA Paper No. 16. Manhattan: Kansas State University Center for Faculty Evaluation and Development, 1986.

Cohen, A. J., and Spencer, J. "Using Writing Across the Curriculum in Economics: Is Taking the Plunge Worth It?" *Journal of Economic Education*, 1993, 23, 219–230.

Colomb, G. G., and Williams, J. M. "Perceiving Structure in Professional Prose: A Multiply Determined Experience." In L. Odell and D. Goswami (eds.), *Writing in Nonacademic Settings.* New York: Guilford Press, 1985.

Connolly, P., and Vilardi, T. (eds.). *Writing to Learn Mathematics and Science.* New York: Teachers College Press, 1989.

Connors, R. J., and Lunsford, A. A. "Frequency of Formal Errors in Current College Writing, or Ma and Pa Kettle Do Research." *College Composition and Communication*, 1988, 39(4), 395–409.

Cooper, C., and Odell, L. (eds.). *Evaluating Writing: Describing, Measuring, Judging.* Urbana, Ill.: National Council of Teachers of English, 1977.

Crosser, R. L. *Instructor's Manual with Lecture Notes to Accompany Concepts in Federal Taxation.* Minneapolis/St. Paul, Minn.: West, 1996.

Daiute, C. "Physical and Cognitive Factors in Revising: Insights from Studies with Computers." *Research in the Teaching of English*, 1986, *20*(2), 141–159.

Davis, B. G. *Tools for Teaching.* (2nd ed.) San Francisco: Jossey-Bass, 2009.

Depew, K. E. "Cyberspace and Digital Writing" (syllabus). Jan. 9, 2009. http://www.odu.edu/~kdepew/eng662s09/index.html

Devet, B. "Welcoming Grammar Back into the Writing Classroom." *Teaching English in the Two Year College*, 2002, *30*(1), 8–17.

Dewey, J. *Democracy and Education.* New York: Macmillan, 1916.

Diederich, P. *Measuring Growth in English.* Urbana, Ill.: National Council of Teachers of English, 1974.

Di Gaetani, J. L. "Use of the Case Method in Teaching Business Communication." In M. Kogen (ed.), *Writing in the Business Professions.* Urbana, Ill.: National Council of Teachers of English, 1989.

Dillon, J. T. *Questioning and Teaching: A Manual of Practice.* New York: Teachers College Press, 1988.

Drabick, D.A.G., Weisberg, R., Paul, L., and Bubier, J. L. "Keeping It Short and Sweet: Brief, Ungraded Writing Assignments Facilitate Learning." *Teaching of Psychology*, 2007, *34*, 172–176.

Drenk, D. "Teaching Finance Through Writing." In C. W. Griffin (ed.), *Teaching Writing in All Disciplines.* New Directions for Teaching and Learning, no. 12. San Francisco: Jossey-Bass, 1986.

Duch, B., Gron, S., and Allen, D. (eds.). *The Power of Problem-Based Learning, A Practical "How To" for Teaching Undergraduate Courses in Any Discipline.* Sterling, Va.: Stylus, 2001.

Elbow, P. *Writing Without Teachers.* New York: Oxford University Press, 1973.

Elbow, P. *Writing with Power: Techniques for Mastering the Writing Process.* New York: Oxford University Press, 1981.

Elbow, P. *Embracing Contraries: Explorations in Learning and Teaching.* New York: Oxford University Press, 1986.

Elbow, P., and Belanoff, P. *Sharing and Responding.* New York: Random House, 1989.

Ennis, R. H. *Critical Thinking.* Upper Saddle River, N.J.: Prentice Hall, 1996.

Ennis, R. H. An Outline of Goals for a Critical Thinking Curriculum and Its Assessment. *CriticalThinking.Net*, 2006. Retrieved from http://www.criticalthinking.net/goals.html

Fagen, R. R. "A Different Voice." *Stanford*, Sept. 1990, 41.

Faigley, L., and Witte, S. "Analyzing Revision." *College Composition and Communication*, 1981, *32*(4), 400–414.

Fawkes, D. Analyzing the Scope of Critical Thinking Exams. *Newsletter on Teaching in Philosophy*, 2001, *00*(2). Retrieved from http://www.apa.udel.edu/apa/publications/newsletters/v00n2/teaching/02.asp

Fink, L. D. *Creating Significant Learning Experiences: An Integrated Approach to Designing College Courses.* San Francisco: Jossey-Bass, 2003.

Flavell, J. H. *The Developmental Psychology of Jean Piaget.* New York: Van Nostrand, 1963.

Flower, L. "Writer-Based Prose: A Cognitive Basis for Problems in Writing." *College English*, 1979, *41*(1), 19–37.

Flower, L. *Problem-Solving Strategies for Writing.* (4th ed.) San Diego, Calif.: Harcourt Brace Jovanovich, 1993.

Flower, L., and Hayes, J. R. "Problem-Solving Strategies and the Writing Process." *College English*, 1977, *39*(4), 449–461.

Flynn, E. A. "Composing as a Woman." *College Composition and Communication*, 1988, *39*(4), 423–435.

Fox, H. *Listening to the World: Cultural Issues in Academic Writing.* Urbana, Ill.: National Council of Teachers of English, 1994.

Francoz, M. J. "The Logic of Question and Answer: Writing as Inquiry." *College English*, 1979, *41*(3), 336–339.

Freie, J. "Thinking and Believing." *College Teaching*, 1987, *35*(3), 89–91.

Freisinger, R. "Cross-Disciplinary Writing Programs: Theory and Practice." *College English*, 1980, *42*(2), 154–166.

Fulwiler, T. (ed.). *The Journal Book.* Portsmouth, N.H.: Boynton/Cook, 1987a.

Fulwiler, T. *Teaching with Writing.* Portsmouth, N.H.: Boynton/Cook, 1987b.

Fulwiler, T., and Young, A. (eds.). *Language Connections: Writing and Reading Across the Curriculum.* Urbana, Ill.: National Council of Teachers of English, 1982.

Garrison, R. D., and Vaughan, N. D. *Blended Learning in Higher Education: Framework, Principles, and Guidelines.* San Francisco: Jossey Bass, 2008.

Gere, A. R. (ed.). *Roots in the Sawdust: Writing to Learn Across the Disciplines.* Urbana, Ill.: National Council of Teachers of English, 1985.

Gilligan, C. *In a Different Voice: Psychological Theory and Women's Development.* Cambridge, Mass.: Harvard University Press, 1982.

Goodenough, D. A. "Changing Ground: A Medical School Lecturer Turns to Discussion Teaching." In C. R. Christensen, D. A. Garvin, and A. Sweet (eds.), *Education for Judgment: The Artistry of Discussion Leadership.* Boston: Harvard Business School Press, 1991.

Gopen, G. *The Sense of Structure: Writing from the Reader's Perspective.* New York: Longman, 2004.

Gopen, G., and Swan, J. "The Science of Scientific Writing." *American Scientist*, 1990, *78* (Nov./Dec.), 550–558.

Gorman, M. E., Gorman, M. E., and Young, A. "Poetic Writing in Psychology." In A. Young and T. Fulwiler (eds.), *Writing across the Disciplines: Research into Practice*. Portsmouth, N.H.: Boynton/Cook, 1986.

Gottschalk, K. K. "Writing in the Non-Writing Class: I'd Love to Teach Writing, But. . . . " In F. V. Bogel and K. K. Gottschalk (eds.), *Teaching Prose: A Guide for Writing Instructors*. New York: Norton, 1984.

Graff, G. *Clueless in Academe: How Schooling Obscures the Life of the Mind*. New Haven, Conn.: Yale University Press, 2004.

Graff, G. "It's Time to End 'Courseocentrism.'" *Inside Higher Ed*, Jan. 13, 2009. http://www.insidehighered.com/views/2009/01/13/graff

Graff, G., and Birkenstein, C. *They Say/I Say: The Moves That Matter in Academic Writing*. (2nd ed.) New York: Norton, 2009.

Grumbacher, J. "How Writing Helps Physics Students Become Better Problem Solvers." In T. Fulwiler (ed.), *The Journal Book*. Portsmouth, N.H.: Boynton/Cook, 1987.

Gunersel, A. B., Simpson, N. J., Aufderheide, K. J., and Wang, L. "Effectiveness of Calibrated Peer Review™ for Improving Writing and Critical Thinking Skills in Biology Undergraduate Students." *Journal of the Scholarship of Teaching and Learning*, 2008, *8*(2), 25–37.

Hairston, M. "Not All Errors Are Created Equal: Nonacademic Readers in the Professions Respond to Lapses in Usage." *College English*, 1981, *43*(8), 794–806.

Hammond, L. "Using Focused Freewriting to Promote Critical Thinking." In P. Belanoff, P. Elbow, and S. I. Fontaine (eds.), *Nothing Begins with N: New Investigations of Freewriting*. Carbondale: Southern Illinois University Press, 1991.

Harris, J. *Rewriting: How to Do Things with Texts*. Logan, Utah: Utah State University Press, 2006.

Hartwell, P. "Grammar, Grammars, and the Teaching of Grammar." *College English*, 1985, *47*(2), 105–127.

Haswell, R. H. "Minimal Marking." *College English*, 1983, *45*(6), 600–604.

Hawisher, G. E. "The Effects of Word Processing on the Revision Strategies of College Freshmen." *Research in the Teaching of English*, 1987, *21*(2), 145–159.

Hays, J. N. "The Development of Discursive Maturity in College Writers." In J. N. Hays, P. A. Roth, J. R. Ramsey, and R. D. Foulke (eds.), *The Writer's Mind: Writing as a Mode of Thinking*. Urbana, Ill.: National Council of Teachers of English, 1983.

Heilker, P. *The Essay: Theory and Pedagogy for an Active Form*. Urbana, Ill.: National Council of Teachers of English, 1996.

Heppner, F. *Teaching the Large College Class: A Guidebook for Instructors with Multitudes*. San Francisco: Jossey-Bass, 2007.

Herrington, A., and Moran, C. (eds.). *Writing, Teaching, and Learning in the Disciplines.* New York: Modern Language Association, 1992.

Hersh, R. H. "Collegiate Learning Assessment (CLA): Defining Critical Thinking, Analytical Reasoning, Problem Solving and Writing Skills" (n.d.). http://www.teaglefoundation.org/learning/pdf/hersh_ctdefinitions.pdf

Hillocks, G. *Research on Written Composition: New Directions for Teaching.* Urbana, Ill.: ERIC Clearinghouse on Reading and Communication Skills and the National Conference on Research in English, 1986.

Hillocks, G., Kahn, E. H., and Johannessen, L. R. "Teaching Defining Strategies as a Mode of Inquiry." *Research in the Teaching of English,* 1983, 17(3), 275–284.

Hirsch, E. D. Jr. *Cultural Literacy: What Every American Needs to Know.* New York: Vintage, 1988.

Hirsch, E. D. Jr. *The Knowledge Deficit: Closing the Shocking Education Gap for American School Children.* New York: Houghton Mifflin, 2006.

Hirsch, E. D., Kett, J. F., and Trefil, J. S. *Cultural Literacy: What Every American Needs to Know.* Boston: Houghton Mifflin, 1987.

Huba, M. E., and Freed, J. E. *Learner-Centered Assessment on College Campuses: Shifting the Focus from Teaching to Learning.* Boston: Allyn and Bacon, 2000.

Hull, G. "Research on Error and Correction." In B. W. McClelland and T. R. Donovan (eds.), *Perspectives on Research and Scholarship in Composition.* New York: Modern Language Association, 1985.

Ireland, P. E. *American Economic Review,* March 1994, p. 47.

Jacobs, L. C., and Chase, C. I. *Developing and Using Tests Effectively: A Guide for Faculty.* San Francisco: Jossey-Bass, 1992.

Janzow, F., and Eison, J. "Grades: Their Influence on Students and Faculty." In M. D. Svinicki (ed.), *The Changing Face of College Teaching.* New Directions for Teaching and Learning, no. 42. San Francisco: Jossey-Bass, 1990.

Jensen, G. H., and DiTiberio, J. K. *Personality and the Teaching of Composition.* Norwood, N.J.: Ablex, 1989.

Jensen, V. "Writing in College Physics." In T. Fulwiler (ed.), *The Journal Book.* Portsmouth, N.H.: Boynton/Cook, 1987.

Johnson, D. W., and Johnson, F. P. *Joining Together: Group Theory and Group Skills.* (4th ed.) Upper Saddle River, N.J.: Prentice Hall, 1991.

Johnson, D. W., and Johnson, R. T. *Learning Together and Alone: Cooperative, Competitive, and Individualistic Learning.* (3rd ed.) Upper Saddle River, N.J.: Prentice Hall, 1991.

Johnson, D. W., Johnson, R. T., and Smith, K. A. *Cooperative Learning: Increasing College Faculty Instructional Productivity.* ASHE-ERIC Higher Education Report No. 4. Washington, D.C.: George Washington University, School of Education and Human Development, 1991.

Keith, S. "Exploring Mathematics in Writing." In P. Connolly and T. Vilardi (eds.), *Writing to Learn Mathematics and Science*. New York: Teachers College Press, 1989.

Kellogg, R. T. "Training Writing Skills: A Cognitive Developmental Perspective." *Journal of Writing Research*, 2008, *1*(1), 1–26.

Kenyon, R. W. "Writing *Is* Problem Solving." In P. Connolly and T. Vilardi (eds.), *Writing to Learn Mathematics and Science*. New York: Teachers College Press, 1989.

Kies, D. "Evaluating Grammar Checkers: A Comparative Ten-Year Study." *Hypertext Books*, 2008. http://papyr.com/hypertextbooks/grammar/gramchek.htm

Kirk, J. J., and Orr, R. L. "A Primer on the Effective Use of Threaded Discussion Forums." ERIC. ED 474 738, 2003.

Kirkpatrick, L. D., and Pittendrigh, A. "A Writing Teacher in the Physics Classroom." *Physics Teacher*, Mar. 1984, pp. 159–164.

Kolb, D. A. *Learning Style Inventory*. Boston: McBer, 1985.

Kolln, M. "Closing the Books on Alchemy." *College Composition and Communication*, 1981, *32*(2), 139–151.

Kroll, B. "Cognitive Egocentrism and the Problem of Audience Awareness in Written Discourse." *Research in the Teaching of English*, 1978, *12*(3), 269–281.

Kurfiss, J. G. *Critical Thinking: Theory, Research, Practice, and Possibilities*. ASHE-ERIC Higher Education Report No. 2. Washington, D.C.: ERIC Clearinghouse on Higher Education and the Association for the Study of Higher Education, 1988.

Larson, R. L. "The 'Research Paper' in the Writing Course: A Non-Form of Writing." *College English*, 1982, *44*(8), 811–816.

Leamnson, R. *Thinking About Teaching and Learning: Developing Habits of Learning with First-Year College and University Students*. Sterling, Va.: Stylus, 1999.

Light, R. J. *Making the Most of College: Students Speak Their Minds*. Cambridge: Harvard University Press, 2001.

Lockwood, J. A. *Grasshopper Dreaming: Reflections on Killing and Loving*. Boston: Skinner House Books, 2002.

Lunsford, A. A. "Cognitive Development and the Basic Writer." *College English*, 1979, *41*(1), 38–46.

Lunsford, A. A. "Cognitive Studies and Teaching Writing." In B. W. McClelland and T. R. Donovan (eds.), *Perspectives on Research and Scholarship in Composition*. New York: Modern Language Association, 1985.

Lunsford, A. A., and Ede, L. *Singular Texts/Plural Authors: Perspectives on Collaborative Writing*. Carbondale: Southern Illinois University Press, 1990.

Lutzker, M. *Research Projects for College Students: What to Write Across the Curriculum*. Westport, Conn.: Greenwood Press, 1988.

MacDonald, S. P. *Professional and Academic Writing in the Humanities and Social Sciences*. Carbondale: Southern Illinois University Press, 1994.

MacDonald, S. P., and Cooper, C. R. "Contributions of Academic and Dialogic Journals to Writing About Literature." In A. Herrington and C. Moran (eds.), *Writing, Teaching, and Learning in the Disciplines*. New York: Modern Language Association, 1992.

MacGregor, J. "Collaborative Learning: Shared Inquiry as a Process of Reform." In M. D. Svinicki (ed.), *The Changing Face of College Teaching*. New Directions for Teaching and Learning, no. 42. San Francisco: Jossey-Bass, 1990.

Maimon, E. P., and others. *Writing in the Arts and Sciences*. Framingham, Mass.: Winthrop, 1981.

Marchitell, H. "Desire and Domination in Volpone." *Studies in English Literature*, 1991, *31*, 287–308.

Meacham, J. "Discussions by E-Mail: Experiences from a Large Class on Multiculturalism." *Liberal Education*, 1994, *80*(4), 36–39.

Meisenhelder, S. "Redefining 'Powerful' Writing: Toward a Feminist Theory of Composition." *Journal of Thought*, 1985, *20*, 184–195.

Meyers, C. *Teaching Students to Think Critically: A Guide for Faculty in All Disciplines*. San Francisco: Jossey-Bass, 1986.

Meyers, C., and Jones, T. B. *Promoting Active Learning: Strategies for the College Classroom*. San Francisco: Jossey-Bass, 1993.

Miller, C. "Genre as Social Action." *Quarterly Journal of Speech*, 1984, *70*, 151–167.

Morton, T. "Fine Cloth, Cut Carefully: Cooperative Learning in British Columbia." In J. Golub (ed.), *Focus on Collaborative Learning: Classroom Practices in Teaching English, 1988*. Urbana, Ill.: National Council of Teachers of English, 1988.

Mullin, W. J. "Qualitative Thinking and Writing in the Hard Sciences." In P. Connolly and T. Vilardi (eds.), *Writing to Learn Mathematics and Science*. New York: Teachers College Press, 1989.

Mulroy, D. *The War Against Grammar*. Portsmouth, N.H.: Boynton/Cook, 2003.

Myers, G. "The Social Construction of Two Biologists' Proposals." *Written Communication*, 1985, *2*, 219–245.

Myers, G. "Reality, Consensus, and Reform in the Rhetoric of Composition Teaching." *College English*, 1986a, *48*(2), 154–174.

Myers, G. "Writing Research and the Sociology of Scientific Knowledge: A Review of Three New Books." *College English*, 1986b, *48*(6), 595–610.

National Conference on Undergraduate Research (NCUR). *Proceedings*. Salisbury University, 2008. CD-ROM available at www.ncur.org.

Nilson, L. B. "Improving Student Feedback." *College Teaching*, 2003, *51*(1), 34–38.

Noguchi, R. R. *Grammar and the Teaching of Writing: Limits and Possibilities*. Urbana, Ill.: National Council of Teachers of English, 1991.

Norman, D. A. "What Goes On in the Mind of the Learner." In W. J. McKeachie (ed.), *Learning, Cognition, and College Teaching*. New Directions for Teaching and Learning, no. 2. San Francisco: Jossey-Bass, 1980.

Nowacek, R. S. "Why Is Being Disciplinary So Very Hard to Do? Thoughts on the Perils and Promise of Interdisciplinary Pedagogy." *College Composition and Communication*, 2009, *60*(3), 493–516.

Palloff, R. M., and Pratt, K. *The Virtual Student: A Profile and Guide to Working with Online Learners*. San Francisco: Jossey-Bass, 2003.

Patchan, M. M., Charney, D., and Schunn, C. D. "A Validation Study of Students' End Comments: Comparing Comments by Students, a Writing Instructor, and a Content Instructor." *Journal of Writing Research*, 2009, *1*(2), 124–152.

Paul, R. W. "Dialogical Thinking: Critical Thought Essential to the Acquisition of Rational Knowledge and Passions." In J. B. Baron and R. J. Sternberg (eds.), *Teaching Thinking Skills: Theory and Practice*. New York: Freeman, 1987.

Paul, R., and Elder, L. *Miniature Guide to Critical Thinking Concepts and Tools*. (6th ed.) Dillon Beach, Calif.: Foundation for Critical Thinking Press, 2009.

Perkins, D., Jay, E., and Tishman, S. "Assessing Thinking: A Framework for Measuring Critical Thinking and Problem-Solving Skills at the College Level." In *The National Assessment of College Student Learning: Identification of the Skills to Be Taught, Learned, and Assessed*. National Center for Education Statistics Research and Development Report (1994, August) (document #NCES 94–286).

Perry, W. G., Jr. *Forms of Intellectual and Ethical Development in the College Years*. Troy, Mo.: Holt, Rinehart & Winston, 1970.

Pinkava, B., and Haviland, C. "Teaching Writing and Thinking Skills." *Nursing Outlook*, 1984, *32*(5), 270–272.

Prince, M. "Does Active Learning Work? A Review of the Research." *Journal of Engineering Education*, July 2004, 223–231.

Prince, M., and Felder, R. "The Many Faces of Inductive Teaching and Learning." *Journal of College Science Teaching*, 2007, *36*(5), 14–20.

Qualley, D. *Turns of Thought: Teaching Composition as Reflexive Inquiry*. Portsmouth, N.H.: Boynton/Cook, 1997.

Ramage, J. D., and Bean, J. C. *Writing Arguments: A Rhetoric with Readings*. (3rd ed.) Needham Heights, Mass.: Allyn & Bacon, 1995.

Ramage, J. D., Bean, J. C., and Johnson. J. *The Allyn and Bacon Guide to Writing*. (5th ed.) New York: Longman, 2009.

Reynolds, J., and Moskovitz, C. "Calibrated Peer Review Assignments in Science Courses: Are They Designed to Promote Critical Thinking and Writing Skills?" *Journal of College Science Teaching*, 2008, *38*(2), 60–66.

Rienecker, L., and Stray Jorgensen, P. "The (Im)possibilities in Teaching University Writing in the Anglo-American Tradition When Dealing with Continental Student Writers." In L. Bjork, G. Brauer, L. Rienecker, and P. Stray Jorgensen (eds.), *Teaching Academic Writing in European Higher Education*. Dordrecht, New York, and London: Kluwer, 2003, 101–112.

Ritter, K. "The Economics of Authorship: Online Paper Mills, Student Writers, and First Year Composition." *College Composition and Communication*, 2005, *56*(4), 628.

Roberts, J. C., and Roberts, K. A. "Deep Reading, Cost/Benefit, and the Construction of Meaning: Enhancing Reading Comprehension and Deep Learning in Sociology Courses." *Teaching Sociology*, 2008, *36*, 125–140.

Roberts, J. C., and Roberts, K. A. "Using Federal Reserve Publications in Institutions and Markets Courses: An Approach to Teaching Critical Thinking." *Journal of Finance Education*, 2004, *2*, 15–25.

Robertson, F., Peterson, D., and Bean, J. C. "Promoting High-Level Cognitive Development: Bringing 'High Bloom' into a Financial Institutions and Markets Class." *Journal of Financial Education*, Fall 2007, *33*, 56–73.

Robinson, W. S. "Towards a Theory of Error." *Teaching English in the Two-Year College*, 1998, *26*(1), 50–60.

Rogers, C. *On Becoming a Person: A Therapist's View of Psychotherapy.* Boston: Houghton Mifflin, 1961.

Rowe, M. B. "Using Wait Time to Stimulate Inquiry." In W. W. Wilen (ed.), *Questions, Questioning Techniques, and Effective Teaching.* Washington, D.C.: National Education Association, 1987.

Russell, A. A. "What Works—A Pedagogy: Calibrated Peer Review." *Project Kaleidoscope.* 2004.

Russell, D. R. "Rethinking Genre in School and Society: An Activity Theory Analysis." *Written Communication*, 1997, *14*, 504–554.

Russell, D. R. *Writing in the Academic Disciplines: A Curricular History.* (2nd ed.) Carbondale: Southern Illinois University Press, 2002.

Russell, D. R., and Yanez, A. "'Big Picture People Rarely Become Historians': Genre Systems and the Complications of General Education." In C. Bazerman and D. R. Russell (eds.), *Writing Selves/Writing Societies: Research from Activity Perspectives.* Perspectives on Writing. Fort Collins, Colo.: The WAC Clearinghouse and Mind, Culture, and Activity, 2003, 331–362. http://wac.colostate.edu/books/selves_societies/

Schwalm, D. E. "Degree of Difficulty in Basic Writing Courses: Insights from the Oral Proficiency Interview Testing Program." *College English*, 1985, *47*(6), 629–640.

Shaughnessy, M. P. *Errors and Expectations: A Guide for the Teacher of Basic Writing.* New York: Oxford University Press, 1977.

Shaw, H. E. "Responding to Student Essays." In F. V. Bogel and K. K. Gottschalk (eds.), *Teaching Prose: A Guide for Writing Instructors.* New York: Norton, 1984.

Slavin, R. E. *Cooperative Learning: Theory, Research, and Practice.* Upper Saddle River, N.J.: Prentice Hall, 1990.

Smith, L. "Grading Written Projects: What Approaches Do Students Find Most Helpful?" *Journal of Education for Business*, July/August 2008, 325–330.

Sommers, N. "Revision Strategies of Student Writers and Experienced Adult Writers." *College Composition and Communication*, 1980, 30(4), 378–388.

Spandel, V., and Stiggins, R. J. *Creating Writers: Linking Assessment and Writing Instruction*. White Plains, N.Y.: Longman, 1990.

Spear, K. *Shared Writing: Peer Response Groups in English Classes*. Portsmouth, N.H.: Boynton/Cook, 1988.

Spellmeyer, K. "A Common Ground: The Essay in the Academy." *College English*, 1989, 51(3), 262–276.

Springer, L., Stanne, M. E., and Donovan, S. "Effects of Small-Group Learning on Undergraduates in Science, Mathematics, Engineering, and Technology: A Meta-Analysis." *Review of Educational Research*, 1999, 69, 21–51.

Stanley, C. A., and Porter, M. E. (eds.). *Engaging Large Classes: Strategies and Techniques for College Faculty*. San Francisco: Jossey-Bass, 2002.

Steffens, H. "Collaborative Learning in a History Seminar." *History Teacher*, 1989, 22(2), 125–138.

Steiner, R. "Chemistry and the Written Word." *Journal of Chemical Education*, 1982, 59, 1044.

Sternberg, R. J. "Teaching Intelligence: The Application of Cognitive Psychology to the Improvement of Intellectual Skills." In J. B. Baron and R. J. Sternberg (eds.), *Teaching Thinking Skills: Theory and Practice*. New York: Freeman, 1987.

Stewart, T. L., Myers, A. C., and Cully, M. "Enhanced Learning and Retention Through 'Writing to Learn' in the Psychology Classroom." *Teaching of Psychology*, 2010, 37, 46–49.

Swales, J. M. *Genre Analysis: English in Academic and Research Settings*. Cambridge, England: Cambridge University Press, 1990.

Swartz, R. J. "Teaching for Thinking: A Developmental Model for the Infusion of Thinking Skills into Mainstream Instruction." In J. B. Baron and R. J. Sternberg (eds.), *Teaching Thinking Skills: Theory and Practice*. New York: Freeman, 1987.

Thaiss, C., and Zawacki, T. M. *Engaged Writers, Dynamic Disciplines: Research on the Academic Writing Life*. Portsmouth, N.H.: Boynton/Cook, 2006.

Tobias, S. "Writing to Learn Science and Mathematics." In P. Connolly and T. Vilardi (eds.), *Writing to Learn Mathematics and Science*. New York: Teachers College Press, 1989.

Treglia, M. O. "Teacher-Written Commentary in College Writing Composition: How Does It Impact Student Revisions?" *Composition Studies*, 2009, 37(1), 67–86.

Troutman, P. "How to Use Sources Effectively in Expert Writing." *University Writing Program, UW 20 News and Notes*, 1 April 2009. http://gw-uw20.blogspot.com/2009/04/how-to-use-sources-effectively-in.html

Villanueva, V. "The Politics of Literacy Across the Curriculum." In S. H. McLeod, E. Miraglia, M. Soven, and C. Thaiss (eds.), *WAC for a New Millennium: Strategies for Continuing Writing-across-the-Curriculum*. Urbana, Ill.: NCTE, 2001, 165–178.

Voss, J. F. "On the Composition of Experts and Novices." In E. P. Maimon, B. F. Nodine, and F. W. O'Connor (eds.), *Thinking, Reasoning, and Writing*. White Plains, N.Y.: Longman, 1989.

Walvoord, B. E., and Anderson, V. *Effective Grading: A Tool for Learning and Assessment*. (2nd ed.) San Francisco: Jossey-Bass, 2009.

Walvoord, B. E., and McCarthy, L. P. *Thinking and Writing in College: A Naturalistic Study of Students in Four Disciplines*. Urbana, Ill.: National Council of Teachers of English, 1990.

Wardle, E. "Writing the Genres of the University." *College Composition and Communication*, 2009, *60*(4), 765–789.

Weaver, M. R. "Do Students Value Feedback? Student Perceptions of Tutors' Written Responses." *Assessment and Evaluation in Higher Education*, 2006, *31*, 379–394.

Weimer, M. *Learner-Centered Teaching: Five Key Changes to Practice*. San Francisco: Jossey-Bass, 2002.

White, E. M. *Assigning, Responding, Evaluating: A Writing Teacher's Guide*. (2nd ed.) New York: St. Martin's Press, 1992.

White, E. M. *Teaching and Assessing Writing*. (2nd ed.) San Francisco: Jossey-Bass, 1994.

Wiener, H. S. "Collaborative Learning in the Classroom: A Guide to Evaluation." *College English*, 1986, *48*(1), 52–61.

Wiggins, G., and McTighe, J. *Understanding by Design*. (2nd ed.) Upper Saddle River, N.J.: Prentice Hall, 2005.

Williams, J. M. "The Phenomenology of Error." *College Composition and Communication*, 1981, *32*(2), 152–168.

Willingham, D. T. *Why Don't Students Like School? A Cognitive Scientist Answers Questions About How the Mind Works and What It Means for the Classroom*. San Francisco: Jossey-Bass, 2009.

Yamane, D. "Course Preparation Assignments: A Strategy for Creating Discussion-Based Courses." *Teaching Sociology*, 2006, *36* (July), 236–248.

Yoshida, J. "Writing to Learn Philosophy." In A. R. Gere (ed.), *Roots in the Sawdust: Writing to Learn Across the Disciplines*. Urbana, Ill.: National Council of Teachers of English, 1985.

Young, A., and Fulwiler, T. (eds). *Writing Across the Disciplines: Research into Practice.* Portsmouth, N.H.: Boynton/Cook, 1986.

Zeiger, W. "The Exploratory Essay: Enfranchising the Spirit of Inquiry in College Composition." *College English,* 1985, 47(5), 454–466.

Zemsky, R. "The To Do List." *Inside Higher Ed,* Sept. 14, 2009. http://www.insidehighered.com/views/2009/09/14/zemsky

Zinsser, W. *Writing to Learn.* New York: HarperCollins, 1988.

Zull, J. E. *The Art of Changing the Brain: Enriching the Practice of Teaching by Exploring the Biology of Learning.* Sterling, Va.: Stylus, 2002.

Index